The Art and Practice of Costume Design

In *The Art and Practice of Costume Design*, a panel of seven designers offers a new multi-sided look at the current state and practice of theatrical costume design. Beginning with an exploration of the role of a Costume Designer, the subsequent chapters analyze and explore the psychology of dress, the principles and elements of design, how to create costume renderings, and collaboration within the production. The book also takes a look at the costume shop and the role of the designer within it, and costume design careers within theatrical and fashion industries. The chapters are illustrated with numerous instructive designs, renderings, and photographs from a variety of designers and productions, making for the most comprehensive coverage of costume design today.

This book features:

- Insights, methodologies, and over 300 full color illustrations from culturally diverse designers.

- Costume design practices pertinent to film, TV, theme parks, opera, and animation careers.

- An extensive glossary of terms that provides clear and instructive information for students and professionals.

- Several interviews with prolific costume design practitioners.

Melissa L. Merz is the Costume Designer at Texas Tech University. She has an MFA in Design from the University of Arizona and a BFA in Design from Texas State University. She has designed over 100 productions of theatre and dance and especially enjoys working on original plays. She feels fortunate to design in several states including California, Arizona, New Mexico, Texas, Oklahoma, West Virginia, Ohio, Michigan, and Vermont. She has been an active member of USITT and sponsors the TTU student chapter. As an advocate of the arts, she encourages growth and education in all areas of art for all ages.

The Art and Practice of Costume Design

Edited by Melissa L. Merz

Routledge
Taylor & Francis Group

NEW YORK AND LONDON

First published 2017
by Routledge
711 Third Avenue, New York, NY, 10017

and by Routledge
2 Park Square, Milton Park, Abingdon, Oxon OX14 4RN

Routledge is an imprint of the Taylor & Francis Group, an informa business

© 2017 Taylor & Francis

Cover photo credits: *The Secret Garden*, Cincinnati Playhouse in the Park
Director: Marcia Milgrom Dodge
Costume Designer: Leon Wiebers
Set Designer: Narelle Sissons
Lighting Designer: Matthew Richards
Sound Designer: David Bullard
Photographer: Mikki Schaffner
Costume Shop Manager at Cincinnati Playhouse: Gordon DeVinney
Draper: David Arevalo; First Hand: Jackie Andrews
Stitchers: David Arevalo, Jessica Hafer, Jackie Andrews
Dreamer Men Construction: Draper: David Arevalo; First Hand: Jackie Andrews;
Dreamer Women Construction: Costume Works, Inc.
Actors: Dan Beckmann, Brandi Burkhardt, Carlyn Connolly, Kevin Earley, Tim McDevitt, Jessica Van Kipp, Michael Yeshion, and Talia Noelle Zoll

Library of Congress Cataloging in Publication Data
Names: Merz, Melissa, editor.
Title: The art and practice of costume design / edited by Melissa Merz.
Description: New York and London : Routledge/Taylor & Francis Group, 2016. | Includes bibliographical references and index.
Identifiers: LCCN 2015042416 (print) | LCCN 2015044292 (ebook) | ISBN 9781138828407 (hardback : alk. paper) | ISBN 9781138828414 (pbk. : alk. paper) | ISBN 9781315738420 (ebk.) | ISBN 9781315738420 (Master ebook) | ISBN 9781317573678 (ePUB) | ISBN 9781317573685 (Web PDF) | ISBN 9781317573661 (Mobi/Kindle)Subjects: LCSH: Costume.
Classification: LCC PN2067 .A75 2016 (print) | LCC PN2067 (ebook) | DDC 792.026—dc23
LC record available at http://lccn.loc.gov/2015042416

ISBN: 978-1-138-82840-7 (hbk)
ISBN: 978-1-138-82841-4 (pbk)
ISBN: 978-1-315-73842-0 (ebk)

Typeset in Gill Sans
by Keystroke, Station Road, Codsall, Wolverhampton

Printed and bound in the United States of America by Sheridan

This book is dedicated to those who mentored the writers:

Alan Armstrong

Peggy Kellner

Patricia Minton-Taylor

Dennis Parker

William Pucilowsky

Dunya Ramicova

Carrie F. Robbins

Beverly Veenker

Fred Voelpel

CONTENTS

PREFACE

Two questions keep coming up for me. The question "what is costume design?" is a constant pursuit and one that seems to change with experience. As an educator, the question "what can I do with a costume degree?" is one I find myself answering to friends, family, and students alike. With this in mind, seven artists have come together to discuss the how, what, why, and what's next of the ever-evolving art of costume design. With the different writers, we have a wider and more varied view of the art, how to approach it, and how to define it. It is our hope that the differences of opinion and thought will excite and inspire, encourage creativity, and help the reader to form opinions as well.

The purpose of this book is to discover the various opinions surrounding the question of what "costume design" means.

It is the exploration of where to begin and where inspiration comes from; the theories of why characters, or people, wear what they wear; the study of the elements of design and how it applies to the craft; the artwork involved in relaying the designs; how everyone involved interacts to make the magic happen; the various places, venues, and situations in which costume practitioners find themselves; and the different ways designers use their talents and knowledge to create the art to which they are dedicated. It is about all of those who work in the world of costumes who have a part in the final creation.

In short, this book is about the art and artists who create the inventiveness referred to as *costumes*.

Melissa L. Merz

INTRODUCTION: WHAT IS COSTUME DESIGN?

Every culture has created its version of performance, and almost always performance has been accompanied by some version of costuming specific to that form, as a way to help tell the story and identify the performers. In some periods, famous fine artists were commissioned to create costume designs; just as often, these costumes were produced by dressmakers, maskmakers, milliners, and other anonymous artists and craftspeople whose names are lost to history.

In modern times, theatre is an art form, and it is entertainment, and it is also a profession. As with any business, theatre involves money—making it and spending it, hopefully in a fiscally responsible way. With the development of costume design as an art form and a profession came the idea of specific training for professional designers.

Costume design is an applied art form, meaning the object itself does not stand alone as an end unto itself. Our work is not destined to hang on a wall or sit on a pedestal (until perhaps years later, as an artifact of theatre history). Rather, it has a purpose, it has a context, it will be used. While creative, costume design has an ultimate purpose, much as a beautifully molded porcelain vase or artfully carved clock does a job while also invoking a response from the viewer on its own aesthetic merits. It will be seen as part of an overall visual statement that is a collaboration between a group of theatre designers. It will also be used to help tell a story, involving a further collaboration between an even larger group of artists.

Asking a group of designers to explain what they do and how they do it will result in a range of answers. While there are certain aspects of costume design that remain constant no matter the practitioner, costume designers and technicians, as do any artists, develop individual approaches based on experience, training, personal style, and the collaborators with whom they work. Often a single designer will use different methods based on the project at hand.

The authors of this book are no exception. Each is experienced, but each has had a different set of experiences. The aspiring designer will read the words of each author and find information that can be applied to the reader's own work in a way unique to him or her.

Theatre students will hear many times that theatre is a collaborative art. The most successful efforts blend the contributions of a group of artists into a cohesive whole. The different definitions of costume design that follow can be viewed in this light—each designer will define the art and the practice of costume design in a different way. The reader can take the essence of each of the definitions and discern a whole that is greater than the sum of its parts . . . a collaboration.

HOLLY POE DURBIN

Holly Poe Durbin is an entertainment costume designer, author, and speaker based in Los Angeles. She has designed for theatre, opera, themed entertainment, and independent film.

The art of costume design is best described with a metaphor: it is creating a world within worlds, very similar to a series of nesting boxes. One opens the largest box to find another inside, and more inside that one. The outermost vessel is the overall project defined by journalistic questions: what, when, where, who, why, and how. What is the project, and why are we doing it? Why tell the story? What artistic point of view best delivers this intention? Who are the characters, and what are the emotional stakes of the story? How will we tell it— a film? A play? A play that thinks it's a film?

FIGURE 0.1 Peter and the Starcatcher. *(Design by Holly Poe Durbin.)*

responses from an audience. And the costume designer does this while balancing both the creative and the logistical demands of the project.

LETICIA M. DELGADO

Leticia M. Delgado is a costume designer, cutter–draper, and educator. Leticia received her MFA in Costume Design and Technology from the School of Theatre at Illinois State University.

Costume design is the interpretation of written character that is created specifically to live and breathe on the stage or screen. The interpretation of characters for each play requires the collaborative effort of many trained individuals. It is the job of the costume designer to synthesize knowledge about art, the human experience, clothing, history, script analysis, and the great theatrical endeavor, into the form of specifically chosen garments that aid in the telling of a particular story. After much reading, research, discussion, budget planning, and deliberation, a costume designer can embark on the creation process. This begins with the two-dimensional design plate and culminates in the creation

On my studio wall I keep an unjustly loose interpretation of Aristotle's definition of *Literature*—it forces me to create an essential structure for any project, or the outermost box.

Literature = Object (subject of imitation)
              + Genre or Mode (manner of imitation)
              + Attitude (degree of awareness about itself)
              + Medium (method of imitation)

No undertaking is this simple, of course, but that initial definition remains a vital lighthouse during the storm of creation. Each smaller, interior box represents another aspect within context— the venue the story will be told in, the production company creating the work, the budgets or support, the storytelling mechanics of the script, the attitude of the script toward itself (omniscient, innocent, ironic, surreal, sassy?), the mechanics of the specific medium, the visual/aural world of the story, the characters inhabiting that world, and the performers inhabiting those characters. Each aspect is a rich microcosm of its own, of course. The costume designer's brain must work simultaneously on all these levels to create characters with complex histories inhabiting a visually unified story world that evokes emotional

FIGURE 0.2 Necessary Losses, *Santa Barbara Dance Theatre International Tour 2007 & 2008. (Design by Leticia M. Delgado.)*

of a specific three-dimensional garment/sculpture that is utilized by the actor, director, and choreographer as a tool that aids in the depiction of an active yet temporal story.

HEATHER A. MILAM

Heather A. Milam is a Professor of Practice at Indiana University heading up the MFA program in Costume Technology.

Costume design is the process by which clothing is imagined for theatre, opera, ballet, or any theatrical, film, or TV production. Costume design defines the period, location, social strata, time of year, time of day, and character development through the use of clothing, accessories, hats, wigs, and makeup. Costume design works with the other design elements to engage the audience in a holistic visual understanding of the production being viewed.

FIGURE 0.3 *Illinois Shakespeare Festival at Illinois State University; Robert G. Anderson as Don Armado in Love's Labour's Lost. (Photo by Pete Guither. Costume design by Nicholas Hartman. Draper–stitcher Heather A. Milam.)*

ESTHER VAN EEK

Esther Van Eek teaches costume design, stage makeup, and rendering at the University of Windsor School of Dramatic Art in Windsor, Ontario. She holds a BFA in Printmaking and an MFA in Design, and is a member of the Associate Designers of Canada.

A costume is anything worn by a performer in a production; costume design is thoughtfully selecting what a performer—actor, singer, or dancer—will wear to convey important information about their character's social status, age, health, temperament, and relationships to the other characters based on the specific artistic and practical requirements of the play. The costume design may include clothing, hair, makeup, accessories, underpinnings, millinery, personal props, and any other aesthetic elements worn on stage. Regardless of period, style, or production concept, costume design's true purpose remains the same: to serve the story and help reveal the heart and truth of it through the meaningful portrayal of the characters in it. The very best of costume design understands itself as storytelling.

FIGURE 0.4 *Flipote in Tartuffe. (Design by Esther Van Eek for the University of Windsor, ON.)*

MELISSA L. MERZ

Melissa L. Merz is Associate Professor at Texas Tech University. She has taught period styles, costume design, principles of costume, costume history, draping, and patterning.

FIGURE 0.5 *Costume designs for Texas Tech University's production of* The Learned Ladies. *(Photo by Ashton Thornhill.)*

You can never replace a first impression. Costumes try to relate much needed information about the characters as soon as they walk onto a stage. While this may be its primary purpose, the path to get there involves several branches. This is an art that involves everyone from the director to fellow designers; to the entire costume shop to the actor; and finally to the audience. It involves integrating a director's vision for a production while serving the play. Costume design incorporates imagery, intuition, desire, communication, creativity, and logic. While these may seem like they would contradict each other, a fine balance of each element goes into designing costumes. Costume design is an art form that, on its own, is limited in its meaning. It is only once it appears on stage with all of the theatrical elements that it comes to life. Each item can be a work of art, beautiful in its own way, but costumes need the energy, context, and grace of a stage to evolve into a unique art form. The design of costumes involves a balance between need, vision, availability, performers, space, talent, and appropriateness to the production.

STEVEN STINES

Steven Stines has taught costume design, costume history, and rendering at the University of Florida, Tulane University, and the University of North Carolina at Charlotte. He is a member of United Scenic Artists Local 829, and holds an MFA in Design from New York University.

FIGURE 0.6 *Costume design for Snowflakes in* The Music City Holiday Spectacular, *Gaylord Entertainment/Opryland, Nashville, Tennessee, 2004. (Design by Steven Stines.)*

For most people, the most familiar aspect of costume design—other than the finished product seen onstage—is the costume rendering. But costume design involves a great many other components beyond the "pretty picture" which is magically transformed into pretty clothes worn by pretty people.

Some designers feel their only responsibility is conceptual, but at some point *someone* must deal with the reality of moving the sketch through the shop and onto the stage. Design requires visual artistry and conceptual thinking, but it is equally about accounting and record keeping, planning and research, and sometimes psychology and babysitting in handling the personalities of performers and directors.

A set designer must, in effect, direct a version of the show. By placing doors and platforms on the stage, the designer affects blocking and movement. In order to design costumes, one must *act* a version of the show, making decisions about the character and his or her motivations, actions, and backstory, often before the actor begins that process. The goal will be to collaborate with the performers to enhance their work with design.

Ultimately, design is a creative cocktail, but there are practical considerations that cannot be ignored:

- Design is Organization. A designer creates and maintains a range of charts and lists and must be expert at time management.

- Design is Communication. This is accomplished verbally and in writing, but most importantly, through the use of graphics.

- Design is Presentation. How does a designer sell an idea? The costume rendering is a crucial element of presentation, but *how* it is displayed and explained is also important.

- Design is Education. A costume designer must be a student not only of theatre and design, but also of visual art, art history, literature, world history, and psychology.

- Design is Realization. Getting the idea on paper is only part of the process of moving that idea to reality, through the costume shop and onto the stage.

Designing for theatre is not a strictly linear process; each element of the process influences others, and the designer often moves back and forth between research, shopping, and drawing.

LINDA PISANO

Linda Pisano is Professor of Costume Design and Head of the Design and Technology program at Indiana University's Department of Theatre, Drama, and Contemporary Dance. A member of United Scenic Artists Local 829, Linda has designed for a broad range of theatre, dance, musical theatre, ballet, and opera.

There is no simple or concise definition for what we do. Costume designers must understand the aesthetic and physiological responses that an audience will discover as they experience a character through the course of dramatic action. A costume designer must understand the nuances and details that will reflect the character outwardly while evoking an emotional response from the audience. A costume designer must have concern for the human condition and an eagerness to engage in collaborative conversation and problem solving with other artists.

QUESTIONS

- Is there a definition that reflects your ideas and ideals of a costume designer?

- Write your definition of what a costume designer is. Can you write a definition of what a designer does without including the meaning of costumes?

FIGURE 0.7 *Design for Hamlet, produced at Indiana University Theatre. (Design by Linda Pisano.)*

Act I

Penny

Act II

FIGURE 1.1 *Rendering of Penny from* You Can't Take It With You. *(Design by Melissa L. Merz, Texas Tech University.)*

CHAPTER 1

THE MAGIC OF COSTUME DESIGN

Melissa L. Merz

Designing costumes can be a wonderful and magical experience, but it also requires hard work and dedication. The desire to please everyone in the process may be prevalent; the ability to do so may be more difficult. Designers must balance the needs of the director, actors, and costume shop without losing their creativity in the process.

In a perfect world, every fabric and trim would be available at a price the designer could afford. Knowing the world is not perfect, designers have to constantly look at what is available, what can be built, what should be rented, what has to be bought, and how to balance everything to create the best show possible. Decisions need to be made often and quickly. Any designer will say time is the rationale behind many decisions, as costumes could be worked on endlessly if time permitted. But productions include deadlines, such as opening dates, which can dictate certain decisions. The audience is hoping for the best show possible, and that means bringing all viable ideas together and compromising as needed in order to create a cohesive and effective design.

> "It [costume design] requires the study of history, knowledge of the decorative arts, an examination of psychology. It's also like painting in motion. A costume designer works with composition, value, and color as does any artist. She analyzes character and monitors behavior as does any social scientist. She identifies theme, plot, and style as does any literary analyst. Not claiming expertise in any of these fields, a costume designer enjoys juggling."
> Marcia Dixcy Jory[1] from *The Ingenue in White*, p. 4

THE COSTUME DESIGNER

A costume designer must possess practical knowledge in a variety of areas, particularly pertaining to the history of clothing. Recognizing the way in which clothing and architecture worked together to create popular styles and movements throughout history is also valuable. Understanding the psychology of clothing, or the reason people wear what they wear, is essential for creating a cohesive design. Its study is both fascinating and valuable. A designer may not find it necessary to be an expert on all aspects of humanity, but continued study into the mannerisms, movements, culture, purpose, evolution, fabrics, construction, and social histories will be useful with different periods of dress. It is important to look at the rules of design while understanding that intuition also plays a part in the final outcome. Since costume design is an art, many of the same tenets apply; a designer knows about composition and balance and allowing imagination to influence creativity.

In addition to the abovementioned skills, one of the most important traits a costume designer can possess is openness and a willingness to change. A designer who feels what they have created on paper is the only choice will continually have problems. They must be willing to focus on the overall image the directors are trying to convey and take into account what the audience will see. They should be willing to work with other designers to understand their views of the play and how their art works within the needs of the production.

While designers cannot help but dream of the ultimate designs, most are faced with the hard realities of budgeting time and money. Almost anything can happen if you have unlimited resources, but few have that luxury. For example, the desire to find that perfect fabric is not always fulfilled. You may want wool made as it was in the 1700s, but instead, the wool blend at a local fabric store may be the only thing that will work within the constraints of your time and budget. Does it make the costume any less appropriate? No. It is important to remember this is a theatrical production. The goal is not to reproduce or create a piece that would fool a museum. At the same time, within the production itself, it might appear to be a work of art that makes the actor feel like they have walked out of a painting, which will delight and enchant the audience. Still, designers must balance what will be effective against cost and the availability of supplies.

Once designers know who has been cast in each role, they have to take into account the actors' natural attributes and understand how to highlight them, not work against them. Different shapes and sizes of the actors' bodies offer wonderful variation on stage. If an actor's appearance differs from that which the designer had in mind, it may require an adjustment in the costume to accent the actor's qualities. For example, if the designer envisioned a short, thin man in a role, but a large, tall man is cast, it could affect the shape, fit, and scale of detail on the clothing.

All of this costuming art does not happen without the help of those who build the costumes. This includes the dyers, who are chemists as well as artists, who give each fabric the perfect shade; the cutters, who begin with a sketch to develop the patterns; the stitchers, who sit for hours at a sewing machine to make everything just right; and those individuals who alter the ready-made garments. It includes all of the artists who contribute to the overall look, which may include wigs and makeup. Whether there is an entire team of people performing these jobs, or the designer is doing it all, the results can be truly magical.

Due to the number of people with whom designers closely work, there is often a need to leave their ego at home and engage their sense of humor. Being a designer means working with different personalities with different needs. Keeping a sense of humor about oneself and the work helps everyone enjoy the experience. Theatre production teams all want the same thing: a production that thrills all involved, including the audience. Most involved feel as though they have put everything into the production. While it may be true that actors feel the most exposed, the designers also feel exposed or vulnerable when it comes to the opinions concerning the overall quality of the production. It is chancy to put your art out there for others to see. Because of this, theatre practitioners can be tense and even insecure at times. Costume designers are no different. This is the time when both understanding and a sense of humor are needed the most. Designers must keep their wits about them, roll with the changes, overcome stress, and, hopefully, still enjoy themselves.

If they can understand this and know that life does not revolve around such things as which buttons to use, for example, they have a greater chance of becoming truly great at what they do. Fine details are a valuable asset as long as the whole picture is kept in focus. Costume designers cannot think they or the costumes are more important than the other elements of the production.

One of the greatest tools in any designer's toolbox is the ability to draw. Whether by traditional means, or with the latest technology, the need to express ideas by drawing is a very important part of the dialogue with a production team. If you have sketches in a meeting with a director, it is important to be able to re-draw or draw over them as needed. The more complete the sketch, the better it will convey your ideas to the production team and the costume shop. The more a designer can draw with confidence, the more believable the drawing will be. Ultimately, while it is wonderful if the **rendering** is beautiful,

FIGURE 1.2 *These simple sketches convey the differences in the styles of dress in a quick manner that allowed open discussion concerning individual chorus members and the actors who would wear them, and they gave the director the opportunity to discuss desired changes. (Sketches of chorus women for Texas Tech University's production of* Women of Troy *by Melissa L Merz.)*

VANYA
and
SONIA
and
MASHA
and
SPIKE

Act 1, Sc. 1

Masha

Act 2, Sc. 2

Act 2, Sc. 3

FIGURE 1.3 *Character collage created for Masha using Polyvore. (Designed by Leigh Anne Crandall, for Texas Tech University's production of* Vanya and Sonia and Masha and Spike.*)*

FIGURE 1.4 *Example of a figure created on a tablet using Adobe Photoshop Touch and Autodesk's Sketchbook Pro. (Artwork by John Conner.)*

the main purpose is to convey information. The more detailed a rendering, the more control the designer will have.

Not all productions require drawn renderings. If working on a production where the costumes will be completely bought or pulled from stock, it might be more effective to show pictures from several resources. If the opportunity is available, showing actual garments may be the most useful. But certainly photos of different garments are helpful as well. Probably the most popular way of expressing initial ideas is through a collage, creating a series of images from magazines, the internet, and even photos of stock costumes, that show a production team a series of ideas about how a character is conceived. The majority of images will probably be of clothing. Images expressing color ideas or even **patterns** can also be included.

Each designer decides how to arrange the images to best fit the circumstances. The most common way of arranging these images is by male/female, lead characters/chorus, or even each character positioned individually. These pictures can be arranged and overlapped in several different ways—whichever method is most effective in relaying ideas. One of the most recent methods is the use of paper dolls. This includes using a figure—found or drawn—with clothing added on top. Images of specific clothing can be used. Other clothing can be cut to shape from a print appropriate to the item. It can be an effective way to get specific ideas across to a director and the production team, especially when relaying more contemporary designs. (See Chapter 4 for more details on rendering).

HOW TO BEGIN

> "What makes costume design so interesting to me is that rather than responding to a work of dramatic literature as a purely intellectual, critical exercise, a theatrical designer joins her own creative sensibility and artistic skill with the poetic genius of the playwright."
>
> Marcia Dixcy Jory[1] from *The Ingenue in White*, p. 4

With any play, the process starts with reading the script, which provides inspiration and information. The written play is the basis for style, rhythm, and characterization. While reading it the first time, movement, images, and emotions should flow through the mind, without any particular reason. Logic, or a sense of correctness, is not important during the first reading. The emphasis should be on experiencing the play as it is written. It is difficult not to form an opinion about the play, concerning likes and dislikes. However, designers must be mindful not to allow their opinions to cloud their judgment in regards to what they have to do. Allow those opinions to form, then push them aside. Think about what the playwright is saying, the plot of the script, and how it all comes together. Absorb the story and encourage the imagination to flow. After the initial assessments and images are formed, some designers like to spend a moment writing down those thoughts or creating sketches which do not limit

What If There Isn't a Script? What If It's an Idea?

Not all productions begin with a script. With devised theatre, it may be a line, an object, or a movement. If that is the case, there is not a play to read before rehearsals or the more traditional design process begins. A theme or idea may be the catalyst for a production. A number of companies have been established that use the devised theatre technique: Blessed Unrest, The Ghost Road, Gecko, and Faulty Optic among others. More than with a traditional play, the process of using the devised theatre technique includes exploring ideas, some of which work, while others are abandoned. In the end, the final product may be completely different from what was started. Maybe the central theme is the only idea that survived from the first rehearsals. Costume designers should contribute to the experience whether they end up having little or a significant impact on the final outcome of the performance. No matter what the situation, the designers have to be flexible and willing to go through several ideas and changes before settling on something that works for the final production.

With dance, movement and music often tell the designer what the costume or costumes need to be. It is possible to start with a costume or items of clothing that inspire

FIGURES 1.5 & 1.6 *Photos of Eurydice's Dream by Blessed Unrest, a company that utilizes devised theatre. (Directed by Jessica Burr. Created by Blessed Unrest. Performed in New York, 2013. Photo by Alan Roche.)*

a dance, although that is not common. The theme, music, and movement often dictate what type of clothing is needed to enhance the performance of the dance. If the music has a hard staccato or heavy drumbeat, it is less likely that a flowing ballet outfit will be desired. But if juxtaposition is needed to make a point, then a flowing costume may be appropriate. More often than not, however, the costume is used to enhance or highlight the performance, not to fight it.

While movement is important for most performers, this is doubly true for those involved in arts such as dance or ice skating. Many ice skaters choose costumes that show the reach and extension of their bodies. They need the judges to see their technique, and their costume should not interfere. The last thing they need is a costume that gets entangled in their legs or arms while doing a triple toe loop, for example. For many dances, the line or extension holds the same importance. The costume can help to express the full emotive purpose of each dancer. It must first serve the movement needed for the piece. An emotion, idea, or even character can become secondary in design importance.

them to one area of design. These ideas and images may remain personal, or they can be shared with others in the production team. They may be the catalyst for an initial design or they may be held until further readings. The whole point is to have these notes available when or if they are needed.

Subsequent readings will include intense scrutiny of the script to discover all the important facts, details, and nuances. After initially allowing the imagination to flow freely, future readings require a closer examination of the script. Research can help with finding specific details concerning the environment and background information as well as script analysis. Script analysis involves characterization and identifies restrictions within the play. Designers have to start considering the limitations of their specific location and production including space, budget, and resources.

RESEARCH

Whether designers engage in research at this point in the process or after script analysis, it is important to be familiar with the playwright, criticism, and the environment surrounding the play. Plays and characters rarely exist within themselves. Playwrights have a reason for setting the story in a specific time and place. It is important to understand the world in which these characters live. This environment includes: architecture, music and art, political climate, and religious situation.

Why study architecture? The short answer is aesthetics. What is attractive to the eye influences architecture and fashion. Similar styles are often reflected in both. As an example, if studying the **Art Nouveau** movement, there are similar patterns within architectural décor and elements of clothing. If a play is set during this time, researching architecture may influence or inspire the look of the costumes. Knowledge of both can influence a designer, even subconsciously.

Taking a look at the art and music of a particular time helps to put the play in perspective. Art, which can include paintings, photos, sculptures, and folk art, is a reflection of what is attractive to the people living during that time. Paintings and photography are considered primary sources of research. Primary research can be anything that is a true representation of the original item. An actual garment is desirable but not always available. For instance, few garments have survived from the 17th century: but if designers look at the art of Peter Paul Rubens and Gabriel Metsu, they will have a better idea of what people of different social status or occupations looked like and how the garments were worn. With an actual garment, people can see all sides, including the inside and how it is made. But how a garment is worn or used is equally important.

Clothing is not the only research focus in paintings, however. The colors used in the paintings can inspire color choices in a production. Furniture, tools, architecture, and lighting depicted in the artwork can also have an influence.

Photography has added volumes to research material. With the ease and price of photography, images of almost anything exist. With a camera in many households, not to mention smart phones, photos have documented almost every aspect of life on earth. The addition of the internet has made these images available to everyone. If someone is searching for 1890s women's swimsuits, numerous photos taken by everyday people appear. Photos allow costume designers to see numerous examples of hard-to-find articles of clothing.

Music is also a representation of the culture of a particular era. The difference between Mozart, Ragtime, and Rock and Roll is significant. Knowing what types of music were popular during a specific time or in a specific place can go a long way toward understanding where and how the characters lived. Listening to the music while designing can help to capture a sense of the overall feeling of the time period. Designing is not only about

FIGURES 1.7 & 1.8 (left) *A dress worn by the Empress Alexandra Romonov showing some of the decorative details reflecting the Art Nouveau style. (Portrait of a Lady by Arthur Ferraris (1856–1936). Auktionshaus Zeller, courtesy of Wikimedia Commons.) (top) Note the detailing on the dress is similar to the details on the Art Nouveau ironwork. (Decorative window designed by Matin Lumineux. Pharmacie Lesage à Douvres-la-Délivrande dans le Calvados (Basse-Normandie, France), courtesy of Wikimedia Commons.)*

visual research—every aspect of a culture or time period is important, and music is a very significant part of understanding the big picture.

When exploring the details of a time period, culture, or location, the political and religious climate can have a huge influence. Is there a war going on at the time of the play? If it does not involve the immediate location, is the connecting country involved? Is there political upheaval within the government? Knowledge of the politics is central to understanding the meaning within the writing. Examples of playwrights who showed a deep understanding of political climate include Augusto Boal, Vaclav Havel, and Peter Weiss; all known for their politically charged plays.

Likewise, religion may be highly significant. It is difficult to truly embrace the characters in *The Last Night in Ballyhoo* by Alfred Uhry without a basic understanding of Judaism. Because the play takes place in the late 1930s, the characters are aware

of the persecution taking place in Europe. It does not affect the characters directly, but connection through Jewish faith makes it important for the family. No matter what the political and religious situation may be, it is important to at least know what or how it affects the characters within the play.

Research should also include information about the playwright. Understanding their background, political and religious viewpoints, and the time period in which they lived can provide insight into the play's overall meaning and help to explain why the playwright chose a particular topic or genre.

Critical research can further a designer's knowledge of the play and the playwright. Search engines within library systems are particularly useful. Databases contain critical writings from everywhere in the world. Accessing and negotiating these databases takes practice, but once learned, it can be an invaluable resource.

AFTER THE INITIAL READING

After reading the play for the first time, the purpose of subsequent readings is to analyze or break down the script. While some of this can be accomplished with the director, **dramature**, and the rest of the design team, each designer should use this analysis to discover the possibilities and restrictions in a script. Betty Edwards writes in her book, *Drawing on the Artist Within*,[2] about the creative process. While Betty Edwards is not directly referring to script analysis, she does outline a process that can be adopted for theatrical designers. She identifies five steps in the creative process: first insight, saturation, incubation, illumination, and verification.

First Insight

Whenever possible, it can be beneficial to understand a director's impression of a script. Some may share these impressions or even provide an in-depth analysis with a concept. Whether the information is given in person or long distance, hopefully there is the opportunity to further discuss those ideas with the entire design team. Characterization, intent, desired message to the audience, and other ideas or goals are important for all designers involved. One of the questions a designer should ask a director is how much importance they place on the italicized words written in the script. In a recently published script, those italicized words most likely came from the playwright, who wrote them to further the understanding of the character's intent, to clarify the scene, or to offer a description that may not be apparent. If you are fortunate enough to know the playwright, you may be able to ask them if their intent was to use the italicized words as a guide or as an integral part of the production. If you are not able to surmise the degree of importance from the playwright, then it should be asked of the director. If you have a highly conceptual production (all black and white, for instance), then a description of a character's green belt, if italicized, no longer applies to that production. While it is true some italicized directions came from a stage manager written during an original production, this is less likely to be true in a recently published work.

The intent may be difficult to ascertain when the description is part of a line. If the line reads "What a lovely green belt," followed by the italicized words, *she says sarcastically,* then those italicized words give great insight into characterization. This could mean the belt is tacky, gaudy, or does not match. Or it could be insight into the character of the one who spoke. Maybe they are judgmental, cruel, or simply rude to point out the possibly odd color. These italicized words should not be ignored, but may need further clarification from the director on the intent.

> "There is no doubt playwrights write, but they also build, make, shape, construct, arrange, rearrange, assemble, level, and even restore and renovate."
>
> Rosemary Ingham[3] from *From Page to Stage*, p. 23

Saturation

When a designer engages in a second reading, it should be used to discern specifics about the play. Rosemary Ingham,[3] in *From Page to Stage*, compares this stage of the process to investigating a crime scene. You collect facts while looking at items that influence the scene, character, and background of the play.

Time, place, and location are often the first details any designer discovers about a play. Playwrights may include this information at the beginning of the script. But if it is not spelled out, then it is important to look for clues within the script. A playwright might include details such as "1969, New England." While this is a great start, it does not tell everything. New England does give insight into climate, style, and possibly attitude. But the more specific the details, the more information and control a designer has. Characters may refer to a landmark or something specific to a location to help determine it is Maine, not Vermont or another New England location. A designer has to become adept at discerning the information from a script that is needed to create a cohesive production. When playwrights do not give specifics about season, location, or time, the director or production team will have to make a decision about each of these aspects. Investigating a play answers many of the questions designers ask.

A costume designer needs to study each character in depth, but this character analysis is not solely the work of the costume designer. The director, the actor, and other designers will do their own analysis. All should communicate their ideas about the characters to be able to come to a cohesive conclusion. Each actor can inspire the look of the character. A designer may have pictured a short, stout person in a particular role, but if the actor who was cast is tall and slender, then those original ideas may not be applicable. The actor who is cast can inspire characterization and therefore a design. It certainly pays for a designer to work with the assets of that actor, not against them. There is nothing more satisfying for a designer than to be in a fitting with an actor and have them say "now I know my character," or "this really adds to my character."

Time of Day

Clothing has a specific purpose, one that often coincides with the time of day. For example, in the Victorian Era, men and women

HEDDA GABLER - Thea Elvsted   Esther Van Eek

JENNY'S HOUSE OF JOY
JENNY

E.Van Eek

FIGURES 1.9 & 1.10 *Renderings of Hedda Gabler (1890) (left) and Jenny's House of Joy (1871) (right). (Design by Esther Van Eek for the University of Windsor, ON.)*

often changed their clothes depending on the time or activity. A woman would not wear her evening gown to accept visitors into the parlor for afternoon tea. A man would not wear his white dress gloves for his morning ride in the park. If designing costumes in the Victorian time period, it is vital that you know which glove was worn to each function. It was not uncommon for a man to wear six different pairs of gloves throughout the day for separate purposes. The rationale may not be clear in the modern world, but it was relevant for that time period and is therefore relevant for the play.

If a character is seen on stage in their pajamas, it is likely to be bedtime or early morning. If a character is wearing pajamas in the middle of the day, it is easy to assume something is awry. The character may be sick, depressed, out of work, or simply lazy. No matter the reason, the audience will note the difference in dress and make inferences as to the hour.

Juxtaposition of time of day and what characters wear can be an effective way to show conflict or a psychological factor in the individual character. If a gentleman on stage is wearing a tuxedo at 7 a.m., while the lighting indicates the sun is rising, chances are that the gentleman has been active all night. Other scenarios could apply, but no matter what the reason, it is unusual to see someone in a tuxedo at that time. An audience would be aware something has kept the gentleman from changing into appropriate clothes for the time of day.

Season

Out of necessity, clothing naturally follows seasons. If it is cold outside, heavier or additional clothing items are needed. Conversely, if it is warm, it stands to reason less clothing is desirable. Raincoats are rarely worn when rain is not involved or anticipated. Clothing and season become remarkable when the desire to be fashionable collides with the needs of the weather. If a man wears a suit in the summer, it could be the need to display social standing or authority matters more than comfort. But a shorter skirt may be worn with tights and boots to make it more appropriate for colder weather. Thus, whether it is a skirt or suit, the fabric choice may be an indication of weather more than the garment itself. Suits can be made of a **tropical weight wool** or wool more suitable for a cold climate. A skirt can be **chiffon** or **corduroy**. Weight of fabric, type, and layers will all contribute to the idea of season.

Season is often not directly stated in the play. A careful reading can provide an answer to this question. Hints about holidays or historical moments may be evident. The question of school taking place or summer vacation will narrow down the possibilities. Does a character mention wanting to swim or build a snowman? When season is unclear, it becomes important for the production team to come to an agreement, as lighting and other aspects of the production can also be affected.

Historical Period

Fashion continually changes and may be defined by movements throughout history. Each period in history adopted a distinct silhouette. It is simple to recognize the broad boxy shape of Henry VIII from all of the other Henrys. The Watteau backed gown of the 18th century offered a grace to the silhouette that included panniers. The "S curve" of the Edwardian period is unlike any other time in history, which shortly moved into the distinct look of the flapper in the 1920s. Fashion, like art, has distinct movements, which can be defined by cultural location and driven by the need for change. Fashion as movements can be divided in many ways. The following is one example: Renaissance, Elizabethan, Baroque, Romanticism, Victorian, Art Nouveau, **Art Deco**, and Modernism. Within these movements, fashion has changed many times as a result of cultural change, advancement in technology, availability of supplies, and even a reaction to boredom.

Towards the beginning of the 19th century, fashion starts to change approximately with each decade. If a play takes place in the Victorian era, the fashion could have several distinct looks. It is therefore crucial to narrow the time period to a specific year or at least a decade.

Moving into the 20th century, fashion for men had more subtle changes, while fashion for women took on different looks more quickly. For instance, the 1920s' dress had a distinct purpose. With the liberation of women, a desire rose to rid themselves of corsets and other restrictions. The need to have attire that was easy to move in brought on shorter skirts and lighter dresses. Women could move, play, and work with greater ease. Special corsets for exercise were dismissed as an item of the past.

With the popularity of the American movie, movie stars started to influence fashion more than the fashion industry or, perhaps, societal factors. The Motion Picture Production Code of 1930 sought to ensure morality for the public. The following is an excerpt[4] under the category of *Costume* that greatly affected the fashion of the time:

PARTICULAR PRINCIPLES:

(1) *The more intimate parts of the human body* are male and female organs and the breasts of a woman.
  (a) They should *never be uncovered*.
  (b) They should *not* be covered with *transparent* or *translucent* material.
  (c) They should not be clearly and unmistakably *outlined* by the garment.

(2) *The less intimate parts of the body*, the legs, arms, shoulders and back, are less certain of causing reactions on the part of the audience.

In reaction to the restrictions, costume designers decided to accent the parts of the body that could be exposed. The result was the beautiful **bias**-cut gowns of the 1930s, with bare arms and backs. The result was that women were now seen as more sensual than ever in their backless dresses.

Men's fashion was also affected by the movie industry. While sales of the t-shirt allegedly dropped after Clark Gable was seen not wearing an undershirt in the movie *It Happened One Night*, the t-shirt made a comeback with Marlon Brando in *A Streetcar Named Desire*. T-shirts and jeans became associated with the "bad boy" or rebel look, as modeled by Marlon Brando and James Dean. This led to young men wearing jeans, white t-shirts, and short jackets in their everyday life.

Knowing the time period can be instrumental in understanding the characters' motivation. Situations arise that are a product of a specific era. For example, in order to understand *Death of a Salesman* by Arthur Miller, it is important that the audience recognizes a time when the door-to-door salesman existed. The end of the door-to-door salesman era in American history is important to the story and should be distinct for the audience. If a company tried to move the play into the 21st century, the play would be confusing and the meaning would be lost.

Along with time period, location, especially geographic area, can influence how a character is dressed, and so will also have a large influence on a production.

Geographic Location

A play takes place somewhere. It may be in a house, for example. That house must exist in a specific location to dictate its style. Even in the United States, the location or region of the play will make a difference in what the characters wear. If a play takes place in Montana in the winter, the clothing will differ from that in Southern California. While the obvious difference will be the weight of clothing (in response to the weather differences), other indications will also exist. For instance, it is not uncommon for someone in Southern California to wear flip-flops year round. But someone living in Montana probably would not consider wearing flip-flops other than during the summer.

Different countries influence costumes. Specific styles can be determined by what is available and traditional. If a play talks about **Wellingtons** and **Burberry**, it is probably based in England. A **kilt**, on the other hand, is commonplace in Scotland. **Shalwar kameez**, **saris**, and **dhoti** denote India as the location. Each item is distinct to the country that brought about its popularity. If a play is set in Mexico, the audience is not likely to see **Hanfu** unless it is a Chinese man or woman who is out of place. (Conversely, if this is the desired effect, then Hanfu may be a perfect choice.) The style of clothing might tell the audience more about the location than any other part of the production.

Political Climate

Extremes in political climate can greatly affect fashion, which was certainly the case during the two World Wars. With restrictions on importing and exporting, and most efforts aimed at the needs of the soldiers, the supplies available to the public were limited, and this in turn affected style. In the United States during World

FIGURE 1.11 *Texas Tech University's production of* Death of a Salesman. *(Costume design by Melissa L. Merz. Photo by Andrea Bilkey.)*

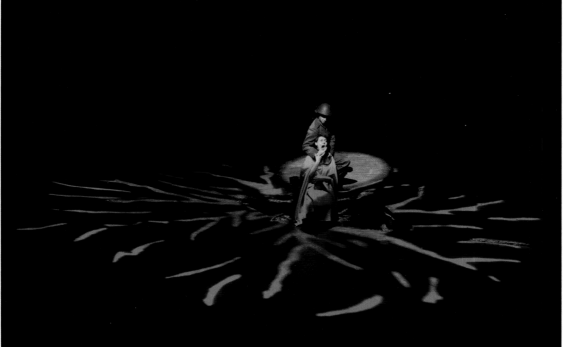

FIGURES 1.12 & 1.13 *Baylor University's production of* Mad Forest. *(Costume design by Sally Askins. Photos by Jarod Tseng.)*

War II, silk and nylon were used for parachutes, tents, and sutures. These materials were therefore not used for stockings, and this shortage led women to draw lines down the backs of their legs to emulate the seam found in stockings of that era. During this War, the conservation of fabrics was ensured with the use of coupons, which limited how much fabric people were allotted. Thus, skirts became shorter and not as full, and men's suits had two buttons and no cuffs. When the War over and restrictions were lifted, supplies became plentiful, and the New Look, created by **Dior**, was popular with its full skirts and added petticoats. Three-button jackets for men were back in style. The political climate no longer restricted supplies and so had less effect on fashion.

Political climate is often linked with geographical location. In studying a play like *Mad Forest* by Caryl Churchill, it is vital to understand what was happening in Romania in the 1980s. The play reflects the attitudes and fears of people facing uncertainty concerning the future of the country. To fully comprehend those fears, one must first understand the details of Ceausescu's reign as Romania's leader. The lack of fuel, food, and supplies rendered him unpopular among the people. Ceausescu and his wife lived in luxury while those around him suffered. Stories of how he would sustain himself by drinking the blood of young people are written into the scene about the vampire and the dog. When designing a play based on real events, it is important to research the mood and feelings of those involved, not just the clothing worn at that time. Glamour shots of Americans will not help tell the story of repression and unrest.

Characterization

While time, place, and location are certainly an important beginning, research of the play does not end there. Characterization is vital to any designer, but arguably more so for a costume designer. Whether a character has the majority of lines in a play, or none at all, it is important to question who they are, what they desire, their purpose, and how they relate to the play and to other characters. The questions can be endless, and it is important to discover each character through what they say about themselves and what others say about them, by studying all interactions.

In *A Streetcar Named Desire*, sisters Blanche and Stella are very different from each other. Recognizing the changes they go through during the course of the play is significant. At the beginning of the play, Blanche appears to be the more sophisticated of the two sisters. She has finer clothes, speaks of grander and more genteel things, and appears to be more worldly than Stella. Eventually, it is revealed that many of these attributes are just a façade. Blanche is actually the more delicate of the two sisters. The script refers to moths and light, diaphanous scarves, the need for quiet, and the desire for softer lighting. Softer lighting is one way to hide her age, but "soft" and "delicate" are used symbolically. In the end, "delicate" describes her mental state. While Stella may initially be perceived as the more fragile sister, eventually she proves to be the stronger of the two. Stella is in a troubled marriage, but she shows great strength in that relationship.

The same analysis must be made for characters that have few or no lines. Although a soldier in a Shakespearean play may not have any lines, how does he relate to others in the play? What is his role or importance? Is it valid to assign rank? Is it someone who will stand in the background looking official, or someone who will have an important part in the outcome of the play? Should he be seen differently because he participates in a pivotal moment in the play? All of these questions should be answered as part of the process of designing the characters.

When considering age, sex, and cultural aspects of a play, casting may have more influence than the script itself. If a director embraces color-blind or cross-culture casting, it could make a significant difference in how to analyze those traits. A character that is written as male, but played by a female, will have a different impact on the production.

Along with the director, costume designers must take all of these matters into account.

Age

Young people tend to move towards the latest fashions and are often more interested in how they look. It is common for young people to want to show their body size and type as well as embrace the adage "beauty is pain." (Think skinny jeans, tight shirts, high heels, and other items that are more fashionable than utilitarian.) As people age, they may adapt a more practical view towards clothing, preferring things that will last over time rather than the latest fashion trend. Many may be more content to wear either classic styles or other items that they enjoyed in the past.

Health also plays an important role in what people decide to wear. As people age, they gain a few aches and pains: whether by experience or necessity, many choose comfort over fashion. Chances are an older person would not want to wear high heels if they have a job that requires them to stand all day. With additional stress on the feet, more comfortable shoes become desirable. Tighter fitting clothes may not be wanted or considered attractive on someone older. Taking all of this into account, it is easy to apply these considerations about age to any time period.

FIGURE 1.14 *Corey Wilson, age 22, playing the older character of Jim in Big River. (Design by Emily Gill for the University of Montevillo, AL.)*

Not all actors are the age of their character, and not all characters act their age. If a character is trying to hide their age, the color and fit of their clothing can indicate this. Wearing the latest fashion or more colorful or bolder prints gives an indication of the character's defiance towards their age, as does how the figure is accentuated. Conversely, if someone younger is playing an older character, they can be assisted in their characterization by makeup, padding, looser clothing, or comfortable shoes. A common way to indicate someone of advanced age is to dress them in an older or former period style.

Sex

A costume designer should work with the director to express the needs of the play when it comes to the gender or sexual orientation of a character. A classic example of this is *Peter Pan* by Sir James Matthew Barrie, which has a lead character that is a boy who never grows up. In many productions, a woman plays Peter Pan; past productions include Cathy Rigby, Mary Martin, Sandy Duncan, and Alison Williams. These women were all playing the part of a boy, but it was never the intent to have the woman be boys, just to represent the spirit of boyishness. On the other hand, the audience is supposed to believe Neil Patrick Harris *is* the character of Hedwig, a botched transgender singer and performer, in *Hedwig and the Angry Inch* by John Mitchell and Stephen Trask. With bold makeup, large hair, and flamboyant clothing, Harris is transformed into this character. For any production, it is important actors are believable in all that they stand for. Similarly, directors must decide how they want to cast the character of Joanne in *Come Back to the Five and Dime, Jimmy Dean, Jimmy Dean,* by Ed Graczyk. Joanne returns for her high school reunion in the small town of Marfa, Texas. After other characters attempt to remember who their fellow schoolmate is, Joanne finally divulges she used to be their friend Joe. If a female is cast as a transgendered male, she is easily believable. If a male is cast in the role, it is important that the audience believe that a female has walked onto the stage.

Occupation

Much has been written about the topic of dressing for occupation. One of the more popular observations has to do with uniforms, both official and unofficial. Official uniforms can obviously indicate a specific job; workers in different professions wear different uniforms. Some military and police wear all one color to appear more authoritarian and imposing. Doctors, medical staff, and scientists still wear white coats to represent cleanliness or sterility. Firefighters wear protective clothing that is recognizable to everyone as the gear needed to perform their job. Robes, stoles, and collars are worn by clerics during religious ceremonies to distinguish them from parishioners. Judges wear traditional robes that differentiate them from others in the courtroom. Today, it is common for most businesses to use some form of uniform to distinguish their employees from their customers. Fast food restaurants and large electronic stores are examples of businesses that have adopted khaki pants and polo shirts with a logo as their uniform.

However, unofficial uniforms tend to be more veiled: these are the type of clothing people readily recognize as a uniform without actually being a uniform. For example, one of the more challenging combinations of dress to put on stage is the classic white button-down shirt and black slacks. White shirts and black slacks have become a recognizable look for waiters: many restaurants have used this combination for years. While this can be used to your advantage when needing a recognizable waiter,

FIGURE 1.15 *Example of a male playing a transgendered female in* Come Back to the Five and Dime, Jimmy Dean, Jimmy Dean. *(Photo from Mitch Baker's production of the play. Produced by the University of Michigan, Flint.)*

it is not as convenient when you would like this combination of colors on an actor who is not playing a waiter. Another example is the American male politician. For decades, many politicians have worn dark, single-breasted suits with a light shirt and red tie. This is so recognizable as a politician's uniform that when President Obama wore a light tan suit, the press made several comments about it. On August 28, 2014, President Obama held a press conference on the threat of ISIS in Iraq and Syria. News and social media immediately talked about the "tan suit" as opposed to the topic of the conference. Twitter reported six thousand tweets about the suit by the time the press conference was over. Interestingly, President Obama had previously admitted to only wearing blue or grey suits in a *Vanity Fair* article in 2012.[5] Although there is no clear reason as to why politicians wear dark suits with light shirts, it can be seen as an unofficial uniform.

Social status, in conjunction with occupation, supplies another kind of unofficial uniform. This uniform has more to do with a culture's expectations of what someone should look like. Stereotypes fall into this category. For example, walking on a college campus, people should be able to tell a professor from a student. Perhaps a professor has more money to spend on wardrobe items, and perhaps a student does not concentrate much on style. In describing a college student, the items would likely include a sweatshirt or t-shirt with the college logo, jeans, and athletic sneakers. In the past, male professors were required to wear suit jackets, and female professors were required to wear skirts. While this is no longer true, it is not unusual to see male and female professors wear a jacket, slacks, and dress shoes. It is therefore fairly easy to recognize the difference between the two occupations of student and professor.

Social Status

For centuries, the clothing a person wore was an easy determinant of social status. The functionality of garments was inherent in the needs of each individual's life. For those with means, practicality was not a priority in their choice of garments or décor. These items required special care to make them last. On the other hand, someone who did manual labor would not be able to wear silks or other delicate fabrics. All workers had to wear clothing that would withstand the needs of their jobs. Those same workers often created their own fabrics, knowing that they needed to be sturdy, long lasting, and warm. Clothing had little to do with what was fashionable at the time and more to do with function, use, and material availability.

Money or riches certainly influenced people's appearance. Only the richest people, or royalty, could afford luxuries. Centuries ago, items like silk and indigo dye were very rare and expensive in the Western part of the world; therefore, they could only be attained by the elite who could afford them. Intricate trims and more detailed styles further set those with high social status apart from the working class. These differences in clothing are apparent throughout history.

FIGURE 1.16 *Jacob Jordaens' painting of Mary of Burgundy,* Mary at Her Devotions. *(Courtesy The Metropolitan Museum of Art)*

In the early Middle Ages, a woman's social status was obvious by the height of her **hennin** or the length of her **train**. Those with a title of Princess had hennins that could be 36 inches tall and a train longer than 20 inches. Noble women would not wear hennins higher than 24 inches, and her maids-in-waiting could have neither a hennin that high nor a longer train. Looking back at these fashions today, it is difficult to understand why hennins and trains were so popular, but it is easy to see how it would divide laborers from those who had the luxury of choosing and setting fashion.

In some cases, changes in fashion evolved as a result of new discoveries or inventions. The **ruff** became popular in the Elizabethan period after the discovery of **starch**. Those who spent time cleaning and re-starching those collars and ruffs did not have the time or need to wear those items themselves. Steam, heat, and sweat all affect starch, so ruffs would not be a good clothing choice for someone who spent time working in a livery, kitchen, or in the fields. This particular look was reserved for the elite. People of the court did not have to do hard labor, and they could afford to have someone cater to their fashion needs.

Some clothing was so complicated that a person needed help to dress, and hence the money or means to pay staff for this help. A character such as **Marie Antoinette** would need more than one person to help her dress for the public. Wearing hair that stood high enough to include a model ship or other decoration took time to create. Ladies-in-waiting might help with various details such as wigs, shoes, and makeup. Only those who had time and money to dress for the purpose of being seen could support this lifestyle. While Marie Antoinette's elaborate clothes is an extreme example, the social differences between someone who could afford numerous individuals to assist in daily routine and someone who could not afford help would dictate the elaborate nature of dress.

Eventually, with a change in commerce, merchants could afford finer materials and so the lines between wealth and class became blurred. But while merchants often copied the styles of the elite, regulations prevented them from using materials reserved for royalty. Laws were passed to separate the socially elite from people with newly acquired riches, thus preventing lower classes from imitating the dress of those with higher status.

As the Industrial Revolution took hold in the 19th century, the invention of the sewing machine provided ready-made clothes, which closed the gap between the social classes even more. Clothing was now readily available to the working and middle classes, bringing fashionable items into the average home. Although differences still existed between fabrics, trims, and practicality of the garments, fashion now had similarities across all classes. Social status began to be influenced by job rather than class position. People started to show their riches in different ways; the elite continued to have garments made by specific designers in order to make certain that they looked better than those of lower social status. By the 20th century, evidence of wealthy men indulging in luxury items could be seen in print. While the suit became standard attire for men, their wives could be adorned with furs and jewels in order to show the wealth within the family. Commonly referred to as "vicarious consumption," men had the ability to show their wealth by embellishing the women close to them rather than themselves.

Culture

Culture is a term used to refer to people with shared beliefs or practices. Those brought up in the same household, same town, or even the same part of the country, are more likely to have shared beliefs. While not everyone will agree completely with everyone else in a family or group, similarities still exist within traditions, customs, morals, and habits.

FIGURE 1.18 *Birkenstocks with socks. (Photo by Fredrick Christoffel.)*

FIGURE 1.17 *Abayas hanging in a store. Note the variety of décor on the garments; even within the simple garment, individuals can express style. (Photo by Melissa L. Merz.)*

Religion is passed down from generation to generation through tradition and ritual. Some people believe that these traditions have not changed since their inception. Traditions can shape the attitudes of individuals, as well as influencing clothing, sometimes based on the ideals of the religion or sometimes based on the culture of past generations. For example, the traditional clothing of Muslims in the Middle East is based on a combination of religion and tradition. The men's dress is commonly known as thobe (thawb) or kundura, which is customarily white, while women wear a black robe called an abaya. Black is considered more subdued or modest, and is therefore a better choice for women. It is not unusual to see some women who only wear the headscarf, known as a hijab, without the abaya. Some women do not wear the hijab and wear the abaya open. The women who wear all of the clothing items are adhering to the requirements of religion and tradition, while those who wear the abaya open are dressing for the purpose of tradition only.

Selectivity can dictate what is considered normal or acceptable in certain cultural groups. Jeans are a preferred item in most American's wardrobes; however, wearing jeans is not accepted in the Amish community. While religion may be a part of this choice, it is further dictated by the belief system within the community. The importance of living a simple life does not include participating in commerce with the outside world, which is represented by jeans. The strict rules of Amish dress are considered normal within this community, though they may be considered odd or strange to other cultures.

Items of clothing that are popular within a community may be a cultural choice. For example, in the northwestern part of the United States, it is not unusual to see someone wearing Birkenstock sandals all year round, including the practice of wearing socks with their sandals when the weather gets cold. This fashion choice is accepted as part of the culture in this area. But acceptable clothing in one part of the world may not be considered fashion in another area. Outside of northwestern United States, it would be difficult to find someone who would wear socks with any sandal for any reason.

Psychological Factors

Psychological factors encompass several considerations, including each character's backstory and state of mind, as well as relevant stereotypes. A designer will need to study the characters' attitudes towards themselves, their environment, how other characters perceive them, and their desire to be attractive to others.

It is not uncommon to dress to make an impression or to present an attitude. No one would take doctors seriously if they walked into an exam room wearing sweatpants, even if they had on a white coat. Doctors dress to portray themselves as professionals with authority. An "emo" or "goth" dresses in dark clothing, heavy boots, and heavy eye makeup. The impression they want others to have is that they are dark, deep, and moody. The problem is that they are all of those things, just like all others who want to portray themselves as "goth-like." While it may seem typical, or even stereotypical, most people tend to dress for the impression they want to give.

Even within the confines of what might be considered typical dress, there are attitudes that influence how something is worn. For example, an actor playing a businessman is wearing a suit. If the actor wears a suit with the top button of the shirt unbuttoned, the tie loosely tied, and the shirttails hanging out, that will give an audience insight into how the character feels about his unofficial uniform. If an actor begins the play wearing the suit in a traditional way but changes to the aforementioned description, that too will give insight into a change in attitude

FIGURE 1.19 *The character of Belise in* The Learned Ladies *is confident that everyone is attracted to her. (Costume design by Melissa L. Merz. Produced by Texas Tech University, Department of Theatre and Dance. Photo by Ashton Thornhill.)*

about the character's job, life, or simply his demeanor. A character who changes from conforming to society's dictates to not caring what others think, is giving an indication of his psychological state. It could be he wants to make sure he does not look like others in society; he may be separating himself or rebelling against the norm; or perhaps he is simply getting ready to relax. For the audience, the way the clothing is worn is as important as the clothing itself.

Being attractive to others is certainly desirable. If someone has a specific body part they like, they might accent that part for others to notice. Conversely, they might try to hide any part that is deemed unattractive. Romantic purpose is an obvious reason to dress attractively. But in actuality, dressing to enhance features can also interest friends because people are naturally drawn to beauty in all things. If someone feels attractive, they are likely to exude more confidence that will attract others. An interesting situation is when a character *thinks* they are dressed to impress, but everyone knows they are not. This not only gives insight into the character's understanding of themselves, but also into how others feel about that character, especially if they make a comment about their look. An even more interesting character is one who dresses how they wish, knowing it may not be attractive, and does not care what others think. While this may seem rebellious, it could also be seen as eccentric. The character of Mame in *Mame* by Lawrence, Lee, and Herman, embodies the concept of doing and dressing how she wanted, rather than how others thought she should.

At times, people dress to deceive or manipulate. A character might want to hide a lack of wealth by choosing to dress beyond their financial means; and a common tactic for defense lawyers is to dress their client in a way that portrays innocence. The question here is not truth, but a chance to guide the viewer's opinion. If a defendant appears in a prison jumpsuit, the jury may be more open to the possibility of guilt. Whereas a defendant that goes to court dressed in a tailored suit gives the appearance of respectability and can encourage thoughts of innocence. Characters may be dressed to betray their true selves in order to further the characterization or plot within a play. A duke may try to hide his identity by dressing as a peasant to be able to move among common people. Under these circumstances, the audience knows the plot while the other characters within the play are not aware of the situation.

Incubation

> "Incubation: the time when thought process happens. Often the time when raw ideas are started and put into visuals, while still mulling over the production as a whole."
> Ming Chen[6] from *Visual Literacy for Theatre*, p. 17

For many designers, this is the most fun, and possibly the most creative part, of the process. It is at this point designers have to take the time to think about the play itself. It is the time when they look over their notes, think about characters, and consider all of the conversations they have had with the director and fellow designers. Designers may recall something that has inspired them and run with it in their research.

Illumination

> "[T]he time, and sometimes the moment, when the thoughts all come together. A designer may feel like 'this is it.'"
> Ming Chen[7] from *Visual Literacy for Theatre*, p. 9

A very exciting part of the process, this stage is often described as the "Eureka moment." After hours, days, and maybe months, all of the thinking, researching, and examination finally pays off. The moment when a designer sees something in their research and everything falls into place is a magical moment. Parts of the designs may simply fall into place. At this time, a designer puts images, sketches, swatches, and other visuals together to show the rest of the team. While it is always important to listen to everyone, they might have that feeling of "I can't wait to show my ideas and images."

Inspiration for a design can come from anywhere. In the process of looking through all kinds of research, inspiration can be seen in anything that has been collected. It is often visual, but does not have to be. As previously discussed, someone on the production team may present an icon, image, thought, question, or sound that might be the catalyst for another designer's process. In working with one of Shakespeare's history plays, the inner workings of a clock may inspire not only a design, but also describe the flow of costume or set changes. In a four character play, perhaps each character is associated with a season.

Color palettes can be inspired by a piece of artwork from the time period. Music can inspire the silhouette of a costume by the flow or the staccato of the beat. Designers are often inspired by nature. Flowers can influence a color palette as well as the shape or décor of a costume. The colors of fall leaves may be the inspiration for a chorus. A still life painting may represent the different characters and their relationship to each other.

Icons, or an object that represents something else, may be presented in a meeting that catches the attention of a designer. A piece of sandstone looks hard, but actually crumbles easily, much like the reign of Macbeth. Yet the objects do not necessitate direct use in a costume or design. In the example of sandstone, it is doubtful sandstone would be used directly on the costume. However, a designer might look for fabrics that appear strong but rip easily. A lighting designer may purposely change the vibrancy of a costume by using a contrasting gel color in a pivotal scene.

A designer might not realize the numerous ways in which their inspiration influenced them in the process of creating a production. On the other hand, inspiration may be seen in every aspect of a production. The level of influence will likely become a part of the discussion with the director and the rest of the design team.

Verification

> "I think of my job as a matter of problem solving. I work within restrictions. The theater space, the play, the director, the set, the actors—numerous factors circumscribe my choices into smaller and smaller concentric spheres."
>
> Marcia Dixcy Jory[1] from *The Ingenue in White*, p. 7

The final part of the creative process involves figuring out if the Eureka moment actually works. Every design has parameters: it needs to work within the concept or ideas set forth by the director and the team. Budget, space, resources, and time are some of the considerations. Many would see the budget as the biggest restraint, but this is not necessarily so. No one feels they have enough time, either in the design process or in the build process.

Working in a large costume shop with lots of amenities is a wonderful thing. It is also rare. Designers can do almost anything if they have access to a dye vat, spray room, craft area, and wig area. It is also a privilege to work with fully staffed shops that include cutters, first hands, stitchers, crafts artisans, wig and hair designers, and all the wardrobe people needed for any quick change. While this kind of costume shop is a dream for many, it is not a reality for the majority of situations.

Designers must keep in mind all of the restrictions while walking their way through the ideas and inspiration for a production. Grand thoughts will not help anyone on a production team if ideas are presented that will cost more than the budget will allow, or the costume shop does not have the personnel to be able to perform the amount of labor conceived. It is vital for the designer to know and understand what it takes to produce what they put down on paper. If the designer is the entire costume department, knowing what it takes to produce an entire production is crucial. This position can be called a Costumer or the "costume everything." This is someone who designs, shops, cuts, stitches, fits, adjusts, trains the costume crew, and, in many cases, does the laundry.

Some would argue that the designer should design what they want, and figure out where to pull back later in the process. The problem with this is managing the expectations of the director and the rest of the team. If they see the dream design, they will expect the dream design. It becomes much harder to make cutbacks after the designs are seen. It therefore helps everyone if the initial presentation is based on some sense of reality concerning what can be accomplished within the restrictions of the production.

Consider the Audience

An important aspect of theatre that designers should keep in mind is the audience. Without the audience, there is no purpose to theatre. If the audience is unable to relate to anything in the play, it is alienated, and the intent of the production is lost. Finding a balance between the desire to connect and the need to entertain can be challenging. While it is important to educate an audience, decisions should be made as to what they will or will not accept. For instance, in *A Streetcar Named Desire* by Tennessee Williams, Stanley is brutish. But when Stanley appears in his silk pajama bottoms, the audience should be aware of his sexuality. If the designer wishes to be strict to the time period, the pajamas would be worn at the natural waist. To the modern eye, this looks odd and does not appear attractive. The designer has to ask the question: is it more important to show the correct period style, or more important for the audience to be able to recognize Stanley as a sexual being? Whether the designer or the director makes the final decision, both will need to take the audience into account.

Is it the job of the designer to push the limits of the budget and labor costs? In some cases: yes. When the director asks for the moon, it is the designer's job to ask what it is about the moon that is important to the director. The problem for the designer is figuring out how to accomplish the needs of the production with the limitations of the venue. In educational theatre, it may benefit the students to push the limits of what can or should be done. The additional build of costumes allows them to get the experience they need to continue in the field after they graduate. Renting costumes may be a necessity to save time. Renting can be a lesson on balance between the needs of the production and the limitations of a costume shop and its personnel. Ultimately, all productions have a limit, whether it is budget, time, labor, or a combination of all three. The needs of the production, the educational needs, and compromise have to balance.

Equally as important as being creative is the need to be organized. Designers have to arrange their ideas in ways that can be explained to others. Not only the images, but thoughts about the play and the designs must be organized. How should the ideas be presented? In what order should they be presented? Would starting with the lead characters make the most sense or starting with overall thoughts about the designs? Would it be better to talk about image/word/inspiration first, or will it become clear as the presentation progresses? Perhaps inspiration came from a specific character: it might be best to discuss that character first and then show how the rest of the characters work within the concept. While deciding how to present, what should be said needs to be determined. Presenting designs is much like "selling" your ideas: confidence will assist in the desired effect. A presentation should not be rehearsed to the point that it sounds like a speech, but some planning will make your pitch succinct and in complete sentences. Be prepared to be interrupted by questions from anyone involved in the production. If the answer to a question is unknown, get back to the team with the answer when possible. If notes help, then use them, but sometimes it is more important to answer questions and deviate from the original plan.

In this age of technology, organizing ideas, thoughts, and images is easily done. Any type of presentation program can be effective for presenting research or designs (for example, Prezi, PowerPoint, Google Docs, or Keynote). These kinds of presentations can be crucial if working long distance. When it is not possible, or cost effective, to have every designer present at early production meetings, programs like Google Hangouts, Skype, and Facetime make it easier to communicate. Research can be sent electronically using a presentation program while the designer is brought into the room by digital means in order to describe to the team what is being presented. If the whole team is present, it may be more convenient to use individual images on a poster or on separate pages. This makes it easier to look at all of the images at once, and they can be rearranged or referenced quickly. But the drawback to this approach could be the bulk of the information: bringing in large posters or several reference books may not be possible or convenient.

Actual articles of clothing can be a valuable visual. Short of using a model, a physical garment can make clear the type of clothing that is desired, as well as the preferred textile. When it is not possible to bring items to the production meeting to show as examples, an individual meeting with the director may be required to further explain the visuals shown in the production meeting.

Throughout this part of the costume design process, there are always points where designers have to step back and see if what they desire is coming to fruition or if adjustments need to be made. Has a new development come up in the rehearsal process? Does this change include costumes, or the speed of a costume change? Has unexpected movement been added that will need to be addressed in the costume itself?

Many designers use a costume chart to help with organization. A costume chart may not be necessary in a show where no one changes. However, if multiple changes take place, as in musicals or complicated plays, the costume chart may be the most important piece of organization for a designer. It is essential to track who is on stage when and what they are wearing. If the play includes a large chorus, a chart may be a good way to determine, for example, if you have mistakenly put several characters who stand together all in the same color. Rarely is it desirable to have a block of one color concentrated on one part of the stage.

The starting point in constructing a costume chart is to make a grid listing each character and each scene. Some designers put a mark in each square where the character is included, and some designers assign a different color to each character. It is important to check in often with the stage manager to see if extra characters have been added to scenes that were not originally listed in the script. Once every character is listed in every scene, descriptions can be filled in as to what they are wearing. The descriptions may start out as generic items such as: suit, shirt, tie, belt, socks, and shoes. This can be changed later when the items become a known factor. The designer can decide how much detail to include. Some designers choose to use great detail so that individual costume plots can be made directly from the chart. When possible, a good addition to the chart is noting how much time there is between scenes. If no scene change is

	Act I	
	Dumbshow	Prologue
Desdemona/Ramona	Desdemona 1: Deep violet gown Slippers Black tights Ramona under gown	
Othello/Claude	O: Guilded breastplate Purple doublet/ purple camica Burgundy tights Purple shoes & turban style hat	
Juliet/Julie	Juliet: Cream gown Ivory slippers White headdress with ferroniere Julie under gown	
Romeo/Iago	Romeo: Royal blue doublet Light blue camica Black tights Black boots	
Constance Ledbelly	Black tweed suit w/skirt Red blouse Red toque w/ pompom Black tights and boots	
Chorus/Ghost		Black camica Black tights Black shoes
Tybalt/Juliet's Nurse	Tybalt Red slash sleeved shirt black lining Black tights Black shoes	
Mercutio/Servant/Soldier		
Notes: Actors don't change tights ">" : change to		

FIGURE 1.20 Sample costume chart or costume plot for Goodnight, Desdemona, Good Morning, Juliet.

taking place, chances are it is only a few seconds. If during this time, an actor exits one side of the stage and enters the other, plus has a quick change, a note needs to be made. In this case, the design may be dictated more by the need for the actor's ability to get back on stage than to try to convey deep meaning through the character. Adjustments will often need to be made in order to aid the play's flow.

DESIGNING COSTUMES FOR A MUSICAL

Musicals include a complex mix of dance, music, and written word, and this complexity entails a different approach than with plays. While all plays require collaboration between the director and the design team, a musical production mandates the inclusion of more artists such as choreographers, musical directors, and sound mixers. Costume designers must work closely with each member of the team, including the actors and all additional artists, in order to ensure a smooth process. One key to success is frequently asking questions at every stage. Many of the aspects

of musicals discussed below could also apply to plays or even operas.

Some designers choose to read the script first without listening to the music simply to understand the plot. Others wish to listen to each song as it appears in the script to obtain the full effect that an audience will get when watching the musical. Either way, the music gives great insight into the mood of each movement within the script. Much like designing for dance, the music will suggest a style of movement and set the mood of the piece. A designer should not begin to think of designing without listening to the music several times, just like the need to read a play numerous times before putting pencil to paper.

Before designing the actual costumes, designers should determine the "givens" involved in a production. Givens are the parameters of a production. All productions have them, but with the complexity of a musical, additional questions need to be answered. The first given involves who is in what scene and musical number. A script may have three characters having a discussion when suddenly a crowd joins them. When did everyone enter? Did they all come in at once, or will the director have them come in at different times during the dialog? How many actors constitute the crowd or background singers? Does the dialog end with a song? How many voices does the musical director need for each particular song? Different characters sing specific lines, but how many singers are needed for the chorus to fill out the sound?

The second given is movement, which is inherent in a musical. Most songs will have some choreography. Does the music call for tap, partnering, or quick movements across the stage? Movement has to be taken into account when considering the design of the costumes no matter what period the musical is set in. When communication is fluid, the choreographer is just as interested in the thoughts behind the costumes as the designer is about the kinds of movements taking place. If the musical number requires tap, the designer should be certain that the audience can see the dancers' feet: therefore no full-length dresses. If the choreography includes partnering, the designer should ask what kinds of dance or lifts will take place. Will the choreography include scissor kicks or other sweeping movement? If so, the costume will have to allow for the movement either with fuller skirts, **gussets**, or possibly slits, or maybe pants will be more appropriate for the scene. Even after this is discussed, designers should attend several rehearsals. Just as directing is fluid, choreography changes with the needs of the production and the individual actors. Choreographers may be enthused by the actors or change the movement based on inspiration in the music. Hopefully, if a change happens during the process, the choreographer

FIGURE 1.21 The Wild Party *requires costumes that allow for choreography and movement. (Costume design by Joe Kucharski. Produced by the University of California, Irvine.)*

FIGURE 1.22 *Flying may not be the only challenge. Blood, severed heads, and other special effects have to be taken into consideration when designing* Re-Animator the Musical. *(Costume design by Joe Kucharski. Starring George Wendt. Produced by Steve Allen Theatre.)*

is considering the costumes that have been designed. But if the designer attends rehearsal and sees how the dance has changed, they can then communicate any concerns. Continued communication throughout the process reduces the chances of mishaps or surprises during dress rehearsals. A keen stage manager will note when a possible concern between costumes and choreography takes place: awareness is key to finding a quick solution.

The third given is movement within the non-choreographed scenes. Are actors running across the stage? Is there a need for a character to do the splits? Will someone crawl across the floor to hide under or behind a piece of furniture? Will an actor trip, fall, or end up on the floor for any other reason? If the actor is wearing a skirt, it is usually desirable to include a dance brief in their wardrobe. If the character is wearing a tuxedo as mandated by the script, crawling on the floor may require replacement pants for the actor. If the budget prohibits replacing pants, then a discussion should take place between the director and the designer before the action is directed into the scene. As with choreography, movement within a scene will change as the director creates. It is helpful if designers attend rehearsals to see how a costume needs to change with the demands of the production. If flying is included in the musical, openings in the costume for the harness wires are very important. Costume designers should be aware of how a harness feels to understand how to make the experience as comfortable as possible for the actor. Designers also need to know how the actor will get into the harness, when it needs to be removed, and how the costume will look with a harness. Once again, a stage manager may be helpful in keeping everyone aware of production requirements.

Space is the fourth given. A musical number that includes hoop skirts of the 1850s can be lovely to watch. A large chorus of 1850s hoop skirts requires a very large space. If the stage is small, it may be difficult to fit all of the women on stage at the same time. A design choice may have to be made to choose smaller hoops associated with the 1840s. Space refers to offstage as much as onstage. Those same 1850s skirts may not fit between the legs or flats for entrances and exits.

Quick changes are a challenge for any production. Discussions of where a quick change can happen should take place early in the production process. Musicals often have large sets that move on and off stage. As these pieces move, costume changes are often taking place. Finding a place for the actors and dressers while allowing for the scene crew to do their job can be tricky. If the wing space is big enough, arrangements can be made for a changing area or booth. If the need for an area is expressed early, technical directors can include it in their plans for backstage space. If the wing space is limited, the scene designer, technical director, and wardrobe will have to rely on creative planning to come up with a viable solution. Working with everyone's needs can be complicated, and often the most efficient solutions come from the backstage crew: the deck chief understands where everyone needs to be in time for the next entrance and will choreograph the crew to move in synchronization.

The fifth given is microphones. Large and small venues use microphones to enhance voices on stage. Accommodating for mic packs, wires, hairstyles, and the actual microphones can take extensive planning. Ideally, a mic pack will be available during fittings so the costume can be adjusted in order to hide the unsightly bulge caused by the depth of the pack. With shirts, jackets, and skirts, the pack is most commonly placed in the small of the back, where the curve helps to hide the pack. If an elastic belt is used, the pack is placed between the belt and the back of the actor, where it is kept secure. In this location, it is usually easy to reach if a problem arises such as a disconnected wire or dead battery. But if the production includes sliding on the back, adjustments will need to be made. The actor may need to slide slightly off the center of their back, or the pack will have to be moved. An actor's safety is the priority in making a decision about

FIGURE 1.23 *Note the position of the microphone at the edge of Caitlin Cohn's hair, as she plays Mary Lennox in* The Secret Garden. *(Produced at the Cincinnati Playhouse in the Park. Costume design by Leon Wiebers. Photo by Mikki Schaffner.)*

the pack's location. Pockets are desirable in most costumes for the possibility of needing an alternative location for the pack. The costume should allow enough space so the pack is not interfering with the line of the costume whenever possible.

Wardrobe and sound crews have to work closely with each other in order to achieve a smooth process for microphone use. If the sound crew is attaching the microphones, the actor needs to know where the crew is stationed to apply them. If wardrobe is attaching the microphones, they have to be trained on how to handle them. A plan should be in place in case something goes wrong with a microphone during the performance. If it is a non-union production, it might be easiest if the dressers are given instructions and training on how to check for immediate issues such as whether the mic pack is turned on, or what to do if it slips out of place.

Once all the givens are taken into account, the rest of the design process can take place. When a musical includes lead characters, secondary characters, and a chorus, it may be useful to think of each of these as separate groups. Much like a Shakespearean piece that has a large chorus, it is important to be able to recognize the relationships between the groups. The chorus does not have to be dressed identically, but should have a sense of belonging or melding together. They should not draw undue focus from the main characters unless it is needed within the scene. If the chorus is thought of as a character, it may be easier to approach the design. This could include color choices, shapes or silhouettes, or a variety of other ways of associating the characters.

Secondary characters should have more distinction than the chorus. Often, they have a story of their own while supporting the primary plot. They can be more complicated than the lead characters but should not draw more attention in their attire. While each one has individual characterization, it may be helpful to initially think of them as a group. For instance, in *Cabaret* by Kander and Ebb, Fräulein Schneider and Herr Schultz share a subplot within the story. Due to their positions, ages, and

FIGURE 1.24 Oklahoma! *Note the similar silhouette of the chorus women while still maintaining some individuality. (Costume design by LaLonnie Lehman. Produced by Texas Christian University.)*

FIGURE 1.25 *Julie Fishell as Fräulein Schneider and Jeffrey Blair Cornell as Herr Schultz in PlayMakers Repertory Company's production of Cabaret, April 3–21, 2013. (Photo by Jon Gardiner.)*

interests, it is appropriate to dress them differently from any other characters in the musical.

While lead characters do need to be recognizable, they cannot stand out to the point of no longer belonging within the realm of the production. They can be set apart by the choice of fabrics, colors, accessories, or other types of flourish. On the other hand, when the musical is more of an ensemble, it may be desirable to have the characters conform to each other.

Other musicals include groups that are distinct by association. In *Crazy for You* by Ken Ludwig and Ira and George Gershwin, Bobby Child goes to Nevada to close a rundown theatre. He meets Polly Baker and falls in love. Meanwhile, there is a chorus of cowboys in the musical that could be treated as a unit. Items could be added to make them individuals, but it may be helpful to initially look at them as a group. A number of Follies showgirls follow Bobby to Nevada. Each girl can be seen as distinct, yet they could be dressed with some similarity. Instead of the chorus all looking the same, each of these groups could be treated

FIGURE 1.26 *In* Rent, *a tight color palette of blacks and greys assists with the ensemble appearance, while adding a bright color separates the individual characters. (Design by Leigh Anne Crandall. Produced by Texas Tech University. Photo by Jared Canada.)*

FIGURE 1.27 *Crazy for You. Note the sophistication of the girls' costumes as compared to the rough look of the cowboys. (Design by Melissa L. Merz. Produced by Texas Tech University. Photo by Andrea Bilkey.)*

differently according to their place of origin. Bobby belongs in the world of the Follies girls. Polly belongs in the more rustic world of the cowboys. The contrast between the two worlds adds the conflict needed to make the show more interesting.

FINAL THOUGHTS

> "Designers are constantly involved in a trance-like process called visual imagination. They mold images in their head—manipulating shapes, colors, material, scales, light, and so on—for artistic purposes ...There is no boundary for imagination. The only difference is that a professional designer knows how to bridge what he or she imagines with reality."
> Ming Chen[6] from *Visual Literacy for Theatre*, p. 19

Whether working on a musical or a play, designers have to consider how best to organize their thoughts and inspiration. In most cases, the script will lead a designer to work in the best or most effective way.

Barbara and Cletus Anderson began their book, *Costume Design*,[8] by saying "There are no absolutes in costume design ...". There are ideas, hints, advice, organizational tools, logic, imagination, and intuition, but no certain way to create costumes in a foolproof manner that will make everyone think the production is brilliant. Working in a specific style on one show does not guarantee success by working the same way on the next show. It is the fact that there are no absolutes that makes the field of costume design forever changing, incredibly challenging, and ultimately greatly rewarding.

On a Personal Note

My mentor, Peggy Kellner, gave me a wonderful piece of advice one day. She told me: "If you want someone to disappear on stage, put them in tan." While I never forgot her words, it wasn't until I did a production of *Twelfth Night* that I understood just what she meant. Within the context of the production, there were two male servants. I dressed them in variations of tan and cream. At a later discussion, an audience member asked why there weren't any male servants, just female. I realized then how easy it was to lose someone on stage.

I've never forgotten those words and have repeated them often to my own students.

QUESTIONS

* Name other examples of "unofficial" uniforms.

* In considering psychological factors, can you recall an instance in theatre where the psychological factor played a predominant role?

* Musicals are not the only situation where microphones are needed. In reading the section about musicals, what else could apply to other types of performance? What remains unique to musicals?

NOTES

1. Marcia Dixcy Jory, *The Ingenue in White: Reflections of a Costume Designer* (Hanover, NH: Smith and Kraus, 2003).
2. Betty Edwards, *Drawing on the Artist Within* (New York: Touchstone, 1987).
3. Rosemary Ingham, *From Page to Stage* (New Hampshire: Heinemann, 1998).
4. See: https//.en.wikipedia.org/wiki/Motion_Picture_Production_Code (accessed February 15, 2016).
5. Michael Lewis, "Obama's Way," *Vanity Fair*, October, 2012. www.vanityfair.com/news/2012/10/michael-lewis-profile-barack-obama (accessed January 21, 2016).
6. Ming Chen, *Visual Literacy for Theatre* (New York: Linus Publications, Inc., 2011).
7. Ming Chen, *Visual Literacy for Theatre* (New York: Linus Publications, Inc., 2011): paraphrasing Paul Zelanski and Mary Pat Fisher's book *Design: Principles and Problems*, 3rd Ed (Boston, MA: Wadsworth Publishing, 2007).
8. Barbara and Cletus Anderson, *Costume Design*, 2nd Ed (Boston, MA: Cengage Learning, 1998).

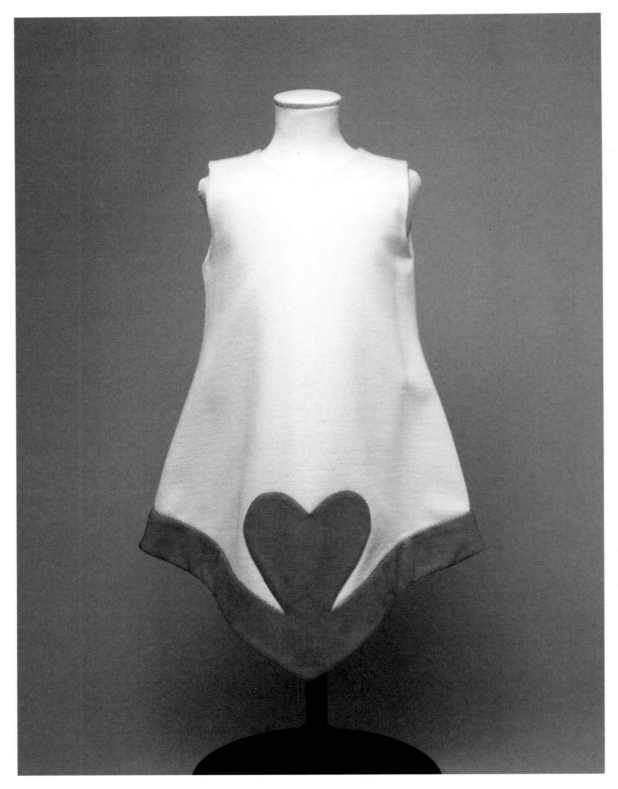

FIGURE 2.1 *1960's Pierre Cardin. Hand and machine stitched and appliqué. (Victoria and Albert Museum.)*

CHAPTER 2

IDENTIFYING CHARACTER THROUGH CLOTHING

Melissa L. Merz

If communication is about sending messages between a giver and a receiver, then costumes are a means of communication. The wearer sends an intended message depending on what they are wearing. People choose what to wear based on the image they wish to portray, the activity in which they are involved, how they feel, or even whom they think they may meet. A piece of advice handed down for generations of daughters is to wear lipstick every time they leave the house; after all, you do not know whom you might run into. The lipstick represents a well put-together and attractive woman. While this is an outdated notion, a specific message was apparent to others. Similarly, if someone is dressing for work, then work-appropriate clothing is important. This could be as easy as a prescribed uniform, or a need to function within the position, or a means to exude confidence and professionalism. Any of the options speak towards the appropriateness of the situation. In each case, the clothing sends a message about the person's occupation and attitude toward themselves and the image they wish to portray.

For the costume designer, questions that come to the forefront are: Is it the actor (wearer) who is communicating or the designer who chooses the clothing? What is the end goal? Is the cut and fit of the clothing suited for the character? Does the style or fit convey the attitude or mood of the character? Is the character comfortable or awkward in their clothing? If the costume is fully communicating, the receiver (the audience) will understand the message. This constitutes communication between the actor and the audience. Is there a guarantee that the audience will receive or understand the message? No. Much like looking at art, each individual will have their own visceral response. Should the audience leave the theatre talking about the messages they attained from the costumes? Probably not. A designer should understand not every piece of clothing speaks volumes. It can be a subtle connection through the use of color, shape, fit, and how it is accessorized.

Dozens of books have been written on the topic of clothing and communication. Theories about the extent of the messages have been debated. The following are a few of the theories or thoughts that pertain to the purpose of costumes.

SEMIOLOGY

> "Three dimensions define culture as part of a communication process: the nature of the communication process, the relations between the communicator and the audience, and the distinction between the communicator and the message."
>
> Kurt W. Back[1] from *Fashion Theory: A Reader,* p. 399

To have communication, those involved must have a commonality or mutual society in order to understand one another. When speaking, a common language must be used. If everyone in a room is speaking different languages, misunderstandings will take place, if there is any communication possible at all. While linguistics is a form of semiotics, it is not the only signifier. Malcolm Barnard[2] defines semiology by quoting Ferdinand de Saussure: "semiology as a 'science that studies the life of signs within society . . .'" (p. 80). Semiotics involves visual signs, sounds, and body language. The idea of clothing in and of itself being a sign or signal, although not a clear or definitive language, has been debated in several books covering the topic of the psychology of clothing. Each item of clothing will not tell the whole story about the wearer's personality, only what the wearer wants to reveal at the

FIGURE 2.2 *What happens if someone wears clothing of a type without knowing it? Examples of hipster men. (Artwork by Marcus Gagliardi, Press Play Productions, August 5, 2014. Courtesy of dreamstime.com.)*

moment. Even then, it is only a type of language between those of a similar society. Consider the different social types you find in Western society: Hipsters, Rude Boys, Rockers, Goths, Hackers, etc. All of these types may be readily recognizable to Westerners, but probably would not have the same meaning to those living in North Korea, for example.

Social groups or subcultures are two or more people who interact and have similar characteristics and interests. In a sense, there is interdependence between the individuals. Not surprisingly, this can include clothing. The purpose of wearing similar clothing is to be accepted by the in-group and coincidentally be recognizable to the out-group. It is a way of advertising "this is who I am." Or at least, who one wants people to believe they are. Dressing similarly is not a complete definition, but it will give an idea with a first impression. Hipsters might wear worn skinny jeans, Converse sneakers, and vintage fashion or thrift store finds. The attitude that goes with it is to conserve earth's resources and

appreciate the arts and sciences. A Bohemian is similar, but should not be confused with the Hipster. The differences may be subtle but generally, a Bohemian will wear looser clothing, purposely unmatched in the classic sense, and more earth-friendly or feet-friendly shoes. For the costume designer, it would be important to understand these differences.

To the average theatre-goer, the differences between Goths, Cyber Goths, Rivetheads, Punks, and Metalheads may be non-existent. To the subcultures, as well as to the costume designer, the differences may be minimal, but these details need attention. Having knowledge of the different yet similar types, a costume designer can make choices in clothing that will not only portray the attitude behind the character, but possibly the ideologies that go with them.

Commonality of all of these groups is the color black, which leads to the confusion between the various groups. However, the ideologies and development of the subcultures is different.

According to subcultureslist.com,[3] Cyber Goths embrace information and how it could lead to a dystopian future. Cyber Goths are inspired by German expressionist films, expressionist paintings, and science fiction that pertains to cyber intelligence. Their artificial and heavily styled look includes the use of black with a bright color accent in their clothing, hair, and accessories. Androgyny feeds into their idea of a utopian society where everyone is treated equally.

Rivetheads would want to make it clear that they are not Goths of any variety. While both Rivetheads and Cyber Goths may wear goggles or facemasks such as respirators or gas masks, Rivetheads wear a more industrial or militaristic look. Instead of accenting the artificial and styled look of the Cyber Goths, they apply less makeup and rely more on their accessories, which can include leather and military accouterments. Androgyny is not needed: women can wear stilettos while men could wear combat or work boots. Both kinds of footwear have a connotation

FIGURE 2.3 *What category would you put them in: Cyber Goths, Punks, or Rivetheads? (Picture of social subculture ©Shutterstock.)*

associated with them, allowing each gender to express themselves as they wish.

CONNOTATION

"It will be noted that, given the associative and subjective nature of connotative meaning, it is almost impossible to be either incomplete or mistaken in giving an account of that meaning. What one person associates with a word or an image can hardly be said to be incorrect or incomplete; nobody is ever taken to task because their connotations are incorrect. As a result of this, connotation may differ widely from person to person . . . . It is also the case, however, that connotative meaning cannot simply be found in dictionaries; one cannot understand connotation simply by looking in a dictionary. This is not to say that dictionaries will not occasionally provide connotative meaning. But, as connotative meaning is the product of a person's sex, age, class and so on, in seeking to understand another person's connotative meanings, one must either be the same sex, age, class and so on as that other person, or one must try to imagine what it would be like to be those things. The understanding of connotation is an intersubjective and hermeneutic affair."

Malcolm Barnard[2] from *Fashion as Communication*, p. 86

While productions, and those involved in making those productions, often wish to send a message, theme, or idea to the audience, all of it is up for interpretation. Age differences of the audience members will bring about different feelings towards images and themes. One audience member might see a polka-dot dress and remember their aunt had one just like it, while another will think of it simply as something from a decade past or even just a fun print. The connotative meaning of the garment can evoke mood or emotion in addition to the desired information about the period, time of day, or activity.

PERCEPTION

Perception, much like connotation, plays an important role in the messages given by clothing. Kurt W. Black[1] wrote "Clothes . . . serve[ing] as cues in impression formation and social perception." (p. 399). As much as designers would like an audience to understand each nuance added to a costume, it does not happen. But are there universal aesthetics that anyone can understand? Certainly. If that same polka-dot dress is hanging on the body, not fitted, and wrinkled, the audience will have a different response than if the same dress is neatly pressed and fits perfectly. Knowing this, the designer can make clearer decisions about fit in relation to the character. Similarly, if the dress fits properly, but is stained and torn, the message to the audience will be one of distress in some form.

> "Temporally, too, there is reason to be cautious about ascribing precise meanings to most clothing. The very same apparel ensemble that "said" one thing last year will "say" something quite different today and yet another thing next year. . . . First, it is heavily context-dependent; second, there is considerable variability in how its constituent symbols are understood and appreciated by different social strata and taste groupings; and third, it is . . . at least in Western society . . . much more given to "undercoding" than to precision and explicitness."
>
> Fred Davis[4] from *Fashion Theory: A Reader*, p. 150–151

When Jean Paul Gaultier costumed Madonna in a longline bullet bra with crotch closures for her Blond Ambition tour, he was able to make a dull 1950s undergarment appear to be desirable and fashionable. Women would not consider going back to wearing these undergarments as they were originally meant to be worn, but once women saw them as outer garments, they had a different connotation. If a woman in the 1950s wore the garments in the same way as Madonna in 1990, the perception would not be that this costume is exciting or fashion forward. Instead, people would wonder why a woman would wear her undergarments in public. Context in this case includes the year, or in the case of a play, the year portrayed on stage.

In the 2010s, it became popular to wear cowboy boots with shorts. While it had a certain charm on women, it was an unusual look for men. Men were seen wearing their boots with basketball shorts. This is truly a case of "one day you're in, the next day, you're out" (to quote Heidi Klum from the TV show *Project Runway*).[5] It was not long before people thought this was a fashion that should not be seen. Hence, this particular costume combination seen in a play could have several meanings. First, depending on the context, it could look a little foolish. A play taking place in another time period might make it look like a man was caught off guard and needed to put something on very quickly and he grabbed some boots. Second, as shorts with boots were seen on college campus, it could have looked

FIGURE 2.4 *Shorts with cowboy boots and Uggs. (Photo by Andrea Bilkey.)*

attractive or normal to the students seeing the play. Third, other audience members might not see the charm or interest and so could see the character as entirely out of place. Fourth, within the context of the play, it might simply be a quirky or funny moment. Depending on the length of time the actor is on stage, it might give a message of humor more than of deep insight into characterization.

COMMUNICATION THEORY

Within the fashion community, several books and articles have been written about the psychology or meaning of clothing. A costume designer can delve into several of the theories going back over a century. The following is a brief overview of some of the more common beliefs behind the meaning of clothing.

Hierarchical Principle

James Laver,[6] museum curator at the Victoria and Albert Museum, further expounded on the theories of Veblen and Flugel by developing his own theory, referring to them as principles: Hierarchical, Utility, and Seduction. Hierarchical involves dressing to prove position in society. As discussed in Chapter 1, fashion plays an important part in distinguishing social classes. While there are arguments for and against the extent of social influences, there is no doubt it had an effect in past centuries, as well as today.

In observing the popular people in the media, it is understandable how the study of emulation of the classes could work to change the fashion of the masses. When Kate Middleton,

> "Once again, we are forced to admit the paramount importance of classes, in this instance class struggles, without which the history of fashion is inexplicable. It is only through a study of emulation, and of the effect of revolutionary crises upon the emulative process, that we can understand fashion in its stages of critical development."
>
> Quentin Bell[7] from *On Human Finery*, p. 183

Duchess of Cambridge, walks in public, the item she is wearing sells out from all shops. The same is said for the dress of the royal couple's children. When the Duchess' engagement ring was revealed, reproductions of the ring were made immediately for sale. Style icons like Beyoncé showed that curves on a woman is a desirable trait, instead of the thinner style of fashion models. The idea of special undergarments or implants to improve the roundness of a woman's backside is currently fashionable. Men who wish to appear higher on the social scale may emulate the dress of Russell Simmons by buying his line of clothing.

While there are arguments for and against the extent of social influences, there is no doubt it had an effect in the past as social classes were trying to find ways to distinguish themselves.

> "... briefly, it describes changes in taste as innovations made by the dominant class, as necessary in order to preserve the 'unity and segregation' of the class, given that modern social codes allow the immediately subordinate group to emulate the tastes and preferences of the one above."
>
> Angela Partington[8] discusses Simmel's work from *Fashion Theory: A Reader*, p. 223

As cultures gravitate more to the popularity of celebrities and a desire to imitate them, the line between the exclusive and the attainable becomes thin. Cheaper versions of some of the most coveted clothing become available as soon as they are unveiled. Companies watch the red carpet styles and work overnight to reproduce versions of the gowns worn by some of the most popular women in the world. The difference is in the quality and uniqueness. Costume designers can capitalize on the cheaper versions when necessary for their limited budgets. Distance and the suspension of disbelief help the audience to understand when a garment can be considered an exclusive style.

Utility Principle

Emphasizing the practicality of a garment and its basic needs, to provide warmth and protection, is the utility principle. Circumstances relating to jobs or finances may contribute to someone dressing in this category. Occupations such as butcher, welder, nurse, laboratory worker, window washer, and others may not wish to dress in the finest of fashion. If one lives in Alaska, a parka of some kind may be a necessity. While practical, a parka is rarely considered high fashion; its purpose is functional. On stage, the use of practical garments may tell an audience the social status or occupation of a character. It may also convey the attitudes characters have of themselves, society, or the importance of clothing and fashion.

Seduction Principle

Sex sells. Whether in advertising or the movies, sex will draw interest. Clothing has a major role in this attraction. Malcolm Barnard includes statements from Rouse to express his ideas on Laver's theories.

> "That is, women's clothes are intended to make the wearer more attractive to the opposite sex because, throughout history and prehistory, men have selected 'partners in life' on the basis of the woman's attractiveness. Men's clothes, however, are intended to display and 'enhance social status' because women, 'for the greater part of human history,' have selected their life partners on the basis of their ability to 'maintain and protect a family' (in Rouse, 1989: 12). So, women's clothes display the woman's sexual attractiveness and men's clothes display the man's social status."
>
> Malcolm Barnard[2] from *Fashion as Communication*, p. 57

Attractiveness is a prevailing factor with several arguments supporting the need for a woman to show sexual prowess to men, while men need to prove social status or the ability to provide. In our modern age, a suit is not a necessity. Suits are constraining, inconvenient, and do not have a function except to show that those wearing a suit cannot do physical labor and are therefore in a place of authority, or for the purpose of formality. Similarly, ties do not serve a purpose except to add decoration. Still, people will be drawn to a well-dressed man in a suit and tie, believing in his official manner and intelligence.

Although the idea of a woman dressing to attract others sexually may seem like an outdated idea, there are several examples to show it does still happen. While the interest in bringing back the longline bra of the 1950s may not be present in its original form, many women have decided to wear supportive undergarments much like the girdle. The body shaper will hold and keep body parts from moving. They are uncomfortable, but women feel they make them more attractive to others. Sales of makeup and hair products reach the billions each year, yet serve no purpose for the health of women's skin. Women spend time each morning to make themselves more attractive to others by using makeup and other products. In looking at prom dresses in a mall, it is unmistakable how these sequined dresses are supposed to help the wearer look more sophisticated and elegant, but the end result is that the short skirts may not be as conducive to dancing as much as looking attractive to others. While mini-skirts are cooler in the summer, there is little reason to wear them in the winter with tights and boots unless the wearer has legs she would like to show off.

It is possible no other clothing item has as many meanings or symbols as the stiletto. The stiletto has been associated with feminism, anti-feminism, rebellion, works of art, signs of submission, or liberation. Despite the advertisements of the 1950s, women did not commonly vacuum in stiletto heels. Instead, women found the opportunity to wear stilettos to be liberating from the day-to-day life of someone who stayed at home. Those who wore

FIGURE 2.5 *The stiletto has varied symbolism. (©Shutterstock.)*

them regularly showed a rebellious nature against the ideas and ideals of the housewife. In wearing a heel of that height, the body shifts to accommodate the stance in the feet. The chest moves forward a bit while the backside shifts back to allow for balance. This stance, as well as the idea that women wear heels, is innately feminine. The fact that wearing stilettos with pointed toes can be painful and tiring can be seen as a symbol of anti-feminism. While women claim to be able to wear heels all day (some even train for marathons or do aerobics while wearing them), an argument can be made that the smaller steps a woman takes, or the need to step carefully, makes a woman submissive. Still other women will claim wearing heels makes them feel empowered. Once again, context allows the symbolism of a stiletto to be revealed.

If seduction or attractiveness to the audience is the end goal, well-dressed actors can "say" more for their character than the lines they recite. Whether an actor is wearing a mini-skirt or a suit that fits perfectly, the idea of what is attractive is somewhat universal. Context will play a part in the situation, but impression also adds to the character.

Tradition and Religion

Quentin Bell writes, "The Sikh, the Muslim and Quaker all exhibit, or used to exhibit, their religious opinions by means of their dress." (p. 101).[7] Throughout time, religion has placed an importance on how someone should dress. A vow of poverty dictated monks and nuns wear simple clothing made of basic cloth. Tradition can also be an influence. Monks do not have to wear brown; nuns do not have to wear black. Yet these colors have become traditional symbols that everyone can recognize. Within the Amish community, hooks are preferred over buttons. Hooks do not work better than buttons; they are a symbol of simplicity. Plain dress shows dedication to humility and helps to maintain a society without social status. Being seen as a part of the community, and not dressing to call attention to oneself, is the Amish way to prevent personal pride. Buddhist monks traditionally did not buy their robes, but were given them. The monastic robe is made up of three parts: an inner robe to cover the lower body, an upper robe, and an outer robe. Like the Amish, there is little variation in the robes or how they are worn. The color does vary from one group to another, but this has more to do with the dyes available in the different geographical regions. The robes are made of pieces of fabric of different lengths depending on where it is worn. The fabric is not cut or sewn, nor does it have fasteners of any kind.

Understanding the subtleties of clothing can be a valuable part of the costume designer's role. Information about why a garment is worn, how it is worn, and how it functions is important. The audience will have certain expectations when it comes to a recognizable religion or group that follows tradition. A designer must take that knowledge and adapt it for the stage. The various robes of a Buddhist monk may not have fasteners, but for use in theatre, fasteners may be advisable for security while appearing on stage. A Sikh dastar or turban is commonly 9 feet in length, wound around the head and hair: but for theatre, it could be fixed in place so that the actor does not worry about the wrap coming apart. Designers collect information about what should be, and adapt it for what it needs to be in a theatrical setting.

> "Moral dangers may also be avoided by the use of thick, dark-coloured and stiff clothing, such as a monk's habit ... He [a Hasidic Jew] said that 'Hasidic clothing serve(s) as a guard and a shield from sin and obscenity.'"
> Malcolm Barnard[2] from *Fashion as Communication*, p. 52

Clothing With Purpose

Separate from the aforementioned principles, clothing can have a different purpose. Clothes that are not adorned with signs that relay an obvious message can still send subtle clues about personality. In most circumstances, they are not meant to scream attitude or be specific, or even to portray every aspect of someone's personality.

Garments are meant to give hints about intent, mood, and attitude. After all, the wearer had a purpose for choosing that particular ensemble for that particular occasion. Despite no obvious message, the observer may subconsciously pick up on the subtle clues, and draw conclusions.

> "Typically a job applicant is not attempting to convey wealth, status or even fashion-consciousness to prospective employers, but personal qualities of ethical or moral significance. In other words these occasions represent attempts to use clothes as a 'language of character.'"
> Colin Campbell[9] from *Fashion Theory: A Reader*, p. 163

If someone applies for a job, they will dress to impress, in hopes of attaining that position. What clothing choices did the applicant make for this particular event? Did the applicant have to walk a far distance and therefore wear more comfortable shoes for travel, while bringing stylish shoes to change into for the interview itself? Is the applicant more comfortable in a t-shirt but wears a button-down shirt and tie to convey a more professional attitude? Is this the only suit the applicant owns? Did the applicant decide to wear the suit to show seriousness of purpose, while the job itself allows slightly more relaxed business attire? An individual may not consciously think through all of these questions. But a costume designer, along with the director and actor, may need to look at each of these questions to establish backstory for the character. As stated before, how the actor wears the clothing may speak more towards the attitude about the interview than the clothing itself. Not only is character involved in these choices, but what happens on stage should be taken into consideration. The action of the scene may play a part in the needs of the costume, how it is worn, and how it needs to function.

FINAL THOUGHTS

Clothing is a basic need for humans. It is important for social norms to wear clothing. The question becomes what does one want to present to the world. Lady Gaga wants to make a statement every time she is seen. Her intention can be interpreted as wild, innovative, eclectic, unusual, self-aggrandizing, or fashion forward. But most people just want to blend in with others. Ultimately, what should be private and what to present to the world is for the costume designer to decide. The difference between a costume designer and someone getting dressed for the day is the costume designer carefully plans the whole ensemble. Consideration might be made for what "matches" or "goes together," but a costume designer will think about each item as a need and as communication. What undergarments are appropriate? What message is portrayed if a t-shirt is worn underneath a button-down shirt? Which shoes help towards creating a character? Is it important for the clothes to "go together" or is a contrast better? For the designer and the actor, the observer is the audience.

The closer to the present time, the harder it is to make a strong statement through clothing. One reason is because everyone who is watching will have an opinion of what they see. If they see something they would wear or even own, they may relate too closely to the character. Likewise, if they see a character wearing something their mother would wear, it may shadow feelings towards the actions of the woman on stage. An audience member might have the same occupation as the actor on stage, and may think "I do that, and I don't wear what she's wearing."

Whether clothing choices are conscious or not, others will receive a message. And this is especially true for theatre and film. The message may be subtle, but the designer has made a choice, and hopes that the receiver is open to the communication.

On a Personal Note

While costume designers want everything to be perfect, it never is. Obsessing is never beneficial to a production. Do pay attention to small details, but know that the color of thread probably won't be seen, so if it's a shade off, it'll be okay. It's great to strive for perfection, but when it doesn't happen, it's fine to let it go. If you know you've done all you could do, then it is perfect in that situation.

Most of all, enjoy yourself and have fun!

QUESTIONS

- Go to a public location. What messages do you read from what people choose to wear?

- Those who have studied the meaning of clothing seem to disagree upon the extent of their meaning. What is your opinion as to how much someone can read about another just by looking at what they are wearing?

- Why is it important for costume designers to understand clothing communication?

NOTES

1. Kurt W. Back, "Modernism and Fashion," in *Fashion Theory: A Reader,* ed. Malcolm Barnard (New York: Routledge, 2007).
2. Malcolm Barnard, *Fashion as Communication,* 2nd Ed (New York: Routledge, 2007).
3. *Subcultures, subcultureslist.com.* (University of Birmingham, Chicago School of Sociology.) http://subcultureslist.com/cyber-goth/ (accessed January 22, 2016).
4. Fred Davis, "Do Clothes Speak? What Makes Them Fashion?" in *Fashion Theory: A Reader,* ed. Malcolm Barnard (New York: Routledge, 2007).
5. *Project Runway,* Lifetime, 2004–, Bunim-Murray Productions.
6. See: https://en.wikipedia.org/wiki/James_Laver (accessed February 17, 2016).
7. Quentin Bell, *On Human Finery,* 2nd Ed (New York: Schocken Books, 1976).
8. Angela Partington, "Popular Fashion and Working-class Affluence," in *Fashion Theory: A Reader,* ed. Malcolm Barnard (New York: Routledge, 2007).
9. Colin Campbell, "When the Meaning is not a Message," in *Fashion Theory: A Reader,* ed. Malcolm Barnard (New York: Routledge, 2007).

FIGURE 3.1 *Costume design for Necessary Losses. (Graphite, marker, and gouache. Design by Leticia M. Delgado. Choreography by Jerry Pearson. Santa Barbara Dance Theatre International Tour, 2007 & 2008.)*

CHAPTER 3

COSTUME & CHARACTER: THE ELEMENTS AND PRINCIPLES OF DESIGN IN THE CREATION OF SCULPTURES IN MOTION

Leticia M. Delgado

THE ELEMENTS OF DESIGN

The elements of design are utilized by all visual artists to inform and influence the viewer. Designers utilize the elements to create two-dimensional and three-dimensional works of art. The successful costume designer has to understand both ways of creating visual art as part of the collaborative and creative process. For the costume designer there is the drawing or rendering in two dimensions and the final three-dimensional costume that is created for the stage. The following is a description and investigation of the design elements that most costume designers utilize in both the two-dimensional and three-dimensional process: **line**, **shape**, **space**, **form**, **color**, **texture**, and **value**. As theatre artists our knowledge of these elements is a vital part of our ability to communicate with each other and with the audience. The principles of design are the manner in which the design elements are organized on a page and ultimately on the costumed actor's body. The nine principles of design that most costume designers and visual artists utilize in the creation of their work are: **balance**, **emphasis**, **movement**, **pattern**, **repetition**, **proportion**, **rhythm**, **variety**, and **unity**. These principles will be briefly touched upon throughout the chapter as the examination of the elements of design in the world of costuming progresses.

Line

Line is the first element utilized by the hand of the designer in the creation of roughs—quick and dirty black and white character sketches—early in the design process. It may also be part of the early research phase. It can help designers and directors describe particular looks they want to achieve during specific parts of the play or particular locales. It can be a good starting point for conceptual discussion. Line also plays a vital part in the actual creation of the costume or garment. The placement of every seam, garment edge, pleat, dart, pocket, cuff, or gather creates a line. The finishing or decorative adornment of a piece of clothing also creates a line. Where the designer draws a line tells us something about the character being depicted and helps inform the work of the costume technicians. It lets the cutter–draper know where seams might be placed and what silhouette is desired. The use of particular types of line will also aide in the placement and selection of particular finishing and/or decorative motifs, such as the placement of piping, braided trim, lace, beading, faggoting, floral appliqués, and fringe. The power of suggestion of one or more lines of varying types can be very persuasive and informative. The different line types and their characteristics work together in the art of costume design to create a cohesive whole.

Characteristics of Line

Line is a mark or series of marks that take your eye from one point to another. Line is used to define shape, contours, and outlines. Specific lines can suggest mass and volume. Lines may be continuous marks made on a surface with a pointed or wide drawing tool. Line may also be implied by the edges of other shapes and forms, like style lines in the construction of a particular garment, the coupling of two garments, or the use of patterned and/or collaged print fabrics in one costume.

In order to better understand the power of line one must first look at the various characteristics of this particular element. Some of the **characteristics of line** which best correspond to costume design are width, length, direction, focus, and feeling. The lines that are utilized by a designer in the sketching and rendering phase are used to convey specific ideas about character, place, time, directorial concept, and the costume construction phase. These lines can be made with an assortment of drawing instruments. Designers may prefer to work with pencil, Conté crayon, charcoal, marker, or ink in this phase. It is up to each designer to pick the drawing instrument that bests suits them and the project at hand. Each drawing instrument has its own particular qualities and this will affect the line that is created and how it is perceived by others. Let us consider the lines created by some basic design tools; a basic sharpened #2 pencil, a broad tip or angled/beveled marker, and a round watercolor brush. Each of these could be utilized to draw a straight line of the same length across a blank page. However the line will not look the same or convey the same type of feeling. Each writing/drawing instrument creates a line that is specific to itself and its own properties. Each line also creates a different relationship to the page. The pencil line is thinner, and feels lighter than the marker line. The marker line has crisp edges, is wider, and has a deep color saturation. The watercolor line is translucent and has an airy quality to it. With this in mind, here are a few characteristics that allow us to see line differently with regard to placement on the page or rendering style.

The first characteristic of line is **width**. Width is the thickness or thinness that can be achieved when drawing a line from point A to point B. The point of a sharp pencil will create a much thinner line from A to B than the side of the same pencil traveling the same distance. The width of a pencil on its side in comparison to a beveled felt-tip marker may be similar but the graphite may create a sense of varied shading while the marker line is solid and dense. Both of these instruments can also create lines that taper into nothingness. Does it begin wide at A and narrow as it travels toward B, or vice versa? A line's width may also be irregular, changing in width from thick to thin (or the reverse).

Length describes the distance a line travels on the page or space. A line can travel a short or long distance depending on the intention of the artist. A line's length can also show inconsistencies. An artist may start a line at point A, travel an inch, stop, and then lay another one inch segment and repeat this pattern over and over until the line finally reaches point B. This creates a broken line. A broken line laid side-by-side with a continuous line will evoke a different power/feeling on the page. Together, width and length are sometimes referred to as the **measure of a line**. In terms of drawing for costume design, length and width can depict different types of fabrics and textures. A varied and cross hatched mixture of wide, long, continuous, and broken lines may help depict lace, tulle, fur, fringe, or patterned fabrics.

Direction lets us know where on the page the line starts and where it is traveling on the page. It is the intentional placement of a particular line with regard to the outer edges of a page or the finished garment on the body of an actor. A line can be horizontal, vertical, or diagonal. A line can radiate from a center. Lines may also curve or zigzag across the page. In simple placement on a page, lines can be perpendicular, oblique, or parallel to one another. The direction of each of these lines will evoke a feeling or emotion in the viewer. Horizontal or vertical lines, alone or together, communicate stability and safety. Diagonal lines may create a feeling of uncertainty and instability for the viewer. Lines that zigzag across a page or the body of a performer may have an air of harsh energy. While softer curving lines may create a feeling of familiarity, relaxation, and sensuality within the viewer.

Lines can have **focus** and **feeling**. Focus is created by the type of drawing instrument, and the pressure or energy applied to the implement at the time the line is put to the page by the designer's hand. This can create a sharp, blurry, fuzzy, or choppy line. Focus produces a particular energy within the line itself. This energy is directly related to another characteristic of line: feeling. Feeling denotes the sharpness, smoothness, jaggedness, and/or graceful nature of a line. The direction, focus, and feeling of a line help to communicate information about a character's inner life. A villain costume may utilize sharp lines like very pointy lapels, hanging sleeves, and a hard zigzag closure across the torso. Whereas the natural shape of a female can be mimicked and accentuated by graceful lines in the portrayal of an Empire gown made with lightweight linen, chiffon, and gauze.

Line Type

The aforementioned characteristics of line can be applied to all art forms. In costume design, they can be utilized in the following **line types**: sketch, gesture, outline, contour, and implied line. Costume designers will often use these types of line to describe their work in its various phases. Ultimately, these types of line also transfer to the realized stage costume with the help of fabric, construction lines, trim, accessories, and the other theatre design areas, such as scenic and lighting design.

A **sketch line** has a short airy quality and it implies the shape of an object. Several of these airy lines are placed next to each other to create the essence or semblance of a particular object. Costume designers may utilize this type of line in the rendering of fabric type and facial features, or in grounding an object. These are just a few uses for sketch lines.

A **gesture line** is filled with motion and energy. Gesture lines can capture movement in the fabric and in the body of the character being drawn. These lines can denote the action of running, laughing, crying, waving, and dancing. Gesture lines enliven a costume rendering and give a glimpse of the character's inner life and their place in the play/plot.

An **outline** creates the outer edge of an object. It captures the silhouette of a particular character and of the clothing that covers their body. It can communicate the time period and the locale that the character inhabits. The outermost edges of a costumed character help to establish and communicate the type of fabric and the character's possible relation to everything else that lives onstage, such as scenery, other costumed characters, and props.

Contour lines can help to describe both the interior portion of an object, as well as its exterior shape. This can be a tricky concept when first encountered by the design student. Contour lines can be used in the rendering stage to lay in shadow and pattern within a draped garment like a shawl. This helps to create depth and life within the established shape, while reinforcing the outer edges of a garment.

Implied line is created when two objects meet. For example, a cream shirtwaist meets the two inch waist band of a deeply pleated navy walking skirt that sits right at the true waist of an actress' torso. Where these two garments meet, in the rendering and on the body of an actor, implies a line, creating a different shape and the beginning of a particular period silhouette. Another cream shirtwaist paired with a gathered and gauzy mint green skirt that begins just under the bust also creates an implied line and a different period silhouette.

Costume designers have to use the element of line in various modes: drawing, painting, and the actual creation of the garment to be worn by a human being on stage. The use of line has to be exacting because it helps to define balance, proportion, and scale. It is also the basis for the next element of design that the costume designer must utilize: shape.

Shape

Shape is two dimensional, self-contained, and created by a single line or several lines that enclose a space. Shapes are utilized throughout the costume design process. They can be seen in rough sketches depicting the human body, pleated and draped garment sections, fabric pattern/print, and accessories. Shapes can

FIGURES 3.2 & 3.3 *Informing the eye of the viewer with line. Both of these artists utilize line to depict the human form and garments with different media. The weight and width of each line invokes a different type of energy. Both artists are depicting motion but not the same speed. (left) In Henri de Toulouse-Lautrec's Jane Avril from Le Café Concert (1893), the skirt outline undulates and is not continuous, creating a feeling of furious and frenetic energy. The medium here is brush and spatter lithograph printed in black on woven paper. (Courtesy of Harris Brisbane Dick Fund, 1923.) (right) The graphite and charcoal figures in Edgar Degas' Sketches of Café Singers (about 1877) also have curvilinear aspects but these are mixed with sketchy vertical and horizontal lines that evoke a heaviness and perhaps even age. (Dimensions: 24.8 × 33 cm. ©Getty Images.)*

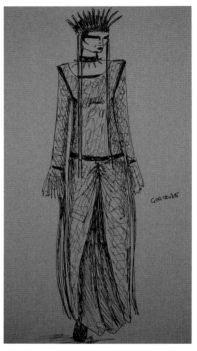

FIGURES 3.4–3.6 *These costume design sketches all utilize different media to create lines that can be associated with time period, a character's inner life, and their place in society. Although graphite, marker, and watercolor are all common in the world of art and design, they each evoke a different energy on paper. (top left) For As You Like It, there is a lofty, soft nature to the graphite and chalk pastel sketch of Celia that highlights her age and Romantic time period. (Miami University of Ohio, 2011. Design by Leticia M. Delgado.) (top right) For Hamlet, the swirling energetic marker lines within Gertrude's costume create a sense of frenzy, while the hard linear nature of the line work on her face and costume outline give the marker sketch a particular gravity. (Design by L. Kay Cotton.) (left) For Les Enfants, the designer has used graphite and watercolor to layer thick horizontal lines over a smooth wash, which both grounds the Narrator and adds a sense of sensuality and intrigue. (Sarah & Ernst Butler Opera Center, 2013. Design by Bich Vu.)*

be categorized as organic, geometric, positive, negative, static, and dynamic.

Organic shapes are free form, irregular, and possess a fluid quality that can convey the energy of movement. These shapes are associated with things we might see in the natural world. They are the gifts of Mother Nature. The shapes of apples, pears, leaves,

shells, or butternut squash are varied in nature. The curvature and flowing quality of organic shape has a calming effect on the viewer's eye. These organic shapes may be seen in the soft scrolling embroidered leaves on a silk chiffon chemise or Empire gown.

Geometric shapes are created by various lines that meet to form an angle. They may also be created with a line that is bent continuously in one direction until it touches itself. Some geometric shapes have angles and all have very clearly defined edges or outlines. Most geometric shapes are created with the help of the human hand. We are all familiar with basic geometric shapes. We learn some of these at a very young age: circles, squares, rectangles, triangles, trapezoids, and ovals.

Shapes in a composition can also be classified as positive or negative shapes. In a two-dimensional composition, the objects on a page are the positive forms and they make up the foreground. Thus, the background is the negative space. A beginning art or design class may employ the simple exercise of placing shapes cut out of black construction paper on a white page and then vice versa. This exercise is intended to help the young artist understand that the placement of objects in a particular picture plane, whether it is the rendering page or the theatrical stage, is

powerful when created with specific intentions and/or choices in mind. It can be used to demonstrate how even the simplest shapes on a picture plane can create implied lines, movement, rhythm, and emphasis. Shapes are used to move the eye and tap into the viewer's personal perceptions. The background and the foreground are both of equal importance in any work of art.

Shapes can also be classified as static or dynamic. A **static shape** is grounded and at rest. A **dynamic shape** is one that appears to be in motion. The depiction of thick or thin fringe with round (geometric shaped) large sequins at the tips, on a dancer twisting and leaping, would give us an example of a dynamic geometric shape. A patterned fabric that repeats ascending or descending shape may also be classified as having or creating dynamic shape. This corresponds to the principles of rhythm, radiation, and possibly repetition.

FIGURES 3.7 & 3.8 *Use of shape in costume can be loose and subtle or big and bold. (left) To create a dancing human figure, Messel (1945) uses charcoal, pencil, gouache, paint, and watercolor to depict the limbs with basic ovals. The sketchy quality of the oval limbs heightens the feeling of motion and the lightness that ballet conveys. (Acquired with the support of the Heritage Lottery Fund, The Art Fund, and the Friends of the Victoria & Albert Museum.) (right) In contrast, for A Flea in Her Ear, Babette is depicted in gouache, marker, and graphite using bright squares and rectangles that pull focus toward particular portions of the character's and actress' body. This tells us a bit about her inner life, the type of establishment for which she works, and perhaps foreshadows the events to come. (Ball State University Theatre, 2004. Design by Leticia M. Delgado.)*

The costume silhouette or outline is often the first shape that comes into the mind of the viewer when thinking about costumes, but it is the sum of many parts. Shape in costume design begins with the depiction of the human form, followed by the illustration of costume garments, adornments/trims, and accessories. The costume designer deals with shape during the early drawing phase, the finishing details of the final rendering, and the selection and rendering of fabric pattern. So some of the first basic geometric shapes may be utilized to depict the two-dimensional human form: the oval of the human head, the trapezoid of the chest area, the trapezoidal lower body, the rectangles or ovals of the limbs, and the possible circular nature of the joints. Some designers may choose to render the torso and limbs with fluid figure eights, resulting in a more organic shape.

After drawing the body of the actor and/or the character, the costume designer can begin the depiction of the garment. Garment depiction on the page, although it is given some depth with the use of shading, is still a basic shape because it is part of a two-dimensional piece of artwork. The depiction of the bodice, sleeves, cuffs, pocket details, and skirt width and length all create distinct shapes that form a whole look or silhouette. The final phase of the costume design on the page and the stage involves accessories and trims, like rhinestone earrings, crystals, belt buckles, lace, fringe, and buttons—all of which are also composed of basic shapes.

Space

In the definition of shape we use the words "space" and "line." Line, shape, and space have a symbiotic relationship. They all help to create each other and cannot exist without one another in a visual composition. So what exactly does space do for the costume design and its success in the theatre?

Space is the area that a shape or form encompasses, together with its surroundings. It is everything that the artist places on the canvas. Thus it is often referred to in association with composition, or the arrangement of objects on a particular plane or canvas. In costume design, the first actual space we may deal with is the actor's body on the page, then the costume they actually wear on their body, and ultimately the stage inhabited by the actor in said costume. The first time a costume designer deals with the element of space is when rendering an actor in costume on the page or picture plane. This is two-dimensional space. In a finished rendering it may look like it has the feeling of volume, mass, or depth, but it does not. Ultimately, the costume designer deals with the space that is the actual actor in the costume on the stage during a production. During this final phase the costume

design is in motion and is also a three-dimensional object that inhabits the space of the stage. This final phase will be discussed further in the examination of the element of form.

Two related characteristics of space in two-dimensional design are positive and negative. These are symbiotic: they cannot exist alone. Positive and negative has already been discussed in the section on shape, but the following is a further examination of these characteristics as they relate to both art and costume design. The **positive space** is inhabited by the primary object that is the focal point of the two-dimensional setting. The focal point is where our eye is being directed to go, and is related to the principle of emphasis (to be covered later in the chapter). **Negative space** is the area that surrounds a primary object in a piece of art. In looking at a costume rendering, the space around the costumed character is negative space. The costumed

FIGURE 3.9 *Using Conté crayon on Michallet paper for* Une élégante (Woman Strolling) *(about 1884), note how Georges Seurat has left a bit of blank space and used less line work all the way around the dark figure. This negative space creates a halo around the figure (positive space), which pulls in the eye and accentuates the curvilinear silhouette. This technique can be used by a costume designer in the rendering phase and perhaps even onstage with the help of a lighting designer. (Dimensions: 31.8 × 24 cm. Courtesy of The J. Paul Getty Museum, Los Angeles.)*

character on the page is the primary image, focus/focal point, and the positive space. If a character in white is placed at the center of a tan or gray **rendering**, they are the focal point of the space. This character is also the primary space. Everything around them on this rendering is negative space. Negative space on a rendering can be very powerful; it can guide our eye to a particular aspect of individual character.

When rendering the character, a costume designer may create a primary or focal space, but it is important not to forget what lies around or surrounds the character on the page. This is not just empty unimportant space. It is vital in the creation of a two-dimensional space that embodies the final area in which the costume will live—the stage. This negative space on the page can help ground the figure and aids in the believable depiction of volume and mass. Traditional perspective drawing techniques and shading create depth on the page. Many of these perspective drawing techniques are utilized by the scenic designer but many still apply to the costume rendering or sketch. A ground line, shadows beneath the body, hatching, ink washes behind the figure, and foreshortening are all vital parts of the rendering space. Some designers even recreate aspects of the set design using perspective drawing techniques to help ground their figures on the costume plate. This can tell the viewer a great deal about the character and their place in the plot/play. It is part of our job as costume designers to help others view the entire world that a character will ultimately inhabit.

Space can convey a feeling of being open or closed. Some costume designers have a very loose and sketchy manner of drawing that can depict the face, limbs, skirt, or full sleeve, with lines that do not intersect or meet in the creation of shape. The costumed figure is the positive space of the rendering, but it is also an open space. Some period/historical clothing depictions like Directoire or Empire profit from such a hand. The depiction of lace, fur, and chiffon fabric is another instance when we may utilize such open space. Some artists choose to employ a much more continuous line style of drawing, in which all shapes and lines meet and are rendered in a definitive and complete manner. A costumed figure rendered in this particular style will obviously be a closed primary space. These two styles can coexist very effectively in a rendering.

The division of space is a vital part of costume design. How the costume designer chooses to dress the actor helps with the physical and mental transformation that is needed to bring the character and plot to life. Space can be divided by line or shape. When drawing clothing on a figure for costume design, the placement of lines creates shapes that are linked to the character's identity in the play. The outline of the character sketch

or rendering is referred to as the silhouette of the costume. The **silhouette** is created by the outer edges of the character's body and the clothing drawn on the body. This silhouette is extremely powerful in the finished costume on stage and in the final design element (to be covered later in this chapter in the section on form). The division of this silhouette in the two-dimensional space and how it affects the depiction of the character on the stage is a crucial part of the art of costume design.

Divisions of the silhouette help to delineate characters and to create mood. Every garment has specific style lines that can tell us a great deal about a character's inner life. Style lines and garment features allow the costume designer to bring out specific character aspects and to play with the distribution of primary space. **Style lines** can be created by a straight seam, different garments meeting, or two distinct and different fabrics meeting on a particular plane. **Garment features** are all of the structural details that create line and shape: pockets, collars, darts, tucks, cuffs, peplums, and various seams and décor. In both art and design, the distribution of space has powerful emotional and psychological effects. Dividing space into equal parts has a neutral or static effect, while dividing the space in an unequal manner creates visual interest. If we divide the human shape horizontally we give the illusion of weight or width, and shorten the body. Some very horizontal costumes like hooped clown suits (or dancing crinolines), very wide Georgian panniers, and certain Elizabethan cartwheel ruffs can add an element of frivolity, hilarity, or severity to the pictorial plane. Conversely, when we divide the human body with vertical lines, creating shapes like rectangles, we give the illusion of length and possibly loftiness. Diagonal tailored lines are often associated with edgier characters. Draped soft diagonals can give an air of grace or even whimsy. All of these divisions of space can also be mixed and matched to great effect.

It is the job of a costume designer to divide the vertical space of the human form in a manner that speaks to both the character and the play they inhabit. The sketch and rendering are the first vehicle for this division. As costume designers, we can utilize structural shape and line to divide the human body in various ways. The most basic space division tool is the garment itself. Where a designer chooses to place seams and change fabrics creates new shapes and spaces that can also be manipulated with line to help emphasize or de-emphasize particular areas on the garment/body, based on character identity. The opulent pattern of a king's or queen's garment will create new spatial relationships and invoke a different feeling from the viewer than that of a dusty, torn, and hewn peasant garment. A designer can also add padding, place trim, and include accessories on specific parts of the body and garments in order to alter our visual perception of the actor's body.

FIGURES 3.10 & 3.11 *Note the emphasis on the vertical nature of these Empire and 1920's designs. The basic outline or silhouette of the costume makes the eye travel up and down (or vertically on the visual plane), even if the pattern of the garment is not strictly vertical, making these characters appear lighter, and less severe. The garment cuts elongate the body of the actor even though some horizontal details exist in the design. (left: Much Ado About Nothing, Ball State University Summer Theatre, 2005. Design by L. Kay Cotton. right: All's Well That Ends Well, Miami University of Ohio, 2004. Design by Meggan Peters.)*

Form

A form is a three-dimensional object, such as a cube, cylinder, sphere, pyramid, or prism. All forms have true height, width, and length. Form for the costume designer is the actor's physical body in costume. It is the final resting place of a costume designer's work. This is where the designer's hand and the hands of the costume technicians breathe life into the rendering. Form unifies line, shape, space, color, value, and texture. It provides the object that will exist in the theatrically lit world of the stage.

The costume designer utilizes the human body as the frame for the structural three-dimensional form: the costume. Costume designers serve the needs of the script and the directorial vision, and this may necessitate the simplification or exaggeration of the human form. If the human form is masked, distorted, enlarged, or elongated, this will capture the eye of the viewer immediately and influence their perception of a character. A designer needs to be capable of assessing whether the body of the actor fits the text and the director's vision for the particular play. Actor measurements and features aid in this assessment, but certain characters may require more involved designs. For example, Shakespeare's Richard III requires a physical deformity to fully recreate the physicality that his psychological complexity necessitates. The actor in the role of Richard III may need to have their shoulder, neck, and upper back padded to achieve what the text and director wish to accomplish. With this information in hand, the designer can begin to think of the next structural layer: the undergarments.

FIGURES 3.12 & 3.13 *When examining the Cavalier and Georgian costumes, note how the eye wants to float from side to side on the page. These images/ silhouettes emphasize the horizontal and round nature of the garments of the period, to highlight mass, weight, and volume. The type of pattern and adornment also allude to the social class and rank of the particular period. Depending on the stiffness of the fabric, we may even hear the rustle of these period garments on stage. (left: Prince Henri De Conde in* The Devils, *Miami University of Ohio, 2004. Design by Meggan Peters. right: Woman's Robe à la Française and Petticoat in silk plain weave (faille) with silk and metallic-thread supplementary weft patterning, and metallic lace trim. Gift of Mrs Aldrich Peck. Courtesy of LACMA.)*

The designer and technicians need to cover the human body with the appropriate male and female undergarments. These undergarments are the foundation of a successful structural three-dimensional form, and ultimately enable the achievement of the desired silhouette. The creation of these undergarments may require a very skilled artisan or technician. An important consideration for any understructure is the actor's ability to live on the stage and bring the character to life without constraint. So costume designers should only accentuate certain parts of the body and/or mold it into the ideal form if it helps with the plot and directorial concept. The first layer against the human form can be as simple as a v-neck undershirt or thin camisole, or as complex as a latex and silicone body altering leotard/animal suit, or a constricting corset and boned cartwheel farthingale. These understructures enhance and necessitate certain construction lines.

In order for the garment to sit properly on the human body, it must have all the right seams, pleats, contour darts, sleeve headers, and gores to hug the undergarment. These special construction needs create lines and shapes within the three-dimensional garment, generating mass, depth, interest, and visual movement. They also enable us to accurately recreate period silhouette. The silhouette in three-dimensional form is aided by the type of fabric from which the garment is constructed, and the manipulation of that particular fabric. Using the cartwheel farthingale as an example allows further investigation of how form brings costume construction together with the elements of line, shape, and space.

The recreation of period silhouette allows the costume designer to create some of the most dynamic forms. The cartwheel farthingale is the basis for what is commonly referred to as the Elizabethan silhouette. This understructure shoots

FIGURE 3.14 *A painting (c. 1606) of Princess Elizabeth (1596–1662), later Queen of Bohemia by Robert Peake the Elder. (Dimensions: 154.3 × 79.4 cm. Gift of Kate T. Davison, in memory of her husband, Henry Pomeroy Davison, 1951. Courtesy of Metropolitan Museum of Art.)*

wool and silk damask can be lined, starched, cartridge pleated, and applied to a stiffened waistband to create a skirt that accentuates and enhances the conical form created by the understructure.

We cannot have a successful Late Tudor or Elizabethan silhouette without the proper execution of the various forms of understructures. The proper execution of this period structure made for the stage is itself a sculpture and its relationship to the other theatrical elements on stage are also critical to its success. Line, shape, and form are powerful communication tools in the world of costume design, but their full power can only be harnessed by the careful understanding and execution of the rest of the elements of design: color, texture, and value.

Color

Color is the quality of light that an object reflects and can be measured by hue, saturation, and intensity. Color is one of the most powerful elements of design. It has strong psychological associations that can inform the viewer's perception and trigger emotional recall. It allows the costume designer to group figures together on the visual plane of the stage by class, rank, and social status. Color can be utilized to highlight the inner complexities of a specific character and their relationship to others on stage. A costume designer utilizes the element of color when creating a color palate in the preliminary design phase, while assembling research imagery, in the creation of the two-dimensional final rendering, and lastly in the construction of the final garment in three-dimensional form.

In order to begin early conceptual discussions with the director and the design team, a costume designer should be familiar with both the subtractive and additive color theories. The understanding of both of these color theories is crucial to the execution of renderings and the final costumed form on stage. The **subtractive color theory** enables us to create in the two-dimensional phase, when painting the costume design renderings. **Additive color theory** deals with the properties of light, allowing the audience to view our three-dimensional costumes on stage.

Many have their first encounter with subtractive color theory when they are learning to mix paint or pigment. When the mixing of two colors/pigments occurs, the removal of certain rays of white light also takes place. This removal or "subtraction" is what allows the new color to be formed. When two colors are mixed together, one of these pigments will no longer reflect a particular color of white light. Subtractive color theory allows the designer to manipulate and transform three pigments—red,

out horizontally from the waist of the actor creating a table-like structure. Then it descends toward the floor maintaining a cylindrical shape with the aid of boning. The table-like portion of the cartwheel farthingale is held up by boning and by the use of a padded structure called the bolster. These undergarments are three dimensional and are a critical part of how the fabric will be molded into a garment with the use of various sewing techniques that are intrinsic to the creation of form. A piece of blue, and yellow—into the various colors we see in our everyday lives. Red, yellow, and blue are the three **primary colors** of the subtractive theory. These three primary colors can be mixed to create the subtractive **secondary colors**: orange, green, and violet. When we mix a primary and a secondary color, we create tertiary colors. The subtractive **tertiary colors** are yellow-orange, orange-red, red-violet, violet-blue, blue-green, and green-yellow. These colors or hues make up the traditional color wheel and can be organized in various ways. A **hue** is the color we experience or see in a color wheel in its purest form: no white, black, or grey has been added. A pure or saturated hue is bright and has high intensity. In terms of paint, like watercolor and gouache, water can be added to dilute the pure or saturated hue, creating luminosity.

We can also add white, black, or grey to the pigments found on the traditional color wheel to create tints, shades, and tones of a particular hue. **Tints** begin as pure hues and have degrees of white pigment added to them. The original hue will get progressively lighter and can be used as low-, medium-, and highlights of that particular hue in a rendering. **Shades** are pure hues that have degrees of black pigment added to them. Shades of a hue work their way toward black and can be utilized to depict shadows and depth on a rendering. A pure hue at full saturation can be muted by adding its complementary color or grey, making the color less vibrant. Reducing a hue's vibrancy is often referred to as **tone**.

Colors can be grouped to create the sensation of temperature, either cool or warm. The **cool colors** are those that are located from green to violet on the color wheel. Cool colors will recede on the picture plane. The **warm colors** of the color wheel are those located from red to yellow; they will advance or appear to move forward on the picture plane. Costume designers can utilize these temperature sensations in the form of color to help depict a character's emotional state or the general feeling of a mass of people onstage. Color can also allow the costume designer to pull the viewer's eye in a particular

FIGURE 3.15 *Tints and shades of the blue hue.*

direction or highlight a portion/part of the actor's body or costume. On a stage filled with navy blue and gray suits, a figure in red will pull focus and pop out of the picture plane, interjecting a sudden feeling of warmth.

Another method used to group color is by color scheme. Some of the most commonly utilized color schemes are: monochromatic, analogous, complementary, split complementary, and triadic. These color schemes are created by grouping colors to create a sense of unity, harmony, or contrast. When studying these color schemes, notice where your eye travels and the associative and emotional recall that such pairings can bring about.

A **monochromatic color scheme** is made up of different shades and tints of one color. An example would be a light lilac, a violet, and a dark violet. This monochromatic scheme can give the illusion of coolness and it may also be associated with images of divinity or royalty, depending on the society you are representing. A monochromatic scheme based on reds may create a feeling of warmth and intensity. Such a color scheme has found its way into the portrayal of the sinful and vivacious characters in numerous plays.

An **analogous color scheme** is made by utilizing colors that live side-by-side on the color wheel and share a primary color. It is often also referred to as adjacent color. A basic example would be blue and blue-green. These colors when used together convey a sense of coolness and serenity. Greens and blues can elicit images of the sky and water in the mind of the viewer, both of which have a renewing sensibility. All analogous colors are most often found in nature and are generally considered pleasing to the eye. Think of that fine citrus fruit which many of you may enjoy on any given morning. The skin of this fruit can vary in color from orange to yellow-orange and possibly all the way to a yellow-green. This is an example of analogous color brought to us by Mother Nature. Analogous color schemes are often used to group families. A designer may use analogous color schemes to depict the Capulets and the Montagues in Shakespeare's *Romeo and Juliet*. Analogous color is also very popular in grouping dancers to highlight particular movements in a dance number.

Complementary colors are located directly opposite each other on the traditional color wheel. These can be blue and orange, yellow and violet, or one of the most famous complementary color schemes in our modern western society: green and red. This combination of colors is often bright and crisp. These colors can create a feeling of alertness and excitement. Such combinations are often utilized in team sports uniforms. This color combination can also be used on one character. One of the colors can serve as the base color, encompassing most of the garment articles, and the other can be the color for the trim and accessories.

Split complementary color schemes are created by taking two complementary hues on the color wheel and adding only one of their analogous or adjacent pairs. The addition of these analogous pairs then omits the complementary hue that they surround on the wheel. An example of a split complementary scheme would be orange, blue-green, and blue-violet. This allows the creation of contrast that is not overbearingly bright to the viewer's eye.

Triadic color schemes are created by utilizing three colors that are equally spaced on the traditional color wheel. A basic example would be the use of the primary colors; red, yellow, and blue. There are three other hues between them on the color wheel. This color combination is best utilized when one of the colors covers a large space and the other two are used in smaller portions as accent colors. This uneven distribution creates visual interest. If all three colors are equally distributed the figure or space may read as static and lose the eye of the viewer. A basic costuming example utilizing this triadic color scheme could be in the depiction of military dress. A military uniform could be made of a blue dress coat and slacks. The blue dress coat could have red piping around the outer seams and yellow braid on the collar and epaulets.

Black, white, and grey are both neutral and achromatic colors. These are not always the most visually enticing colors for costume design when used alone. They are often used in combination with other more dynamic color schemes. Black, white, and grey can also be added to all twelve hues to reduce the purity and brightness of any hue, creating a neutral color like moss, puce, slate, or mauve. These neutral palettes are often quite pleasing to the eye and find their way into many theatrical productions. Neutral colors in costume design can become beautiful canvases when the theatrical light dances on them. Some combinations of neutral colors may also be appropriately used to depict dream states or flashbacks in the theatre. Certain neutral combinations with a good degree of distress are also ideal for depicting a character that is down and out, or a group of people who have fallen on hard times.

Now that some of the basics of subtractive color have been covered, the investigation into the power of color to convey a character's emotional state, social status, and their place in the advancement of the plot can begin. Knowledge of color psychology and culturally specific color associations can be just as valuable to a costume designer as they are to a marketing design firm. As human beings we associate certain colors with particular events, places, or moods we have experienced in our lives. As designers we can tap into the viewer's subconscious by utilizing certain colors. Everyone has different life experiences, but as a Western culture we have assigned specific emotive significance to particular colors. When we see a character in solid black we feel a sense of gravity, possibly evil, or maybe melancholy. A figure in glowing white may cause us to feel peace and a sense of purity. A pure primary blue may have a calming affect on us and is often associated with the cleansing powers of water. These three particular colors can also have different meanings in a religious context. Such religious color signifiers may prove helpful when dealing with particular plays. Understanding color psychology in our Western culture strengthens a designer's ability to create and communicate.

Color is a powerful design element. We begin our understanding of color as infants and the understanding of its meanings grows with us, evolving as we age. Color is integral to both the design process and the completed product. Color mixed with the style and cut of garments can significantly alter an audience's perception of a character and their understanding of the event that is being presented before them. The choice of fabric is tied to color and another essential element, texture. Having discussed subtractive color theory and the possible perceptions and uses of the twelve basic hues, the tactile nature in which these colors may exist on the stage should be considered. Interesting and engaging color in costume design relies on the tactile nature of fabrics, or texture, that is revealed through the use of theatrical lighting. What are the implications of texture for a costume designer?

Texture

Texture is what the surface of an object feels like to the human hand. With regard to fabric in costume and fashion design, it is often referred to as the hand of the fabric. It is the perceived tactile nature of an item or fabric; what it feels like against skin. Texture, like color, depends on theatrical lighting design to reach the audience member's eye. It has a strong psychological effect on the viewer. Texture is a great tool for the designer to utilize when depicting class or locale because it ignites a tactile recall in the viewer. This can help convey specific feelings attributed to soft, rough, or uneven surfaces that can be equated to character relationships or the depiction of active and successive events on the stage. A character swathed in shiny snakeskin, metallic spikes, and stiffened horsehair will create a sense of anxiety, uneasiness, and possibly doom. While a woman in a smooth silk paneled charmeuse skirt and fluffy angora sweater may read as soft, warm, alluring, and inviting. The clanking and banging of armor onstage will not only aide the intensity of a fight scene, but the reflective quality may sting the eye of the viewer creating a sense of pain and urgency within.

Texture is depicted in the two-dimensional phase of the costume rendering or sketch and is a vital part of the early collaboration and communication process. This type of texture, in the two-dimensional phase, is sometimes referred to as implied or visual texture. Two dimensional or **implied texture** is created by using various drawing techniques to make a blank page look as though it is smooth, rough, soft, or any necessary consistency. Implied texture can be achieved using a variety of media and the previously covered elements of line, shape, color, and even form, depending on the painting technique or method. Texture and the principles of pattern, repetition, and rhythm can make a design lively and engaging in both the two-dimensional format and in the three-dimensional product for the stage. The two-dimensional aspects of texture and how an artist might go about interpreting the tactile nature of surfaces can be quite versatile. The rest of this investigation of texture will be based on the three-dimensional aspect of texture; its real existence on the body of the costumed actor.

Texture can accent specific areas, spaces, and forms, to create focal points in a composition. Certain textures are an innate characteristic of particular fabrics. Pairing a highly textured garment or costume piece with a flatter, more matte garment will create contrast and movement in the viewer's eye. Pairing opposites makes for a dynamic character ensemble, but one must understand the inherent hand of fabrics to make a pleasing aesthetic choice. The use of texture creates visual interest on the costume and helps pull it away from its surroundings. In the world of costume design, texture can be created by fabric type, pattern, manipulation, and the adornment of a particular fabric. A costume's final life under the stage lights is enhanced by the use of texture. The following is an examination of how fabric is created, as this process directly correlates to its tactile nature and its vital role in the creation of a sculptural form for the stage.

Fabric Manufacturing

Fabric texture is created by its fiber, its yarn content/structure, and its finish. **Fibers and filaments** are the smallest components of a fabric. They are used to create threads or yarns. These yarns are then braided or twisted together. Next, two strands of yarn are woven at a ninety degree angle to create the fabric. Yarns can vary based on how many and what types of fiber are twisted together prior to the weaving process. The type of fiber and filament, as well as how many of each are utilized, will create the first layer of texture on a piece of fabric. Fibers and filaments can be plant based, animal based, or synthetic. Each type of filament has particular characteristics that we will

briefly detail later in this section. Plant-based, animal-based, and synthetic filaments are woven or twisted in a particular direction in the early part of the fabric creation process. Some basic yarn creation methods are S-twist or Z-twist. The S-twist is created by single yarns that are twisted to the right. Some common S-twist fabrics are cotton and linen. The Z-twist is created by single yarns that are twisted to the left. Wool is a common Z-twist fabric. This twisting and weaving will create another layer of tactile characteristics that affect the eventual hand and drape of the fabric. The fabric weave makes yarns adhere to one another, creating a stronger fabric. The three basic fabric weaves are plain weave, twill weave, and satin weave. These all have numerous variations that help to create fabric texture.

Fabric weaving is said to have started in China and other Eastern regions as early as 500 BC. This was achieved by the use of human hands on a loom. In its most basic form, fabric is woven using a warp and weft yarn on a loom. The **warp** thread is pulled taught lengthwise or longitudinally on a loom. We often refer to this as the straight of grain on a piece fabric. Warp threads are usually stronger and of a higher quality, allowing for the tensions incurred on them when they are stretched on the loom. **Weft** or filling yarns are woven over and under the warp and run **cross grain** on a piece of fabric. These weft yarns are usually fuzzier and more uneven due to the twisting of filaments. This particular characteristic of weft yarn contributes considerably to the texture of a fabric. Today, the manufacturing of fabric still uses the same principles but includes solutions and heating techniques that give us fabric finishes. These finishes include, but are not limited to: printing, dyeing, mercerizing, embossing, flocking, permanent press, glazing, and moire. With regard to texture, these finishes make use of line, shape, and the layering of color shades and tints in the two-dimensional rendering of costume plates. This depiction directly correlates to the absorption and reflection of theatrical lighting.

Basic Textile Compositions, Textures, and Use in Costume

There are certain fabrics that are quite common in the costume design world. Further examination of these fabrics requires some knowledge of fabric composition. Fabrics are composed of fibers and filaments. A number of these fibers and filaments occur naturally in our world and help to create some familiar fabrics: the plant-based and animal-based fabrics or textiles. Some commonly used fabrics from the plant-based world are cotton and linen. They are also often referred to as the natural or cellulosic fibers or fabrics. Some of the common animal-based fabrics or proteins are wool and silk.

Cotton is the most prominent fabric in our modern world. It is used in the world of costume design in many ways, from the early stages of constructing the muslin mockup, to period understructures like corsets and petticoats, and of course in the actual creation of a costume garment like a period shirtwaist, chemise, or a gingham dress. With regard to the creation of texture on a costume, several properties make cotton a good choice: it takes dye well and can be overpainted nicely; and numerous sewing techniques can be applied that allow for an added layer of textural dimension, such as gathering, pleating, embroidery, smocking, and trapunto. Some familiar plain weave cotton fabrics are chambray, gingham, percale, lawn, and poplin. Denim, drill, gabardine, and chino are common twill weave cotton fabrics. Cotton fabrics like terrycloth and velvet also have the added texture of pile, which is created by the weaving process. Eyelet embroidery is another common texture added after the weaving process. Most cotton fabrics absorb light with the exception of sateen (a cotton-based satin weave) or a mercerized cotton. These types of cotton have a sheen on their surface which reflects light.

Linen is another plant-based cellulosic fabric. It is created from the flax plant and its fibers and yarn have a natural sheen to them that appears either as a smooth or a mottled matte texture depending on the weaving process utilized. Its yarns can contain slubs: gathered raised sections that do no press out. Such slubs can appear prominently in some natural ecru, ivory, tan, or gray linen fabrics. These slubs, and linen's natural tendency to wrinkle easily, can give linen a very primitive texture, allowing for its use to depict costumes of the early Biblical, Egyptian, Greek, and Roman historical periods. Linen dyes well but may bleed color in particularly hot situations if not set properly and laundered prior to stage use. Unlike cotton, linen does not always lend itself to heavy stitching and manipulation. Its fibers may break and show stress when handled excessively; for example, when a high heat dye vat and wire brush are used to distress this type of material.

Silk is an animal-based protein filament derived from the cocoon of the silk worm. Silk fabrics have an attractive drape and an inherent luster. Silk dyes well and can be an ideal surface for various painting techniques like batik and block printing, which are beautiful ways of incorporating the principles of pattern, repetition, rhythm, and unity. Silk does tend to wrinkle easily, but it takes well to pressing and can get its shape back easily. Some common silk fabrics used in costume design are noil, chiffon, organza, charmuese, satin, crepe de chine, georgette, shantung, and some brocades. Most silks are plain weaves and are not resilient over time, but other attributes like hand and drape make them useful to the costume design world. The lightweight silks like habotai, georgette, and chiffon give us a range of delicate movement and are ideal for dance, the portrayal of ethereal characters, or even the layering of fabrics for the Empire or Directoire silhouettes. Noil and shangtung fabrics have slubs on their surface. This lends a texture to the fabric surface that can be enhanced by painting and dying techniques. Noil is often used in Medieval female costumes and in the depiction of various t-shaped ancient dress items, from Biblical to Roman. Noil also takes well to the layering of spray dye for distressing garments. This method of adding color creates another layer of implied texture that is ideal for depicting individuals who are on the fringes of society, plays that take place prior to our modern revolution in hygiene, or the enhancement of movement in dance pieces.

Wool is a protein textile fiber. It is derived from the fleece of certain sheep breeds. Wool fabrics are split into two families; woolen and worsted. Some common woolen fabrics in the design world are tweed and flannel. The fibers of woolen fabrics are much shorter and contain a good deal of crimp, hence creating a fuzzier, more uneven, surface. Such a surface can create a distinct textural interest when revealed to the viewer by the lighting design. Worsted wools are smoother because they are created using longer fiber yarns that are also stronger and lighter. Commonly used worsted wools are gabardine and crepe. Most wool fabrics are created using either the twill weave or a variation, like herringbone, which may mix yarns of several hues, shades, or tints. Such a mixture will help enhance the pattern and texture of the fabric. Wool can also be used to create jersey and knit fabrics. Wool drapes well and holds structure. Seams, pleats, and gathers have a nice crispness to them on a worsted wool fabric. Some wool fabrics can help to ensure a structured fit for the purpose of replicating military uniforms, tailored suits, and historically accurate coats for the stage. Wool is highly absorbent and retains body heat: one should consider this with regard to the actor. Wool dyes well with the use of reactive chemical dyes. It will also take a direct dye like Rit but the high heat setting required with this method may destroy or break the fibers, causing the surface to become distorted. However, the creation of such distorted textures may work to one's advantage when designing for characters of little means, or individuals who require the layering of several hewn fabrics, like witches or mystical creatures in the bog.

There are numerous synthetic fabrics in our modern world. They have been, and continue to be, created to mimic some of the tendencies of natural fibers. These synthetic fibers help to make what we often refer to as the manmade fabrics. Some of these are rayon, acetate, spandex, triacetate, metallic, acrylics, and modacrylic. Many of these fabrics are utilized in the world of design due to their availability, ease of use, and cost effectiveness. In the costume design world, budget, time, and location play a huge part in fabric choice, meaning that fabric selection may sometimes have to be altered to accommodate restrictions. For such instances, there are a variety of blends that allow us to give the illusion of a linen, wool, or silk that may be out of our reach. Some common blends that are used include: polyester-cotton, terry-wool suiting, and polyester viscose rayon. The varied percentages used in the manufacturing of each blend ratio will affect the texture, hand, and fit of the fabric: they each have their own properties and surface texture.

Utilizing Print and Applied Décor

Texture can also be fabricated with a print. Fabrics can be manufactured with prints that are heat bonded to the fabric fibers. Certain fabrics may allow for more of a dimensional print depiction. For instance, a pile fabric like velvet that has a metal or lace pattern pressed into it with heat embossing will have an eye-catching three-dimensional quality that can be depicted through line, shape, shades, or tints on the page, which in turn will translate into engaging repetition, rhythm, and variety of movement on the stage. Print that is used to create texture can also be woven into the fabric or achieved with factory printing solutions. An elaborate print may also be applied to a fabric by costume artisans using airbrush, stencils, stamping, silk screening, or embossing techniques. These methods can create a three-dimensional quality to the fabric surface. Depending on the theatrical space and the lighting, this texture or three-dimensional quality can be heightened or diffused. Dyeing techniques can also add a layer of depth and texture to a costume. Some fabrics may be dyed before they are cut. Others may be painted after they have been sewn in order to add decorative detail, show age or distress, or add stylized visual accent for dance or whimsical theatrical characters. The size and contrast of prints or fabric patterns can tell the viewer about the inner life of a character, reveal their socioeconomic status, or highlight an event or locale. Print leads the eye of the viewer, so placement should be exacting because it will emphasize specific structural lines and parts of the actor's anatomy. A stomacher with elaborate print and embroidery will pull the viewer's eye into the torso and lead them to the décolletage, collar, and the underskirt.

The manipulation of particular fabrics through the use of layering, cutting, sewing, painting, and dye techniques can also add texture to a costume design. A costume designer and technician can utilize numerous sewing techniques to alter some of the natural tendencies of a fabric and create texture that reconfigures its drape. The placement of piping between seams, trapunto stitching, smocking, elastic casings, slash and puff, and embroidery are just a few methods by which fabric can be manipulated to create surface texture. Such surface textures can be used on various garments, from Renaissance chemises and doublets to children's clothing, and can even be used to create a quilted armor effect.

All of these techniques add to the interest of the visual plane of the costume by remolding the fabric's surface area, and altering the drape, to create a new texture and added depth. The use of such techniques may also allow the designer and technician to sculpt the fabric into a particular silhouette that speaks to the character, time period, or particular event.

The use of decorative trims, appliqués, and certain types of closures also add a layer of texture and dimension to the fabric of a costume. The placement of trim can emphasize the silhouette and style lines. Trims can match or contrast with the fabrics; in either case, they add dimension. A hint of silver sparkle on the cream lace appliqués that sit on the bodice of a white ballet tutu helps to accentuate the graceful movement of the torso and limbs by gently capturing the light. The same lace appliqué on a fitted deep blue, black, or plum Belle Epoque hour-glass gown will also create an alluring texture that captures the viewer's eye. The use of faux or real fur and feathers on hats and capes can add that perfect finishing touch of class or scandal to a costume, while also adding a fluffy and lofty air to the textural plain. Some appliqués and buttons may have a high sheen on their surface that creates a reflective impression when revealed by theatrical lighting, and this can aid in the depiction of flashiness, decadence, or opulence, depending on the occasion and the character they adorn. Such finishing details have been left to the end of this section because they sit upon the fabric and have a direct connection to the next element of design that is crucial to the completion of a costume for the stage or screen: value or light.

Value

In the art world, value often refers to the lightness or darkness of a color and ultimately the entire composition. At its most simple, value is used to reveal the true shape of an object. A three-dimensional object may be depicted through the use of the tints (light values) and shades (dark values) that make up the value of an individual color. A recognizable colored form under a directional light will have all values represented within the form itself and its cast shadow. Lines and shapes will be created within the form as the tints and shades border each other in their depiction of the three-dimensional form on the plane. Any

FIGURE 3.16 *In* Romeo and Juliet, *note how the silhouette of the costume and the limbs of the dancer work with the light to create an elegant yet severe character. Beams of light travel through the dark and the flowing skirt to create a balance of softness and fierceness all at once, capturing Lady Capulet as both a mother and a force to be reckoned with. (Santa Barbara Dance Theatre, 2007. Costume design and photo by Leticia M. Delgado.)*

irregularities in the surface of the form will have variation in value and create texture. The realized costume under the stage lights is similar to a sculpture in the art world; it has value that is heightened or created by the reflection of light.

Theatrical Lighting and Costume

Since the costume is a part of the stage picture, the various elements of design employed in the construction of a costume can only be fully realized when they are revealed by light. Thus the form or moving sculpture we refer to as a costume for the stage must be composed in such a way that it remains dynamic when living under the stage lights; it must have inherent value. Every choice, from the color of the fabric, to the stitch line placement, and to the layering of fabrics and the addition of trims, creates a form that has value and can live in harmony with the lighting design, and may help the performer to hold the viewer's eye on the stage. Ultimately, a costume is a sculpture in motion whose success on the stage relies on the manner in which the stage is illuminated. What the viewer will see is a scientific and symbiotic relationship between the surface of the object, the direction and

intensity of the waves of light transmitted upon it, and the light that bounces off the object into our eye. In order to understand this relationship, let us briefly discuss how we see color, some functions of lighting design, and basic color theory for theatrical lighting design. This will afford us the terminology to further investigate the close relationship between value and form as it relates to costume design. How does the human eye work? What allows us to see the dimensions created by value?

Value is created on the stage by the rays of light that bounce off an item or form, and enter into our eye. We have light receptors called cones and rods on the retina of our eyes. These receptors send messages to our brains, where they are deciphered. It is important to note that white light contains the entire visible spectrum of color: red, orange, yellow, green, blue, and violet. These separate colors only exist because of the way our eyes and brains work together. The color we see is transmitted from our eyes to the brain by cones that are centrally located on the retina. Rods are located on the sides of the retina and transmit mostly black and white. The combination of these allows us to see tints and shades, which create value and depth. The color or colors our brains decipher depends on the pigment saturation of the object, and the color of the light that is directed at the object. The relationship between light and an object's perceived color revolves around the absorption, refraction, and/or reflection properties of color. We will discuss this process and how it works with fabric later in this section. The manipulation of white light by the lighting designer can be achieved by mixing light wavelengths, the use of filters, and various other components of stage lighting design.

In its most rudimentary form, theatrical lighting design is rooted in the additive color theory. The primary colors of the additive color theory are red, green, and blue. These colors are often referred to as RGB and are also utilized to create color on computer screens. The secondary colors of additive color theory for light are cyan, magenta, and yellow. When these six colors overlap, white light is created. A lighting designer can utilize filters to alter and create all of the colors of the visible spectrum. These filters will live in a variety of instruments and can be directed or focused to fill particular areas on the stage with color or particular intensities of white light. The objects on the stage will reflect the wavelengths of color that cause their pigment or hue and absorb the other wavelengths. If a blue light source and a red light source are both focused on a particular area of the stage and a lady in a blue satin gown appears, the gown will absorb the red wavelengths and reflect the blue wavelengths into our eyes. The blue cones in our retina will then send this information into our brains. This can be altered by fabric dye composition, garment trim, texture, and the intensity and direction of each of the light beams.

Illumination is one of the basic functions of theatrical lighting; it allows the audience member to see a particular area of the stage or object. Illumination has to be finessed to give true depth or three-dimensional value. The creation of lighting areas and color palettes can make this finessing a smooth process for all involved. Sharing of swatches and pulled garments is essential to guarantee that the texture, color, and form of your garments can best be served by the lighting design. Selective visibility and the distribution of light are other important functions of light that a costume designer should understand. They aid in the viewer's reception of form or silhouette. They can help bring out the intricacies of specific construction techniques that are pertinent to character creation, or omit particular costume or scenic accents.

The silhouette will be revealed by the direction and angles of the beams of light that come in contact with the costumed actor. If an object is only lit from the front of the stage with white light, it will appear flat in the eye of the viewer. It may even get lost in the scenery. This is not usually the effect we want to achieve with most of our costume designs, but it may be useful for certain avant-garde productions or within a setting meant to suggest uneasiness. If light is directed toward an object at angles from the front, side, and back, it will reveal a more textured costume with several degrees of value represented within its form. It will also provide the highlight and shadow needed for an optimum three-dimensional form. The creation and execution of a true three-dimensional form requires an understanding of value and how it correlates to the other elements of design.

If an audience member sees a character in solid white at the centermost lip of a thrust stage, standing all alone in the middle of a single beam of light surrounded by dim light, then everything around this figure on stage is negative space, painted by the selective placement of light beams on the stage. Meanwhile, that character clothed in white is the positive space or primary object in the picture plain. The beam of light accentuates the focal point of this solemn setting: the costumed character in white. It leads the eye of the viewer to this sculptural form and highlights all connected design and directorial choices. The use of color filters can paint color on the white garment and accentuate existing textures. A metal gobo will cast shadows and create patterns on a garment. Both filters and gobos can change the mood of a particular scene. With this in mind, let us discuss other relationships that light and fabric maintain on the stage.

The element of texture has already been discussed, along with the inherent tactile qualities of various fabrics or textiles.

Additionally, fabrics are selected by the costume designer with several aesthetic factors in mind, including color, surface texture, print size, and drape. None of these factors would be visible without light. The surface area of a costume, and the light projected upon it, work together in three manners. Fabric surface refracts, reflects, or absorbs the wavelengths of light, causing texture, value, and depth to be revealed. When wavelengths of light pass through particular fabrics like silk chiffon, habotai, gauze, or very lightweight cottons it sets the stage for a magical moment. This is particularly stunning when a costumed figure is in motion, evoking a light and airy mood that permeates the stage and mind of a viewer.

All colors absorb some wavelengths of light, but the fabric density also affects what happens when a wavelength of light is projected upon it. When light hits a heavy, opaque, or dull surface (like velvet) the fabric will absorb an optimum amount of wavelengths. Reflection is another way in which light and fabric surfaces engage. We have already talked about how color is reflected, but certain textural surface finishes can add to the reflection of wavelengths. A smooth fabric with a high amount of luster or sheen—like satin, metallic, and vinyl—will bounce back wavelengths at an optimum level. A women's matte red gabardine sheath dress will not reflect back as many wavelengths of light as a red satin sheath dress if placed under the same lighting instrument. The fabric color and texture, as well as the light that is directed upon it, will make one dress appear brighter on the spectrum of red light than the other.

The element of value is crucial in the theatrical world because it is directly tied to the lighting design, an area of design that is not necessarily under the costume designer's purview. It is wise to understand how form and value work together in order to better navigate all the choices in fabric, texture, line, and color. This type of knowledge will aid in the collaborative effort and allows us to create costumes that will enhance the visual experience and stage compositions. The deliberately costumed character can inhabit the specific space that the plot necessitates. Value carries the three-dimensional vision into the eyes and minds of the viewers and audience members.

The traditional elements of design aid the costume designer and coexist with the other components of theatre. Each of these elements, along with the principles of design, can be further explored and our knowledge of them will evolve as our artistic capabilities grow. Theatre itself has seen a shift in the use of the theatrical space, narrative, and design. Today the theatrical experience may not be limited to the stage alone. The breaking of the fourth wall and extensive use of actor–audience interaction brings with it its own set of rules, which are still being formalized.

Nevertheless, the elements of design are the foundations for successful visual communication, and the success of our sculptural creations depends upon our understanding of the physical and psychological emotions they can harness and activate in the audience member. A basic knowledge of the elements of design is but a springboard for successful art or design. One must also understand their relationship with the principles of design.

THE PRINCIPLES OF DESIGN

The **principles of design** are used to organize the elements in a work of art. They include balance, emphasis, movement, pattern, repetition, proportion, rhythm, variety, and unity. Some of these principles have been referenced briefly in earlier sections of this chapter as they directly correlate to certain elements of design. The following summaries are rudimentary in nature, but will allow young designers to understand the principles and to apply them to the visuals in the world around them and in their own designs.

Balance is the placement of shapes, forms, colors, textures, and space in a way that makes the work of art feel steady and even. Balance can be symmetrical, asymmetrical, or radial. Symmetry in design would require the positive and negative space of two halves of the visual plane to be equal or to appear equal in terms of weight. Asymmetrical balance requires that the two halves differ in appearance. A basic example of asymmetry in costume is the use of a baldric to cut the torso in half or a diagonally draped bodice. Radial symmetry will have all lines, shapes, colors, forms, and values originating from the same focal point, perhaps the center of the visual plane. A basic example of radial symmetry could be the mandala or perhaps something found in nature, like a succulent or dahlia. In the world of costume design crafts, radial symmetry can be found in the creation of ribbon rosettes.

Emphasis is created when a section or part of the art piece pulls in the viewer's eye. This can be achieved by specifically placing contrasting shapes, colors, values, and textures in a work of art around a focal point. The **focal point** is the exact area of a composition that the artists has deliberately chosen to accentuate. The areas around the focal point may be less intense or muted, thus drawing less attention to themselves in the compositional plane. This muting of other elements is called **subordination**. Hence focal point and subordination are symbiotic aspects of emphasis.

Movement directs the viewer's eye through the picture plane. This can be achieved with the various types of line or implied line created by specifically arranged shapes, shape edges, color, and value in a work of art. Movement or the feeling of

motion is part of a successful sketch or rendering for dance, and specific garments in straight theatre. Movement can also be seen in sculpture, installation art, and of course among a group of characters onstage. So the costume design can intensify or work against the active stage picture created by a director, depending on the situation.

Pattern is the replication or reiteration of shape, line, or form throughout the plane of the entire work of art. It works closely with the principle of repetition. **Repetition** utilizes a pattern of objects, forms, and value to create a feeling of activity in the work of art. When pattern and repetition work well together, there is a sense of unity in the artwork. Pattern and repetition are essential considerations for fabric choice, clothing placement on the human form, and the creation of cohesive groups on the stage.

The principle of **proportion** deals with the size and relationship of all the individual parts of a whole object or single form. It is important to note that ideal proportions have changed through time. The costume designer regularly deals with the proportional planes of the human form. The costume designer first deals with proportion when drawing the human figure. Often the head is utilized as a unit of measurement to make sure that the figure is a particular number of heads tall and wide. This helps ensure that the figure itself is proportionate. For example, we can say that a figure needs to be eight heads tall, so the torso from chin to crotch is three heads, and the legs from crotch to the floor must be four heads. The figure is also part of the scenic designer's two-dimensional world when rendering perspective sketches, painter's elevations, and their three-dimensional scale models. The costume designer can redraw or manipulate the proportions of the actor's figure with the use of various style lines, construction techniques, patterned fabrics, and accessories to depict a certain time period or to accentuate a part of the torso. Proportion is a crucial part of both the costume construction phase and the realized costume's existence on the stage. In terms of art and in the world of theatrical design, proportion usually exists in conjunction with the principle of scale.

Scale is the size relationship of one object to another object in a single work of art or a given visual plane. A sculpture of the human body can be a mathematically proportionate form or object, but if it is twice the height and width of the average man then its scale can be referred to as giant or grandiose. When looking at this looming figure next to an actual human being they help to define each other in terms of size. Proportion and scale is also important when choosing fabrics with print for the stage. One must consider the appropriate scale with regard to the performer's size, the character, the period, the production concept, and the size of the performance arena. Grandiose scale is commonly utilized when depicting a costumed character for young audiences or even the depiction of a historical character like Queen Elizabeth I. The size or scale of pockets, lapels, and buttons are also rooted in the symbiotic relationship of proportion and size. The revers and lapels on the coat of an Incroyable or Dandy are almost laughable to some audience members but are crucial in the depiction of period fashion.

Rhythm creates mood and is created by the carefully orchestrated repetition of one or more elements to create energy and variety on the visual plane. Some basic types of rhythm are linear and gradation. Linear rhythm deals with the manner or timing in which lines are placed on the visual plain. This can be found in basic gesture drawing or sketches. Gradation employs value, shape, and color to create a sense of progressive or recessive motion within a work of art. Rhythm through gradation is often employed in the world of fabric manipulation for dance in the manner of dip dyeing wet silk or linen garments at timed intervals in the same color of dye. Rhythm works hand-in-hand with variety.

Variety is the combination and calculated use of several design elements organized by various principles to create difference. Variety creates visual interest and keeps the viewer's eye engaged and moving through the work of art. If the viewer is engaged in a manner that keeps the eye and the mind active and receptive to the visual plane, then the elements and principles of design have been utilized in a successful manner and unity, the final principle of design, has been achieved.

Unity is the achievement of a sense of oneness within the work of art. It is a finished and complete artistic experience. It may be achieved through common uses of space, pattern, line, and color. When all of the elements in the work of art can live on the same visual plane and relate to each other, visual harmony has been achieved.

On a Personal Note

Both the elements of design and the principles of design work together to communicate mood, place, personality, and (especially in theatre) an active and cohesive visual. From a very young age, we are exposed to these elements and principles, including line, color, shape, pattern, and repetition. They are essential in the creation of art and they are also readily visible in everyday life in the modes of interior design and advertising. Our everyday lives are so engulfed in some of these elements and principles of design that there is a tendency to forget the power they have to influence and guide the human mind.

The careful, educated, and calculated creation of character for the stage is strengthened by the understanding and utilization of the power that lies in the elements and principles of design.

QUESTIONS

- Choose a character to sketch. Choose two different media. Now draw this character twice, once with each medium. Experiment with line, shape, and form, as well as the organizing principles. Share these designs with another artist and discuss.

- Stretch your capabilities and explore the possibilities. Think about which elements and principles you utilize the most frequently when designing. Now create a design that utilizes *only* the elements and principles that you *rarely* utilize or find difficult to explore.

- Create a design that utilizes color, value, proportion, and scale. Pair up with a partner and analyze the design.

Carol Burnett as
"Charlotte" as
"Roxanne"

Bob
Mackie 1995

"Moon
Over Buffalo"

FIGURE 4.1 *Costume design for Carol Burnett in* Moon Over Buffalo. *(Marker on paper. Design by Bob Mackie, Martin Beck Theatre, New York, 1995.)*

CHAPTER 4

COSTUME RENDERING

Steven Stines

THE PURPOSE OF THE RENDERING

"I like to compare the costume sketch to a road map. The sketch, like the map, is not an end in itself; it is a limited guide."

Patricia Zipprodt[1] from *Contemporary Stage Design U.S.A,* p. 29

Though costume **renderings** are often judged by how effectively they demonstrate the designer's prowess with drawing and painting, the primary purpose of the rendering is communication. A successful rendering will also provide an indication of the style of the design and of the show. A rendering is used to "sell" the designer's idea to the director, to the other designers, to the performer, and to the producer who ultimately will foot the bill to turn the drawing into an actual costume.

Some designers prefer the term "**sketch**," reflecting its purpose as a working document, to be revised and even discarded as needed along the way; merely a part of the entire process of creating costumes. Other refer to "costume **plates**," much the same as a sheet of scenic drafting. "Rendering" may seem too formal, and could be defined as a work of visual art that is an end unto itself instead of a step along the way, albeit a significant step.

"I prefer to call my drawn and painted costume designs, 'renderings,'" says Dunya Ramicova,[2] who has designed for the Metropolitan Opera, the Royal Opera, and director Peter Sellars, and has taught at Yale and the University of California. "The precise meanings of words and their origins have been important to me from the beginning of my career. Rendering is defined as 'depiction or interpretation by artistic means', and its origins include 'to give back' and 'to present.'

FIGURE 4.2 *Costume designs for Vaudeville Performers in* Whatever Happened to Baby Jane? (*Design by Eduardo Sicango, Theatre Under the Stars, Houston, TX, 2002.*)

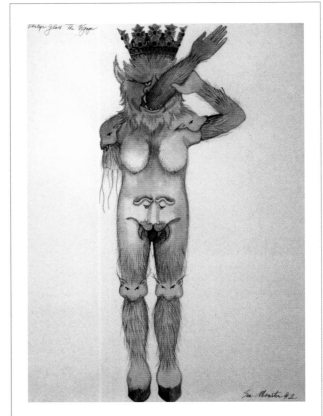

FIGURE 4.3 *Costume design for a Sea Monster in* The Voyage. *(Graphite pencil, watercolor, metallic watercolor on watercolor paper. Design by Dunya Ramicova, Metropolitan Opera, New York, 1992.)*

"From the beginning of my education . . . I learned to treat costume renderings very seriously," says Ramicova. "Both [my teachers] Virgil Johnson and Ming Cho Lee were dedicated to teaching the importance of the rendering as a communication tool. I learned to understand that renderings have to work on many levels to motivate all those involved in the creation of a production. My goal is to inspire all those who have to refer to my renderings in order to mount the production."

"A costume sketch is all about communication." says Jess Goldstein,[3] costume designer of *Newsies* and *Jersey Boys*, a Tony Award winner, and faculty member at the Yale School of Drama. "It needs to be a simple and direct way to establish my point of view about the character and also about the material. While I believe the sketch might have a particular attitude, I also think it can't overwhelm the character and leave little room for further exploration by the actor and director.

"As I go through the process of creating and fitting the actual garments, I certainly reference the sketch at all times, but I will sometimes diverge from my original notions in a fitting if I see that the proportions or other details are not quite helping the actor to become the character . . . The sketch is never to be thought the final product. Directors should never feel like they can't reject a design in the early stages of the process."

Regardless of the chosen term, therefore, this piece of graphic communication must serve both as a piece of visual art and as a source of information. How the sketch is created will depend on personal taste, individual skill level, approach to the overall design process, and the abilities of the costume shop. While many costume renderings are visually striking as fine art or illustration work, many designers find it useful to add notes, fabric **swatches**, reference material, and research directly to the sketch. This kind of pragmatism becomes practical and effective given the ultimate goal of a costume rendering.

FIGURE 4.4 *Costume design for Mrs Malaprop in* The Rivals. *(Ink and colored pencil on paper. Design by Jess Goldstein, Vivian Beaumont Theatre, New York, 2005.)*

Do Designers Need To Draw?

> "Of course there are many tools at the designer's fingertips today that can help tell the story of the costume. However, nothing is as exciting as a beautiful sketch that begins the process toward a fulfilling production."
>
> Ann Hould-Ward[4] from an email interview

The quandary when reviewing design work is deciding to what extent rendering is a job requirement for designers. Increasingly, it seems design training sidesteps the notion that the costume designer should be adept at drawing and painting. Teachers allow, or even encourage, tracing figures or using *croquis* (outlines of

FIGURE 4.5 *Costume design for Countess Aurelia in* Dear World. *(Watercolor, gouache, ink, and pencil on vellum. Design by Ann Hould-Ward, Charing Cross Theatre, London, 2013.)*

bodies to which student designers can add clothing). Whether this is an acceptable long-term practice or a stop-gap measure while the student develops figure-drawing skills depends on the individual academic philosophy.

Some designers find that directors relate more to photos and period research than to a sketch. With the increasing reliance on shopped garments and pieces borrowed from fashion designers, some **style** the costume directly from the racks.

There are costume designers—very successful designers—who do not draw as part of their process. Some of these designers come from a background in fashion design or styling; this is more common in film and TV than in live theatre. In truth, there are famous and successful designers who function primarily as "editors" of the work of a staff of other designers, assistants, shoppers and **sketch artists**, as is common in the fashion world. Whether this is a result of a heavy workload, a hierarchy that requires a large staff, or a lack of specific skills can be debated.

Some designers may be capable of producing a sketch that will provide the necessary information for a shop, but that may not be an effective selling tool when presented to a director or performer. The "editorial" designer may rely on sketch artists to provide ideas or flesh out concepts. Still others—the lucky ones—may be so busy and have so many projects simultaneously that they use a staff to focus on details, which may include sketchers.

Though designers may use the skills of a sketch artist to create renderings, not only must the designer sometimes arrange payment for this from the design fee, but does a designer who does not draw also forfeit an important responsibility or the pleasure of a good deal of the creative process? Perhaps the answer to this is best considered on an individual basis because it reflects the working methods of the designer.

Tradition, however, seems to demand that the costume designer possess some degree of rendering skill, as the costume sketch remains for most of us the primary means of communicating our ideas, be they quickly scribbled onto a napkin at lunch, or as masterfully drawn and painted as fine art.

"Good drawing is essential for a designer because it is the tool we use to communicate," explains Goldstein.[3] "Obviously, it is what sells the design, both to the director and to the actor. But good drawing doesn't necessarily mean anything fancy. Once again, I think sketches have to be simple and direct. Proportions need to be correct."

Carrie F. Robbins,[5] costume designer for *Grease, Agnes of God*, and Irving Berlin's *White Christmas*, and a faculty member for more than 20 years at NYU's Tisch School of the Arts, says, "I can only answer for me. I know there's another side to this issue. But I think drawing is crucial. Drawing is supposed to come out of the thinking process, so how can you not do it? Many people have figured out a way around this, but I think it's valuable. It makes you take the time to think through each design decision as you draw it.

"We're paid so little that we're almost automatically in a position of doing more than one job at a time. The designer must then delegate certain hunks of the job. Because it's reasonable and important and right to be able to make a living. One of the things people seem to find easiest to delegate is the drawing, rather than sitting down and facing a blank piece of paper. For me, drawing can be enjoyable. The second way to delegate is if you have enough money to hire a good shop, then you don't have to find the fabric, or worry about the detailing or the back view. A good shop will solve it."

"Drawing is as important a skill for the costume designer as elocution is for the serious actor," says Ann Hould-Ward,[4] a Tony-winner for her costume designs for *Beauty and the Beast*, whose work also includes *Into the Woods* and, with Patricia Zipprodt, *Sunday in the Park with George*. "It is the method by which we tell our story and communicate the nuances of it to our fellow collaborators and the shops that are making the costumes."

Information and Communication

Set designers have a range of graphics with which to communicate their ideas—the color sketch, the model, various kinds of drafting, **paint elevations**—and often are provided an assistant to complete the design package. While costume designers may also provide detail and technical sketches, and even full-size drawings of **embellishment**, most often we are restricted by time and practicality to one sketch per costume.

This single sketch, then, must provide a wide range of information. The successful costume rendering includes a

FIGURE 4.6 *Costume design for Violetta in La Traviata. (Gouache, watercolor, and charcoal. Design by Cait O'Connor, Lyric Opera of Chicago/ Canadian Opera Company/Houston Grand Opera, 2014.)*

FIGURE 4.7 *Costume design for Falstaff in Henry IV. (Ink and colored pencil on paper. Design by Jess Goldstein, Lincoln Center Theatre, New York, 2003.)*

clear idea of the structure and **silhouette** of the garments, along with indicating the weight and color of the fabric and other components, and where each element is used. A costume shop will need views of both the back and the front of the costume, which many designers find easiest to include on a single sketch. Renderings may incorporate written notes to the shop to make sure the idea has been explained. Other detail drawings might clarify shoes and accessories, hair, and makeup (see Figure 4.9).

"Clarity is essential for the shops making the clothes," says Goldstein.[3]

Ultimately, says Robbins,[5] "The shop depends on that sketch being serious and meaningful and providing enough facts to have budget numbers attached. We're asked to do something that is going to be **bid** on, and to which money will be attached. We have to communicate the idea. You're discussing ideas with your director or choreographer, both of whom are deeply involved in what the show will look like. If the image on the page is unreadable, how do they know? I'm not talking about creating a John Singer Sargent, but something that is legible. [A sketch that

is unclear] is like writing something in shorthand and giving it to someone who can't read shorthand."

Examples of research, whether historical or inspirational, might also be included as part of a rendering. Some designers include a great deal of research as part of the sketch, feeling that seeing the sketch in this context is more informative, or provides the costume shop with the most comprehensive and concentrated understanding of the design. Attached research should be consistent and well edited. A potpourri of photos and diagrams with no clear relation to the design will confuse the director and the shop.

The costume sketch, says Hould-Ward,[4] "is the reference through which we have funneled all the research, both historical and creative, along with the conversations between director and designer—in fact all the designers." She frequently attaches reference material directly to the sketch, or prepares a **research board** to accompany the drawing.

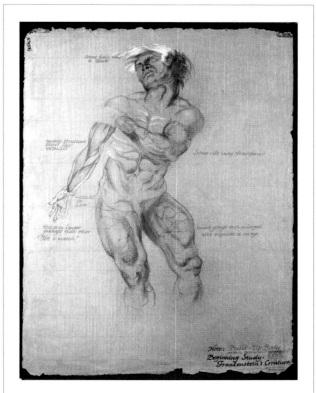

FIGURE 4.8 *Costume design for the Creature in* Frankenstein. *This costume was made using layered body suits, built up to form musculature, then detailed with cording,* **trapunto,** *and paint. The face and neck were applied* **prosthetics.** *(Colored pencil, chalk, gouache, and calligraphic marker on paper. Design by Carrie F. Robbins, Palace Theatre, New York, 1981.)*

FIGURE 4.9 *Costume design for Estelle in* No Exit. *(Design markers on vellum. Design by Rafael Jaén, American Repertory Theatre, Cambridge, MA, 2006.)*

of the production and the design concept. Ultimately, though, the designer or an assistant will have to work with the shop to fill in the blanks that allow the costume to be built.

Some designers prefer to work with a vague sketch and to determine details as the costume moves through the shop. Goldstein[3] argues, "I don't think a single sketch can always have all the information a shop might require; but I believe truly great **drapers**, **milliners**, and crafts people can bring so much to a design that I don't want to stifle them with only the details in my sketch. And that's what shop meetings should be about— discussing all the details, and the exchange of ideas with the sketch as a springboard for the creative process."

For the costume shop, "the verbal description of the design is important in understanding the rendering," according to April

Conversely Goldstein[3] asserts, "Perhaps some vital piece of research can accompany a sketch but I don't think it should be crowded with a lot of other images unless it really helps to explain the designer's choices. I usually put research pictures together in another display that can be kept in the rehearsal hall, as well as copies for the people making the clothes."

Annie O. Cleveland,[6] a costume designer and author of the book *Digital Design for Costume Designers: Pens, Pixels, and Paint*, says, "Taking the time to do a rendering gives the designer an opportunity to focus on the research and make decisions based on what serves the needs of the play and not what is just a cool piece of research. With digital design, pieces of research can be placed directly onto a rendering, scaled to size, and their effectiveness assessed within the entire design."

Each designer develops a personal way of presenting the idea, and determines what is most successful for their way of working. But the list of information required by a shop in order to successfully translate that idea into reality is fairly consistent. Some renderings could be classified primarily as evocative; they are beautiful pieces of visual art and effectively convey the spirit

FIGURE 4.10 *Costume design for Kaschei in* The Firebird. *The designer has included small detail sketches to explain that the performer will use stilts and how his body will be built out. (Watercolor with acrylic, colored pencil, pen, and graphite. Design by Zachary Titterington, University of Florida, 2014.)*

FIGURE 4.11 *Costume designs for Nabob in* Peter Grimes. *(Ink, watercolor, gouache, with attached reference images. Design by Ann Hould-Ward, Metropolitan Opera, New York, 2008.)*

McCoy,[7] who has worked as a costume maker at many opera and ballet companies, including the Boston and Atlanta ballets, and, as a member of **IATSE**, on numerous films. Highlighting the need for designers to understand costume technology, McCoy cautions, "Just because you have drawn it, doesn't mean that it is buildable. Be prepared to work out a Plan B."

"Costuming is a collaborative process and the renderings, to a certain extent, lay the foundation for that collaboration," says Stacey Galloway,[8] a costume designer and technologist, and a faculty member at the University of Florida. "The amount of specificity in the renderings requires or allows a draper to have more or less input in the choices that are made to create the character that appears on stage."

In some cases, the draper is instrumental in creating the design. According to Amanda Whidden,[9] assistant designer for *Wicked* and subsequently the costume supervisor as the show embarked on its long life on Broadway as well as touring and international companies, the input from the costume shop for those costumes was "tremendously important. The sketches were a jumping-off point." She explains that the drapers were viewed as "collaborators" in the realization of the costumes, and that, in fact, with the closing of Barbara Matera Ltd, the original shop for the show, making sure replacement costumes look as intended was "more difficult; their work was so important."

FIGURE 4.12 *Costume design for Desireé in* A Little Night Music. *(Watercolor on paper. Design by Stacey Galloway, Seaside Music Theater, Daytona Beach, FL.)*

FIGURES 4.13 & 4.14 *Costume designs for a Brave (left) and Tinkerbell (right) in Peter Pan. Two sketches by the same designer, one drawn and painted tightly, the other much looser in style. (left: Digital painting. right: Pen and ink, watercolor, and digital painting. Designs by Judanna Lynn, Milwaukee Ballet, WI, 2012.)*

FIGURES 4.15 & 4.16 *Costume design for Belle in The Peony Pavilion. (left) The sketch includes drawings of each of the many layers of garments, plus accessories. (Watercolor and gouache. Design by Lauren Gaston, University of Missouri–Kansas City, 2014.) (right) The costume was draped and built in Hong Kong from the rendering by American designer Lauren Gaston, working without meeting in person. (Draped and built by Christina Wai, Hong Kong Academy of Performing Arts, 2014. Model: Graziela Bastos. Photo by Sarah M. Oliver.)*

Not all designers will be able to work with a shop like Matera's; often in academic or summer theatre, and even in fully professional venues, the shop staff is not experienced or reliably gifted. Ideally the draper brings to the process not only a firm understanding of construction and costume history, but also a high degree of artistry, with an eye for proportion and detail. But when this is not the case, the designer should be prepared to include as much specific information as possible in a sketch. This can be imperative not only as a means of communication, but also to ensure that the designer's intentions have been clearly delineated in advance should the final result be less than expected.

In some cases, the designer and the costume shop have worked together previously and have developed a "shorthand" in their way of working that requires less specificity in the sketch. Judanna Lynn,[10] a costume designer who specializes in design for dance, explains that her approach to rendering "depends on the skill set of the [costume] maker. If they aren't that experienced I will be more detailed with the sketch." When she works with highly skilled costumers, Lynn says, "I can be much 'sketchier' about the sketch. I don't have to spell out all the details."

On the other side of the coin, there are designers whose sketches are almost draftings; very specific guides for how the clothes will be made. Though the draping and construction process may include revisions, sketches like these could conceivably allow a shop to build the costume without additional consultation. Some design teachers include projects with this specific goal in mind, to test the students' understanding of structure and communication.

"As a draper, I prefer a rendering to have clear information on silhouette and proportion," says Galloway.[8] "The more information that is provided, the more likely it is that the costume will replicate the designer's idea. Specificity in details, trim, seam placement, etc., varies greatly within rendering styles and, as long as the information is provided in some format, such as conversations or sketches, drapers can generally work with that variance."

Beyond the costume shop, the costume sketch provides information to others involved in the production. Collaborators, including the director, choreographer, and design team, need to see a clear indication of the costume concept, usually presented in a series of production meetings, or at times by long distance when the team is not centrally located.

Costume sketches are usually presented to actors during the rehearsal process, and are also on display during fittings. Many actors find the costume to be an intrinsic part of their characterization, and seeing the sketch is part of that process. According to Hould-Ward,[4] the rendering "allows us to facilitate the group of actors and other collaborators going forward with the concept of where we are headed. It helps the actors to imagine themselves for the first time in the character. [That's] one of the reasons I always draw with the actor's photo right there with me at the drawing table.

"If you do not draw well enough to elaborate the story of the clothing, you are inhibiting your ability to tell your story," continues Hould-Ward. "The other designers see where you feel the production is headed, and with great drawings we are all able to continue to grow the production. You want to draw well enough to make the team you are working with salivate with anticipation of what the final product you will all conjure up together will be."

FIGURE 4.17 *Reference images for Countess Aurelia in* Dear World. *In addition to period research for the sketch seen in Figure 4.5, this collection of images includes a list of costume pieces and photos of actress Betty Buckley, who will play the part. (Design by Ann Hould-Ward, Charing Cross Theatre, London, 2013.)*

COSTUME RENDERING IN THEATRE HISTORY

From the beginning of Western theatre in Ancient Greece, performers have worn costumes. Looking at performance in any culture, one usually finds clothing, masks, makeup, and headgear that are developed as part of the performance. In ancient times, someone was presumably called upon to communicate the idea for a costume; our understanding of ancient theatre costumes comes from scenes recorded in sculpture, vase painting, and mosaics. By the Renaissance, we have surviving examples of actual costume renderings, and in time, some of these were signed and can be attributed to specific designers like Inigo Jones (1573–1652) and Daniel Rabel (1578–1637).

Our image of the Romantic era ballerina is preserved through lithographs printed for middle-class homes, picturing famous dancers in their notable roles. These illustrations include detailed representations of the ballerina's costume, seen through the filter of Romantic sensibilities.

FIGURE 4.18 *Figurine of an actor wearing the mask of a slave. (Terracotta. Hellenistic period, 2nd century BC. Courtesy of the British Museum, London. Photo by Jastrow.)*

FIGURE 4.19 *Kabuki theatre actors in the Edo Ichimura-za production of Kyō-ganoko Musume Dōjō-ji. (Japanese, 1852. Courtesy of Wikimedia Commons.)*

FIGURE 4.20 *Actors in masks playing two women and a witch. (Mosaic from the Villa del Cicerone, Pompeii. Dioscorides of Samos, Roman, c. 1st century AD. Courtesy of Wikimedia Commons.)*

FIGURE 4.21 *Costume design for "A Star" in a Masque, early 17th century. (Design by Inigo Jones. Courtesy of Wikimedia Commons)*

FIGURE 4.22 *Costume design for "Music" from the* Ballet des Fées de la Forêt de St. Germain *(Ballet des Ridicles), c. 1625. (Watercolor, ink, pencil, and gold paint on paper. Design by Daniel Rabel. © Victoria and Albert Museum, London.)*

FIGURE 4.23 *Marie Taglioni in* La Bayadère. *Hand-colored lithograph, c. 1830. (Artist: Alfred Edward Chalon. Lithographer: Richard James Lane. ©Victoria and Albert Museum, London.)*

FIGURE 4.24 La Dame aux Camélias. *Lithographed poster, 1896. (Design by Alphonse Mucha. Courtesy of Wikimedia Commons.)*

During the late 19th century, Alphonse Mucha (1860–1939) designed costumes, scenery, jewelry, and personal wardrobe for the most famous actress in the world, Sarah Bernhardt, immortalizing both her performances and his design work in a series of **Art Nouveau** style theatre posters that are still reproduced. These were advertisements rather than costume renderings. But in this period, other designers, notably "Wilhelm" (William Charles John Pitcher, 1858–1925), created what theatre artists today would instantly recognize as costume sketches.

Rendering sometimes reflects the prevalent style of fine or decorative art popular when the designer was working. Echoing a highly stylized or distorted movement in art can be hazardous in a costume rendering. Ultimately, a designer's work will be seen on the human form, which is three dimensional and subject to the proportions determined by nature. The illustrator Erté and other artists of the 'teens and '20s are beloved by many designers, and

FIGURE 4.25
*"Wilhelm" pantomime
design, 1890.
(Watercolor over pen
and ink. Design by
William Charles John
Pitcher. © Victoria and
Albert Museum, London.)*

their costume renderings are beautiful examples of
Art Deco illustration. Looking at these costumes as
they appeared onstage, however, can be disappointing
in comparison. The elongated, flattened geometry
of the Deco figure simply did not translate onto a
flesh-and-blood performer. The costume designer is
wise to adapt the rendering style to acknowledge the
reality of the human body.

One of the most famous costume renderings
is Léon Bakst's design for the dancer Nijinsky in *The
Afternoon of a Faun* (see Figure 4.28). Bakst began
his career as a painter in Russia; he incorporated
his expertise in ancient Greek art history into
the drawings for this and other ballet designs. His
costume sketches for the **Ballets Russes** also gave
his collaborators a full array of information and his
designs are still used by dance companies more
than 100 years later. The *Faun* sketch is a beautiful
painting with a clearly-considered composition, yet
we can understand the costume's structure, the
embellishment of fabric, the wig, the makeup, the
footwear, and the design for the long scarf that is
used as an integral part of the choreography
(see Figure 4.29).

FIGURES 4.26 & 4.27 (left)
Program illustration for Nuit de Folies,
*1920s. (Design by Alec Shanks. Courtesy
of Wikimedia Commons.) (right) Lilyan
Tashman in the* Ziegfeld Follies. *Publicity
photo, c. 1916–1917. The design in the
photo is similar to that illustrated by
Shanks, but the reality of fabric, feathers,
and flesh is quite different to the stylized
deco painting. (Unknown photographer.
Courtesy of Wikimedia Commons.)*

FIGURES 4.28 & 4.29 (opposite and above) *Costume design for Vaslav Nijinsky as the Faun from* L'Après-midi d'un Faune, *1912. (Graphite, watercolor, tempera, and gold paint on board. Design by Léon Bakst. Wadsworth Atheneum Museum of Art, Hartford, CT.) (above) Vaslav Nijinsky in* L'Après-midi d'un Faune. *(Walery Photographie, 1912. Courtesy of Wikimedia Commons.)*

By the 20th century, designers like Bakst were viewed as important collaborators in the development of new kinds of theatre, and the costume rendering became a document worthy of archiving and even collecting. While earlier theatre designers came from fine art or fashion backgrounds, eventually theatre schools viewed the discipline as specific and began to offer programs devoted to developing designers. This training ideally includes courses that address rendering.

DRAWING AND PAINTING MEDIA

Rendering is communication and rendering is art. The designer, as an artist, will develop individual methods and preferences. Some designers, though rarely, elect to work in three dimensions, much as a set designer uses a scale model. But the prevailing mode is a two-dimensional sketch.

There seem to be two primary philosophies about the desired nature of the costume rendering, which might be classified as the *purist* vs. the *pragmatist*. The former approach focuses on the use of **watercolor** as the traditional and only acceptable medium for a proper costume sketch (see Figure 4.30). The pragmatic school of thought, however, allows the use of any material or medium that will successfully convey the idea and the information (see Figure 4.31).

Watercolor is often viewed as the most difficult paint medium to master. It also can be time-consuming, requiring the layering of washes of color and the time for each application to dry. In the hands of a designer who is competent with watercolor, the final product is effective and can be dazzling. But reality—in the form of deadlines, lack of painting skill, or simply preference

FIGURE 4.30 *Costume design for Lavinia in* The Heiress. *(Watercolor. Design by Lauren Gaston, University of Missouri–Kansas City, 2014.)*

FIGURE 4.31 *Costume design for a Ghost in* Follies. *(Gouache, dimensional paint, and glitter on watercolor paper sprayed with liquid watercolor and pearlescent gouache. Design by Gregg Barnes, Marquis Theatre, New York, and Kennedy Center, Washington DC, 2011.)*

FIGURE 4.32 *Costume design for a Female Native on an Alien Planet in* The Voyage. *(Graphite pencil, watercolor, metallic watercolor on watercolor paper. Design by Dunya Ramicova, Metropolitan Opera, New York, 1992.)*

for other media—can point to the need to accept the use of other materials; a **mixed media** costume sketch can be effective and practical.

Ramicova[2] says, "I was taught the love of watercolor by Ming Cho Lee, who is undoubtedly one of the finest watercolorists in the history of stage design, though he actually never taught the skill to his students; we had to do that on our own. He taught us that watercolor is the best medium to reproduce the effect stage lighting has on colors and textures of the set and costumes. Having been very fortunate to work with some of the finest lighting designers in the world, I can attest that watercolor is the best medium to utilize for costume renderings. Nothing on stage is ever truly flat or completely even in tone, and no other medium but watercolor can reproduce the effect of lighting on both scenery and costumes.

"I have used other media in addition to watercolor: color pencils and also pastels, but never markers or acrylic. I like to mix my own colors so markers hold little interest for me. Acrylic is too heavy for my way of working."

When Robbins[11] was a student at Yale, she remembers, "The costume design teacher mandated that all sketches be drawn on white watercolor paper, 8½" × 11", with figures something like 8" tall. Watercolor was the medium he required. This never made any sense to me except that it was a compact size to carry around and made for easy arrangement in portfolios. I say draw on what ground you want in a size that feels comfortable to your hand. Choose something that aesthetically feels 'good' with the play."

As the costume designer moves from rough sketches on napkins and legal pads to a finished rendering that can be proudly presented to collaborators and the producer, there are, then, more decisions to be made.

to saturate the paper repeatedly, should that be the required approach, as the paper will return to its original, controlled shape as it dries. But this process is time- and space-consuming.

A blow-dryer and an iron become art supplies when using a wet medium. The blow-dryer, of course, circumvents the need to literally watch paint dry. Careful use of a steam iron can eliminate most (though usually not all) of the wrinkles created when oversaturating watercolor paper or when painting on a paper not intended for wet media. (Always place a clean piece of white paper between an iron and a sketch. Do a test with the kind of paper on which you have painted. You may want to use a dry iron on a sketch that is still slightly damp, or use steam on a dry sketch.)

Watercolor is made in "hot press" and "cold press" finishes. Cold press paper has a rougher texture and absorbs water more quickly; hot press paper is smoother and allows more time to manipulate the paint, as the surface stays damp for longer. Keeping watercolor paper damp creates a softer effect with the paint, while using dry paper allows a hard edge to a painted shape, or a **drybrush** technique that is effective for rendering hair and fur.

Papers designed for pastel and pencil, like Canson's "Mi-Tientes," come in a range of colors and shades. With care, one can paint on some of them without a great deal of buckling. **Bristol board** is a sturdy, cost-effective paper, available in a range of weights and in both smooth "plate" and rougher "vellum" finishes. Some designers select actual **vellum**, as is used in hand-drafting, finding its smooth finish and transparent nature useful. There are also multi-purpose papers, like Stonehenge, that work with many different drawing and painting media.

FIGURE 4.33 *Costume design for The Lamplighter in* The Little Prince. *(Watercolor, pencil, pastel, and acrylic paint. Design by Vera Katharina DuBose, University of Applied Sciences, Hamburg, Germany, 2011.)*

Paper

The watercolor purists, of course, will select a weight and type of watercolor paper. The heavier the paper, the more water it can withstand without distorting, buckling, or wrinkling. Properly used, watercolor paper is taped down to the drawing table or even soaked and stretched while wet on wooden stretchers (the way canvas is prepared for oil or acrylic). This allows the designer

FIGURES 4.34 & 4.35 *(left)* Watercolor on cold press paper and *(right) watercolor on hot press paper.*

FIGURES 4.36 & 4.37 (left) *Layers of watercolor applied to wet paper and* (right) *layers of watercolor applied to dry paper.*

the size of the finished sketch, the weight of the paper, and even the horizontal or vertical orientation of the sketch.

The weight of paper is designated by the term "pounds" or "lbs." The larger the number, the thicker and heavier the paper will be. Paper is usually made by compressing wet fibers in a mold. Papers that are made of cotton fiber are considered the highest quality.

Papers made specifically for marker rendering are very smooth and tend to be lightweight; these papers may be difficult to use if the rendering technique requires significant erasing of a preliminary drawing. Thin paper may need to be mounted on a sturdier backing either before or after the rendering is completed. While some designers use rubber cement, spray adhesive, or masking tape to mount their work, these are poor choices over time, as the adhesive will soak through and stain the surface. Low-tack white paper tape or double-sided tape are better choices.

Occasionally a designer may decide to use illustration board or mat board for costume sketches. While board is sturdy, it is also thick and, if there are a number of sketches to be completed, a stack of costume renderings can be inconveniently heavy. The designer should always have an eye on how a costume sketch will be included in a portfolio. This practical consideration will affect

FIGURE 4.38 *A range of half-tone and colored paper. (Photo courtesy of Canson.)*

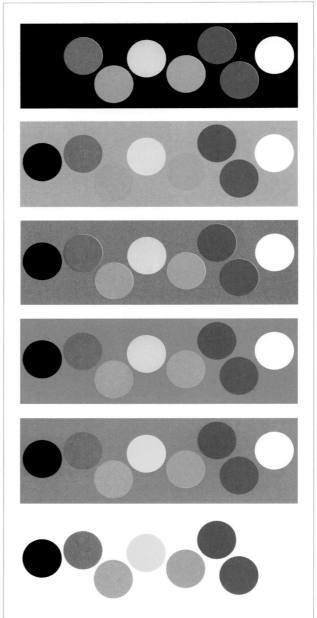

FIGURE 4.39 *The appearance of color is relative to the colors with which it is juxtaposed.*

While many costume sketches are produced on plain, white paper, the designer may want to consider if this is the most effective way to present a sketch. The most basic tenet of color theory is that color is relative (see Figure 4.39), and this includes color as it will be seen by an audience. Unless a stage is designed to be predominantly white, costumes are more likely to be viewed against a darker or more colorful background. The way this affects the color of the costume should be reflected in the choice of background for the sketch.

"White rarely has anything to do with the tones of the set the costumes would be seen against," says Robbins.[11] "So it seems logical to me to get yourself onto an appropriately toned paper after talking with the set designer."

There is a range of solutions to this challenge, including washing in a basic background (see Figure 4.40), echoing the style or elements of a scenic design in the costume sketch (see Figure 4.41), or using half-tone or colored paper (see Figure 4.42).

Half-tone usually refers to a neutral shade of paper—beige, tan, or gray. There is a wide range of papers, including watercolor

FIGURE 4.41 *Costume design for the Statues in* Beauty and the Beast. *(Ink and acrylic on paper. Design by Alun Jones, San Antonio Metropolitan Ballet, TX, 2004.)*

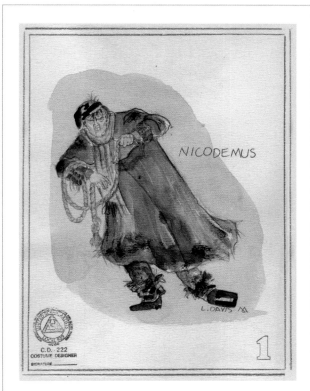

FIGURE 4.40 *Costume design for Nicodemus in* The Mystery of Irma Vep. *(Graphite and watercolor. Design by Lindsay W. Davis, Actors Theatre of Louisville, KY, 1991.)*

FIGURE 4.42 *Costume design for the Witch in* Hansel and Gretel. *(Pen and ink, and gouache on paper. Design by Judanna Lynn, Hartford Ballet, CT, 1983.)*

FIGURE 4.43 *Joan Crawford in* Grand Hotel. *(Costume design by Adrian. MGM, 1932.)*

paper, available in half-tones. One of the most important reasons to avoid a pure white background is that white draws the eye to itself. The 1930s movie costume designer Adrian was famous for using white collars and cuffs on black dresses to pull focus to an actress's face and hands. Rendering white costume details (or indeed costumes that are predominantly white) on white paper will not accurately convey the impact this will have onstage. A white costume is more accurately shown on darker or colored paper (see Figures 4.44 and 4.45).

Black paper can be used to dramatic effect; it is not unusual for a show to be performed on a black or very dark set. For a costume rendering, black paper makes colors "pop" (another application of color theory), although it also requires an opaque medium. Colored pencil is also effective on black paper. Some designers paint in a black background as the basis for a sketch.

A painting surface can be collaged or printed prior to adding the character, either for pure artistic effect or to help tell the

FIGURE 4.45 *Costume design for a Loveland Chorine in* Follies. *(Gouache, dimensional paint, and glitter on watercolor paper sprayed with liquid watercolor and pearlescent gouache. Design by Gregg Barnes, Marquis Theatre, New York, and Kennedy Center, Washington DC, 2011.)*

FIGURE 4.44 *Costume design for the Dionysus in* The Bacchae. *(Pencil and watercolor on drawing paper. Design by Zack Brown, Circle in the Square Theatre, New York, 1992.)*

story (see Figure 4.46). There are designers who use printed paper, like scrapbook paper, real or dollhouse wallpaper, and book-making paper, as the surface for costume renderings. This is more effective with an opaque paint. Printed paper can also be used as a background for mounting the finished sketch (see Figure 4.47). Select a pattern that relates to the look or setting of the production.

FIGURE 4.46 *Costume design for Bessie Burgess in* The Plough and the Stars. *Each sketch for this show uses a different background of collaged clippings, letters, and documents related to the plot and character. (Collage, ink, marker, and colored pencil. Design by Susan Tsu, The Huntington Theatre, Boston, MA, 1985.)*

FIGURE 4.47 *Costume design for Mechanical Woman in Sing Sing Sing. (Pencil and gouache on paper, mounted on decorative paper. Design by Alison Burris, Tulane University, LA, 2011.) The designer has selected a scrapbook paper as the border for her rendering. The cogwheel motif on the paper reflects her design concept, which features a dance costume inspired by robots and machinery. This is one of many decorative papers available at local craft stores.*

DRAWING AND PAINTING

> "Draw tight and paint loose. Draw what you see and not what you know."
>
> Fred Voelpel[12] from a lecture

Theatre designer and teacher Fred Voelpel often told his students to "draw tight and paint loose." This wise advice allows the designer to indicate clearly the structure and details of the costume while avoiding the need to create a photo-realistic painting of fabrics and trims. Color can be applied almost impressionistically.

Voelpel also told his students to "draw what you see and not what you know." While the artist may know intellectually the structure or elements of the subject matter, these may not be visible or apparent, and to include them is distracting or superfluous.

Teaching someone to draw is beyond the scope of a single chapter in a book covering the entire discipline of costume design. There are step-by-step manuals covering both drawing in general and figure drawing, which is the most important art background for a designer who wants to create beautiful, informative, and accurate costume sketches. One should begin by accurately drawing the human form before dressing it.

"I always create the figure first," says Cleveland.[6] "The act of determining body shape, creating a pose that conveys emotion or action, and adding a facial expression instead of a neutral

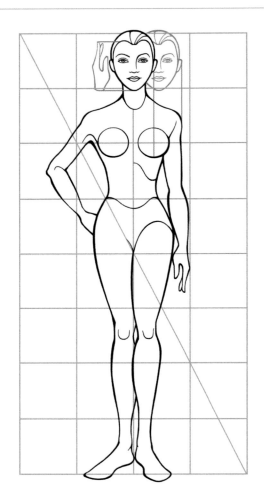

FIGURE 4.49 *The classical proportions of the human figure include a body that is eight heads high. The shoulders are two heads wide. From hairline to chin is the same length as the hand. The center of the breast is aligned with the width of the head and is two heads down the body. The waist is three heads down, the crotch four heads, or half-way, down. The fingertips reach to mid-thigh.*

THE RAKE'S PROGRESS

FIGURE 4.48 *Costume design for a Lady of the Night in* The Rake's Progress. *Although the structure of the costume and headpiece are clear in the sketch, the color is applied loosely. (Gouache, watercolor, and charcoal. Design by Cait O'Connor, New York University, 2009.)*

FIGURE 4.50 *Costume design for Gay Wellington in* You Can't Take It With You. *(Digital rendering with Corel Painter. Design by Annie O. Cleveland, Little Theatre of the Rockies, University of Northern Colorado, 2000.)*

FIGURE 4.51 *Costume design for Ondine. (Gouache. Design by James Bidgood.)*

FIGURE 4.52 *Costume design for the Fashion Show in* Roberta. *(Watercolor and ink. Design by Jen Hebner, Boston University, MA, 2012.)*

face, is the closest I get to the same kind of understanding of the character that the actor has. Once the figure is defined it becomes the armature that influences the shape of the clothes."

In addition to anatomy, a costume designer should study still life drawing, in order to communicate the weight and drape of fabric (see Figure 4.51). Analyzing the structure and construction of clothing by drawing is also necessary. The book *Character Costume Figure Drawing* by Tan Huaixiang (Focal Press, 2010) specifically addresses costume rendering techniques in depth.

Costume design students may not have a background in drawing. It is not unusual for designers to begin as performers, or to find that skills in sewing or crafts can be applied in costuming. Newcomers to drawing often find the approach developed by Betty Edwards helpful, as explained in her book *Drawing on the Right Side of the Brain* (Tarcher, 2012). Her techniques give a basic foundation in a limited time, using a set of exercises and assignments found in the book. The underlying philosophy is that one must accurately draw what is observed, rather than basing a drawing on pre-determined knowledge about the subject matter.

FIGURE 4.53 *"The Lantern Bearers," illustration for Collier's Magazine, 1908. (Oil on canvas mounted on cardboard. Design by Maxfield Parrish, Crystal Bridges Museum of American Art, AR.)*

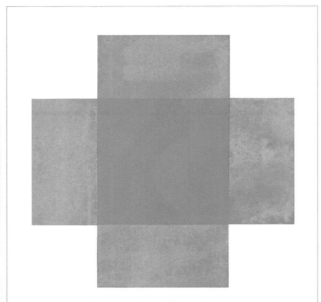

FIGURE 4.54 *Layering washes of different shades creates a richer and more complex color.*

While some designers may choose to move immediately to the brush when rendering, most begin with some degree of drawing. Typically, this will be done with a pencil, though some may choose ink (see Figure 4.52)—felt-tip pens, technical pens, pens with metal nibs, even ball point pens can be used for effective drawing. If you plan to paint over the ink, a quick test to be sure the selected ink is waterproof or can withstand the paint may save a great deal of agony.

Standard **graphite** ("lead") pencils are sold by letter (B or H) and number—3B, 2H, etc. The traditional yellow school pencil is called a #2. The higher the number of a B pencil the softer the graphite; the higher the number of an H pencil, the harder the graphite. The softer the graphite, the darker the line will appear to be, and the harder, the paler. Most artists will have an array of soft and hard pencils. The harder lead is easier to erase and to keep sharp, but it can also create a permanent indentation in the paper.

Ramicova[2] says, "In the last ten years I have used primarily erasable terracotta pencils instead of graphite pencils to do my drawings. I discovered that there was good reason why artists used terracotta pencils and crayons before the invention of graphite pencils in the 19th century. Terracotta pencils eliminate the hard line of graphite and in this way the effect is more lifelike, since no object in nature has hard edges; instead there is a softer, less-discernable outline. This reproduces the effect of stage lighting perfectly."

Ink can also be brushed on like paint, and diluted like watercolor. It is available in a variety of colors, as are transparent dyes like Dr. Ph. Martin's. Using dye is not for the faint-of-heart; it is permanent (on paper and on clothes) and not particularly easy to control. But in the hands of an artist who is comfortable with the technique, dye can produce brilliant colors with speed.

Paint tends to be a preferred color medium for costume designers. Watercolor, as mentioned, is the traditional choice, and is available in the cake form most children use. The less expensive it is, the more "filler" is included in the paint along with the more expensive pigment that provides the color, and hence the less satisfying the effect. The more professional choice is watercolor in tubes; it can be expensive, but the color is concentrated so a tube will last for some time, as well as being more useful for concentrated or intense values.

Watercolor is more successful when applied in layers; this means achieving a dark or bright color will take time. The artist Maxfield Parrish, famous for the brilliant blue of the skies in his illustrations, achieved the effect by layering very thin washes of oil paint in a variety of shades of blue, one on top of the other (see Figure 4.53). The eye then perceives each layer separately and the effect is one of jewel-like vibrancy. Watercolor works the same way. Layering washes of color rather than mixing it on a palette creates a more complex and richer result. Mixing wet color can muddy the tone. This has the effect of subduing the vibrancy of the paint, which can be useful also, but should be chosen as an intended result.

If you elect to mix wet watercolor, use a plastic or metal palette rather than paper; that way, the paint will not soak into the surface and can be remoistened and used until it is gone (which can be years). A plastic cover helps preserve the paint and keep it clean.

Depending on the desired effect, a designer painting with watercolor will determine how often to change the water being used. In general, a large container is preferable. As you work, the paint rinsed from brushes stays in the water and eventually colors it. If the goal is clear or pure colors, the water should be changed frequently; in rendering a show where the costumes are dirty or the colors muted, the paint residue in the water can be an effective way to create that look. Basic color theory tells the artist that water tinted by one color of paint has a specific effect on paint from the opposite side of the color wheel.

Designers are often dissatisfied with watercolor as it is hard to "control" and will not produce a slick, untouched-by-human-hands result. Most paints can be applied with an airbrush but this technique is so time-consuming as to be impractical for most designers.

Watercolor, like most paints, cannot be controlled like a pencil. One must accept that the paint will do what the paint does, and accept the effect as part of the beauty of the medium. Artists work for years to develop painting technique and are rarely satisfied, though the effect to the fresh eye may be beautiful.

Gouache is another water-based paint; while watercolor properly used is translucent, gouache can be used as an opaque medium or diluted to be translucent. Undiluted gouache, applied too thickly, will crack and flake off. Many designers find gouache easier to use than watercolor, or prefer its versatility.

Certainly the costume rendering can make use of the standard approach to scene painting, using transparent paint for shadows and opaque paint for highlights. Even when using watercolor for costume sketches, gouache is quite useful for

FIGURE 4.55 *Costume design for Ferrando in Così Fan Tutti. (Pencil, pen, watercolor, and watercolor pencil. Design by Yao Chen, University of Texas at Austin, 2011.)*

FIGURE 4.56 *Costume design for Mrs Warren in Mrs Warren's Profession. (Watercolor and gouache. Design by Tyler Wilson, University of Missouri–Kansas City, 2015.)*

FIGURE 4.57 *Costume design for Male Ensemble/Fancy Man in Something Rotten! (Gouche and dimensional paint on watercolor paper sprayed with liquid watercolor and pearlescent paint. Design by Gregg Barnes, St. James Theatre, New York, 2015.)*

FIGURE 4.58 *Costume design for "Goldfinger" Dancer in a James Bond themed halftime show. (Graphite pencil, watercolor, gouache, and metallic gouache on watercolor paper. Design by Steven Stines, Dallas Cowboys Cheerleaders/Corporate Magic proposal, 2012.)*

FIGURE 4.59 *Costume design for the Ladies Corps de Ballet in* The Merry Widow. *(Ink and acrylic on paper. Design by Alun Jones, Louisville Ballet, KY, 1997.)*

painting details and highlights. Gouache is available in metallics; these can have a flat appearance if used alone. It can be more effective to lay in shadows and highlights, even colors (metal reflects color), in watercolor or gouache, then wash a metallic gouache or acrylic over that to add the iridescent or reflective effect.

Gouache is also available in an acrylic formula. While standard gouache can be rewetted on the paper or in a container, acrylic gouache dries into a permanent finish. The advantage is that one can paint on top of dried acrylic gouache without the moisture from the second application turning the surface back into wet paint that will mix with the new coat. The advantage of water-based gouache is that a painted surface can be wetted and reworked, or colors blended after drying. As with most color media, the advantages seem often to be simultaneously the disadvantages.

Some designers select **acrylic** paint as their medium. This can pose a problem with some papers; as the acrylic dries it will pull the paper and create wrinkles. On a surface that can withstand acrylic, it is a medium that allows the painter to create dimensional texture and depth. It can also be diluted to be transparent like watercolor.

Given how quickly some renderings must be completed, designers may select markers as the medium, for both drawing and painting. Some designers find markers much easier to control than paint and brush. The primary disadvantage is that the difficulty of mixing colors with markers requires the purchase of many different colors in order not to limit the design palette, and often in both fine- and wide-points.

Markers can be used effectively on most papers, though usually a smooth surface is required; again, a quick test is wise in order to avoid bleeding ink. One must work rapidly in order to create an even application of color and avoid the overlap onto color that has already dried. Marker is translucent; to create a smooth coat of color requires blending the strokes before the ink

FIGURE 4.60 *Costume design for Cher. In the 1970s, when Bob Mackie was designing two weekly TV shows, along with movies, nightclub acts, and other projects, he turned from paint to marker as his medium. (Marker on paper. Design by Bob Mackie, Caesar's Palace in Las Vegas, NV, 1981.)*

dries. Going over a dried area of marker darkens the color, and doing so as one colors creates the typical streaky "magic marker effect." Colorless blender markers are also available to help soften edges and mix colors. Using markers, the designer can embrace the medium for its own properties, or learn to control it enough so that it can simulate watercolor.

Dry media can be time efficient but present some drawbacks. Chalk or dry **pastels** cover quickly but are fragile. Using fingers or a clean cloth to rub pastel is an efficient way to spread or blend color, but again, the advantage is the disadvantage, as pastels are easily smeared. Pastel dust can be collected and "painted" with a brush, and pastel pencils are harder and produce a finer line. Using a spray **fixative** is a necessity with pastels; this is a clear, protective coat that will not affect the colors. Fixative is sold as being "workable," meaning it is possible to protect the piece and continue working on top. In reality, the fixative will make the surface harder and resistant to water. Once a rendering in any medium is complete, fixative is a good idea. Oil pastels can be blended and, with a solvent, painted, but they take a period of days to dry and are thus not practical for most costume renderings.

FIGURE 4.61 *Costume design for Ariel in* The Tempest. *(Ink, pastel, and watercolor. Design by Christine Reimer, Bard on the Beach, Vancouver, Canada, 2008.)*

FIGURE 4.62 *Costume design for the Queen of the Night in* The Magic Flute. *(Colored pencil and marker on colored paper. Design by Larissa McConnell, University of Missouri–Kansas City, 2010.)*

FIGURE 4.63 *Costume design for* The Duchess of Malfi. *(Collage of photocopied and resized fine art images. Design by Jen Hebner, Boston University, MA, 2011.)*

Colored pencils are another dry medium. They are perhaps most useful for detail work, adding texture, and articulating shapes, rather than for large areas, which require layering softly applied coats of color. Colored pencils are very useful for quick color roughs. In selecting a pencil, more expensive brands like Prismacolor or Derwent are much higher quality, with a waxier formula and richer colors than those found in the school supply aisle. Colored pencil tends not to scan or reproduce well in print; subtlety and detail are lost and the background paper is more apparent. Working on colored or half-tone paper helps reduce some of these problems. Select a paper color that reinforces the color palette of your design, and make it part of the rendering.

There are also watercolor pencils, which are applied like colored pencil then wetted with a brush. Designers sometimes select watercolor pencils believing they don't require as much skill as paint, but in reality, like all media, they require some technique and experimentation to be effective.

Resourceful designers turn to any number of additional materials to convey their ideas; craft paint, puff paint, spray paint, nail polish, and body glitter spray are some of the non-traditional substances useful to create specific effects.

The **collage** can be a useful way to create a design rendering; in this case, collage may refer to a presentation board of separate photos or sketches of clothing, or to a piece of collage art. A collaged costume rendering may use photos, sketches, painted paper, commercially available printed paper (like scrapbook pages or dollhouse wallpaper), and fabric. Some costume renderings use the actual costume fabric on the character's figure in the sketch; this, however, gives an inaccurate idea of the scale of any pattern or texture. Collages can also be created digitally.

Of course, an increasing number of costume designers are turning to digital rendering, using Photoshop, Illustrator, Corel Paint, and other software graphics programs. The digital rendering may be created entirely with the computer, usually using a stylus and draw pad, or may begin with a traditional drawing in pencil or ink which is then scanned, modified, and colorized.

DIGITAL COSTUME RENDERINGS

> "Just because the computer is a neat tool, it can't draw for you."
>
> Carrie F. Robbins[5] from a telephone interview

Digital rendering has a number of advantages. The blue bodice that might look better in green? Or the blob of paint that dripped onto a flawless rendering? A computer scan allows the designer to change, correct, or enhance the costume sketch, whether the original is digital or traditional. Colors can be changed with the click of a mouse rather than by repainting. Costume details can be modified, added, or eliminated. Figures can be cloned and redressed.

Scanning the drawn-and-painted rendering allows the designer to clean up the sketch, to alter details with relative ease, to label the sketch, to archive it, and to create an effective addition to a portfolio. The wide array of available fonts, including many on free font-sharing websites, allows consistent, attractive labels and titles.

Some designers remain faithful to traditional techniques. "I have to admit that I have absolutely no interest in computer-generated designs," says Ramicova,[2] "but I do understand why designers today resort to this medium. I understand that it saves time, and certainly costume designers today are so poorly paid that just to survive they have to work on multiple productions, often two or three at a time. Such a schedule does not allow for the now old-fashioned approach to design that I was taught."

FIGURE 4.64 *Costume designs for "Hot Chocolate" (Spanish Variation) in* The Nutcracker. *(Digital rendering. Design by Carrie F. Robbins, Cincinnati Ballet, OH, 2011.)*

FIGURE 4.65 *Costume design for Barbra Streisand as Fanny Brice in* Funny Lady. *(Marker sketches with digital labels. Design by Bob Mackie, Columbia Pictures, 1975.)*

FIGURE 4.67 *Costume design for Cupid in a chroma key promotional video. (India ink on Bristol board, scanned and colored in Photoshop. Design by Steven Stines, Corporate Magic for Rite-Aid, 2005.)*

FIGURE 4.66 *Costume design for Lilli Vanessi/Kate in* Kiss Me Kate. *(Digital rendering using Photoshop CS5. Design by Rafael Jaén, Lyric Stage Company of Boston, MA, 2009.)*

But as the digital portfolio becomes a requirement for designers, even those who choose to create in a traditional medium find mastering some computer skills useful. Unfortunately, some digital renderings take on a primitive look, given the degree of skill required to create effective art electronically. Simply scanning and reproducing pattern gives a rendering the flat appearance of a paper doll or an old-school comic strip. Possessing a computer is not a substitute for artistic skill. *The computer in costume rendering is another medium; it is not a replacement for artistic ability.* The most effective computer costume renderings are created by designers with a solid background in drawing and a mastery of the elements of design.

Digital rendering author Cleveland[6] believes that "using a computer will not suddenly give one the ability to create evocative, aesthetically pleasing costumes if the user does not have a foundation in the art of costume design and has not developed some skill in sketching techniques.

"Most designers, myself included, who have come from traditional rendering training, still use a pencil and paper to make the preliminary sketches and then use the computer primarily to

Working

Rose
The School Teacher

FIGURE 4.68 *Costume design for Rose the School Teacher in* Working. *The patterned fabrics were created by photographing garments and manipulating the photos as part of the sketch. (Digital rendering using Corel Painter. Design by Annie O. Cleveland, Ohio State University, 2008.)*

color the renderings. There is something about the organic feel of pencil on paper that helps me to access that window into the character's soul."

Despite working entirely in a digital medium in recent years, Robbins[5] says, "If you can't draw with a pencil, it's three times, four times, harder with a stylus in your hand. It's more slippery, so you have to know what you're doing. It doesn't do it for you.

"There's something harder about the computer. The feeling you get when you're drawing and you feel the pencil bite into the paper—you don't get that with a computer. The resistance you get from the paper when you're drawing is helpful, like a landmark. That landmark is gone with the computer. It won't draw for you. I don't know why people think that."

Judanna Lynn[10] is formally trained in drawing, but creates some of her costume sketches digitally (see Figure 4.14). She explains "Oftentimes I like to make a pencil sketch first and then scan it in. Then maybe I color it in, erase, add to it. I can't imagine doing this without knowing how to draw. Moving around all these little gadgets is not a substitute. But there are effects you can get quickly. I like it sometimes just because it's fun.

"Too much stuff I see all looks like a bad cartoon, or like Manga [a Japanese comic style with distorted bodies and large doll-like eyes]. It all looks alike. Having a good foundation where

MAN OF LA MANCHA

MOOR
CENTRAL CITY OPERA • 2015
BY DALE WASSERMAN; LYRICS BY JOE DARION; MUSIC BY MITCH LEIGH
GENERAL AND ARTISTIC DIRECTOR PELHAM G. PEARCE • DIRECTOR PAUL CURRAN
SET AND COSTUME DESIGNER COURT WATSON

MAN OF LA MANCHA

MOOR
CENTRAL CITY OPERA • 2015
BY DALE WASSERMAN; LYRICS BY JOE DARION; MUSIC BY MITCH LEIGH
GENERAL AND ARTISTIC DIRECTOR PELHAM G. PEARCE • DIRECTOR PAUL CURRAN
SET AND COSTUME DESIGNER COURT WATSON

MAN OF LA MANCHA

MOOR
CENTRAL CITY OPERA • 2015
BY DALE WASSERMAN; LYRICS BY JOE DARION; MUSIC BY MITCH LEIGH
GENERAL AND ARTISTIC DIRECTOR PELHAM G. PEARCE • DIRECTOR PAUL CURRAN
SET AND COSTUME DESIGNER COURT WATSON

FIGURES 4.69, 4.70 & 4.71 *Costume design for a Moor in* Man of La Mancha. *Like many digital costume sketches, this one begins with a traditional drawing. (left) It is then scanned and colored using a computer (right). (Digital rendering. Design by Court Watson, Central City Opera, Colorado, 2015.)*

you can do it the old-fashioned way provides the basis for creating effective renderings regardless of the method."

Designer Rafael Jaén[13] is a member of the National Association of Photoshop Professionals (NAPP). He says, "I always tell my students that it is indispensable to learn how to paint classically first. If they know how to create transparent layers with watercolors and opaque layers with acrylics; if they know how to add gritty textures with colored pencils and soft values with pastels; and if they know how to include line weight and create **ombré** effects with design markers; then they can definitely use digital tools to render costume sketches."

"By far the one digital function that is nearly impossible to replicate with traditional media is the use of layers," asserts Cleveland.[6] "Layers give the designer the ultimate flexibility in design. [By separating elements onto individual layers] each part of a digital sketch can be manipulated or changed without affecting whatever is underneath."

According to Robbins,[5] the ability to alter a single layer while the remainder of the rendering remains consistent is a time-saving device. "You can very quickly try out numerous things," she says. "You can see it in green, or red, or shorter, or longer, put on a hat, change the hair. You can print out a few variations and show the director so they can understand and you haven't made three complete drawings."

Cleveland[6] adds that "when changes [in a design] crop up, as they invariably do, changes in a digital drawing are almost instantaneous as compared to creating another hand-crafted rendering."

Another feature of computer graphics, according to Cleveland, is "the amazing power of the 'undo' command. The

FIGURE 4.72 *Costume design for Man 1 in Marry Me, a Little. (Digital rendering using Photoshop Elements. Design by Rafael Jaén, New Repertory Theatre, Watertown, MA, 2012.)*

FIGURE 4.73 *Costume design for Bessie in Baden-Baden 1927: Mahagonny Songspiel. (Pencil sketch with Photoshop. Design by Court Watson, Gotham Chamber Opera, New York, 2013.)*

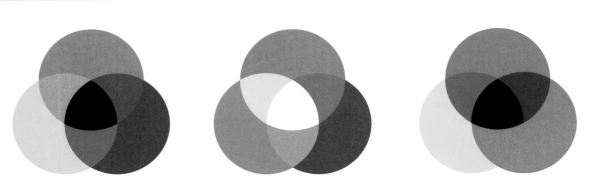

FIGURES 4.74, 4.75 & 4.76 *The color wheels of: (left) pigment (RYB); (center) light (RGB); and (right) printing (CMYK). In pigment and ink, the mixing of all three colors theoretically results in black; while in light it results in white.*

ability to erase without destroying the underlying sketch takes away the fear of making mistakes. A hand that just doesn't look right can be redone with just a few keystrokes." And, she adds that digital rendering is ultimately more accident-proof than traditional sketches on paper: "Gone are the days when putting the finishing touches on a rendering resulted in a smear or blot of ink destroying an image in which one had invested many hours."

Speed and ease of long-distance communication are clear advantages of using the computer in costume design, whether to create the entire rendering or to archive the traditional sketch. Jaén[13] says, "I still love drawing, painting, and hand-drafting, but in today's competitive world I need to produce renderings really fast in order to stay productive and complete projects in a timely manner. I also need to readily have digital files to communicate with production teams who are sometimes overseas or in a different state. Digital rendering facilitates this process."

Cleveland[6] concludes, "For those of us who were taught traditional media and had to relearn how to sketch on the computer, the learning curve is still steep. But for designers who have grown up in the world of computers and have used Photoshop to manipulate images for their Facebook pages, adapting to digital design is relatively simple. It is easy to say nothing beats the spontaneity and organic quality of a sketch made with a pencil on paper, but manipulating a digitizing pen and tablet is no longer an alien technique. The computer may not completely replace the pencil because a designer must have the necessary skill to tear off a piece of craft paper in the middle of the construction process and quickly sketch a new idea. But if nothing else, digital design opens a vast window of possibilities that stimulate the imagination, and is a terrific addition to the designer's toolbox."

Digital rendering requires an understanding of differences in color using paint, light, ink, and the three different associated color wheels. Visual artists learn early on that the three primary colors of pigment are red, yellow, and blue (RYB); while lighting designers work with the primaries red, green, and blue (RGB), which sounds odd to the painter. Adding yet another set of primaries—the cyan, magenta, yellow, and black (CMYK) of four-color printing with ink—is necessary when printing digital renderings.

One must understand that the vibrant colors seen on the computer screen, which uses light, will be significantly muted as they roll out of the ink-jet or laser printer. Due to the difference in mixing RGB and CMYK primaries, the colors will also often be quite different in hue than those that have been meticulously selected while working with digital graphics software.

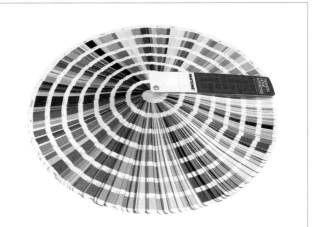

FIGURE 4.77 *Color specifier swatch book. (Courtesy of Pantone®.)*

FIGURE 4.78 Femmes au bord de l'eau, 1885–1886 *by Georges Seurat. (Oil on panel. Courtesy of Wikimedia Commons.)*

FIGURE 4.79 *Enlarged detail from the vintage comic book* Zegra, Jungle Empress. *(Fox Feature Syndicate. Courtesy of The Digital Comic Museum.)*

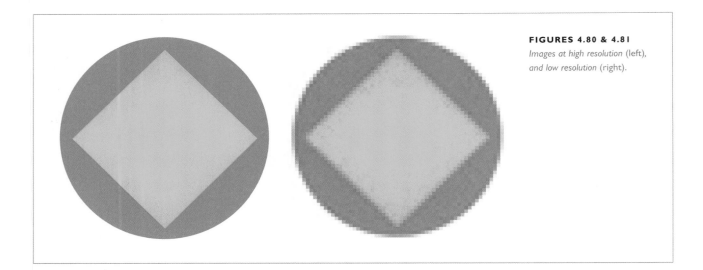

FIGURES 4.80 & 4.81
Images at high resolution (left), and low resolution (right).

Pantone, a company which creates custom inks and color systems, produces "color specifiers": fan-style books of color swatches (see Figure 4.78) that include the CMYK ink formula required to produce the swatch color when printing. These books can be expensive, but ultimately are a wise investment. Working with digital renderings that will be printed for presentation or for a portfolio requires having faith in selecting colors from the specifier rather than trusting the screen display. Of course, if the rendering will be presented only digitally, then using the RGB colors seen onscreen is fine. If accuracy is important for both printed and digital display, this may mean creating two versions, or tweaking one, to be effective in all forums.

When printing the digital rendering, the higher the quality of the original file and the better the printer, the more effective the printed result. Printing is done with a series of tiny dots, using the same principles as **pointillism** (see Figure 4.78) to give the illusion of mixed colors. The fewer the dots per square inch, the less effective the illusion. Think of the way an old comic book looks (see Figure 4.79): the same effect is used in large scale by the Pop Art painter Roy Lichtenstein.

The dots are measured by the inch, known as DPI (dots per inch) in printing and PPI (pixels per inch) on the screen. The more dots or pixels per inch, the smoother the effect of the pointillistic spray of ink in the four colors: cyan, magenta, yellow, and black. Current computer screens display in 72 or 100 PPI. A magazine or book is usually printed at 300 DPI, while a very fine printing job is typically 600 DPI. This is called the **resolution**.

Much like an Etch-a-Sketch toy, computers can only create images using horizontal and vertical lines. The higher the resolution, the smaller each of these lines will be, giving the

illusion of a smooth curve. When printed at a low resolution, the blending of colors and the delineation of the edges of a shape are less precise than may be desired. Printing at a low resolution produces a jagged or "pixilated" edge.

The higher the resolution—i.e. the greater the number of dots or pixels per inch—the more space a digital file will require on a drive or disk. In most cases, printing at 300 DPI produces a very acceptable final product. Of course, when archiving your work for a website or digital portfolio, there is no point in using additional file space to save it beyond 100 PPI. So, the wise designer may choose to have two versions of any sketch created, enhanced, or archived digitally—one suitable for printing, and the other, less greedy with space on the drive, for viewing on a screen.

REFERENCE MATERIAL

Having crossed the hurdle of selecting a color medium and a surface material, and deciding between a traditional or a digital approach, now the designer is ready to move to the next step of creating the rendering.

When creating a costume sketch, the designer should begin with the figure beneath the clothes. The commonly held view is that the most important part of a costume is the underwear. Undergarments shape and sometimes distort the anatomy, determining the silhouette of the clothing on top. An understanding of anatomy is crucial for the costume designer, and the drawing of the body is the foundation on which the costume will be drawn and painted. Draw the character naked or in underwear, work out the proportions of the figure, and only then begin to draw the costume.

There are numerous books offering advice and instruction for figure drawing, some focused on fashion and costume design. Fashion illustration, though, uses specialized techniques that elongate the figure to beyond what is realistic. The goal in drawing a costume sketch is to work out, among other considerations, the proportions of costume elements as they relate to the person who will wear them.

Fine artists doing figural work traditionally work from models, and a costume designer should endeavor to study still life drawing as part of design training. The most basic element of any costume created for an actor is the human body, and a basic understanding of anatomy is crucial to almost any aspect of costuming, including rendering.

Working from live models to create renderings is rarely practical for a costume designer; the time and money involved are unlikely to be available. Some designers try to work from full-length photos of the cast, but this is not often feasible; the cast may not be available or even selected when sketches must be done.

Although experience allows the costume designer (or any artist) to draw the figure without viewing a model, having some sort of reference is valuable. It is useful to compile files of assorted body types and various poses. Of course, the internet search is a great tool, but having a photo reference at hand without relying on the screen, or without the expense of printing it out, is also handy. Digital images, however, can be catalogued and archived for quicker access.

There are a number of books and digital collections for artists; they include photos of models in a range of poses and activities. Cleveland[6] says, "Digital rendering has provided me with the ability to assemble a library of poses that can be used for a variety of characters." Yet understanding how to modify the reference material is also necessary. Photos of people in an assortment of poses, holding objects, moving, or dancing can be used to add variety to the rendering.

Magazines and catalogs are useful sources of traditional reference material; but so many of these involve professional models with ideal or even computer-enhanced body types that they are not reflective of the bodies you will likely be costuming. Grab any photo that provides a clear view of the body when it is older or heavier, or of unusual proportions. Again, an understanding of anatomy allows the designer to modify the genetically-blessed underwear model into a normal human being, even adding sags and rolls to the flesh.

FIGURE 4.82 Following the Fashion *by James Gillray. Gillray is satirizing women who adopt Empire-period fashion regardless of whether it flatters their body type, and how proportions of clothing have a different effect on various bodies. (Hand-colored etching, 1794. Courtesy of Wikimedia Commons.)*

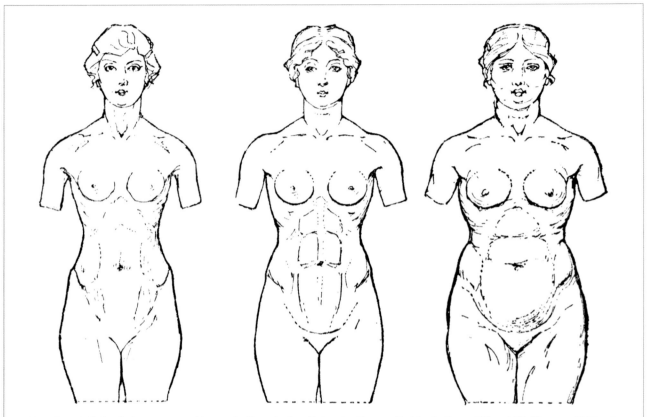

FIGURE 4.83 *Various body types portrayed by an artist. Illustration from* L'education Physique féminine *by Georges Hébert, 1921. (Courtesy of Wikimedia Commons.)*

Photo files—paper or digital—of faces are also invaluable in terms of rendering character. Some designers begin by determining what the character looks like, setting aside period or concept, to focus on the personality or physical type.

FROM ROUGH SKETCH TO FINAL RENDERING

> "Clearly there is a difference between preliminary renderings and final renderings. I do not say 'finished' designs because a design is not finished until the production is out of previews or opened—and in certain instances, not even then!"
>
> Dunya Ramicova[2] from an email interview

The degree to which a designer uses rough sketches and then adapts them to a finished sketch will be determined by the individual approach to rendering; there are no right-and-wrong guidelines for this process. Some designers transfer the rough to create a polished final sketch, while others prefer to work with a more spontaneous style, applying color to the same sketch they have used to work out proportion and detail.

Ramicova[2] says, "Preliminary renderings which help me to communicate with the director during early stages of the production process have to allow the director to feel comfortable with rejecting any or all of them. At the same time, preliminary renderings have to be clear enough to avoid confusion and ambiguity. I usually present my preliminary renderings unpainted with a selection of fabric swatches to give a sense of color, or I make reduced size copies of the costume renderings and paint those so as not to spend too much time on painting."

When discussing the rough sketch, there are distinctions to be made between kinds of rough. Many designers find themselves doodling on any available surface, from napkins to notebooks, or in the margins of a script, in order to think on paper or keep a record of initial ideas or modifications. This kind of sketch could

FIGURES 4.84–4.87 Costume design for Julia in Lend Me a Tenor. The design progresses from the "personal rough" (top left); to a clear pencil sketch (top right); which is then scanned, cleaned, labeled, and augmented with research and swatches for presentation (bottom left); and finally results in the finished color rendering in graphite, watercolor, and gouache (bottom right). (Design by Steven Stines, Tulane University, LA, 2010.)

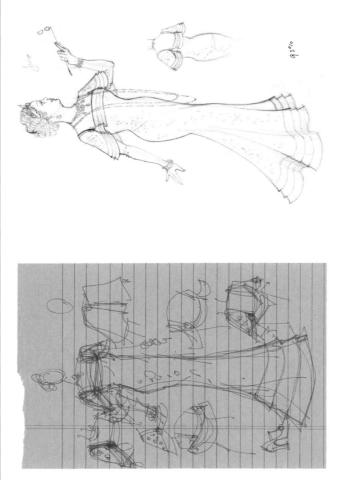

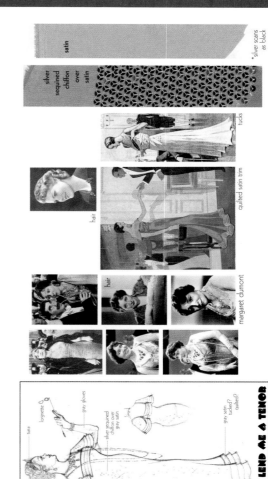

FIGURE 4.88 *Thumbnails of costume designs for Queen Lear. (Fiber-tip pen and pencil. Design by Tracy Grant Lord, Melbourne Theatre Company, Australia, 2012.)*

be termed the "Personal Rough Sketch". Often directors and actors are not visual artists—or they visualize in a different way than designers—so would not likely be able to understand these quickly drawn ideas. This requires a "Presentational Rough Sketch," something that can be shown in a production meeting or as part of an approval process. Any sketch that will be presented should be an indication of the designer's professionalism, and reassure collaborators that the quality of the costumes will be high. A presentational rough sketch should be neat, and the details "**readable**".

The computer is a valuable tool in preparing a rough sketch for the production team. It can be used to clean up the sketch, to add labels and notes quickly and legibly, to cut and paste research images, and to add scans of swatches. Today, the creative team often meets through technology rather than in person, and preliminary ideas need to be sent long distance. Digital versions of the rough sketch are therefore clearly an advantage.

Color roughs or **thumbnail** sketches can save time and anguish by allowing the designer or others on the production team to see an overview of the entire show, checking the palette and color relationships, and making sure that the use of color attracts attention as desired. Printing or photocopying drawings, full size or reduced, allows a quick way to create color roughs, using a medium like colored pencils or markers, or paint washes of the predominant colors. Presenting options to a director or choreographer during the rough sketch phase is a time-saver, avoiding redesigning or revising finished renderings.

The rough is used to work out the design—line, proportion, construction, and details—as well as the shape, proportions, and position of the figure. At precisely what point in the process the

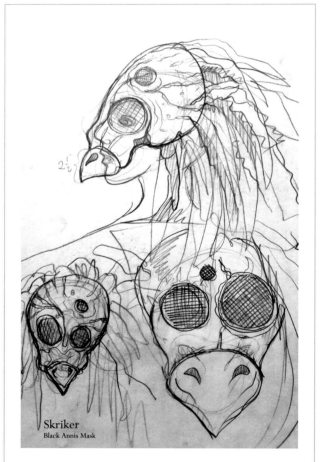

Skriker
Black Annis Mask

FIGURE 4.89 *Studies for Black Annis from The Skriker. (Pen and ink. Design by Casha Jacot-Guilarmod, Tulane University, LA, 2012.)*

FIGURE 4.90 *Costume designs for the Angels from* Jersey Boys. *(Ink and colored pencil on paper. Design by Jess Goldstein, August Wilson Theatre, New York, 2009.)*

designer moves from rough sketch to finished rendering, and just how that is accomplished, is a matter of individual working method.

Ramicova[2] explains, "Once the director and I come to an understanding, I work hard to create compelling renderings, often taking the time to draw the faces and body types of the actual actors or singers, since this makes the process of communication with them go more smoothly."

Some designers prefer to create the final rendering directly onto the paper in one step, simply redrawing the rough, refining and correcting as they go. Others choose to refine the sketch, then transfer it as a very clean drawing. As noted previously, the drawing may be done in a variety of media.

Transferring a drawing can also be accomplished in a variety of ways. Transfer paper, which is similar to the old-fashioned carbon paper typists used to make copies of documents, is available in graphite and in several colors, including white, which allows the transfer of a sketch to black or dark paper. The transfer paper is placed between the rough sketch and the selected paper, and the rough simply traced over, making the line work visible. Another method uses a light box (or light board or light table). Placing the sketch under the paper chosen for the final rendering allows a rough to be traced directly onto the selected paper, unless the paper is dark or extremely heavy. The name of

FIGURES 4.91–4.93 *Costume design for Moritz in* Spring Awakening. *The pencil sketch is scanned and refined in Photoshop (left), then printed onto colored paper (center) and painted with watercolor and gouache (right). (Design by Steven Stines, University of North Carolina at Charlotte, 2013.)*

FIGURE 4.94 *Costume design for Spring Waltzes. (Watercolor, gouache, and colored pencil on brown-line print. Design by Steven Stines. Choreography by Beverly Veenker, 1993.)*

the device is fairly self-explanatory; the basic form is a metal box containing a light source, with a glass or plexiglass cover onto which the drawing materials are placed. The layers of paper are backlit and can be seen through for tracing.

Goldstein[3] says, "I sketch with the help of a light board which allows me to trace over my initial drawings to perfect the lines (see Figure 4.90). Most sketches go through a series of at least three or four versions. The lines are drawn with a Pilot Razor Point black pen and the color is mostly done with Prismacolor pencils and occasionally fine-pointed color ink markers. No erasers . . . just resketching until it's done to my satisfaction."

If a black and white sketch is deemed satisfactory, it can be photocopied or printed directly onto art paper—with some restrictions (see Figures 4.91–4.93). The paper should not be significantly heavier than card stock, and the size must usually be consistent with standard paper sizes: 8.5" × 11", 8.5" × 14", or 11" × 17" (it can be trimmed later as needed). The paper will likely need to be individually hand-fed through the copier, and it is advisable to prepare extra sheets in the case of paper jams. But once the photocopy is accomplished, it is an effective and quick way to move your drawing onto the selected paper. In most cases, the copy is waterproof, and so can be painted over with any medium. A wise designer may print multiple copies of a sketch, as a means of experimenting with color, or guarding against the perils of painting mishaps without having to redraw.

Some designers like drawing on vellum, which is useful for both graphite and ink. Vellum is not an ideal choice for wet

FIGURES 4.95 & 4.96 *Costume design for Philip Bosco as George, sober (left) and drunk (right), in Moon Over Buffalo. This pair of sketches shows how both design and rendering can help to tell the playwright's story. (Marker on paper. Design by Bob Mackie, Martin Beck Theatre, New York, 1995.)*

media, but dry color and marker can be applied to both front and back. In the same way as hand-drafting, vellum drawing can also be printed in black-line, brown-line, or blue-line; then painted (see Figure 4.94). The setting of the printer can be adjusted for darkness depending on the desired effect. Dark settings will create a half-tone effect for the entire page, while a light setting will keep the background white or pale and provide a reproduction of the darker parts of the original line work. If a dark or murky effect is desired, making the print towards the end of the day when the fluid is old produces a darker, splotchier result. When exposed to light over time, however, the page will darken or yellow.

Any of these printing methods is useful if your design requires multiples of a single costume in various colors, or a basic garment with variations. The basic costume can be drawn and reproduced, with details and variations added to that base drawing.

Each stage of the rendering process has value in communication. According to Jaén,[13] "A line drawing, for example, can serve as a preliminary sketch to talk about silhouette and period style with a director. It can also serve (with notations) as drafting that a draper can use for seam placement and such. A finely executed color sketch can speak volumes about a character's qualities, via palette and textures, and it can also guide in the procurement of the proper fabric weight and type. In addition, final sketches are a great tool to communicate with actors; when they see 'themselves' in character it makes the fittings that much smoother." The costume sketch, Jaén says, "gives the director, the other designers, the actors, and the technicians a clear picture of the story that the designer wants to tell."

COMPOSITION

As with any work of visual art, composition is a basic element of the costume rendering. And, as is so often the case with components of a costume sketch, composition must be viewed from both an artistic and a practical standpoint. The natural instinct is often to place the figure in the center of the page; but the costume designer needs to think ahead and remember how many functions the rendering must fulfill. When laying out the sketch, one must factor in room for additional elements like back views, detail drawing, attached research, and swatches of fabric and trim (see Figure 4.97).

In most cases, costume sketches feature a single costume or a single character. This has a practical aspect, since at times more than one shop or more than one team of shop personnel will construct a show. But there can be cases when a designer opts

FIGURE 4.97 *Costume design for Old Henry in* The Fantasticks. *(Graphite, watercolor, and gouache on watercolor paper with attached swatches. Design by Steven Stines, Riverside Theatre, Florida, 2003.)*

to show two or more characters in a single rendering. This can reinforce a visual or character relationship (see Figure 4.98), or offer multiple viewing angles for costumes that are structurally similar (see Figure 4.99). In some cases, a designer may show the arc of a character's costume changes in one sketch (see Figure 4.100).

Care must be taken in a group plate not to obscure information about a costume by hiding it behind another figure. Placing all the figures on the same plane is one way to avoid this, but it creates a more dynamic visual to work out ways to group figures other than in a straight line, while still communicating the necessary information.

Group plates can present costumes as they will be seen together onstage. Goldstein[3] describes how using smaller figures "allows me to draw groups of characters on a single page, which can be helpful in presenting how a particular scene might look, especially in large shows like Shakespearean plays, musicals, and operas."

FIGURE 4.98 *Costume designs for Gwendolyn and Lady Bracknell in The Importance of Being Earnest. (Fiber-tip pen and pencil. Design by Tracy Grant Lord. Based on the original production designs by Tony Tripp. Melbourne Theatre Company, Australia, 2011.)*

FIGURE 4.99 *Costume designs for Ladies of the Night in The Magic Flute. (Ink, pastel, and watercolor. Design by Christine Reimer, Vancouver Opera, Canada, 2006.)*

FIGURE 4.100 *Costume design for Don Quixote in Man of La Mancha. (Ink, watercolor, and gouache. Design by Ann Hould-Ward, The Shakespeare Company, Washington DC, 2015.)*

FIGURE 4.101 *Costume designs for Basilio in the ballet Don Quixote. (Ink, acrylic, and gold paint on paper. Design by Alun Jones, Louisville Ballet, KY, 1999.)*

FIGURE 4.102 *Costume designs for Newsies. (Ink and colored pencil on paper. Design by Jess Goldstein, Nederlander Theatre, New York, 2012.)*

FIGURES 4.103–4.106 *Costume designs for Agamemnon, Athena, Orestes, and Pylades in Agamemnon and His Daughters. These sketches were completed in black and white because the designer felt the line work provided crucial information for the drapers. The finished costumes were dyed with ombré or mottled effects in a neutral palette. The sketches were created as interrelated images. (Pen and ink. Design by Lindsay W. Davis, Arena Stage, Washington DC, 2001.)*

Costume plates for a show should be viewed as a group even when they depict only one character on each page. The designer's work will often be presented or displayed as a whole because this gives a clearer indication of the effect of a stage full of costumes—an indication of character relationships, along with relative scale, silhouette, and color palette. One should try to establish a consistent scale for the entire group: if a tall character fills the page, a shorter character would not; and a child would fill less space on the page than an adult.

How large should the figure be in a costume sketch? Students often seem to want assigned parameters. Scenic designers may establish a mathematically based scale (for example, ¼" = 1'0") for their renderings, and certainly for set models; but costume designers more often work at a size that feels comfortable. Although a designer like Lucille (Lady Duff Gordon), in the early 20th century, could produce very small renderings full of exquisite detail, other designers may need larger dimensions in order to include all the necessary components. Conversely, extremely large renderings may be effective in the moment, but they will ultimately need to fit into a portfolio.

FIGURE 4.108 *Costume design for the Crab Faerie from* The Skriker. *(Pen and ink. Design by Casha Jacot-Guilarmod, Tulane University, LA, 2012.)*

FIGURE 4.107 *Costume design for the Singing Teacher in* On the Town. *(Watercolor and pencil. Design by Zack Brown, Hamburg Statsoper, Germany, 1991.)*

FIGURE 4.109 *Costume design for Male Ensemble (Marketplace) in* Aladdin. *(Gouache and dimensional paint on watercolor paper sprayed with liquid watercolor and pearlescent gouache. Design by Gregg Barnes, New Amsterdam Theatre, New York, 2014.)*

Robbins[5] says, "I've found, after many years of teaching, that each person develops an affinity for a certain size figure. One student is comfortable drawing twelve inch figures; someone else prefers five inchers. I say draw the size figure that makes you most comfortable and you'll get all your drawings done faster and easier. The one proviso is that, of course, drawing larger takes a bit longer, but will show more details, and also more drawing flaws. Drawing small has a certain charm, which is seductive."

STRIKE A POSE

> "The sketch is the first inkling of where the attitude and energy of the show will go. In fact, I spend hours figuring the stance of the body in the sketch as, to me, it's my first chance to have a conversation with the actor about who this character is. If I do it well I can facilitate the roadway for the director and actors to go down by what I tell them about the spirit of the production in the sketches."
>
> Ann Hould-Ward[4] from an email interview

A good costume rendering is a character study, not just a diagram of garments. As with all elements of a costume sketch, the pose is a combination of art, information, and salesmanship.

For some designers, simply getting a clear sketch of clothing on a figure in a frontal pose is an achievement; this may be all that is needed. But the goal should be greater, and for a variety of reasons. An actor uses movement and posture to convey character—and so does the costume designer. Costumes themselves can be designed to affect the way an actor moves or stands, or to shape the body, and the rendering should use the same approach.

Selecting the angle from which the costume is viewed and the position of the figure makes a statement about the character, but it is also determined by the information deemed important for the shop. If a design has a significant detail on the side or back, a strictly frontal view is inadequate (see Figures 4.109 and 4.110). In art history, following several centuries of frontal or profile portraits, Italian Renaissance painters discovered the charm of the ¾ view (see Figures 4.111 and 4.112). That angle often allows the costume designer to include more information about the costume (see Figure 4.113).

FIGURE 4.110 *Costume design for Prospero in* The Tempest. *(Watercolor. Design by Susan Tsu, Oregon Shakespeare Festival, 1994.)*

FIGURE 4.111 *Portrait of Cecilia Gallerani (Lady with an Ermine), 1483–1490, by Leonardo da Vinci. This painting is considered to be the first portrait using the ¾ view of the head. (Oil on panel. Czartoryski Museum, Poland.)*

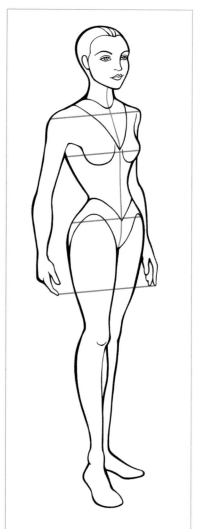

FIGURE 4.112 *In ¾ view, it is important to adjust the centerline of the body. This position also places shoulders, hips, and limbs onto lines angling away from the viewer.*

MS. NELLY MIRCIOIU

MANON
ACT III · SC. 1
Washington Opera '90

Zack Brown '90.

FIGURE 4.113 *Costume design for Manon. (Watercolor and pencil. Design by Zack Brown, Washington Opera, 1990.)*

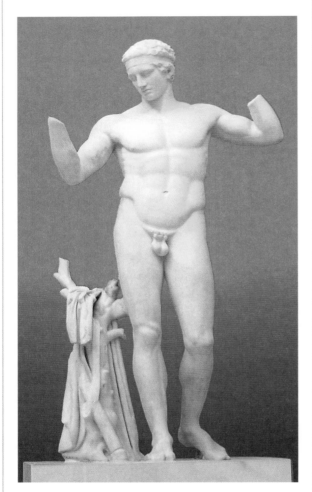

FIGURE 4.114 Diadumenos by Polykleitos. Roman marble copy of Greek original, 5th century BC. (National Archeological Museum of Athens, Greece. Photograph by Ricardo André Frantz.)

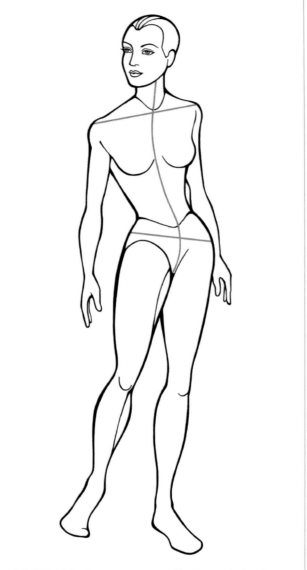

FIGURE 4.115 In a contrapposto position, the curved spine affects the angle of the hips and shoulders.

Ancient Greek sculptors introduced the idea of **contrapposto** to art: in this position, weight is shifted from two feet to one foot, which creates a sideways curve in the spine, tilting the shoulders and pushing one hip to the side. Keep in mind that "the backbone's connected to the hipbone," so moving one part of the anatomy out of alignment will affect the other parts.

Incorporating gesture and movement also allows the designer to simultaneously make a statement about the character and convey information about the costume. Certainly the weight and drape of fabric is more effectively demonstrated when the character is moving. Small gestures like lifting a skirt to display a petticoat or a shoe, pushing a jacket back to reveal a vest or

a lining, or partially hiding the face behind an open fan—all are more interesting than a static figure, and at the same time are ways to display costume details (see Figure 4.117).

The use of props (whether or not these are costume props) can reflect the script, reveal the character, or simply create interest. Holding a flower, reading a love letter, applying lipstick—all are business for an actor, whether onstage or in a sketch (see Figures 4.118 and 4.119).

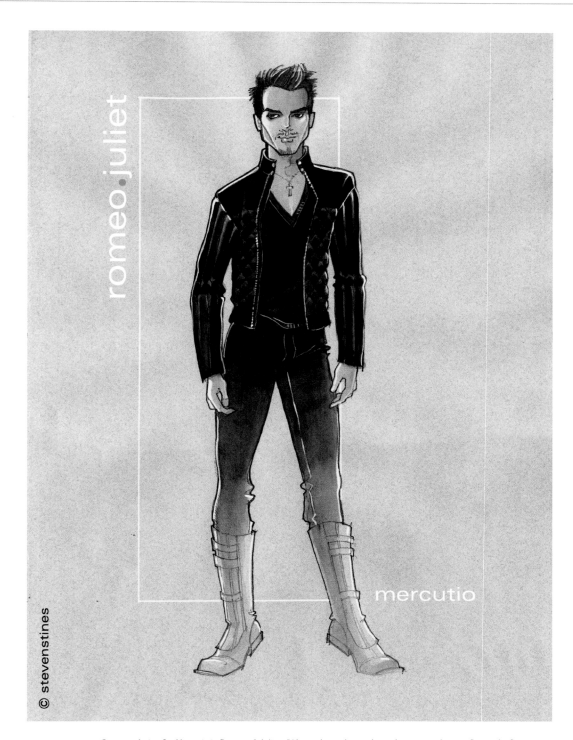

FIGURE 4.116 *Costume design for Mercutio in Romeo & Juliet. (Watercolor and gouache on laser-printed paper. Design by Steven Stines, University of North Carolina at Charlotte, 2013.)*

FIGURE 4.117 *Costume design for Female Ensemble/Prologue (Day Look) in Something Rotten! (Gouache and dimensional paint on watercolor paper sprayed with liquid watercolor and pearlescent paint. Design by Gregg Barnes, St. James Theatre, New York, 2015.)*

FIGURE 4.118 *Costume design for Sonia in* They're Playing Our Song. *(Graphite, watercolor, gouache, and gold acrylic on paper. Design by Steven Stines. Concept sketch for Arts Center of Coastal Carolina, 2004.)*

FIGURE 4.119 *Costume design for* The Importance of Being Earnest. *(Gouache. Design by James Bidgood.)*

FIGURE 4.120 *Costume design for Martha in* The Gospel According to the Other Mary. *(Terracotta pencil and watercolor. Design by Dunya Ramicova, Los Angeles Philharmonic, 2013.)*

FIGURE 4.121 *Costume design for Anna Petrovna in* Platonov. *(Watercolor on watercolor paper. Design by Steven Rotramel, Yale School of Drama, CT, 2013.)*

FIGURE 4.122 *Costume design for Eliante in* School for Lies. *(Pencil and Photoshop. Design by Yao Chen, University of Texas at Austin, 2013.)*

As noted at the beginning of this chapter, a costume designer must, in effect, act a version of the show as part of the design process; similarly, applying elements of acting, like movement and posture, when creating the rendering will result in a far more interesting and effective result.

RENDERING STYLE

For designers for whom rendering is not a strong point, the goal is to communicate information about the costume so it may be realized. But for designers adept at drawing and painting, being able to bring a specific style to the rendering is a decided advantage in presenting and selling the idea.

Rendering style may influence the choice of media, or may be a result of that choice. Some designers have a distinct, personal rendering style that marks their sketches immediately as their own. Others develop a stylistic versatility that allows the rendering style to reflect the nature of the production or the design concept.

Even within the parameters of a single, recognizable style, it is beneficial to be able to modify the work to reflect the specific design. It is hard to envision a single style that serves *Threepenny*

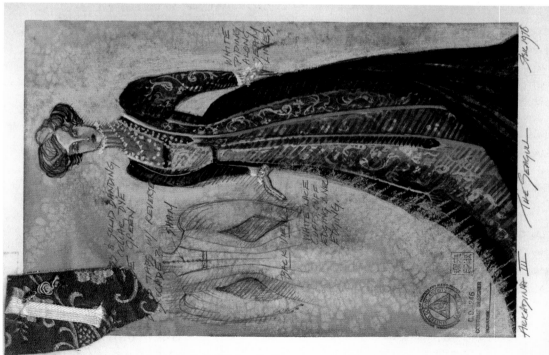

FIGURES 4.123 & 4.124 Costume designs for (left) Arkadina in The Seagull, and (right) Gwendolyn in The Importance of Being Earnest. The same designer, working with the same historical period, uses two distinct styles of rendering as a response to two very different plays. (Designs by Susan Tsu. (left) Watercolor, pencil, chalk, and salt, The Indiana Repertory Theatre, IN, 1978. (right) Watercolor and pencil. The Alley Theatre, Houston, TX, 1995.)

FIGURES 4.125–4.127 *These renderings convey a range of different moods, reflecting the literary source, the character, and the design concept.* (left) *Costume design for Lee in* True West. *(Colored pencil, marker, and watercolor pencil. Design by Lauren Nigri, Wallis Theatre, Northwestern University, IL, 2015.)* (center) *Costume design for Oronte in* The School for Lies. *(Pencil and Photoshop. Design by Yao Chen, University of Texas, 2013.)* (right) *Costume design for Lavina in* Titus Andronicus. *(Watercolor and gouache. Design by Tyler Wilson, University of Missouri–Kansas City, 2015.)*

Opera, Coppélia, and *Volpone* equally. Mastering drawing and painting, studying the history of fine and decorative art, and taking every opportunity to observe photography, film, advertising, and graphic design will develop a frame of stylistic reference for rendering.

Evoking a mood or atmosphere is a more abstract concept when discussing the costume sketch, and moves into the area of artistry as opposed to information. It goes beyond step-by-step instructions into the realm of Supreme Court Justice Potter Stewart's words, "I know it when I see it." A costume sketch for the witches in *Macbeth* would, logically, require a different visual atmosphere than a sketch for Miss Adelaide in *Guys and Dolls.* Creating a mood with a costume sketch goes beyond indicating structure and materials, and makes a statement about artistic interpretation of the literature or music. Like a director or an actor, the designer must have a theatrical response to the project, and costume rendering that can demonstrate that viewpoint becomes an art form.

RENDERING EFFECTS

Beyond the drawing and painting of the character in the costume, there are considerations of details and effects that will make the sketch more successful. In basic terms, these are adding to the costume sketch elements that make it more theatrical, and can better reflect the way a costume will be seen onstage.

In the section of this chapter about paper selection, the use of half-tone or colored paper was recommended because it more accurately conveys the effect of a costume on a set and will allow the designer to better judge the color relationships between scenery and costume and within the costume itself. But there are other rendering methods that both allow a more accurate consideration of color and value relationships, and make the costume sketch more effective as a form of presentation and communication.

Adding a background is a common rendering technique. This can be as simple as a wash of color or tone added, but depending on painting skill can become more complex. Knowing

FIGURE 4.128 *Costume design for The Moon in Blood Wedding. (Watercolor, gouache, and ink. Design by Casha Jacot-Guilarmod, Tulane University, LA, 2011.)*

the predominant color of the scenery is very helpful, not just in determining what colors to use for fabrics, but also in selecting a background for the renderings.

The background can be added after the character is painted, working around the figure. But it is simpler to add a background to the line drawing, or at the beginning of the rendering process. When this idea is introduced to students, they often shy away from adding color to an unpainted sketch. "Won't the color show through?" they ask.

In some cases, designers will use an opaque paint over a colored background (see Figure 4.57); in others they will apply the background paint, avoiding the area where the figure will be. It is possible to use the nature of layered transparent paints to simulate the effect of the lighting designer's color gels and **gobos** (see Figure 4.133). One can use the nature of watercolor to create aqueous effects, to drybrush, or to create a mottled surface by dropping clean water or bleach, or sprinkling salt to soak up wet color.

As with figure drawing, there are a number of instructional books about using paint, and techniques such as **scumbling** and **gradients**, to create effects. **Spattering** with a toothbrush adds texture. Allowing paint to drip or run (see Figure 4.134), ripping or burning the paper, layering papers, beginning with a dark background and painting in a white or pale figure (see Figure 4.45)—all of these are approaches which can be used to indicate the overall style or dramatic effect of the design.

Designers sometimes include a framing element for their sketches, like rule lines or a background with a defined edge

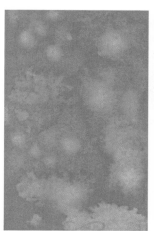

FIGURES 4.129–4.132 *Effects achieved with watercolor by* (from left to right): *dropping clear water; scumbling and blotting; sprinkling salt on wet paint; and spattering with a toothbrush.*

FIGURE 4.133 *Costume design for Von Rothbart in Swan Lake. (Watercolor, ink, and bleach on Bristol board. Design by Zack Brown, American Ballet Theatre, New York, 2000.)*

FIGURE 4.134 *Costume design for the Absinthe Fairy in* Dreams of Oblivion. *(Graphite, watercolor, and gouache on watercolor paper. Design by Steven Stines, Tsunami Dance Company, New Orleans, 2009.)*

INCLUDING INFORMATION ON THE SKETCH

"You know what I love? I love clear labels. A sketch without a label is not meaningful. If you're in a shop and there are 30 things going through at the same time, they don't know what it is without labels. Include the name of the show, the name of the character, when it's worn. Put the name of the actor on the sketch if you know it. Isn't it about not making mistakes?"

Lindsay W. Davis[14] from a telephone interview

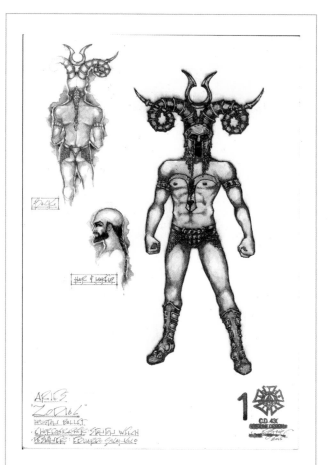

FIGURE 4.135 *Costume design for Aries in* Zodiac. *The sketch includes front and back views and a detail of the hair and makeup, is thoroughly and completely labeled, and is numbered for the shop's reference. (Design by Eduardo Sicango, Houston Ballet, TX, 2015.)*

(see Figures 4.123 and 4.124). Allowing the figure to break the line and extend into the border can add dynamism or dimension. This device was often employed by Walter Plunkett, the designer of *Gone with the Wind*.

Containing the painted background within a border is easy. Simply tape off the border; regular Scotch tape works well, but one should first apply the tape to scrap paper or fabric and pull it up to make it somewhat less sticky, and therefore less likely to tear the paper as it is removed after the paint dries.

Learning to convey the effect of lighting on the figure and on the fabric is not just a means of creating a more theatrical costume plate. Using shadow and highlight creates dimension, and also provides information about the kind of fabric used in the design. Imagine the different ways satin, velvet, wool, and metallic lamé reflect or absorb light; this information should be part of a costume sketch.

FIGURE 4.136 *Costume design for* Dracula. *The elaborate design of this cape is most effectively shown in a back view. (Pen, ink, and gouache. Design by Judanna Lynn, Houston Ballet, TX, 1997.)*

FIGURE 4.137 *Costume design for Ilia in Mozart's* Idomeneo. *(Ink, pastel, and watercolor. Design by Christine Reimer, Pacific Opera, Victoria, Canada, 2007.)*

As noted at the beginning of this chapter, the primary goal for a costume rendering is to provide information. To that end, many designers include a range of supplementary sketches and notes. Some designers may prefer to preserve the rendering as a painting, but this proves impractical for most. Even collectors who acquire theatre design sketches often express a preference for renderings that include swatches and notes: the costume plate is a "living document" with an end use, and designers must understand that they are creating something different than pure or fine art.

The first question most drapers will ask a designer is "What does the back look like?" Costume maker McCoy[7] cautions that "if you don't include a rendering for a back view, be prepared to let your cutter come up with how it should look."

A costume shop could certainly create the back of the costume independently, but the costume designer is responsible for designing a three-dimensional piece, which more likely than not will be viewed by the audience from many angles. Including a rear view is smart and responsible (see Figure 4.9). It need not be a full, colored rendering, but can be a small sketch of the costume back, or rear detailing. Some costumes may make a statement when

seen from the back, and so designers may choose to make a back view the primary image in the rendering (see Figure 4.136).

"If you have a specific idea of a detail of the design, don't hesitate to include the specific example with the rendering," suggests McCoy[7] (see Figure 4.61). Unusual structural components or special effects will require detail sketches and often technical drawings, which may be incorporated into the rendering.

Hair and makeup are crucial components of a costume design. While makeup or hair designers may function as independent artists, in theatre (as opposed to film) their work is often subject to the approval of the costume designer. A wise designer, when afforded the luxury of collaborating with hair and makeup artists, will welcome their knowledge and input, and there should be a discussion of period and character with the goal of creating a unified look. A costume rendering should always include an idea of how the character will look above the neck.

As with most components of the costume sketch, there is no single "right" way to render hair. Looking at the examples in this chapter, one will see hair rendered in an articulated manner (see Figure 4.9) or more impressionistically (see Figure 4.151). Hair, like clothing, should be viewed first in terms of overall form,

The Rocky Horror Picture Show
The Floor Show

FIGURE 4.138 *Costume design for Rocky in The Rocky Horror Picture Show. (Marker, watercolor, pencil, and rhinestones on paper. Design by Alyssa Couturier-Herndon, University of Florida, 2013.)*

with areas of light and shadow (see Figure 4.94), rather than as a collection of individual hairs. Once the overall structure of the hairstyle is rendered, one can add indications of direction or texture of the strands of hair (see Figure 4.160), and indicate whether the style is controlled (see Figure 4.122) or loose (see Figure 4.52). As with fabric, one should imagine hair responding to the movement of the actor or blowing in the wind (see Figure 4.149).

Beyond artistic or construction considerations, the design sketch is a tool to sell an idea, and should include a clear indication of the type of person the character will be. Costume designers should learn to draw faces. Facial features, expressions, ethnicity, age—all of these are factors in creating a character, and are affected by the work of the costume and makeup team. They should be noted in an effective costume rendering (see Figures 4.140–141).

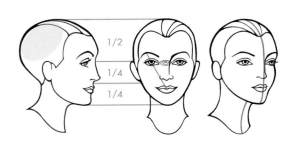

FIGURE 4.139 *For a face with ideal proportions, the face can be divided into quarters, with the eyes halfway down and one eye width apart. The ear aligns with the eye and nose. A diagonal line from the center of the lip through the iris indicates the arch of the eyebrow. As with the full figure, an adjusted centerline is required for a ¾ view, and the features further from the viewer are foreshortened. In profile, the features fall on the same guidelines as in the front view.*

FIGURES 4.140 & 1.141 *These designers have included very specific character faces as part of the sketch, which also functions as information about makeup. (left) Costume design for Judge Turpin in Sweeney Todd. (Pencil, watercolor, colored pencil, and collage on watercolor paper. Design by Matt Iacozza, University of Connecticut, 2012.) (right) Costume design for the Governess in Cyrano. (Gouache, James Bidgood.)*

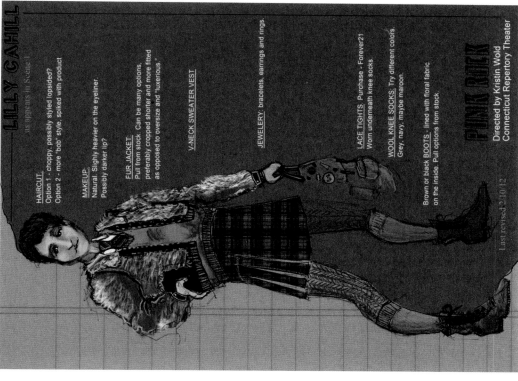

FIGURES 4.142 & 4.143 *For hundreds of years, costume designers have found it useful to add notes to their sketches; only the medium has changed. (left) Costume design for the Ballet de la Délivrance de Renaud, c. 1617. (Watercolor, ink, pencil, and gold paint on paper. Design by Daniel Rabel. ©Victoria and Albert Museum, London.) (right) Costume design for Lilly Cahill in Punk Rock. (Pencil, Prismacolor pencil, and Photoshop on watercolor paper. Design by Matt Iacozza, Connecticut Repertory Theatre, 2013.)*

As clearly as a costume sketch may be drawn and painted, designers often find it desirable to include notes—sometimes *lots* of notes—to explain elements of the idea or construction (see Figures 4.142–4.144). If the desire is to preserve the original sketch as a piece of illustration, then the computer is convenient; the rendering can be scanned and labeled as needed. But most costume designers are happy to include notes directly on the sketch.

Labeling and notating a costume sketch can be simple and informative, or it can be integrated into the design and the rendering style. Labeling includes adding the title of the show and the identity of the character, along with the act and scene if there are costume changes. A designer's signature or **union stamp** also becomes part of the composition. Alongside such practical considerations, written information on a costume sketch can also explain the designer's thoughts on construction and materials to be used.

Labels and notes should be legible, whether they are practical or design-based, hand-written or computer-generated. Some designers use the show's logo, or create a title treatment based on the design style. Others feel simply including the information is sufficient; this is a personal, creative choice.

FIGURE 4.145 *Costume design for Sophie Scholl in* Weiße Rose. *The sketch includes a photo reference of the historical person portrayed in the fictional plot of the opera. (Pencil sketch with Photoshop. Design by Court Watson. Project for Camerata Nuova opernregie Preis – Kölner Kinderoper, Germany, 2014.)*

RENDERING FOR SPECIALIZED GENRES

"The drawing is the bridge in the conversation with the artistic director or choreographer and the costume makers. It's me interpreting the artistic director's or choreographer's vision. I see it as a team sport."

Judanna Lynn[10] from a telephone interview

When designing for certain kinds of performance, the costume sketch should be adapted to better reflect the nature of the production. Dance design requires sensitivity to the physical nature of the performance. Costumes for dance should always be designed with an understanding of how they will appear when moving. Similarly, the costume as drawn should be portrayed in motion. The figure itself should be accurately drawn in a position consistent with the dance technique employed by the performer.

FIGURE 4.144 *Costume design for Finale Showgirl in Paradis. (Design by Eduardo Sicango.)*

FIGURE 4.146 *Costume design for the North Wind from* The Nutcracker. *(Pen and ink, watercolor, and digital rendering. Design by Judanna Lynn, Carolina Ballet, 2001.)*

FIGURE 4.147 *Costume design for Cecile Volange, from Dangerous Liaisons. (Watercolor, acrylic, and pencil. Design by Jennifer Symes. Choreography by Sasha Janes, Charlotte Ballet, NC, 2012.)*

Dance training alters the anatomy to facilitate technique. Ballet dancers, for instance, work with the legs in a turned-out position, the feet pointed, the shoulders lowered and the arms rounded. As a former ballet dancer, designer Lynn[10] says, "I'm very aware of turnout and hip placement and where the hands and feet are. It does annoy me when these are not right."

Modern dancers and musical theatre performers have particular poses and movements, often specific to a choreographer or style. Referring to photos of dancers is helpful for the costume designer, but care must also be taken to select a pose that does not obscure important information about the costume.

Fabric will also be affected by movement. "If the design has particular issues of fit or movement, it is very beneficial if the rendering indicates the type or hand of the fabric," says Galloway.[8] As mentioned earlier, rendering fabric in motion helps communicate the type of fabric specified. Certainly, the choice of fabric is crucial when designing dance costumes, and the sketch should provide as much information as possible about that choice. When sketching a dance costume, imagine that there is a fan blowing the fabric; how and where does the costume move?

High-style or fashion-based costume designs also call for a specific approach to the sketch. Some designers view creating a costume sketch as essentially the same as doing a fashion illustration, but there are some fundamental differences involved.

New York-based fashion illustrator Robert W. Richards works in a classic style founded on the golden age approach of illustrators like Eric and René Boucher, who depicted Dior's "New Look." According to Richards,[15] depicting fashion means "learning to eliminate anything that's not important. If you're drawing a dress, just do the basics so it reads. Illustration depicts clothes better than photography does. It cuts right to the bone. Elongating the figure, that's a very strong component of fashion illustration. You get more grace when you elongate, and fashion should be graceful."

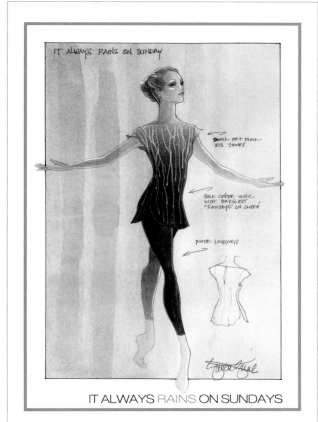

FIGURE 4.148 *Costume design for It Always Rains on Sunday. (Graphite, watercolor, and gouache on paper. Design by Steven Stines, Newcomb Dance Company, New Orleans, 2012.)*

FIGURE 4.149 *Costume design for Carmen in the ballet Carmen. (Watercolor, acrylic, and pencil. Design by Jennifer Symes. Choreography by Sasha Janes, Charlotte Ballet, NC, 2013.)*

FIGURE 4.150 *Fashion illustration. (Watercolor and pastel. Robert W. Richards, 2008.)*

FIGURE 4.152 *Costume designs for Joan Eastman in Okay. (Gouache. Design by James Bidgood, Green Mansions Theatre, New York, 1960s.)*

FIGURE 4.151 *Costume design for "Sisters" from Irving Berlin's White Christmas. Designing costumes based on what she terms "'50s glam," Robbins uses the look of mid-century fashion illustration for this sketch. (Digital rendering. Design by Carrie F. Robbins, Marquis Theatre, New York, 2009.)*

"As opposed to costume design, for which you have to keep the proportions." With an extremely elongated figure in a costume sketch, Richards says, "a performer would say, 'I don't understand, I don't look like that.' For theatre, I think you have to portray the person who's going to wear it. In fashion illustration you can make up the person, or it's a model. Fashion models have a definite purpose. They have great figures and they know how to pose and, generally speaking, they're gorgeous.

"Doing a costume sketch is more literal. And you have to do more rendering, you have to design. Fashion illustration is based on things that already exist. They send you the dress. Costume design is more of a creative process."

Some shows are set in a world of high-end or couture clothing—*Private Lives*; *The Women*; any show where the characters are wealthy, urban, modern people. It is these shows where *Vogue* becomes a logical source of research (see Figure 4.151). Other shows are cast with showgirls, who have very tall proportions. The performer will likely be statuesque (see Figure 4.152). Creating the sketch may entail elongating the figure, but take care to limit this. The classical proportion of a body that is eight heads high is, in fashion illustration, exaggerated to 10, 12, or even 14 heads high (see Figure 4.153)—but not even a supermodel can provide a body quite like that.

The actors cast in a show with couture clothing will hopefully be in good shape and know how to wear clothes, but they are still human beings, and, as noted, part of the goal of the costume sketch is to work out the proportions of clothing in relation to the body on which it will be seen.

FIGURE 4.153 *"Petite robe de Jardin," by Georges Barbier, from Costumes Parisiens, 1913. (Pochoir. Courtesy of Metropolitan Museum of Art, New York.)*

FIGURE 4.154 *Costume design for Hildy Johnson in His Girl Friday. (Gouache, pen, and pencil. Design by Tracy Grant Lord, Melbourne Theatre Company, Australia, 2012.)*

FIGURE 4.155 *Costume design for Chauncey Deville in* Dracula, a Musical. *(Watercolor. Design by Susan Tsu, Alley Theatre, Houston, TX, 1993.)*

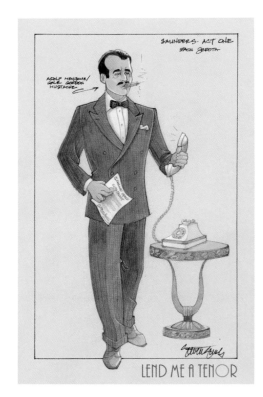

FIGURE 4.156 *Costume design for Saunders in* Lend Me a Tenor. *(Watercolor, gouache, and graphite pencil on paper. Design by Steven Stines, Tulane University, LA, 2010.)*

Rendering a show that uses tailored clothing or uniforms requires a particular approach. Line work becomes important (see Figure 4.154). The French designate clothing either as tailored clothing or as *flou*, a term that fashionistas find hard to translate but which is understood to refer to the light, mobile, soft, or draped aspects of clothing. *Flou* can be rendered much more vaguely than tailored clothes, whether worn by men or by women. In theatre, tailored costumes are often built by a separate shop or team, and these costumers are quite focused on precise shape and placement of the structural and decorative details of the clothing (see Figure 4.155).

Some designers have difficulty rendering male figures and particularly the specifics of lapels, pockets, button placement, and seaming that is inherent in tailored clothes. Designers should study the standards employed in menswear. Depending on the period, there are defined rules about the length of a jacket or the **break** of pants, the amount of shirt cuff visible, where the buttons are positioned, and how a tie is knotted. The width of

lapels, hat brims, ties, and shirt collars is interrelated and should be rendered accurately. How many jacket or vest buttons should be left open? Is this a **peak lapel**, a **notch**, or a **shawl**? Is the shirt collar standard, spread, or wing? Men's hats and military caps have very specific shapes and proportions, and the costume sketch which is not drawn clearly may result in an inaccurate final product. With tailored clothing, the designer might consider including clear research materials to supplement a sketch.

Actors are often advised to "never work with children or dogs." When costuming the former, the designer's sketch should reflect the correct proportions of a child. Looking at paintings from Colonial America, the viewer is often struck by how odd the children look (see Figure 4.157). Painters had not mastered the ability to portray children and simply presented them as miniature versions of adults, with adult proportions. Yet the head develops its full size sooner than the rest of the body; and an adolescent girl has full-size feet before she reaches her full height. The rendering should also maintain a relative

FIGURE 4.157 Portrait of Two Children *by John Badger (attributed), Boston, Massachusetts, 1755–1760. (Courtesy of Wikimedia Commons.)*

FIGURE 4.158 *Costume sketches of designs by Theoni V. Aldredge for the Orphans from the film Annie. (Watercolor. Sketches by Lindsay W. Davis, Columbia Pictures, 1982.)*

proportion to the other renderings in the show, as explained in an earlier section. Children have particular postures and movements that can be used in costume renderings, and of course, mastering the ability to draw a face includes an indication of age.

Certainly, if casting is completed before the rendering process, the sketch can reflect the appearance or type of actor in any given role. Manipulating and disguising appearance is in the arsenal of both costume designer and performer, and the sketch should indicate the *character's* body type, hair color, skin condition, and age. In some cases, when an actor is well known, the identity of the performer is required to be recognizable or consistent with a public image.

Designers who work with celebrity performers may find that the actor has approval over the costume design. Some actors are knowledgeable about costumes and can articulate in a conversation with the designer the way in which clothing can help to develop their idea of the character. They can see past a rendering and understand the actual design.

FIGURE 4.160 *Costume design for Diana Ross. (Marker on paper. Design by Bob Mackie, 1970s.)*

FIGURE 4.159 *Costume design for Al Pacino as Herod in* Salomé. *(Pencil and watercolor on drawing paper. Design by Zack Brown, Circle in the Square Theatre, New York, 1992.)*

It may be cynical, but it is also true that other actors are more focused on the portrait aspect of a costume sketch. Here in particular, designers may employ sketch artists. With this category of actor, it is wise to present a sketch where the face and body are portrayed in a flattering light.

In addition to fashion illustration, Richards[15] has also created many celebrity portraits, including posters and ads for theatre and musical performance. When asked how best to draw a star, he laughs and says, "If it's a woman, resemblance-wise, just eliminate

FIGURE 4.161 *Fashion illustration. (Gouache. Robert W. Richards, 2010.)*

Using painting and drawing techniques, the design sketch should include indications of the surface texture of fabric and other materials, as well as of any pattern or print. Some designers prefer to render meticulous scale reproductions of the actual print (if fabric has been sourced) or the desired fabric (see Figure 4.164). Others work more impressionistically, either as an artistic choice or as a matter of expediency; drawing and painting detailed fabric patterns is time-consuming, or they may not want to commit so specifically to a fabric that may not be available. But giving an indication of the color, pattern, and type of fabric is necessary so the shop knows which fabric to use. If a shopper or an assistant is locating fabric for the designer, they will need this information.

While the purist will prefer that all detail be painted in with fine brushes, the pragmatist will use all manner of media to render stripes, patterns, and special effects. Colored pencil, felt-tip marker, or gel pen on top of paint seem the simplest ways to indicate fur, pinstripes, flyaway hair, and small patterns.

Using pattern, one can enhance the illusion of dimension in a costume sketch. The way a pattern turns a corner or hangs in folds indicates shape and volume. Most patterns can be broken down into geometric shapes, in order to lay out the way they wrap around the figure, and then be completed more precisely (see Figures 4.169–4.171).

Fur is easily rendered using painting techniques like drybrushing, or with colored pencil. Of course, a designer needs to know the various types of fur—short-haired like mink, long-haired like fox, spotted, or striped—and often how to simulate them with synthetic materials. The kind of fur should be clear from the rendering, and is as simple as selecting a stroke length for the lines (see Figures 4.15 and 4.128).

Similarly, there are many kinds of feathers; the rendering should let the viewer see a difference between soft, full feathers like ostrich and stiffer or narrower feathers like pheasant. Again, varying the painting or drawing technique is key (see Figures 4.172 and 4.173).

Sheer fabrics like chiffon or lace reveal what lies beneath, whether that is anatomy or another fabric. When rendering a costume made of sheer fabric, a wash of paint is usually the easiest solution (see Figure 4.174). Just as the color of the fabric deepens in folds or when the fabric falls over itself in layers, use paint to build up a more intense color in shaded areas, while painting in glimpses of the body or the fabric below. For lace, using a pencil, thin brush, or gel pen, add an indication of the spirals or floral motifs common to lace.

A changeable fabric like iridescent taffeta can be rendered much as a sheer; if you examine fabric like this, the shadows are one color and the highlights another. Paint what you see. The

everything but the eyes, mouth, and hair. With women, you don't put in a lot of detail. With men you do. There are certain rugged things that identify them."

RENDERING FABRIC

For costume designers, our primary medium is fabric. Aside from human anatomy, the most important subject matter we must learn to render is fabric. A costume sketch tells the viewer what kind of fabric is used, what color, what pattern, how it responds to light, and how it drapes or moves—or doesn't drape or move.

In the creation of a costume, designers also use metal, plastic, fur, and leather, and, with advances in technology, high-tech materials and even light. The costume sketch must indicate where and how all these materials are employed.

Costume materials may echo the shape of the body or undergarments on which they are used; some fabrics and other costume elements are stiff and will take a structural shape of their own. These effects need to be communicated.

FIGURE 4.163 *Costume design for Masha in* The Three Sisters. *(Watercolor, pencil, pastel, and acrylic. Design by Vera Katharina DuBose, Longstreet Theatre, University of South Carolina, 2013.)*

FIGURE 4.162 *Costume design for Gilette in* The Game's Afoot. *(Design by Eduardo Sicango, Asolo Repertory Theatre, Sarasota, FL, 2013.)*

FIGURE 4.164 *Costume design for Desdemona in* Othello. *(Graphite, watercolor, and gouache on paper. Design by Alyssa Couturier-Herndon, University of Florida, 2015.)*

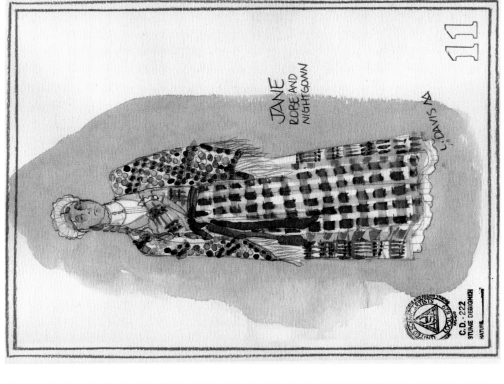

FIGURES 4.165 & 4.166 These renderings show two very different approaches to rendering checked fabric: one tightly painted, the other almost impressionistic. (left) Costume design for a Toy Shop Showgirl in The Music City Holiday Spectacular. (Graphite, watercolor, and gouache on watercolor paper. Design by Steven Stines, Gaylord Entertainment/Opryland, Nashville, TN, 2004.) (right) Costume design for Nicodemus in The Mystery of Irma Vep. (Graphite and watercolor. Design by Lindsay W. Davis, Actors Theatre of Louisville, KY, 1991.)

FIGURES 4.167 & 4.168 These renderings show similar floral patterned costumes; one rendered with traditional media, the other digitally. (left) Costume design for Giulietta in King for a Day. (Pencil sketch with Photoshop. Design by Court Watson, Alice Busch Opera Theatre, Glimmerglass Festival, NY, 2013.) (right) Costume design for Luisa in The Fantasticks. (Graphite, watercolor, and gouache on watercolor paper. Design by Steven Stines, Riverside Theatre, Florida, 2003.)

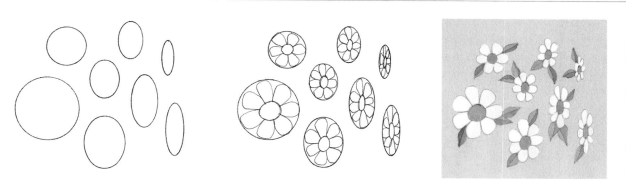

FIGURES 4.169–4.171 *A repeated pattern of daisies on a skirt begins as a series of circles (left). Viewed from the front, the shapes are round, but as they travel around the body, the shapes become ovals. (middle) Once the basic shapes are sketched in, the petals begin as spokes, and the angles can be figured out. (right) Then the actual flower can be fleshed out, and the effect is more accurate than drawing each flower as seen from a front view, which has a flattening effect.*

FIGURE 4.172 *Costume design for Ain't Misbehavin'. (Watercolor, gouache, and pencil on paper. Design by Steven Stines, Riverside Theatre, Florida, 2003.)*

FIGURE 4.173 *Costume design for Finale Showgirl in Paradis. (Design by Eduardo Sicango.)*

jacquard is another painting challenge and the solution is similar. If you look at a jacquard as it is draped into folds, the design is brighter or shinier than the background in one area and the reverse is true in the opposite direction. The design becomes a highlight in the sections that fold inward, and the background is the highlight as the fabric curves outward (see Figure 4.94). Shiny costumes like satin or lamé require large areas of highlights, and more contrast with the shadows (see Figure 4.58).

Costumes with metallic or jeweled elements are eye-catching on stage, precisely because they reflect light. The effect is actually quite simple to achieve on paper. It requires a small brush and a tube of white gouache, used to render random dots as points of light (see Figure 4.56). Logically, the highlights would be more densely concentrated on parts of the body that curve outward and catch the light (hips, bustline, or thighs, for instance), and scarcer in shadowed areas. Using broken lines, the rendering can convey the use of beading in a pattern or strip.

As skills develop, the designer can use the same techniques in a variety of colors to echo the multi-colored reflections of light on lamé or beading. Looking at design sketches by jewelers like Cartier or Tiffany, one can see how simply but effectively the artist has indicated the sheen of metal, the sparkle of gemstones, and the luminosity of pearls.

Opaque pens in white or metallic can also be easily employed to make dots on the rendering as points of light. A finely-sharpened colored pencil or a gel pen used to make cross marks gives the effect of a star filter in photography (but note that all the angles should be the same) (see Figure 4.87).

Rendering white costumes can be quite simple. Here, the designer should definitely consider either a half-tone paper or a background wash (see Figure 4.44). Unless the scenery is all white, rendering white costumes on white paper is deceptive in terms of the visual effect of the costume onstage. And in terms of rendering, there is nowhere to go! Working on a darker background, the designer works up from shadow to highlight.

FIGURE 4.174 *Costume design for Jorey Remus in* Love Nest. *(Gouache. Design by James Bidgood, Writers Stage Theatre, New York, 1963.)*

FIGURE 4.175 *Costume design for Cher. (Marker on paper. Design by Bob Mackie.)*

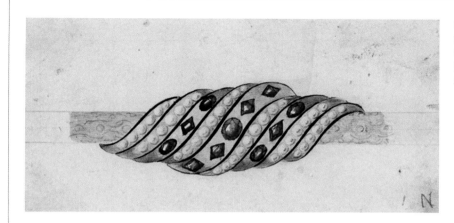

FIGURE 4.176 *Design for a bracelet for the firm of John Brogden, c. 1860s. (Pencil, watercolor, and ink on card. Design by Charlotte Isabella Newman. © Victoria and Albert Museum, London.)*

White gouache is a simple means of layering and building up the white of a costume, while indicating shadowed areas by using thinner coats of paint. The designer may wish to include areas of color indicating the way white reflects colored theatrical lighting.

RAPID RENDERINGS

Time is money, they say. In theatre, time is often *your* money. Designers are cautioned never to calculate their earnings per hour, given how time-consuming most costume design projects become. While costume designers often want to create the most beautiful renderings possible, in some cases deadlines require the focus to be on other responsibilities. Even so, there are techniques and media that allow good-quality renderings complete with all the necessary information.

Developing the ability to draw accurately but quickly is an important design skill. Before the 1980s, fashion illustrators were often dispatched to runway shows to capture images of clothing as it was modeled. Classic fashion illustrations of the mid-20th century are often beautiful, seemingly spontaneous images; these artists had to note both the essence of the design and any important details. A designer can sharpen these quick-draw skills by sketching from video or even TV shows as a rendering exercise. You may be surprised how much information you can capture, and how effectively, when drawing quickly. Of course, one key is to avoid overthinking the process. *Draw what you see.*

In combination with developing the ability to see and draw quickly, there are materials available that facilitate quick renderings. Dry media, or those which dry quickly, speed up the process for most designers, as does eliminating the need to mix color. Markers and colored pencil are the most popular means

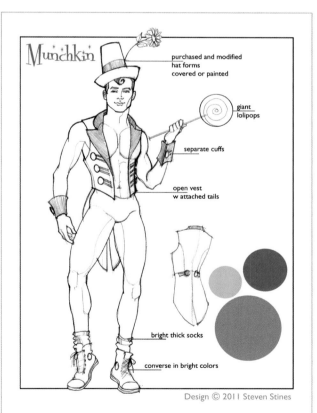

FIGURE 4.177 *Costume design for a Munchkin from* Wickedly Ever After. *(Pencil sketch and Photoshop. Design by Steven Stines. Choreography by Diogo de Lima, Project Lazarus, New Orleans, 2011.)*

FIGURE 4.178 *Costume designs for Depression Scene in* Swingin' on a Star. *For a scene using pulled costumes, this quick rendering gave an idea of the look. (Watercolor, gouache, and graphite on paper. Design by Steven Stines, Riverside Theatre, Florida, 2001.)*

of creating rapid costume sketches (see Figures 4.60 and 4.88). Markers in particular require that the artist work quickly. There are brands of marker that come with two different felt tips, a fine point at one end and a wider point at the other; this allows the designer to select the tip that produces the desired coverage or effect. Colored pencil is quick and easy to use as a rapid indication of color or texture: creating a fine art effect, though, takes time and skill. Dry pastels can be quite quick, but, as noted, are fragile and easily smeared.

In cases where time is very scarce, it seems perfectly acceptable to modify the traditional approach to the design rendering. Perhaps a line drawing in pencil or ink can be used to indicate silhouette and construction, with color swatches added to indicate palette (see Figure 4.177). Whether these are areas of paint or marker; paint swatches from the home improvement store; Pantone color chips; actual fabric swatches; or areas of

color applied with Photoshop to a scanned sketch; it is wise to include them in some relative proportion as they will be seen on the stage. In other words, for a red costume with blue and purple details, a larger red swatch with smaller areas of the additional colors would be in keeping with the final product.

Designer Jeanne Button[16] has told of being pressed for time on a project and using Dr. Ph. Martin's dyes to solve the problem. Working with an assistant, she soaked watercolor paper in plastic dish tubs of the diluted dyes so each sheet of paper was tinted the predominant color of a costume. She then drew her sketches in pencil and used white gouache to create highlights.

Goldstein[3] sketches in a smaller scale than many costume designers. "I started doing small sketches when I got out of grad school and found myself designing big shows, often with little time. I also started using colored pencils then (instead of paint) because I found I could sketch faster in that medium. And a four inch figure seems to be able to get away with less detail than a ten inch figure. The sketch becomes more about the silhouette and the color." (see Figure 4.90).

When time is short, depending on the nature of the production concept, photo research boards or computer collages may take the place of the sketch; this is much easier to do for contemporary shows, though period research may be collaged if the design will reproduce that research. Designers may also draw or paint details over photocopied reference material. For a bought or pulled production, the designer can style costume looks on a dress form or an actor, and photograph them. In the digital age, this becomes a very rapid way to disseminate information about possible costume options. Of course, this is not feasible when the costumes are to be built by the shop.

Regardless of the medium selected, there is one approach that will help save time when rendering a show; use an "assembly line" method of drawing and painting costume plates. Keep each design sketch at the same state of progress as you proceed. Finish all the drawing before beginning to apply color. Then apply like colors to each plate as you continue.

Begin with the flesh; for a costume designer, the color of skin is a crucial element of color relationships. In general, all skin tones are warm, but beyond that, the array of options is vast. Casting can affect the success of color choices for costumes, and applying skin tones to the sketches first will help in balancing other choices.

Some designers advocate moving next to white, as it tends to draw the eye more than any other color onstage. Moving from color to color and painting each article of clothing that will be that shade is an efficient use of time. Beyond time management, when the renderings are viewed as a whole, the designer can check the entire array as work continues. Are the colors balanced? Does any particular design draw the eye away from the whole? Where does the palette become monotonous and need an accent?

When the larger areas and background colors are completed, move on to pattern, details, and accessories. Not only does this approach help to organize your efforts, but it also keeps each sketch at a similar state of completion. Imagine having finished half of the plates to a detailed state and then running out of time, not having begun the other half. An assembly line worked for Henry Ford and it can work for the costume designer.

BODY TYPE

Determining a body shape appropriate for the character is part of the design process. **Prosthetics**, padding, and construction can create inflated body parts, from breasts to bellies, and should

FIGURE 4.179 *Alice Jennings in a beaded flapper dress: from* Brewster Magazine, *English, 1921. (Photo by Nickolas Muray. Courtesy of Wikimedia Commons.)*

FIGURE 4.180 *Betty Grable: pin-up for 20th Century Fox, 1943. (Photo by Frank Powolnoy. Courtesy of Wikimedia Commons.)*

FIGURE 4.181 *Elizabeth Taylor: studio publicity portrait, c. 1955. (Photographer unknown. Courtesy of Wikimedia Commons.)*

FIGURE 4.182 *Model in a knit dress with patterned tights. For the Durene Association of America, 1967. (Photographer unknown. Courtesy of Wikimedia Commons.)*

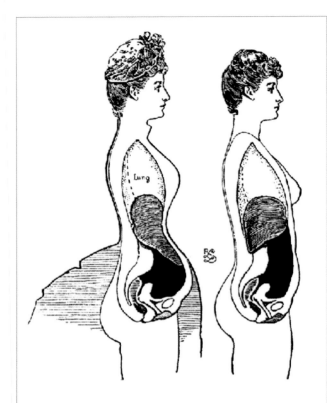

FIGURE 4.183 The tilting of the liver in certain cases of tight lacing. *(From the* New York Medical Journal, *1887.)*

The prevailing body type of any period must be acknowledged by the costume designer. Of course, actors dressed in a period silhouette face the same question as most people living in the actual period—do they have the ideal body for the time? And many of the tools available to achieve this ideal body are the same for the actor as for the historical figure. The difference is that contemporary actors have not grown up wearing garments like corsets that, over time, reshape the body; nor have they grown accustomed to the physical restrictions or distortions that result. Moreover, through the years, the human body has become larger, both vertically and horizontally. For this reason, actual period clothing seen in a museum seems almost miniature to modern eyes, and vintage clothing often will not fit the contemporary performer.

When rendering costume designs that require body modification, the designer faces the decision as to how precisely to portray that distortion. How small, reasonably speaking, can an actress's waist become using a corset? The safest bet may be be indicated in a sketch. This is a method of creating a character visually using costume and makeup. The actual casting can affect those decisions, of course. There is a limit to what can be achieved given anatomical reality.

Throughout history the body has been variously revealed or distorted by clothes. Part of costume history is differentiating between clothing that accepts the natural form of the body and clothing that creates modified shapes through the structure of a garment.

The ideal size and shape of the body also varies through time. In the 1920s, women were encouraged to be boyish, flat-chested flappers (see Figure 4.179). The 1940s offered the choice of pin-up girls or broad-shouldered Joan Crawford types (see Figure 4.180). In the 1950s, highly exaggerated hourglass curves were the goal (see Figure 4.181), supplanted in the 1960s by a return to the flat chest epitomized by Twiggy and other models (see Figure 4.182). Underwear, exercise, and plastic surgery have all been employed to modify the body into the desired shapes.

FIGURE 4.184 *Costume design for Jane in* Whatever Happened to Baby Jane? *(Design by Eduardo Sicango, Theatre Under the Stars, Houston, TX, 2002.)*

to acknowledge the change in silhouette that will be created by the costume, while at the same time acknowledging that a contemporary performer has not reshaped the anatomy over a lifetime to adhere to a period ideal (see Figures 4.94 and 4.98).

Body type is also a factor in casting, so costume designers learn to draw bodies and postures that are far from idealized, as well as eccentric faces (see Figures 4.184–4.186).

PREPARING FOR PRESENTATION

An important aspect of time management when creating renderings is allowing time to prepare the sketch for presentation. This is often more time-consuming than a novice designer expects. It entails everything from trimming the edges of sketches, to labeling, to attaching swatches. If the work is to be sent digitally, the time for scanning and formatting must be estimated and factored into the rendering schedule.

Swatches are generally viewed as a necessary element of the costume sketch as it moves into the shop. Sometimes these will be attached after the fact, particularly for a design that uses dyed or painted fabric. But including some indication of either the actual fabric or the kind of fabric the designer hopes to find is important in submitting costume designs for discussion and approval. Swatches should be neatly trimmed, and ideally included with an eye to their relative proportions as used in the costume. Having a huge swatch of trim next to a tiny swatch of the primary fabric is not an accurate indication of how these materials will be seen onstage (see Figures 4.140, 4.162, and 4.172).

As mentioned when discussing composition, the best approach is to leave space on the sketch for swatches; this avoids the conundrum of covering portions of the design with fabric samples. How to attach the swatches is a matter of personal taste, but remember that some methods are forever—glue will stick and staples leave holes. Paper clips, low-tack white tape, or drafting tape are more forgiving if you foresee moving or removing the

FIGURE 4.185 *Costume design for Leopold in* Her Seat Is Vacant. *(Watercolor. Design by Malgosia Turganska, short film, New York University, 2010.)*

FIGURE 4.186 *Costume design for Eddie in* Tango. *(Gouache, watercolor, and charcoal. Design by Cait O'Connor, Trinity Repertory Company, RI, 2012.)*

swatches. It may be useful to attach the swatches to a separate card that can then be easily clipped or taped to the sketch.

Scanning images allows the designer both to archive sketches and to send them digitally to any pertinent collaborators, including shops that may be bidding on the job or building the costumes. Working larger than 8½" × 11", as most costume designers do, requires learning how to piece together smaller scans (which is quite simple once the technique is learned) or having access to a large-format scanner. Carefully photographing sketches is another way to make them available for digital work, though a direct scan produces a higher quality image.

For better or worse, the presentation can affect a collaborator's opinions as much as the actual content. It conveys an idea of the designer's professionalism, organization, and command of the job. Poor design work is sometimes, unfortunately, camouflaged by slick presentation; good design work, even more unfortunately, can be derailed by poor presentation.

Directors tend to respond to presentations that are easy to follow, clear in intent, and perhaps have an element of the interactive. This may be as simple as making the swatches accessible to the touch. Ideally, the sketch itself will be protected behind vinyl or acetate. Although the designer may place sketches in some kind of portfolio, it is recommended that they also may be displayed as a unit, whether on a wall or on a table, so that the other designers and the director can view them as a whole, to see the scope of the design concept, the entire color palette, and the visual manifestation of the character relationships. Even when presenting designs in class, the designer should show work in as professional a manner as possible; class is a preparation for the "real world," which includes production meetings with collaborators.

WORKING AS A SKETCH ARTIST

> "Theoni Aldredge had four assistants, three of whom did nothing but draw; that's how much work she did."
> Lindsay W. Davis[14] from a telephone interview

Earning a living in the arts is not easy. Many theatre professionals spend long years building careers while also working at other jobs to pay the bills. Designers are luckier than actors in that we have

FIGURE 4.187 *Costume sketches of designs by Theoni V. Aldredge for the Orphans from the film* Annie. *(Watercolor. Sketches by Lindsay W. Davis, Columbia Pictures, 1982.)*

a range of skills that can be applied to other areas, and because there are costume-related jobs which can be a source of income while designing for little or no money to build a résumé and portfolio.

Working in costume shops or on wardrobe crews, working in rental houses, or assisting established designers can all be sources of financial stability as well as part of the apprenticeship aspect of design training. If a designer is skilled at rendering, there are other applications like illustration and graphic design, although these are also very competitive fields. Some costume designers employ **sketch artists**. Working as a sketch artist in costume design can be a useful step in establishing a career and earning a living.

As mentioned at the beginning of this chapter, some costume designers function as editors. In fashion, designers like Ralph Lauren and Calvin Klein work with a large staff of designers to ensure that a consistent aesthetic is applied to each season's collections. This is also not uncommon in movie costuming, beginning in the "golden age" of the 1930s.

While designers like Adrian and Walter Plunkett created their own sketches, the most famous movie costume designer, Edith Head, barely drew at all. According to Jay Jorgensen's book *Edith Head* (p. 200–201 and p. 364),[17] her office at Paramount employed a staff of sketch artists; not only did Head sign all their sketches, she also usually took credit for their work. For at least two movies, *Sabrina* and *The Sting*, she accepted Academy Awards for costumes she did not design. What Head did do quite successfully was to negotiate politics, soothe egos, and garner publicity—for the costumes and for herself.

The job duties of a sketch artist range widely, depending on the working methods and preferences of the designer. Some designers need a sketch artist to prepare presentational versions of their very specific designs, often provided to the sketch artist as drawings to be referred to in the creation of a glossy final product. Many film designers have an illustrator on their design staff because there are so many layers of approval and so many revisions required during the production process. The Costume Designers Guild, based in Los Angeles, recognizes Illustrators as a category distinct from Designers.

In theatre, a costume designer may also employ sketch artists, and the kind of work the sketch artists do and the nature of their contribution varies depending on the working methods and personality of the designer. For some designers, using sketch artists is a pragmatic solution to a heavy workload. Some projects are so large that rendering or even designing the entire piece is

too much for a single individual, and the sketch artist completes some of the rendering process, or may be hired to actually design some of the costumes. For others, it is a means of most effectively communicating their own design ideas when rendering is not their forté. Some designers are stylists and simply don't draw, but find themselves in a professional situation where renderings are necessary.

And then there is the not-so-secret secret: that some sketch artists are the de facto designers of costumes attributed to other, better-known or more experienced designers. In other words, the sketch artist is essentially doing design work, with or without receiving credit. Bob Mackie, Lindsay W. Davis, Martin Pakledinaz, and Gregg Barnes all spent time in their careers as sketch artists whose work was attributed to other designers. Those designers may or may not be generous in giving credit where it is due, but the astute viewer may be able to recognize the style of the sketch artist regardless of the signature.

Davis was one of the sketch artists employed by Patricia Zipprodt and by Theoni Aldredge, who, in the 1970s and 1980s, was one of the most successful designers on Broadway, also working in film. Davis[14] says, "For [the movie version of] *Annie*, she didn't even go to California. She was doing *Dreamgirls* [on Broadway] at the time. I was in California for six months. She said 'My allegiance is to [*Dreamgirls* director] Michael Bennett,' because her work for his *A Chorus Line* had been both financially lucrative and important to her career.

"Marty [Pakledinaz] did all the principals for *Annie*." Davis explains. "I did all the orphans, I just did children. Marty was working on *Dreamgirls* too, so I went to California. Theoni had that many projects."

Using a minimal amount of reference material that Aldredge provided, "we would do line drawings. She would make a few changes, then after that she would choose the fabrics, and then we'd paint from the fabrics she picked. She gave us maximum flexibility about how we would approach it and she would make certain changes. She couldn't draw as well as we could."

But Davis continues,[14] "I don't want to sound like I was claiming the design as mine. I was very, very grateful for that job. Of all the people who have had 'factories,' design factories, she probably had the most successful one because she had great people working for her." According to Davis, assisting and sketching for an extremely successful designer aided in developing an understanding of what was possible at that level. "Theoni bought almost nothing, everything was always custom made. We got so much experience with the beaders and the fabric painters."

The flip side of working as a sketch artist is that some designers refuse to acknowledge that contribution. "I've drawn three whole operas at the Met, major, major work," says Davis. "Twice I was put under a gag order not ever to tell anyone that I did the work . . . They made one of my sketches into the poster for the show. The designer said 'you cannot tell anyone, and I'm going to sign the sketch.'"

Should you elect to take a job as a sketch artist, be prepared to negotiate some kind of credit if that is possible, or an amount of freedom to pursue your own projects. In many cases, though, drawing for a designer is a means of advancing a design career, seeing first-hand how the process works at a higher level, and earning an income.

WHAT COMES AFTER . . .

Fine art is purchased and placed on the wall of a home or museum, hopefully providing pleasure or provoking thought. But it has no practical purpose beyond its own existence. The costume rendering, when it is drawn and painted and labeled and swatched and approved, still has a job to do. As the designs move through the costume shop en route to the stage, the designer, the draper, the director, and the actors continue to refer to that "pretty picture," as the costume takes form and, finally, makes its appearance onstage as an intrinsic part of theatrical collaboration.

> "The function of sketching in the design process is to allow us to dream."
>
> Ann Hould-Ward[4] from an email interview

On a Personal Note

Show is an adjective. Business is a noun.

QUESTIONS

- If a designer does not have well-developed skills in drawing and painting, what are some ways to effectively communicate the ideas for the design with collaborators and the costume shop?

- What are the purposes of the costume sketch in the design process?

- What is the most important aspect of a costume sketch for the designer? For the director? For the actor? For the costume shop?

FIGURE 4.188 Costume for a Dancer *by J. Howell Russell, 1894. (© Victoria and Albert Museum, London.)*

NOTES

1. Elizabeth Burdick, Peggy C. Hansen, and Brenda Zanger, eds, *Contemporary Stage Design U.S.A.* (Connecticut: Wesleyan University Press, 1974).
2. Dunya Ramicova, email interview with author, January 22, 2015.
3. Jess Goldstein, email interview with author, January 19, 2015.
4. Ann Hould-Ward, email interview with author, January 26, 2015.
5. Carrie F. Robbins, telephone interview with author, January 25, 2015.
6. Annie O. Cleveland, email interview with author, January 21, 2015.
7. April McCoy, email interview with author, February 14, 2015.
8. Stacey Galloway, email interview with author, February 15, 2015.
9. Amanda Whidden, telephone interview with author, February, 2013.
10. Judanna Lynn, telephone interview with author, January 16, 2015.
11. Carrie F. Robbins, email interview with author, February 15, 2015.
12. Fred Voelpel, lecture to design class, New York University, 1984.
13. Rafael Jaén, email interview with author, January 14, 2015.
14. Lindsay W. Davis, telephone interview with author, January 18, 2015.
15. Robert W. Richards, telephone interview with author, January 27, 2015.
16. Jeanne Button, lecture to costume history class, New York University, 1984.
17. Jay Jorgensen, *Edith Head* (Philadelphia: Running Press, 2010).

FIGURE 5.1 *Featured in this image is the character of Akhnaten in the opera of the same name by composer Philip Glass. This image demonstrates the collaboration between the design team in order to create an elevated space with back lighting, which illuminates the silhouette of the actor's body through a fabric that transmits light. The performer also collaborated by using LED rings that he could control during the action to coordinate with particular moments in the music. (Akhnaten. Composer: Philip Glass. Performer: Nicholas Tamagna. Conductor: Arthur Fagen. Costume design by Linda Pisano, Scenic design by Doug Fitch, Lighting design by Todd Hensley, Stage direction by Candace Evans. Produced at the Indiana University Jacobs School of Music Opera & Ballet Theatre.)*

CHAPTER 5

COSTUME COLLABORATION

Linda Pisano

COLLABORATION

Defining collaboration as it relates to the work of the costume designer is complex. The number of people that a costumer must work with on a daily or per-production basis can be staggering. From initial contracts with artistic directors, company managers, and production managers, to directors, design teams, dramaturges, costume personnel, vendors, performers, and stage managers, costume designers work with a wide range of individuals to bring their work to fruition.

In its most simplistic form, collaboration is the relationship between two people working toward the same objective. Etymology of the term **collaboration** leads us to the Latin roots for *together* and *to work*. More specifically, collaboration is the manner of working with others with diverse visions and processes toward a unified outcome.

Collaboration requires preparation and compromise; it requires skills in communication, quick decision making and problem solving, and the ability to listen well. In our fast-paced industry we often overlook the importance of taking and making time to have face-to-face meetings, telephone calls, or Skype conversations regarding ideas and questions about a production. Not only do these meetings create the groundwork for strong designs, but they also make the process of designing more meaningful and rewarding. It is all too common for the ease of digital transmission to remove the human aspect from our very human discipline.

Collaboration is the key for every theatre practitioner. Strong collaborative relationships among members of a creative team lead to more invigorating and inspiring discussions and greater investment from all parties in producing a powerful production. This chapter will outline some of the skills, processes, and people involved in making the collaborative journey of the costume designer successful, sustainable, and meaningful.

COMMUNICATION IN COLLABORATION

> "The single biggest problem with communication is the illusion that it has taken place."
> George Bernard Shaw,[1] Playwright

Communication is the key to any successful relationship. This holds true in both our personal and our professional spheres. Costume designers must not underestimate the power of communication in conveying their ideas in such a way as to evoke enthusiasm, trust, and commitment from the many people involved in a particular production. The *Oxford English Dictionary's* list of etymological sources for the word "communication" lists this definition: "the fact of having something in common with another person or thing (late 13th or early 14th century in Old French)."[2] This seems particularly fitting for our industry, which attracts a diverse group of thinkers. Looking at communication from this **vantage point** means that despite differing perspectives, we must find common ground upon which to build our teamwork through language and visual research.

For our purposes, successful communication can be defined as a transfer of ideas and thoughts with clarity and interest that arouses a curiosity and enthusiasm resulting in action. Action is the result of effective communication. If costume designers present their ideas in a particular way, they can provide a vision that results in others contributing their time and talents to making those ideas a reality. Indeed, the enthusiastic action steps that

FIGURE 5.2   *There are many facets and steps involved in collaboration to create the costumes for a production. Figure 5.2 demonstrates the work of a costume department in not only interpreting and executing the construction based on the designer's costume rendering (on the left), but also the process of ensuring the fit of the garment and additional pieces. This costume for the character of The Genie includes not only the layers of a stylized garment, but also custom-built ballet boots, gloves, and a foam headpiece. The costume will need to last through many seasons as ballet is often remounted, yet it must be able to fit many dancers with minimal modification over its lifetime. The dancer must be able to move unhindered and with complete confidence in their safety. Communication between designer, costume department, choreographer, and performers is critical during the execution stage with particularly complex and/or unusual pieces. (BalletMet Columbus original ballet production of Aladdin. Choreography by Gerard Charles with special choreography by Jimmy Orrante and Justin Gibbs, Script by Steven Anderson, Costume design by Linda Pisano, Scenic design by Dan Gray. Costumes created by the BalletMet Costume Department.)*

result from effective communication make for some of the most satisfying collaborative experiences.

Communication Skills

Collaboration is only as effective as the communication of those involved; hence a discussion of a variety of communication skills is necessary to understand this process.

Developing Verbal Communication Skills

The way in which we articulate ourselves elicits an immediate response from those with whom we speak. For better or for worse, people will assess us, even judge us, by our regional dialect, accent, or speech impediment. Without denying our self-identifying traits, it is possible to consider ways in which we might best verbalize our ideas to a broad audience.

Some important priorities to consider before presenting our ideas include:

- Find confidence and take pride in your work. A successful designer has taken time to develop truly meaningful research and sketches; that effort is deserving of time and respect from the viewer. Never apologize for your work, your drawings, or your nervousness.

- Let your work speak for itself. Avoid overly detailed descriptions early on in the discussion. If the detail is already in the research or the sketch, it is more effective to allow your audience time to study your research and/or your renderings and then ask questions.

- Focus on the storytelling. Demonstrate through the sketches and research how the costumes will tell the story in the context of the action of the production. Allow the details of individual costumes to be expressed in a more focused group meeting, or address them in your answers to the questions you will inevitably be asked about the costumes. Speak to the art and the overarching themes of how the costumes fit into the world.

- Be prepared. Always be prepared.

- Understand your audience. Will you be speaking with a small group or a large room filled with people? How familiar are you with the group? Is the room filled with producers, a board of directors, and an artistic director, or are only the director and other designers present? Are you standing in a formal presentation setting or around a table? The more formal the setup, the less intimate the presentation will feel to the audience. Regardless of the intimacy or formality of the presentation, a designer should be prepared to describe their ideas with clarity, efficiency, and enthusiasm.

- Practice your presentation and have note cards if needed. If you feel uncomfortable speaking in front of a large group or in formal settings, learning to overcome, or at least manage, your nervousness is essential. Many people find that writing the ideas that are most important to convey on index cards or in some bulleted format helps them to stay focused on their task. Writing every word down in a speech is antithetical to the process, as you risk reading, rather than sharing, your presentation. Finding the spontaneity and the joy of presenting your ideas will make for a more rewarding experience.

Developing Visual Communication Skills

More experienced designers have learned that effective visual communication is as much the result of the designer learning how to "see" as it is providing visual imagery for others to look at. The more designers are able to view the world from a variety of vantage points, the more effective they will be in creating unique and poignant choices as they work. Learning to "see" the world requires taking time from our schedules to experience art, performance, and nature, and generally observe life as it moves about us.

Students of design should spend a good portion of their studies in learning how to research effectively and to express their ideas through visual means. Even early-career designers

can schedule an hour or two a week to seek out and compile a bibliography of books, paintings, photography, websites, and other reliable resources for costume research. When possible, they could fit in an hour or two at a museum, local exhibit, or archive. The more references that designers uncover, the greater the breadth of sources they have upon which to draw when developing ideas for a project. Furthermore, it is expected that a designer keeps a journal that doubles as a sketchbook and a place for taking notes or recording thoughts on impulse. Some designers keep a journal for each production they work on, while others keep an entire library of journals from month to month or year to year. There are no hard and fast rules for a designer's journal. The objective should be to fill it with any and all quick sketches or more elaborate plans that may have absolutely nothing to do with a current project, but allow one to express ideas as they come, and not to forget them. Journals are also effective tools when visiting libraries, museums, and nature. The more one sketches and writes about what one sees, the more one retains and absorbs the surrounding world.

Once designers develop the aforementioned habits, they will find inventive ways to share their research and their sketches with each creative team on each project. Communication by visual means will become comfortable and efficient. Sketching in a journal on a daily basis develops a sense of spontaneity in drawing style, with a focus on those elements of the design that are particularly important to the storytelling.

The skills of a master painter are not necessary in order to be an inspiring designer. One simply needs to be prepared to have research and sketches that are commensurate with the ideas being communicated. If one's illustrations do not provide adequate clarity, then one may augment the sketches with research that defines the details, the color palette, and the silhouette. As long as designers have the knowledge, skill, and passion for locating and sifting through visual research, they have the foundation tools needed to communicate their ideas effectively.

Developing Social Communication Skills

Despite our love for the performing arts, most who have chosen a profession in design have little or no desire for a career on the stage. Being on stage and having strong social skills in communicating ideas, however, are two very different things. Social communication has much in common with performance, but with different objectives. Some basic groundwork to consider includes the development of a sense of sincerity and honesty when conveying one's thoughts and ideas about one's work, listening objectively and intently, making eye contact, and confidence in a comfortable and casual way to ensure affability and approachability. A creative team needs to shed the boundaries of social formalities quickly through honest, meaningful, and collegial rapport. Many companies will have a meet-and-greet for the creative team to get to know one another; others will have the entire group meet for a two- or three-day retreat, where they share meals and social time between work sessions, and will often read through the script, **libretto**, or score together. These opportunities should be embraced, as they help to establish creative camaraderie and potentially long-term professional relationships among team members.

The designer's job on the creative team is to provide a specialized skill in analyzing characters from a visual perspective. The psychology of dress is profound; each culture and each time period has a very specific social order regarding what and how clothing is worn. The designer has mastered where to look and what to look for in their research, and can relate it to individual characters within a story while considering the overall aesthetic of the ensemble—for instance, a particular stylization of silhouette to emulate a particular art movement, or the respect of a classical ballet tradition. Whatever the production, this specialized skill is unique in the group and requires a positive and hands-on approach to sharing that knowledge with ease and pleasantness. It does not require a know-it-all demeanor, or pontification about one's knowledge, but rather an enthusiasm to share what one has learned about a subject and listening to others' thoughts and ideas about the topic. Students of design are often surprised to learn that many seasoned directors have an extensive knowledge of costume history and the psychology of dress, but reserve sharing their expertise as they enjoy seeing what young designers bring to the table as part of the collaboration.

Presentation of Self

As costume designers we are quite aware of what clothing we wear and how we wear it. Yet designers may sometimes be unaware of how they are perceived by others. Clothing becomes a part of our self-identification and self-expression. When meeting with a new creative team, collaborating with a new director, or presenting for a group of producers and a company, it is important that we convey a sense of professionalism and trust. Walking into a meeting looking frazzled, disheveled, or careless, risks giving the impression that a designer does not respect the creative team or the project. Whatever our style and however we express ourselves through clothing, we should provide a look that is thoughtful, clean, and exudes a sense of being well prepared.

After all, if costume designers are unable to dress themselves effectively, how can they be trusted to dress others?

Students of performance design should have many opportunities to engage in group discussions, meet new people, and have professional interview experiences. These are significant opportunities for developing self-confidence. Meeting new people and conversing about our work provides opportunities for us to be introspective about how we and our ideas are perceived. Do we find that we dominate the conversation? Does our shy quietness come across as arrogance? How do we find the best balance between listening and understanding? Costume design students and emerging designers must take the time to receive feedback on how they interact with other professionals in conversations and presentations. This feedback should include personal exchange, clarity in articulating oneself verbally, and our outward appearance in terms of professional demeanor.

Here are some questions a student designer might begin to consider as they work on new collaborative projects:

1. Expectations:
   — What are the expectations of my role in this team?
   — With what are the producer and director entrusting me?
   — What do I expect from myself as a professional?
   — Would I hire me to do this job? Why?

2. Trust:
   — Do my words and my communication style communicate a sense of trustworthiness and confidence?
   — Do my research and renderings demonstrate a strong sense of preparedness?
   — Am I providing honest and clear answers to questions?
   — Am I approachable and pleasant to collaborate with?

3. Organization and Commitment:
   — Am I on time?
   — Am I flustered or disorganized in my discussions and/or presentations?
   — Is my work organized and presented in a clear and cohesive way?

THE ARTISTIC TEAM: COLLABORATIVE ROLES

It is vital that the artistic team work together to create a cohesive and successful production. The following is a summary of the key members of an artistic team, who will all need to collaborate with the costume designer.

FIGURES 5.3–5.5 *The three images from La Traviata demonstrate the collaboration of an artistic team in creating images that express storytelling through visual composition. The approach to the production overall was to reimagine the story with Violetta, like other female characters in her sphere, as a butterfly. There was a decision that it would be a merging of contemporary and late 19th century aesthetic in the visual style of the scenic and costume world. The lighting practicals were also part of this post-modern sensibility. (top) The monochromatic palette selected for Act I evokes a sense of sameness in the world in which Violetta moves. (middle) A brighter and more sensual world is depicted at a later party where Violetta is wrongly accused and begins her descent into her tragic demise. (bottom) Falling between the action shown in the previous scenes, this is starkly different in terms of color, pattern, and texture. A tranquil, subdued and quiet haven is created in which Violetta has escaped her world with the man for whom she has fallen in love. (La Traviata. Music by Giuseppe Verdi with libretto by Francesco Maria Piave. Conductor: Joseph Rescigno. Choreography by Rosa Mercedes, Costume design by Linda Pisano, Scenic design by Cameron Anderson, Lighting design by Patrick Mero, Stage direction by Jeffrey Buchman. Produced at the Indiana University Jacobs School of Music Opera & Ballet Theatre.)*

Director

The **director** leads the overall artistic vision and approach to a particular production. Their work with the actors, the design team, and any other applicable roles such as the choreographer or musical director, will ideally all come together in a unified and evocative performance. The director's role is to "see the big picture" and lead the whole team in a process that preserves the integrity of the underlying themes and ideas that are to be the focus of the production. Many directors hire designers that they especially enjoy collaborating with and will ensure that they work with them often. It is important for designers to foster strong artistic relationships with directors in order to create their most successful work and safeguard their career interests.

Artistic Director

The **artistic director** may or may not also be the producer of a company. However, in the capacity of artistic director they are the person who selects a particular director and design team for a production or a season. In many companies the artistic director finalizes a season of titles that aligns with the core mission of the organization, and works with the director to define the parameters of how an approach to a particular production will work with the overall season. The artistic director may attend rehearsals and provide feedback to the director. Like a producer, an artistic director is not only interested in the mission of their company, but also in the community that they serve, and consequently may have a particular perspective on how the style of a production is perceived by their audiences.

Scenic Designer

Aside from the director, the **scenic designer** may work the most closely with a costume designer in the early stages of artistic development. Their role is to create the environment in which the characters will live. They will work to create the parameters of this world: that is, they will create the environment based upon a series of values and ideas that the script and/or the director suggest are most important to the storytelling. For example, a director may choose to place a Shakespeare play in a world that has experienced an apocalypse. The director and the designers would need to determine what that society values. Are they low on water or food? Whatever is of value to the characters becomes important to the visual theme and then all other attributes of the world travel on either side of that commodity. This value will inform what the characters wear, what the clothing is made of, and how it is worn. Collaboration with the scenic designer is ongoing throughout opening night.

Lighting Designer

With increasingly sophisticated advances in lighting technology over the past several decades, the role of the **lighting designer** has become paramount in the development of the world of the play early on in the process. In the 21st century their contribution is no longer tertiary, coming in during the last steps of the artistic process, but rather as a co-creator in the early stages of developing the approach to a production design. The work of the lighting designer can have an incredible impact on costumes, from the perception of color by an audience to the transmission of light through a fabric at a dramatic moment in the action. The impact of effective communication between a costume designer and a lighting designer should not be underestimated and should be fostered through meetings and the sharing of ideas as they develop.

Sound Designer

Aside from microphone and mic pack placement, costume designers rarely spend much time in direct collaboration with a **sound designer**. This does not mean that sound does not have an artistic contribution to the costume design and visa-versa; indeed, the sound of a woman's heels clicking across a raked wooden deck or the sound of a large taffeta skirt rustling in a silent moment can either break or make the impact that a character's action has in a scene. The sound designer is an excellent place to start the conversation with the director about how those elements may or may not work with the storytelling.

Projection Designer

A relatively new member of the artistic team, the **projection designer**, like the lighting designer, is an important part of the initial approach to creating the physical world of the play. Their work impacts on every design area to differing degrees. Interaction with the costume designer is usually minimal except when costumes become a surface for projection. If this is the case, the costume designer and projection designer must communicate about everything from the composition of the textile chosen, to the surface texture, and to the color and pattern. Unique and exciting opportunities can arise from this sort of collaboration. Problem solving and brainstorming through trial and error are to be expected, so planning and preparing for some time just

FIGURE 5.6 *This image of a Parisian bar in the late 19th century illustrates close collaboration between costume, lighting and the projection/production designer in order to coordinate the director's vision for recreating the world in which Vincent Van Gogh painted. Careful attention is given to matching colors in the fabrics, the painted scenery, the lighting, and the projected painting. Moreover, this is a new work with the composer and librettist in residence during the design phase and the rehearsal process. This meant that changes in dialogue, music, transitions, and movement were routine and required constant communication between the artistic team and the production departments. (World Premier of new opera Vincent. Composer: Bernard Rands. Librettist: J. D. McClatchy. Conductor: Arthur Fagen. Stage direction by Vince Liotta, Production & Projection design by Barry Steele, Costume design by Linda Pisano. Produced at the Indiana University Jacobs School of Music Opera & Ballet Theatre.)*

to play with fabric under projection should be built into the schedule early on. There may also be occasion when one or more costumes may need to match the costumes in the image being projected. Under these circumstances it is important to agree upon color early on, bearing in mind that projection requires a palette of light and costume utilizes a palette of pigment, creating a slightly different effect on the interpretation of color on stage.

Composers and/or Playwrights of New Works

Working on a **new work** can be simultaneously thrilling and challenging. Some **composers** and **playwrights** are encouraged by the commissioning company to be a strong voice in the production process from inception through to opening.

Other companies ask the director and designers to take the lead in producing the new work and the director becomes the liaison between the composer/playwright and the artistic team. Whatever the framework of the process, there are some fundamental similarities with all situations. For example, the costume designer will need to stay flexible regarding changes to the score or the script. Characters may come and go, scenes may be cut or added, and directorial approaches may change. As long as the costume department and the production management have clearly outlined a schedule of deadlines, budget parameters, labor availability/costs in regards to scope and scale, as well as other important management issues, then the costume designer, working within that outline, should be able to embrace a certain degree of flexibility in the artistic choices as they relate to the costume design. Before a designer accepts a contract for a new work, especially if they have never worked with new plays before, it is important to investigate thoroughly the schedule, policies, labor, budget, and practices of the company before accepting the contract. New works require a designer to jump in and take on a great deal of unknowns. If a designer does not feel committed to, compelled by, or interested in this process, it is better to pass up the opportunity and move on to something else.

Choreographer

The **choreographer's** collaboration with the costume designer takes a similar priority to that of the director. In musical theatre and especially in contemporary dance or ballet, the choreographer's input is vital to a successful costume design. Aside from obvious movement and safety concerns for the dancers, which are paramount to the design and construction of the garment, the choreographer often takes a major role in determining the style and silhouette of certain costumes, since they directly affect the art of the dancer and the choreographer. The costume designer, along with the costume makers, should be in continual communication with the choreographer throughout the build process regarding fabrics, fit, and rehearsal pieces. Many

choreographers appreciate attending fittings. This should be according to company or costume department policies and the comfort level of the performer and the designer.

Fight Director

Like the choreographer, the **fight director** will have important input into certain attributes of the costume design. The first areas of interest to a fight director will be the weapons and their holders (such as sword belts, baldrics, and holsters), as well as the shoes planned for the performers. The most effective communication between a fight director and a costume designer takes the form of questions. The fight director should be completely aware of shoe styles, capes, coats, headwear, or anything that could endanger the safety of a performer or impede the planned action and movement. The costume designer should proactively seek out as much information as possible regarding the style and use of weapons, belts, holsters and so forth, along with information about who oversees the maintenance, fittings, and budget of the weaponry and weapon accessories. In some companies the fight director may oversee weapons; in others it may be the prop department; or it may be costume crafts, depending on the expertise of the personnel. One of the most important parts of collaboration between the fight director and

FIGURE 5.7 *This collage of rough sketches expresses how a designer and a choreographer brainstorm. In these representative sketches, the designer is quickly sketching ideas as the choreographer discusses thoughts about possible characters that might appear in a new ballet based on the story of Alice in Wonderland. The pencil sketches are not meant to be commitments to any particular idea, but rather impulses that might generate other ideas or directions in the collaborative thinking about the world of the story. (BalletMet Columbus original ballet production of Alice in Wonderland. Choreography by Gerard Charles, Script by Steven Anderson, Costume design by Linda Pisano.)*

the costume designer is access to fittings where the weapons and accessories will be fit with the final or near-final costume and accouterments. Costume designers should be very clear on when relevant pieces are due in rehearsals so that the performers can have adequate time to ensure safety in all pieces while actively engaged in choreographed movement.

BRAINSTORMING: EFFECTIVE DEVELOPMENT OF IDEAS

Like collaboration, **brainstorming** is the process of coming together with other experts or advisors in a discipline to consider issues and ideas. Brainstorming usually implies critical evaluation of a particular situation or idea and ways to resolve a conflict or something that is not working. So if collaboration is defined as working together, then brainstorming might be considered a tool to be used in the collaboration process. It involves confident and forthright approaches from all participants, utilizing best practices in an intensive discussion or series of discussions.

In Stephen Covey's book *The Seven Habits of Highly Effective People*,[3] he discusses in-depth strategies (or habits) which help people to be strong and influential communicators. *Habit 6: Synergize* is particularly applicable to our collaborative brainstorming processes when creating a production.

Covey's *Habit 6: Synergize*

"To put it simply, synergy means 'two heads are better than one.' Synergize is the habit of creative cooperation. It is teamwork, open-mindedness, and the adventure of finding new solutions to old problems. But it doesn't just happen on its own. It's a process, and through that process, people bring all their personal experience and expertise to the table. Together, they can produce far better results than they could individually. . . . When people begin to interact together genuinely, and they're open to each other's influence, they begin to gain new insight. The capability of inventing new approaches is increased exponentially because of differences. Valuing differences is what really drives synergy."

Stephen R. Covey[3] from *The Seven Habits of Highly Effective People*

When meeting with one or more of your production team to have a brainstorming session, whether in person, electronically, or by telephone, it will help to consider the following:

- Make the time. Although you may need to schedule a beginning and ending time, make sure you plan the meeting for a time when you will not be interrupted or rushed. Include it in your schedule so that nothing else gets in the way.

- Be prepared. Have any sketches, research, or paperwork with you to discuss challenges or issues that need to be resolved. Write out your questions and topics of discussion if you think you may forget them.

- Practice listening. Listening is the key to understanding someone else's viewpoint. Ask them about their ideas, but avoid making comparisons between your ideas and theirs. Each person on the team deserves time to be heard.

- Make notes. Walk away from the session with notes and take a few minutes immediately after you leave the meeting to write down your response to the discussion. What stands out as most important or key to your next steps? Take time to incubate the ideas and follow up with any questions after a day or two.

EFFECTIVE USE OF RESEARCH

Cultivating a successful and fulfilling career as a costume designer requires that one embrace the process of research. Research topics for the designer range from fine arts, anthropology, textiles, and design, to history, psychology, and social and religious traditions throughout the world. Given the impossibility of deeply mastering such a broad range of subjects and all of their potential implications for costume design, it follows that *how* a designer researches can be almost as important as *what* they research. One must also consider conceptual research—sometimes referred to as "evocative" research—that stimulates the designer's impulse to create.

For effective collaboration with your team, research must be presented in a way that is accessible and relevant for a given production. If a designer is working long distance, sometimes creating a PDF of a PowerPoint can provide the director with a quick reference via email, or that same PowerPoint can be produced at high resolution via an online storage site like iCloud or Dropbox. But although digital images can provide a wide range of visual resources, in face-to-face meetings a set of printed images and/or books with strong color visuals lends itself more readily to browsing, conversation, and thoughtful reflection on the research, just as picking up a book in a library or bookstore entices the reader to turn pages and browse the contents for further inspiration. Designers will often add research images to their renderings to provide a frame of reference for the sketch and to offer the director and costume department a variety of lenses through which to view a particular costume.

A word about digital images: resolution is crucial. Be certain that images are not only taken from a reliable source, but that they transfer to the digital or print medium. Clarity should be paramount after content, and images should not be torqued or skewed. Take the time to learn extensively about transferring images to presentation programs like PowerPoint, inserting them into documents, attaching them to emails, or uploading them to various sites for sharing. Printed images should be in full color, well laid out on the page, and of a size that is large enough to view from a couple of feet away. Labeling is very helpful, whether it is laid out in the document, printed, or clearly handwritten. Be sure that spelling is correct and penmanship is legible.

Thoughts on Digital Images

- Don't rely on the thumbnail image from a search engine in your presentation. Always go directly to the site and get the highest resolution image possible. Thumbnails do not transfer or print with a high resolution and therefore look unprofessional.

- When re-sizing an image in presentation programs like PowerPoint, always enlarge from the corner or by using the tool bar; otherwise images can become distorted.

- Emailing presentations such as PowerPoint can be precarious. It may be best to save the presentation as a PDF and mail it in this format. If using storage sites like Dropbox, it is also good to compress the file and save as a PDF. This method allows others to open it easily on a mobile device such as a tablet or smart phone, and preserves the integrity of the layout of images that you have created within the presentation.

Place and Time

A director or choreographer may or may not have a strong understanding of historical silhouettes. With experience, a designer can gauge this knowledge in the first meetings about the script. Some directors and choreographers will readily admit to a lack of experience with period costumes, while others may have a strong sensibility in the area. Either way, it is useful for costume designers to utilize their research to clearly outline notable

attributes of a particular period and how they are relevant to some or all of the costumes designed. Occasionally a designer must be specific in defining the evolution of a period as well. For example, it may not be enough simply to refer to the decade of the 1920s; the nuances evident in the evolution of men's and women's fashions between 1920 and 1929 is significant; not to mention socioeconomic class, location, and further considerations about who wore what and how they wore it. Thus it is of the utmost importance that designers provide consistent research throughout their presentation, unless the time period is still under discussion.

Mood and Spirit

Presentation can be everything. The research presentation cannot simply demonstrate a particular time or place, but must also give the sensibility of the mood and spirit of a genre, a production approach, or of the characters. Provide the director with research images that elicit an emotion or evoke the milieu of the play or dance. Offering shallow, trite, or animated images as research for a dramatic, tragic, or otherwise serious genre can be detrimental to the integrity of the designer's work and will diminish the trust a director or choreographer has in the collaborative process.

Color

Swatches of fabric in early meetings are not always possible, nor are they necessarily important at this stage. Providing a strong sense of color through research images, existing paintings, or even prints of textiles can sometimes be far more influential. A swatch of fabric should be carefully considered before being presented to a director as an option if the designer has no intention of using that particular textile quality but is only referring to color. Our tactile senses are too strong to keep from being influenced by the fabric itself. Color is often considered to be the most powerful element of design as it has a physiological impact on the viewer; hence the designer should focus on communicating the color in a variety of sources, unless they can secure the exact desired fabric.

Other elements such as line, mass, texture, and pattern can also be effectively communicated by referring to images, paintings, and prints. Unless something highly unusual is requested in terms of texture, or the costume department is expected to manufacture something specific, swatches with texture and/or pattern can be introduced later in the design process, perhaps after initial silhouettes have been discussed.

EFFECTIVE USE OF DRAWINGS AND RENDERINGS

Not all designers are illustrators. Some excellent designers simply have little or no skill in the area of drawing. Although this can be a disadvantage for young designers to be hired on portfolio alone, this should not sway a talented early-career designer from developing creative ways to effectively express their ideas in two-dimensional form. One of the most effective visual communication tools is providing a sense of storytelling through research and some sort of rough sketches. Outlined below are some fundamental terms used for various steps in the illustration process. Young designers are encouraged to consider how they can successfully utilize their strengths in research to augment their sketches and renderings if illustrating the human form in costume is not a skill they possess.

Thumbnail Sketches

These are small, quick sketches that are particularly helpful for the designer to work through ideas. It is a form of storyboarding in a sketchbook, using little or no erasure; indeed, designers often find that working in pen keeps the **thumbnails** raw and intuitive.

FIGURE 5.8 *This example of a preliminary costume sketch of the character Violetta in Act III of the opera* La Traviata *by Verdi provides both a front and back view of the costume. When working with complex costumes and/or costumes which will require a great deal of movement, it is often helpful for the costume designer to work with the director, in person if possible, and sketch through ideas. This sketch is black ink pen on ivory parchment. Pen sketching allows for rapid visceral drawing responses to ideas, which is conducive to fluid conversation and brainstorming. (Costume design by Linda Pisano, Stage direction by Jeffrey Buchman. Produced at the Indiana University Jacobs School of Music Opera & Ballet Theatre.)*

They can use these thumbnails to quickly work through basic silhouettes and accessories, compare and contrast shapes and forms, or otherwise work through initial ideas with the director on hand. Sketching next to the director or choreographer in a brainstorming session or initial meeting can provide a casual but effective way to communicate ideas in an informal way without the director feeling compelled to commit to a finalized and formal rendering.

Preliminary Sketches

These sketches are more detailed and may or may not include color. Very often designers may go through several sets of **preliminary sketches** until they are confident that choices are ready to be finalized into a fully executed rendering. Preliminary sketches are most effective on a drawing paper, rather than on watercolor paper or **Bristol board**. These often include written notations, research images, working drawings or line sketches of accessories, headwear, and even diagrams of complicated items like wings, masks, or rigged special effects. Designers should never consider their preliminaries precious artwork, as they are meant to be sketched on, mulled over, and modified as tools of communication.

Final Renderings

The use of the word "final" in this context can conjure up the idea that the designs are unchangeable; and indeed, contracts may require signatures of approval from the director or even from the costume department on the back of each rendering. **Final renderings** are based in contract and must be honored by all parties; however, with mutual agreement, final designs are sometimes modified when the **realization** of such designs is directly affected by a change in casting, issues with fit, or an overall change in the approach to a particular character approved by the director and producer. In any case, final renderings are expected to be fully colored drawings that also include detail, working drawings, and special instruction and research, either directly on the plate or accompanying it. Every costume for every character must be rendered and provided to the costume department. Each rendering should include a plate number, identification of the character, act, scene or musical number, and the signature of the designer along with the title of the play or dance production. If the designer is under union contract, the **union stamp** should be visible on all renderings.

Final renderings are most effective when a set of color copies is provided to stage management to post in the rehearsal room so that actors can study them. Another copy, either digital or print, should be provided to the director to refer to as the rehearsal process begins, and the overall composition of each scene is considered.

The original set of renderings, or a high resolution printed set, must be provided to the costume department and should include quickly identifiable swatches that correspond to the pieces being built, along with samples of trim, buttons, and other items to be manufactured. Assistant designers, shoppers, craftspeople, and wig personnel should also have access to the original renderings or high resolution prints. Cutter–drapers in particular like color copies as it allows them to take notes directly on the printouts in their meetings with the designer. They can also add their own

research images or thumbnail sketches of back views or interior structures, to enhance their own working notes of a particular item.

In addition to clearly delineating the items to be built, final renderings should provide a sense of the mood and spirit of the characters. Once fittings start, they should be available in the fitting room as part of the communication between director, costumers, and performer. They can also be valuable when discussing quick changes with the dressers and backstage wardrobe running crew.

Ultimately the final renderings become a tool utilized by every area of the production team, management team, and performer(s) throughout the rehearsal and build processes. Their

FIGURES 5.9 & 5.10 *Like the preliminary sketch, these examples of costume design renderings for the character Violetta in Act III of the opera* La Traviata *by Verdi provide both a front and back view of the costume. With color and detail, the rendering also includes a slight movement of the arm so the cutter–draper can better interpret the proposed butterfly wing design. The use of watercolor concentrate enhances the vibrancy of the suggested color. Yet it was also chosen for practical purposes: it has quick working and dry time because operas and musicals often require dozens of renderings to communicate all of the costumes. Note the inclusion of information about the production, the designer's USA Local 829 stamp and signature, as well as a title block. These are standard notations on costume renderings that are important in communication and organization with the costume department and stage management as they track changes for the director and performer. (Costume design by Linda Pisano, Stage direction by Jeffrey Buchman. Produced at the Indiana University Jacobs School of Music Opera & Ballet Theatre.)*

importance cannot be underestimated and should be clearly outlined in contracts and/or riders.

Sometimes the marketing department will also request to use renderings that have a high quality of illustration and/or style. If a contract clearly states that the designs are copyrighted by the producing agency, then the marketing department should make it clear that the physical renderings/art work belong to the designer. If it has been otherwise agreed, it is in the designer's best interest to understand how the actual renderings will be used in marketing and publicity materials, especially if the contract stipulates surrender of the original work.

EFFECTIVE USE OF ORGANIZATIONAL SKILLS

Costume designers are usually balancing several production designs at once. Each may be in a very different place in the creative process, but often there comes a point when one must schedule a day full of tasks that encompass multiple projects. Aside from being subject to contractual dates for each project, designers must be self-motivated and able to skillfully navigate priorities and deadlines without supervision of their daily work schedules, as they often work in the comfort of their own homes. Whatever one's personal life may entail, such as a roommate, a single lifestyle, a partner, or a family that includes young children and/or teens, it is important to establish a professional routine that creates a life/work balance. Scheduling and time management are important skills needed to make it all work effectively for everyone, including the designer.

Keeping a detailed calendar is not an option; it is an essential tool. In order to find time for meaningful phone meetings, research, and rendering, a calendar can help the designer create personal deadlines and goals. A daily task list prioritized into an achievable number of undertakings each day can allow the designer to work on multiple projects without feeling buried under mounting deadlines. Moreover, scheduling creates a framework that allows for personal time, which is critical to continually infuse the creative groundwork necessary for a successful design career.

Designers should make the time to study the professional management skills required for a healthy business model. A freelance career is sustainable only when designers can be their own managers and understand everything from contracts, riders, and taxes, to overseeing their priorities and maintaining strong professional relationships. One must make time to give every project and creative partnership one's most creative and talented self, which is achieved through a healthy work/life balance.

Other organizational tools, such as paperwork, are crucial for productive collaboration in all areas of the costume design process. The **action chart**, sometimes called a scene breakdown, is a foundational tool utilized by the costume designer at the very beginning of the process of script analysis. It provides the framework from which all other documents can stem, from the costume plot/piece list to quick-change tracking, check-in sheets, and even pulling and shopping lists. Once a solid action chart is in place, the costume designer is prepared to engage in detailed discussions with all areas.

Not only is the **costume plot** (sometimes called a "piece list") crucial to the work of the costume designer, but it is also required by contract with almost all theatre, opera, and dance companies. It is considered so important to the collaboration between the designer and the costume department that it is almost always due at the same time as the final renderings. This itemized list of every costume piece will be influential in costing out a production, managing the budget, bidding, outsourcing, rentals, and communicating with associate costume designers, assistant costume designers, and the entire costume department.

FIGURE 5.11 *Various research images were provided to the craft artisan by the costume designer to describe the scale and color of the shawl collars required for multiple characters in the opera* Akhnaten *by Philip Glass. The director approved this research with the understanding that the opera was a somewhat stylized approach to the historical period of Egyptian history in which Akhnaten reigned. As this approach was clearly articulated with the crafts department, the artisan was given some autonomy in creating the realized design as seen above. Materials were used to emulate the faience from the historical period. (Shawl collar created by crafts artisan Lani Tortoriello for the Philip Glass opera* Akhnaten. *Costume design by Linda Pisano. Produced at the Indiana University Jacobs School of Music Opera & Ballet Theatre.)*

It also ensures that the details and nuances that comprise the aesthetic of a designer's work are not forgotten once it moves into the build process.

EFFECTIVE COLLABORATION WITH THE COSTUME MAKERS

It would be possible to combine discussion of collaboration with a costume maker and a similar discussion of collaboration with an actor, because both deal directly with the physicalization of the costume. Accurate fit of a costume affects movement, range of motion, breathing, physical endurance, characterization, and storytelling. The collaborative relationship between the designer and the technologist or costume maker in their three-dimensional interpretation of the design is readily apparent; an actor, however, will often need to understand fully why and how to wear the garments, and it is often the designer who explains the historical or social significance, the meaning as determined by the director, designer intentions, and different ways to use the costume pieces.

The costume department is made up of a wide range of personnel, and those working most closely with the designer include some, if not all, of the personnel listed below, depending on the size of the company, the bidding costume company contracted to manufacture the designs, or possibly one of several companies hired to build various parts of a design. In the latter case the costume associate, with the help of assistant designers, will negotiate the day-to-day requirements and tasks of a given production design.

It is important that designers maintain an open channel of correspondence with their associates and all of the personnel listed. Some collaborate extensively with the designers, while others may only have a moment with them. The designer's personality sometimes sets the tone of approachability with the various personnel, but it is still important to the process for designers to acknowledge each of the roles that go into realizing a design. This serves as best practice for the workplace and makes everyone more involved in a collaborative effort to create something of value and quality.

Shop Managers and Assistant Shop Managers

Designers must maintain constant communication with either or both of these roles. In larger companies or professional shops, the associate designer will be the liaison on a day-to-day basis, but open communication is very important when scheduling fittings and setting up early meetings with the makers.

Assistant Designers

If a designer is working with an associate designer, the assistants are often working directly with the associate. However, often an assistant designer, whether part of the company's staff or hired independently by a designer, is in constant communication with the designer to shop for fabric and ready-made pieces, provide research, or navigate the shopping and swatching. A well-organized, savvy, proactive assistant who practices good management skills will rarely be in want of employment, and it is an excellent entry-level position for a young designer that provides a great real-life learning opportunity.

The **United Scenic Artists** define the assistant's duties as "The work of the Assistant shall be to assist the Designer in the work of the Designer." An associate position is known to take on more leadership in the day-to-day organization and implementation of the costume design process; sometimes making some decisions when the designer is unavailable and/or being a liaison with various vendors and businesses that are executing the design. An assistant designer will work their way into the role of an associate designer.

Some smaller regional theatre companies have costume staff in the role of assistant costume shop manager or assistant wardrobe supervisor. There are varying titles, but these positions will often serve unofficially in an assistant capacity with a costume designer on a particular production. If the scope of a position at a theatre company includes duties one might expect of an assistant designer, indispensable traits include excellent verbal and written communication skills, a basic understanding of historic costume if pulling from existing stock, and a fundamental knowledge of fabrics.

Shoppers

Most companies have a shopper who communicates with the designer (and/or their associate or assistant), and is also willing to find creative solutions while working directly with the management to stay within budget and on schedule. The designer's renderings, visual research, and a strong knowledge of fabrics and ready-made pieces can make the shopper's work more effective.

Cutters–Drapers

Cutters and drapers are perhaps the most crucial members of the costume department with whom a designer will discuss garments in detail. Not only will this relationship include initial meetings regarding construction, but frank discussions, quick and creative problem solving, and continual cooperation throughout fittings and technical rehearsals are required. The role of the cutters and drapers is to interpret the designs. Not merely translate them, which can imply duplication. Cutters–drapers contribute their expertise to realize the designer's ideas in three-dimensional form through interpretation of the drawings.

This relationship has the potential to exemplify collaboration at its very best. It requires that the designer acknowledge the cutter–drapers' function of asking questions and sharing perspectives and ideas based on their experience and expertise. The successful designer will not only provide cutters and drapers with sketches and research, but will be open to studying research provided by knowledgeable and experienced tailors and dressmakers. Relinquishing a sense of sole ownership of the designs may be one of the most difficult decisions a designer will need to make, but the sooner they recognize the essential role of collaboration in the design and implementation process, the more they will celebrate the success of a strong partnership with many artisans along the journey.

Below are some considerations a costume designer should make when communicating with the cutter–draper and tailors:

- What is the storytelling of each character from look to look and how does the fit of the garments change throughout the action?

- Once the production is cast, how do the measurements of the actor translate into the garments being made for them? Will they require foundation garments or augmentation to enhance or manipulate their silhouette?

- Are there textual references to costume that must be adhered to?

- Are there special effects involving costumes? Are there quick changes that require unique closures?

- Is there a stock of costumes to work from, or will they be manufactured, purchased, or rented?

- What is the length of the run of a production and what maintenance will be provided? Is there time, labor, and budget for daily laundry and/or dry-cleaning, or are there back-to-back performances which may require two of each item?

- Are there any contractual agreements from specific performers about their costumes and/or shoes? (It is not unusual to see this in performers' riders, so be sure to consult with the production or company manager for details.)

- Have performers been asked via contract to modify their look in any way to play a role?

- Is there any dance or fight choreography, or any changes on stage that may require assistance in removing or adding costume pieces?

First Hands

Collaboration with first hands is usually directed by the cutter–draper, and although there may be some meetings with the designer regarding certain details, it is not to the extent that occurs with the leads of each construction team.

Stitchers

Although there is often no direct communication or collaboration between the designer and the stitchers when a full construction team is available, the designer should seek out opportunities, no matter how brief, to acknowledge the value of the work provided by the stitchers in creating the garments. Best practices and a healthy work environment are best served when every member of the team is recognized for having value in the overall outcome of a project.

Crafts Artisans

Often overlooked in smaller companies or academic costume departments, costume crafts can make the difference between an adequate design and one that provides every facet and nuance of a complete and powerful artistic endeavor. Costume crafts run the gamut from millinery, jewelry, shoes, and armor, to special effects, bags, purses, glasses, adornments, and other accouterments. The successful designer will have research, sketches, and notes prepared for the crafts artisan upon their first consultation. Moreover, like cutters and drapers, experienced and expert crafts artisans can provide their own ideas, research, and skill to enhance the designs and problem-solving challenges in safe, effective, and sometimes poignant ways. Their cooperation is a necessary part of achieving a polished overall finish for a design through their dedication to mastering the distinctions in the details of the design in question. The communication between designer and crafts artisans is ongoing throughout technical rehearsals. Every fitting that involves headwear, jewelry, or other accessories should be given the courtesy of time and consideration by the designer.

Dyers and Painters

If there is one area where a designer is bound to learn the most from another artisan, it is in the area of dyeing and painting.

Master dyers and painters sometimes seem like a rare breed, and when a designer has the fortune of working with someone skilled in this area it is important to glean as much knowledge as possible from the relationship.

Even with the best knowledge, dyers and painters often have to work through a great deal of trial and error to achieve ideal solutions. A designer must be attentive and try to respond as quickly as possible to dye swatches, so as not to hold up the sometimes long and arduous process of dyeing fabric in time for a cutter–draper to begin work. Furthermore, the designer must understand that the colors achieved with watercolor renderings or research printouts can sometimes take time to achieve in fabrics, especially if they select textiles that are difficult to dye. The more knowledge that a designer has of the intrinsic properties of textiles in terms of how well they dye and retain color, the more effective the collaboration will be between the designer and the dyer–painters. The less experience a designer has with basic union and/or fiber reactive dyes, the more difficulty they will have expressing what they want achieved with a given fabric or garment, and this may not end well for the final outcome or integrity of the proposed design.

Designers cannot simply be "illustrators" or "designers"; their very ability to communicate their ideas hinges on at least a basic working knowledge of the processes that go into realizing a garment from textile to finished silhouette. Perhaps nowhere is this better exemplified than with their work with the painters and dyers.

Shoe Masters (Ballet/Dance)

In professional ballet the designer does not contribute in any capacity with modifying the shoes of a dancer. The safety, health, and art of the dancers may all lie in the custom fit and maintenance of their shoes, especially when en pointe. If budget allows, some companies may give the costume designer liberties in changing the color of the shoes and even adding pattern or **motifs**, provided it is done with the appropriate dyes and does not interfere with the safety and function of the shoe. It is also not uncommon in more traditional ballet for spats that emulate boots to be added to men's shoes. But like other areas of construction, it is important for the designer to trust the expertise and experience of those who work most often with the shoes to make any modifications. Indeed, a well-executed contract or letter of agreement will remove all responsibility for safety and execution of the costumes from the designer, and thus the designer must not only be willing, but also to expect, to follow the advice of those who will carry the responsibility for ensuring the safety and health of the shoes, garments, and ultimately the performers.

Wardrobe Crew (Professional and Non-Professional)

The costume designer, or their associate or assistant, will provide the head of wardrobe or the costume manager with all the necessary paperwork for the wardrobe crew. In a smaller company, the designer may be welcome backstage during technical rehearsals, **ten-out-of-twelves**, or dress rehearsals, depending on the schedule and practices of the given organization. In this case, it is usually beneficial for the designer to stay out of the way between "call" and "go" while the crew gets acclimated to the costumes and the needs of the cast, waiting until questions are addressed directly to them. It is best to leave notes regarding maintenance and minor repairs to the wardrobe crew, and take only notes that directly affect the design, or answer questions that relate directly to the way in which a garment is worn or used on stage. Despite it being a time of high energy and even stress, it is in everyone's best interest to be calm and professional at all times.

For union designers, it is highly recommended and often required that they not enter the dressing room or backstage area, but rather wait in the house unless and until the wardrobe crew calls for them. The production or stage management for each particular company can advise the designer on policies. Research and understanding is good professional practice.

Wig and Makeup Department

Collaboration with the wig and makeup department will vary from company to company. In some companies, a wig designer or wig master may be "jobbed in" per production as needed; in others they fill one or more full-time positions. But there are some companies in which someone within the costume department oversees this area. Unfortunately, this negates the absolute importance of expertise required for fine quality workmanship, but the lack of a specialist in wigs and makeup is a reality for many companies today. This challenge makes it crucial for university curricula and practicum work for today's young costume designers to offer as much history and training as possible in the area of wigs and makeup. Early-career designers often find themselves left to figure out how to provide wigs, period makeup, or special-effects makeup, on little or no budget and with no real knowledge of the craft.

The difference between a production with and without the expertise of a wig and makeup specialist cannot be underestimated. It can mean the difference between a merely serviceable design and a provocative, unforgettable, and powerful visual in the context of the storytelling. No matter how phenomenal a costume design may be, it is unfinished without an investment in the hair and makeup of each and every character. Too often this area is considered an afterthought, when in reality it is an essential part of the overall look of an ensemble.

When a costume designer is provided with the expertise of a wig master and/or wig designer (and better yet, a department that can support the entire production), a good collaborative series of discussions from very early on in the design process is imperative. But where does a costume designer begin, and what is the relationship between the two departments?

Professional contracts, riders, and/or negotiations between a costume designer and an employer should clearly indicate what expertise will be available in the area of wigs and makeup, and that budget should be separate from the materials budget for costumes. Knowledge of these factors will assist the designer in creating the most effective and skillful overall look for a design within achievable expectations. The costume designer works directly with the director and artistic team to pursue an approach to the overall production design; the wig and makeup department, like cutters–drapers and tailors, assist in achieving this goal. Their expertise in interpreting the designer's work can increase the possibilities and choices available to the designer. Although the designer has the final approval on the overall look of the ensemble, of each character, and the cast at large, it is important that they collaborate with the specialists to understand ways in which they might work to realize each look.

A costume designer should include in their research packet extensive images and information regarding the styles, colors, and specifics of the hair and makeup required for the production. For example, an 18th century Western European opera will require extensive information about styles, wigs, wig uses, colors, social class, and many other variables from the costume designer to assist in early conversations with the wig department. Because the hair and makeup of Western Europe in the 18th century was directly related to gender, socioeconomic class, occupation, and even religion, it becomes a major part of the early communication. If the opera is based on a more traditional approach, this research becomes imperative in achieving specific looks. However, if a play is being highly stylized, it is possible that less comprehensive but more evocative and abstract research could be combined with some strong interpretation on the part of the wig and makeup specialists.

As with any costume maker, the costume designer must develop a rapport with the wig and makeup specialists, and

clearly outline how closely the research should be followed and how much room for interpretation is possible; and this can only be done if the designer has come well prepared with research images, historical and textual context, and a clear vision of the overall approach.

Below are some considerations a costume designer should make when communicating with the wig and makeup department:

- Is everyone wigged, and if so do any characters require multiple looks?

- Are current headshots available of each performer that clearly show their hair color, complexion, and features such as hairline and facial hair?

- Are there textual references to hair or makeup that must be adhered to?

- Are there special effects involving wigs or makeup? (One look at Stephen Sondheim's *Into the Woods* will provide examples of these challenges.)

- Is there a stock of wigs to work from, or will they be manufactured, purchased, or rented?

- Do all the styles require lace-front, or could some get away with a less expensive hard front?

- Are there any contractual agreements from specific performers about their hair and wigs? (It is not unusual to see this in performers' riders, so be sure to consult with the production or company manager for details.)

- If necessary, are performers with facial hair willing to shave it or grow it according to the design?

VERBAL AND VISUAL COLLABORATION WITH THE PERFORMER

At this point, it is important to acknowledge that a performer in both live performance and film/TV may have particular idiosyncrasies and even contract riders or clauses that outline specific preferences or rights when it comes to their costumes or the way they appear. It is imperative that contractual agreements are respected and certainly reasonable requests should be heard. Most importantly, the young designer should recognize that an empathetic approach to working with a performer, whatever the genre, is an ideal way to create a meaningful collaborative environment.

The Actor

Historically, the importance of collaboration between costume designers and actors has been underestimated, if not sometimes ignored. This is detrimental to the entire production process, and both artists must regard the other with respect and dignity. Indeed, the combined creative resources of both parties can lay the groundwork for some truly inspired choices.

There are many ways that costume designers can assist actors in their process. A well-prepared designer can advise a female actor on how to sit in a 19th century bustle, or a male actor on how to glide through an entrance in a Restoration costume wearing three inch heels, a wig, and a long coat. Navigating pieces like these can be overwhelming, especially to a young actor still learning to develop character, so this is an important part of the work that a costume designer must be prepared to do. The designer must learn to put the actor at ease and to commit to learning the actor's process and their exploration of physicality in the role. A comprehensive understanding of this type of collaboration with the actor and the costume maker exists after the design student has gone through fittings with many actors and has established a comfortable dialogue in this all-important setting. An actor must trust the designer, and the designer must earn that trust.

Finally, with all union-represented performers, it is important for designers to familiarize themselves with the rules and expectations surrounding fittings and dressing room procedures for each company and/or the performers unions such as **Actors Equity Association**.

The Opera Singer

First and foremost, opera singers are concerned with having the capacity and health to perform vocally to the best of their abilities. If their voices are not perfect or nearly perfect in performance, it can be detrimental to their careers. The degree of physical endurance that some of the great operatic roles can require of a singer is remarkable. So in the context of an essentially 20th century approach to a role (sometimes called the "park and bark"), which does not require much physical action on the part of the singer, or a more 21st century sensibility where the singer may be pushed to some true physical extremes while singing, the costume designer must always keep in mind the health and comfort of the costume for the singer to fully expand with their breathing through the neck, shoulders, and abdomen. With this in mind it is clear why fittings of these anatomical regions must be prioritized for opera singers, and why the designer should speak frankly with singers about their action and work while wearing particular looks.

The opera singer—student, emerging professional, or established veteran—requires many of the same considerations as the actor. Many singers, however, lack the background that most actors have to understand the role of the costume designer, or they are accustomed to singing in companies that mostly remount older designs from their stock or rent existing designs from a large rental company. The quality of costumes and professional practices they have experienced varies widely, depending on where they have worked and studied. More established companies that focus on mounting new works will still use designers, or have fully staffed costume departments, and will therefore provide opera singers with experiences in the fitting process, reading designers' renderings, and developing a role with at least some contact with costumers. Singers who have worked in companies that rely on rental packages or existing stock may not have gone through a process of fittings and having costumes built or modified in design for them, and they may never have seen any research, sketch, or representation of the costume they are to wear until they put it on for final fitting or technical rehearsal.

In an academic setting, voice teachers may or may not want some involvement with students' process, including costume fittings. The same can be true for children and children's choirs that may be brought in for a particular production. In these cases, it is good to have knowledge of the company's policies and perhaps to have a conversation with the company manager or production manager, in order to understand fully the expectation of collaboration between the designer and the teacher or the children's parents. In the case of children, most companies will have a child wrangler (sometimes an assistant stage manager), but in any case there should always be a parent or guardian present at all fittings, dressing rooms, and conversations with child performers. This also holds true for theatre and dance.

There are some specific challenges that can sometimes be part of working with opera. Double casting, understudies, and last-minute changes, particularly in a chorus, are not unusual with some companies and in academic environments. Directors often cast two people for the same role who are not in any way physically similar. This may require that one designs two different looks for the same costume to enhance the physicality of the different singers portraying the same character. As opera performers are cast for their vocal abilities, their physical appearance frequently differs from what designers might expect in age, size, or other attributes. In any case, designers must remember to serve the character as it relates to the storytelling, while keeping the comfort and safety of the performer in mind.

Finally, guest artists who are hired to come in and play a role usually have that character in their repertoire, having played it several times with various companies in many different costumes. Indeed, it was not long ago that an opera singer would travel with costume in hand! However, in the 21st century we embrace change, and it is important for the designer to prepare in advance for the physical needs of the singer, as sometimes there is only one fitting and very little time to prepare. Most opera singers have an opinion about their costumes in comparison with other costumed versions of the role, but a professional performer should understand the critical role of the designer in creating a costume suitable for the character, the overall look of the production, and the stylistic/thematic approach of the staging.

The Ballet Dancer

Like all performers, ballet dancers are cast in specific roles due to their expertise and ability to achieve the highest degree of technical and artistic virtuosity in their given profession. One fall or mistake could not only cost them the respect of their patrons, but it could also result in a career-ending injury. This is why ballet requires the upmost respect for the dancer's work and may involve multiple discussions and possibly multiple fittings involving the choreographer. Ballet also has a long tradition that is celebrated through the pedigree of dancers and their ability to emulate very specific choreography. This does not mean that choreographers, designers, and dancers are not eager to transform and expand the boundaries of tradition, but it does mean that a costume designer must be aware of the objectives and expectations of a specific company and/or ballet title. Designing a full production or new section of *The Nutcracker* may mean a fairly traditional approach intended to satisfy audiences and underwriters; yet the same company may have a season of cutting-edge approaches to many old and new works. No matter what the approach or the expectation, there is a heightened sense of specialization needed for truly high quality ballet design.

As a costume designer for ballet, one should spend time becoming familiar with the history of ballet, the dance company for which one is working, and the work to be produced. One must, in a sense, be one's own **dramaturge**. This is prior even to beginning research toward the design and execution of the ballet in question. It is essential to understand the difference between the many variations of the tutu costume, the endless variations of construction and fabrics, partnering and floor work, and the specialization of shoes. In a ballet company, the costume designer should never supervise the pointe shoes; they are overseen by designated staff with professional experience. The only exception

to this would be if the choreographer agrees to take them to another color, which can be an expense but simply requires a color or decorative decision by the designer, who even then will never handle the shoe. There is too much specialization and customization in the pointe shoes of a dancer for anyone other than an expert to deal with this area.

Ballet fittings can be complicated. A designer should work with the drapers, cutters, and anyone else involved with the fitting to ensure that enough time is reserved for looking at the fitting of foundation garments, taking care to allow the dancer to work through a full range of motion, and for discussion of the fabrics. The designer should request, if the draper–cutters have not already made this decision, to have mockups created from fabric that is similar in stretch and weight to the design. Conversations with the costumers should include how construction will affect design in terms of seam lines, **bias cuts**, and the finishing and placement of any trims. If tutus are utilized, the designer must clearly outline the fabrics to be used with the costumers, and bear in mind the budget. How many years are these expected to last? Will these costumes go out for rental? How often will this production be remounted in these same costumes? It is a truly unique experience for a designer to revisit their costumes 20 years after their design and to see what fabrics and what choices stood the test of time, both practically and artistically, and what could have been reworked and rethought. These choices regarding budget, fabrics, trim placement, and so forth all directly affect the design. It may behoove a designer to look closely at their research and sketches, and ask "What will I think of this if I were to come and see it 20 years from now?" This is a difficult and rather sobering consideration, but a very necessary one.

When preparing for fittings, the designer should expect that the dancers might have with them a small entourage of supporters, or possibly the choreographer, present. Each look should be given a specific amount of time and all correct undergarments should be worn, especially at the mockup fitting. If specialty items such as headdresses, unusual jewelry, or rigged pieces are to be worn, it is essential to have the makers of those pieces present and ready to fit early on. These items cannot be afterthoughts in ballet, as they can completely change the balance and technical performance of the dancer.

Always begin fittings with a brief description of the approach to the costumes if they are non-traditional or in any way highly stylized. Have the renderings, research, and swatches available to share with the dancer. A designer must be positive and personable, as this will allow the dancer to feel comfortable, and more forthcoming with questions, in order to understand how the costume will fit and move. It will also allow them to value the enthusiasm that designers have for their work and the efforts they make to create the looks for each production. Like opera singers, not all ballet dancers have worked with professional costume designers; some may be young, coming out of programs where the costumes were ready-made from catalogues or rentals. In this case, they may not understand the expertise and artistry that is involved in a costume designer's work or the integrity of the designer's position as part of the artistic team. Designers cannot and should not take offense, but rather educate and share what they do. It might be helpful to ask emerging dancers if they have ever had a costume built for them; some younger dancers that are in companies with dance academy affiliations are not even aware of what a mockup is. This is an excellent opportunity to share the process with dancers (and, in the case of children, the parent or guardian who might be accompanying them).

Finally, there are some traditions with stage makeup and hairstyles in ballet that may or may not be appropriate for the style in which the production is being designed. Be sure that discussions with the choreographer and the wig and makeup department happen early on, and clarify those expectations at all final fittings so that the dancers understand how the hair and makeup approach will be directly related to the costume design.

The Contemporary Dancer

Designing for contemporary dance is an ideal collaborative process for those designers who enjoy what some might call an "organic" process—i.e., one that is potentially always changing right up to the final rehearsals. Such a process permits exploration within rehearsal and a collaborative approach to design that allows choreographer, designer, maker, sometimes even dancer, to be part of the natural development of the ideas. This requires patience, problem-solving skills, and clear expectations of deadlines for the labor.

As the costume design is so integral to the movement and progression of the story, it is ideal for those individuals who are as innovative in costume making as they are in costume design. Indeed, it is an ideal venue for the costume maker who would like to explore design. Knowledge of a wide range of fabrics (particularly stretch fabrics), and the techniques that they require—coupled with a creative approach to draping, seaming, and layout of garment shapes—is crucial.

Contemporary dancers are usually very athletic, and because of the variety of techniques they employ, there may be a wide range of body types within a single company. Many within the contemporary dance community celebrate this physical diversity, which creates many opportunities for the costume designer

and costume maker to explore silhouettes that enhance the choreographer's imagery.

As with all of the other performer–designer collaborations, fittings should be well organized and welcoming. The contemporary dancer, like the ballet dancer, has similar considerations such as safety and artistic tradition. However, contemporary dancers may often have much less on their bodies or may even be nude or near nude on occasion, which requires discretion, the upmost professionalism, and a closed fitting only for necessary staff. It is not uncommon for fabric and costume pieces to be draped directly onto a contemporary dancer in a fitting if the production has a stylized approach. This is why it is beneficial to have research, sketches, and any other visual narratives of the approach and look of the piece available in the fitting room. Designers should prepare to talk through the whole look of the design with each dancer, and if the choreographer is present, there could be an opportunity for a collaborative discussion.

Prior to each fitting, it is critical for the costume designer and the costume maker to communicate clearly about the style of each of the costumes in terms of how they will look on the individual dancers. This will result in more efficient use of time and unified creative force in the fitting room, which in turn will achieve a strong and effective look and instill confidence in the performer.

In summary, it is critical to acknowledge that any application of costume design—whether it be film, TV, live performance, or entertainment—requires the same fundamental skills in preparation, organization, storytelling, and goals upon which the aesthetic choices are made.

POTENTIAL CHALLENGES IN THE COLLABORATIVE RELATIONSHIP

Successful collaborative relationships require work and commitment. The following discussion outlines specific challenges that may be encountered during the process of developing a production.

Group Dynamics

Every group differs depending on the people involved and the project at the heart of the creative development. Sometimes one or more members of the creative team emerge as leaders due to their experience, their strong vision for that particular project, or both. In other cases no apparent "leader" will emerge from the group, but rather a fairly equal collaboration will develop, either spontaneously or over time. Whatever the group dynamic, it is important that everyone on the team is allowed to share their work and contribute ideas; yet it is also vital for everyone to listen and attempt to understand. Naturally the director should ultimately take the lead on the overall vision of the production, and the design team can greatly assist in this role by providing a strong foundation of ideas, research, and consideration as to how to put those ideas in the service of the overall theme and story to be produced.

Long-Distance Collaboration

As mentioned earlier in this chapter, digital media can create a sense of taking the human quality out of our very human field. Therefore, utilizing media such as webinars, online meetings with cameras, and phone conversations can create a stronger sense of unity and collaboration among a design team. It is the responsibility of the emerging generation of designers and directors to take the initiative to keep abreast of the most personable and user-friendly programs for meetings and digital communication. Long-distance collaboration is here to stay, and as the cost of air travel rises in a time of dwindling financial resources, it will be utilized more and more as arts organizations struggle to balance budgets and eliminate excessive expenditures. The more comfortable the designer is at interacting effectively and personally via various means of long-distance communication, the better prepared and informed they will be during the artistic development of a project. Furthermore, digital communication requires verbal and visual clarity that continues to be readable after multiple copies, such as emails and other digital transmissions. The upside of moving to more digital communication is that in some ways it is providing a path to more environmentally sustainable theatre processes, and it is bringing together people from around the world in ways that may not have been possible for previous generations of theatre practitioners.

Approaches to Conflict Resolution

With the diverse and strong personalities that are attracted to careers in the performing arts and entertainment industries, it is inevitable that conflicts will arise—some over small misunderstandings, others rooted in deep philosophical and/or artistic differences. Each individual must be ultimately responsible for their actions and reactions. Professional practice requires not compromise of one's self or principles, but rather a sincere effort to understand and to educate.

Communication or lack of communication can make or break a project, and can be the difference between a powerful and poignant production, or a dismal and haphazard effort at storytelling. Thus members of each team are responsible for their reactions to one another, and how well they listen to and value each other. This is why the first few social interactions become so important in establishing a personable yet professional rapport; it provides an opportunity to get to know and respect each other even with strong differing opinions or work processes.

Ultimately, if communication breaks down, the production manager or a mediator must step in if contracts are involved. If the conflict leads to marginalization or remarks that cross the line into harassment, an impartial third party who is trained to deal with conflict resolution must be sought out. Despite the personable, artistic, and sometimes informal nature of our industry, it is still a profession and it is still a place where creative minds should be safe to express ideas and approaches in a community of fellow artists.

Civil Discourse in the Fitting Room

It is important to remember that everyone has a hard day occasionally. When fittings occur during a stressful period for the costume department, or rehearsals are becoming challenging, it can cause frustration and aggravation, which could manifest itself in the fitting room. The designer must do all that they can to set an optimistic and calm tone for a fitting. This is why clearly acknowledging performers is important. Greet them, create a secure place to laugh and to be themselves, introduce them to everyone in the room, and provide them with a comfortable and safe environment. The fitting can be challenging for performers, as they are literally baring themselves in front of people they may not know and watching their bodies transform into the character while standing in front of a full-length mirror. If the performer is a well-known artist or celebrity, discretion should be a top priority; only those people whose presence is absolutely necessary should be present, and privacy from recording devices or from anyone who might take advantage of the situation should be secured.

Starting a fitting with a positive and professional attitude is key. This requires confidence and preparedness with the pieces to be fit and with the order in which they will be fit. Allowing the cutter–draper and the first hand to get the garment on the performer gives the designer time for some casual discourse with the performer. It is an excellent opportunity to ask them about their character and for the designer to share thoughts as developed with the director. The designer never comments or makes judgments on a performer's body, as it is highly inappropriate in any situation, and unethical. Only clinical assessments of how a garment fits a body are appropriate. If a performer is very casual about talking about their body, it is all right to listen, but it should not open the gate for discussion about the person's physicality unless it directly relates to the clinical fit of the garment.

If healthy communication has been established between the costumers and the designer, this will create a sense of trust that the performer may perceive. However, some performers may still become frustrated and lash out—perhaps because they are having a bad day or, more commonly, due to struggles with body image, insecurities about their physical appearance in general, or lack of confidence in their ability to portray the role convincingly on stage. Even some of the most seasoned performers may never overcome insecurities about their body or develop a mental maturity to face areas with which they are dissatisfied. As unfortunate as this may be, the designer's role is not to be a therapist or motivational coach, but rather to listen and assist in addressing real issues with a clinical and practiced attitude as it affects the costumes for that production.

If a performer begins complaining about a costume, costume piece, or fabric choices, the designer should be a good listener and be concise and forthright about asking what exactly the performer is having trouble with. Trust and honesty are hand-in-hand, but this is only possible when the words used are kind and not belittling from either party. No one should ever be disrespectful to the other's choices or ideas. Just as the designer must listen to the concerns of the performer, the performer must listen to the reasoning from the designer. If abusive or disrespectful language is used, the designer should confront it in a calm tone and ask the performer to start at the beginning and talk it through. If abusive language or commentary continues, it is best to cut short the fitting and let the performer know you will reschedule at a time when the director or a production manager can attend.

No matter how gifted a designer, how talented a performer, or how skilled a costumer, no one is above civil discourse. A creative, passionate, and strong personality does not negate the necessity of kindness and civility, nor does it ever excuse disrespectful or judgmental comments about others or their work.

FURTHER CONSIDERATIONS

"Teamwork is the ability to work together toward a common vision. The ability to direct individual accomplishments toward organizational objectives. It is the fuel that allows common people to attain uncommon results."
Attributed to Andrew Carnegie,[4] Scottish–American industrialist and philanthropist

Creating a Meaningful Process for All Involved

Producing stage productions in any genre of the performing arts is not for everyone. But those who have the impulse to create, and partner with others who share that purpose in their lives, may find the field of production to be artistically and professionally satisfying. With each project often completely different from the next, members of creative teams continually moving on to other projects, and the wide range of personalities within the field, there is indeed something for everyone. With professional practice and team members who focus on listening, understanding, and contributing, there is no reason that each project, albeit sometimes stressful and difficult, cannot be rewarding in some way. If we walk into a project with the goal of making it a positive outcome for all involved, we are more likely to find that the collaborative process becomes professionally and personally gratifying.

Maintaining Professional Contact after Opening Night

Opening night may be a time for celebration, for the departure of the artistic team, and for the performers, musicians, conductors, run crews, and stage management to take over maintaining the integrity of a production—but it is not an ending point. A designer will no doubt have made some good professional connections that have been meaningful. To keep these connections strong, it is important to occasionally stay in contact with those with whom you have worked. Even a postcard with images of your most recent work and a personal handwritten note on the back can renew the fire of a successful collaboration and encourage contact with a view to working together again. It is important that early-career designers remember that even working relationships that seemed less obvious may mean a connection with a future director, designer, or producer. Keeping in contact with a costume manager or maker could be the difference between them mentioning you, or forgetting about you, when speaking with the

FIGURE 5.12 *Based on the ancient Vietnamese folk tale of* Our Benevolent Buddha Thi Kinh, *the creative team for this opera approached the production as a folk tale with reference to the unique distinctions of Vietnamese culture in the architecture and the clothing. Special attention was paid to the use of the color yellow, and the important references it made about the culture and the tale itself. Once lighting was introduced, the collaborative effort that was made regarding the color palette, its tone, and its intensity was evident in ensemble compositions such as this. (World Premier of new opera* The Tale of Lady Thi Kinh. *Music and libretto: P.Q. Phan. Conductor: David Effron. Stage direction by Vincent Liotta, Scenic design by Erhard Rom, Costume design by Linda Pisano, Lighting design by Todd Hensley. Produced by the Indiana University Jacobs School of Music Opera & Ballet Theatre.)*

artistic director or production manager at the theatre in which they work. Never underestimate the importance of professional friendship in our field. Everyone enjoys a collaborative and positive work experience and will seek after those practitioners and artisans with whom they feel confident.

Embracing Change as an Opportunity

Designers are often heard either lamenting or celebrating the closure of an artistic process on opening night. If it was difficult and challenging they might celebrate moving on to another process; if it was particularly rewarding they may lament having to say goodbye to their team. Either way, the performing arts are always about change, and change requires risk, which is the best way to progress and develop. Consider change as an opportunity to learn about new ideas, create new relationships, and experience new processes. The more we embrace change,

the more we can move confidently and steadily into new projects. It is important to foster professional practices in all aspects of one's career, and part of that is being open to a changing world, remaining positive, setting goals, and enabling new and sometimes unusual opportunities to come into our lives.

On a Personal Note

The field of costume design is always evolving. From current fashion trends, our understanding of history, and the ways in which our industry produces performing arts and entertainment; we are always evolving. Embrace change by viewing each collaborative opportunity and project as an opportunity to challenge yourself, thereby gleaning experience and knowledge. A positive perspective and happiness leads to success, not the other way around.

QUESTIONS

- What attributes are critical to successful collaboration with a stage director?

- What experiences could best prepare a young designer in developing confidence in their communication and collaboration?

- What are some considerations a costume designer should make prior to speaking with their cutter–draper or tailor?

- In what ways can a designer help to create and foster a healthy environment for performers in fittings?

- In reviewing the chapter, what are some memorable best practices or attributes that a young designer might cultivate to ensure their success in the field of costume design?

NOTES

1. See: www.brainyquote.com/quotes/quotes/g/georgebern385438. html (accessed February 19, 2016).

2. See: "communication, n." Oxford English Dictionary online. www. oed.com/view/Entry/37309?redirectedFrom=communication (accessed June 19, 2015).

3. Stephen R. Covey, "Habit 6: Synergize," in *The Seven Habits of Highly Effective People*, www.stephencovey.com/7habits/7habits-habit6.php (accessed January 5, 2015).

4. See: www.goodreads.com/quotes/251192-teamwork-is-the-ability-to-work-together-toward-a-common (accessed February 19, 2016).

FIGURE 6.1 *The costume design process for Jaquenetta in* Love's Labour's Lost—*from rendering, to fabric samples and mockup, through to the finished costume. (Final rendering by Nicholas Hartman. Draper: Heather A. Milam. Actor: Sara J. Griffin at Illinois Shakespeare Festival at Illinois State University. Photo by Pete Guither.)*

CHAPTER 6

IN THE COSTUME SHOP

Heather A. Milam

One of the most exciting and scary moments of being a new costume designer is interacting for the first time with a costume shop. The potential for making magic is palpable. It is exhilarating to see drawings become three-dimensional costumes for the first time with a new team. Some designers are well trained in costume making in addition to design, and others have focused more on the art in design, but developing a positive working relationship with the costume shop is very important in either case. The primary focus of this chapter assumes the designer will be working with the expertise of a costume shop to get final costumes on the stage.

> "The designer brings the vision, the spirit, the concept, the color, the back story. We [the costume shop Tricorne] try our very best to bring all of that to reality. In the best world to me, it happens with a great deal of back and forth dialogue; work in 3D on the form as well as in the fitting room."
>
> Katherine Marshall,[1] owner and draper at Tricorne

COMMUNICATION

A costume designer and a costume shop, maker, or artisan will work together, capitalizing on each other's strengths to fully realize a design. The importance of developing and maintaining this healthy relationship cannot be emphasized enough. The success of a designer will be exhibited in the realized design of a show, so establishing best practices in interacting with costume shops will only benefit the designer's future. Creating a strong,

trusting, collaborative relationship is the goal: clear, precise, and specific communication is at the core of the best shop–designer interactions. Being able to clearly articulate what you expect to bring to the table, and what you expect the other party to provide, is the first step.

There is a series of questions a costume designer might pose as they begin working with a new team:

- Do you know how *you* define costume design?
- What are your expectations about how you are going to work as a team?
- Do you know who is responsible for what part of the process?
- Do you know how to talk about your artistic vision for the costumes?

And then the practical questions:

- Do you know how much fabric will be needed, and what trim you are looking for?
- Do you understand your budget and how you are supposed to use it?
- How much time do you have to give to the shop?
- What is the fitting request policy of the shop you are going to work with?
- How does the shop handle shopping/return receipts?

It is always better to ask a lot of questions, rather than assume. Asking questions might seem obvious enough, but interviewing shop staff illustrates that a lack of communication is usually at the root of a disappointing experience. Knowing yourself is the key; and then you can talk about what you need to do the best job.

Communication happens in three different ways: through conversations and explanations; through the rendering, sketch, and research; and through gesturing. There are three distinct methods by which people communicate or understand ideas: auditory, visual, and kinesthetic. Each person might respond better and more accurately in any one of these ways. Learning what works for you and the people you are communicating with can go a long way. Take the time to go back and forth until all parties are satisfied with understanding each other. Continue to ask for clarification or for someone to repeat back what you said in their own way, so you know that they understand what you mean. If the communication seems at all uncertain, it is good practice to send an email restating what you understood from the conversation. If communication is still misunderstood, hopefully the email will help to fix it, and there is also a record of the decisions agreed upon.

Trust

> "The most important thing is really setting it up from the beginning: that they [the costume designers] are confident that we [the shop] are going to make their designs beautiful. Make sure they know that we are as invested in their vision as they are."
> Susan Davis,[2] costume shop manager at Seattle Opera

Trust is such an important factor in the designer–shop relationship. Art is personal. Design aesthetic is personal. The shop work that is created is personal. So emotions are high and feelings can easily get hurt. The designer must trust that the shop will bring their ideas to fruition; that the draper will interpret from the renderings and research what the designer has imagined for the show. Ideally, the designer can expect that the shop knows how to expertly construct a garment to appropriately fit an actor. They can also expect guidelines on budget, fabric, builds, and timelines from the costume shop manager. The size of a shop and the skill level of the workers or volunteers greatly affect the work environment. Larger shops employ professionals who can handle any scope and scale of design, while smaller shops may have less experienced staff. It is possible a designer will need to step in to instruct on construction. Particularly upon first leaving a training program, a designer may need to have enough knowledge to get

their show up on stage. But this, hopefully, will not remain how they have to work for the span of their career. Working with a professional shop, a designer can concentrate on the design and allow the shop staff to handle construction.

DIFFERENT SHOP ENVIRONMENTS

There are several different types of costume shops. There are the large professional costume shops; small to medium professional costume shops; specialist shops like craft-focused shops or tailoring shops; regional theatre costume shops; summer stock costume shops; community theatre costume shops; and academic costume shops. The difference is often the number of employees, the technical skills of these employees, show and maintenance budgets, and other related expectations. How does a costume designer work differently in different shop environments? The experience differs from person to person and shop to shop, but there are some generalizations that offer guidelines on the different kinds of designer–shop experiences and where you might encounter them.

The smallest costume shops manage to create costumes despite very limited resources, space, equipment, and stock. These are usually associated with community theatre and utilize volunteers or independent contractors who are newly trained designers or technicians. The actors need costumes and these shops provide them. The dynamic is often led by the person hired as the designer. Then there are smaller shops; specialty shops, professional shops, or regional shops. At the opposite end of the spectrum there are the large professional regional, summer stock, or private costume shops.

Academic costume shops have the most complex set of parameters. Many schools aim to be a professional training ground. This is noble, but often difficult to achieve. The designers (students) in many instances are still learning; they are in the midst of educational development and need a place to figure things out. They need to gain their confidence as a designer, learn about design and construction, evaluate their personal strengths and weaknesses, and be taught how to trust a draper and yet still feel comfortable speaking up when something is not right. Conversely, in a professional environment, it is expected that at least half of these issues are already resolved. There is less room for discovery and experimentation. This is not referring to design specifics, new media, or out-of-the-box concept experimentation; it is about a designer finding their voice and knowing how to move a show through a shop. A young shop technician and a young designer still need the space to learn what works for them in the collaboration process. Most of the people involved in academic theatre are also juggling both production and educational responsibilities. They are not just designers or just shop personnel; they are students with homework and outside projects.

The small summer stock costume shop often has a team of employees and interns or volunteers who work long, hard hours in a fast-paced environment. The designer(s) work with the shop to produce many shows in a short amount of time. Summer stock costume shops are a team thrown together for a short amount of time to work on several shows. Young designers and technicians should always have some summer stock experience because of the pace and intensity. It is an experience unlike any other. Decisions must be reached quickly and the construction speed is heightened. If a young designer can be an assistant or design intern in this situation, they will learn a lot from someone who is more experienced. The hours are long and the people working as a team are with each other all day, every day, for several weeks. They often live together or very near each other and are removed from their everyday lives. This forces a unified focus, and is far removed from an undergraduate or graduate academic experience. There are also fantastic networking opportunities with theatre people of varied experience levels. Some large and established summer stock costume shops (for example, Utah Shakespeare Festival, and Santa Fe Opera) function much more similarly to the large professional shops.

In independent shops (large or small) the shop employees work for the individual who owns the costume shop. These shops can be specialty shops that provide an expertise in tailoring, beading, millinery, corsetry, or crafts; or they can provide all aspects of general costume production. The shop bids on costume jobs available from different designers which are being produced by different companies. A designer might choose a specific shop to work with, according to reputation or a positive previous working relationship. They may have discovered there is a draper that understands implicitly what they are trying to create. Or they might go to a specialist simply because they have specialist work. Frequently, the guiding factor will be budgetary. The bid process allows a show to be divided amongst different shops, catering to their specialties, and allowing the work to be spread out (particularly in a place like New York where there are many shop options, all within easy travel distance for the designer and the actors that need to attend fittings). Craft pieces can be made in one place, tailored jackets in another; the chorus in one shop and the leads in a different one. The owners of the shop are very hands on in the business of their shop and are involved in making the decision about how much things cost, who is going to shop for the fabric, what each of their drapers will work on, and how quickly they can expect to get a show in and out of the shop.

RENDERING AS COMMUNICATION

> "Your drawings are a tool. If you think you have to do the incredible, artful pictures for the producers or backers, do the drawings you need for the presentation. But then you have to have a much more informative sketch for the draper/shop. This can sometimes happen right as you are talking with the draper and you discover what they need to know that they don't see in the sketch."
> Mary Nemecek Peterson,[3] freelance costume designer

The foremost communication tool between the costume designer and the draper or shop is the costume **rendering**. The shop manager usually gets rough sketches from the designer very early on in the process in order to assess the general needs of the show so that they can assign budget constraints and personnel. However, when a show officially "comes into a shop," it is usually accompanied by drawings of each of the costumes for which the shop is responsible. The designer can provide a myriad of options to portray their ideas (collages, Photoshop, painted renderings, etc.). However, the primary purpose of these tools is to communicate with the people responsible for making the costumes happen so that they know what the designer wants as a final product.

The draper views the rendering as a piece of information, an important piece of information for sure, but just a means to the end product. The drawing is the designer's way to get their idea about a costume out on paper in order to share it with the shop, so the shop can create it. The draper can appreciate an artistic representation of a costume, but if they cannot glean the relevant information from it in order to make the costume, it is not a very useful tool. It is therefore very important to the shop that they see not only the artistic drawing, but also the research and specific detail that inform the designers' vision.

A rendering can miscommunicate what the end result will look like. If a rendering has a long thin figure to represent a costume that will essentially go on a short, curvy actress, the director may not ever see what they thought they were going to get from the costume. This is where a draper and designer work together to make the actor that has been cast look more like the character the director has envisioned. The designer should keep realistic body shapes in mind when making design choices, and the draper refines their eye for proportion to get the best possible look from the costume. If a young designer struggles with this, they might consider getting full body, front, side, and back photos of their actors. That way they can look at the real bodies

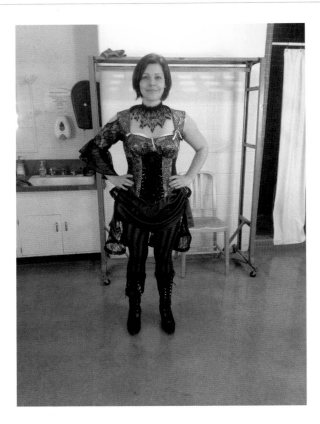

FIGURES 6.2–6.4 *Costume design for Jaquenetta in Love's Labour's Lost. (top left) Final rendering by Nicholas Hartman. (top right) Actor Sara J. Griffin in the final fitting. (right) Sara J. Griffin in performance at Illinois Shakespeare Festival at Illinois State University. (Photo by Pete Guither.)*

cast in the show and this might help them design most effectively for them.

Drapers will work with the rendering you give them; they want to give the designer the costume they designed. They are successful at what they do when the final product, the costume on an actor on a stage, looks like the rendering provided. Good drapers take great pride in their ability to analyze and replicate a sketch. They work hard to reproduce the style, shape, and proportion of a designer's drawing. In their training and experience they have hopefully worked with all varieties of rendering styles. The more they transform what they see in a rendering into an actual garment, the better they get at doing it. Young drapers should be encouraged to take basic drawing, sculpture, or figure drawing classes. Aside from learning some specific language from the fine arts, it is excellent training in how to translate proportion. They learn how to reinterpret what they see right in front of them. Doing this over and over again in a variety of formats is, surprisingly, as helpful for a draper as it is for a designer.

A designer can expect a draper to analyze a rendering quite literally. Drapers may take proportions, height, and width directly from the drawing. Drapers have been known to measure each piece in a rendering to figure out the proportion in relation to the other pieces. The initial goal of a draper is to recreate (as exactly as possible) the designer's drawing: they should not "correct" for historical accuracy or be influenced by their personal aesthetic. Mary Nemecek Peterson,[3] explains, "I count on the draper to not try to improve on the design, but try to get the best out of the designs in cooperation with the designer." A good draper will have extensive knowledge about costume history, and what is right and wrong for a period. Therefore, a designer can expect a dialogue about historical idiosyncrasies if the show is not authentically period accurate. The informed draper will want to confirm that what is put on paper is exactly what the designer wishes to see. It is not the job of the draper to change any of the details, and so if something seems inaccurate, they should query with the designer. As mentioned previously, clear and open communication is the key to a successful working relationship.

THE SHOW IN THE SHOP

> "The idea I try to pass along to students is that it is always good to walk in as a designer knowing at least one way to execute the idea—but then be open to see and hear amazing ways to implement your vision that you could not begin to imagine."
>
> Campbell Baird,[4] Professor, Department of Design for Stage & Film, New York University

Shop Staff

There are many people working in a costume shop because there are many specialized steps in the construction process. A specific job title does not always mean exactly the same job description from shop to shop; there are regional variances and colloquialisms. For example, the person who is the head of a costume construction team is known as a draper, a cutter, or a cutter–draper depending on which part of the country you are in. All of the shop personnel are valuable artists in their own right, and are knowledgeable about areas in which the designer is not an expert. Many designers are very good drapers or tailors, but when they come into a shop as the designer their role is specifically defined. Being able to let the shop do its job will most often get the project done most efficiently and, sometimes, even better than the designer could have imagined.

The costume shop manager or **costume director** is the person in charge of how the shop is run on a day-to-day basis. They are in charge of the overall shop budget including labor, materials, office supplies, and items required to keep the shop running. This position is often the liaison with other production positions and management personnel. Costume shop managers have to keep track of the entire shop's working budget, as well as the show-by-show breakdown. From initial conversations with designers, production managers, and directors, they will ascertain the major needs and expectations for each show, and divide up the budget appropriately. Costume shop managers oversee all work as it occurs, from each team and for every show.

> "The costume shop manager supervises the entire costume shop, including wardrobe, to ensure a consistent standard of work and product. He/she oversees all of the daily 'business' for the costume shop and for each production; he/she works to create a cohesive costume look for every event that Arizona Opera is associated with."
>
> Kathleen Trott,[5] costume shop manager at Arizona Opera

FIGURE 6.5   *The costume shop at Illinois Shakespeare Festival at Illinois State University.*

The **cutter–draper** is responsible for overseeing the creation of the designed costumes. They alter and fit costumes that are pulled from stock or rented. They plan the embellishments for existing garments. They build garments that do not yet exist. This position has extensive contact with the designer. It is the cutter–draper's job to figure out the mechanics of a costume so that it works on stage. When building a costume, they will create the patterns and the structure and shape of a costume so that it looks like the rendering on the actor who wears it. The cutter–draper is the prevalent artistic supervisor responsible for the construction or alteration of their assigned costumes.

The **first or second hand** works alongside the cutter–draper in order to take the patterns from the cutter–draper and fit the pieces of the puzzle onto the chosen and appropriate fabrics. They are the "first hands" on the chosen fabric, making sure it is prepared properly; whether the fabric is just washed

and dried, ironed and steamed, or if they have to administrate the coordination with a dyer–painter. The first hand will assist the cutter–draper in fittings, and then interpret the cutter–draper's pins, marks, and words. They will collaborate with the cutter–draper to determine the best construction methods for creating each piece. The stitchers look to the first hand for instruction or direction on how the pieces of fabric go together to make the costume. As they are often the work distribution channel from the cutter–draper to the stitchers, the first hand is a key player on the shop team, but they do not always have a lot of interaction with the designer.

The **stitcher** is the person responsible for sewing a costume together or stitching the alterations. They must be proficient in a variety of hand stitches and be skillful in using a sewing machine. (Although in larger shops, the machine stitching and the hand stitching are sometimes two different jobs done by two different people.) Stitchers must possess basic garment construction knowledge, have an understanding of what fabric can and cannot do, and know how to cleanly finish a costume. They usually work under the direct supervision of the first hand and/or cutter–draper during the build process, rarely having any direct contact with the designer. It is often the entry-level position for a costume shop employee. But stitching is an art and talent in itself: specialists can sew and manipulate fabric to create the most stunning garments. Specialties include: tailors who make primarily menswear and create structured, finely finished garments; finishers, who are expert at hand sewing and complete the final detail work on a garment, creating a beautiful finished masterpiece inside and out; and beaders, who meticulously apply beads for embellishment. Most of these skills are needed in every shop, even if one person holds several of these specialties.

FIGURE 6.6 *A draper, Artur Allakhverdyan, at his work for* Wicked *on* Broadway. *(Design by Susan Hilferty. Photo by Tova Moreno.)*

FIGURE 6.8 *A tailor, Artur Allakhverdyan, pressing a jacket for* Nice Work if you Can Get It *on Broadway (Design by Martin Pakledinaz. Photo by Tova Moreno.)*

FIGURE 6.7 *A first hand, Svetlana Poplavska at Artur & Tailors Inc., strikes a pattern onto fabric for* Cabaret *on Broadway. (Design by William Ivey Long. Photo by Tova Moreno.)*

FIGURE 6.9 *A stitcher, Tetyana Uhlitskykh, at her work for Spider-Man: Turn off the Dark on Broadway. (Design by Eiko Ishioka. Photo by Tova Moreno.)*

What's in a Role?

Natalie Kurczewski,[6] Staff Draper at Signature Theatre, Arlington, VA (and Former Principal Men's Cutter at the Royal Shakespeare Company, UK) explains:

"At the RSC [the shop manager] was called Head of Costume. He was also the liaison between the costume department and the outside world. Because our shop was so expansive, there were also several HODs (Heads of Department). As Principal Men's Cutter, I was the Deputy HOD.

Draper is not a term that is used in the UK. I was a cutter, as was my HOD. The cutter did the jobs of both the draper and the first hand. I was responsible for interpreting the rendering, creating the patterns, and cutting the fabric. I also prepped any fabric and chose interfacings and linings.

"There were several levels of Maker [stitcher is not a term used in the UK] at the RSC. Makers were responsible for taking the cut pieces and not only putting them together, but *knowing* how to put them together. I very rarely had to give instruction to the makers. They also cut basic pieces, such as pockets and flys, so my time was better spent elsewhere. This was *not* an entry level position."

materials. This position often has extensive contact with the designer because there are specific visual design elements that need to be conveyed, and possibly mechanical action that needs to be addressed related to the movement of the actors in the show.

Craft work can be carried out within a costume shop by a separate team, an existing member of the team, or a separate craft shop. Crafts can involve a variety of items or pieces that the designer has specified that do not encompass traditional sewing or garment construction. It might be dyeing fabric to match a specific color; painting fabric to give it a print; or modifying fabric to resemble embellishment. Hat-making techniques will be required if there is **millinery** work that needs to be done. Exceptional three-dimensional elements needed for some craft work involves mechanics and exotic forms, hence the use of less traditional materials and mediums rather than fabric and thread. These might include foam, glue, felt, thermoplastics, wire frames, plastics, metals, wood or bamboo, rods and reeds of all sorts, and more. The craft person should have interest and knowledge in these other areas and in the safety of using these non-traditional

Sucessful Craft Work

Killer[7] is a phenomenal craft artisan who has worked for years in New York City. She has worked for the larger professional shops and has opened her own craft specialty shop. She describes her craft process and how she works with designers in the following way:

"The designer should provide complete sketches, research, and inspiration while I help problem solve their ideas and make them a reality. The most important thing I need from designers is inspiration! The rendering should give good proportion and be well thought out as far as how the costume will work on the body, especially when it comes to craft work. Craft work is very difficult to price out and if it is not well thought out, the cost to me can put me out of business. I have turned down huge productions because the design team and the director were clearly not on the same page.

"Small clarifying sketches of different views are also very helpful in crafts. Often craft designs need to be more three dimensional. It is also very important for the designer to know their materials and let me know how they want the costume to move and feel. I need to understand how the piece works in the show. Sometimes it can be very helpful to understand the context of the scene that the piece is in. Knowing how the choreography is going to be is crucial from a craft work perspective. The designer and the director should be very in sync on choreography. When it comes to mechanical pieces, it is crucial for the mechanical guy and/or lighting guy to participate in the discussions from the beginning. The designer and director can get more of what they want if they do that."

FIGURE 6.10 *A craft space at Indiana University, showing wigs that have been prepared for a production.*

Wig Complexities

The person handling wigs or hair goes by many different titles. Martha Ruskai,[8] co-author of *Wig Making and Styling: A Complete Guide for Theatre & Film*[9] had this to say about the title complexity:

"'Hair/Wig/Makeup Designers' communicate with the director and cast, and consult with the costume designer, but they are not bound to their renderings or choices. This position/title is rare in regional theater but more common in regional opera where costumes are rented and fit by local wardrobe heads. The title should only be used in situations where the person functions as a member of the design team and does all the design work expected including script analysis, attending meetings, and discussions with the director and other members of the team.

"'Wig Master' or less commonly 'Wig Mistress' or 'Wig Artisan' are the titles for the person who builds, fits, alters, styles, and is ultimately responsible for the upkeep of the wigs. Wig Masters are akin to drapers and work from costume renderings and research. This position is most common when a company has someone in position as full time/seasonal staff.

"'Hair & Wig Stylist' would be used for someone who is there every day handling both performer hair and the styling and upkeep of the wigs.

"'Wigs by'/'Wigs provided by'/'Wigs built by' are for those times when a wigmaker is brought in specifically for a production, is not on staff, and is not running the show."

Martha also had excellent advice for costume designers who want to participate in the design of hair and wigs: "1) Render based on the performer's hairline, skull shape, and facial features so that the hairstyle details will be proportional. 2) Provide usable front, side, and back research and sketches including any hat skeletons. 3) Be prepared to discuss what you want it to look like in detail, but do *not* tell the wig person how to achieve it."

The **wardrobe person** is responsible for maintaining the costumes once the show has progressed to dress rehearsal. This position works primarily backstage and handles getting the actors ready for the show and helping them get in and out of the appropriate costumes, sometimes very fast. They are also responsible for laundry and fixing items that break during the run of the show. The wardrobe person must think quickly because if

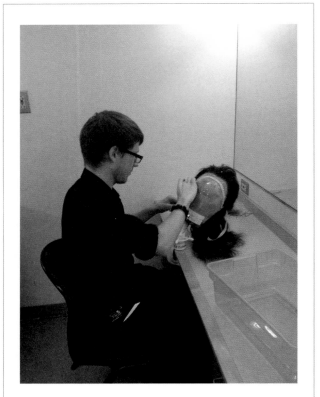

FIGURE 6.11 *James Renton taking care of a wig for a production of* Hedda Gabler *at Indiana University.*

FIGURE 6.12 *The women's dressing room during a production of* Hedda Gabler *at Indiana University.*

a problem with a costume occurs during the show, it is usually just minutes before the actor must be onstage again. The role involves extensive interactions with the shop, the actors, and stage managers. A wardrobe person will also have interaction with the designer during dress rehearsals.

Some other shop personnel work very closely with the designer, and a new designer might seek these positions in order to work with a more experienced designer. A shopper is the person who makes local or virtual purchases to meet the needs presented by the sketch of the designer. They are accountable to both the designer and the draper, and must make appropriate fabric, trim, and other purchasing choices. A design assistant is sometimes employed by a costume shop (for example, at Santa Fe Opera), or they might be employed directly by the designer.

Design Assistance at Utah Shakespeare Festival

Jennifer L. Bach[10] is Costume Shop Supervisor at Utah Shakespeare Festival, and interprets design assistance as follows:

"In the Costume Shop here at Utah Shakespeare Festival, we do not hire Design Assistants for our Costume Designers, generally speaking. The Costume Shop Administrative staff offer a lot of design assistance as part of our day-to-day jobs.

"I know the costume stock better than anyone and can often inform the designers whether or not something could be pulled rather than purchased or built. I also go to stock with the Designers to help pull things—and I transport the costumes back and forth. Jeff Lieder knows [all the] resources for purchasing materials and actual costume pieces (dance wear, western wear, etc), and often orders materials for the shows after consulting the Costume Designers. Lori Hartenhoff sources the shoes for nearly all of the productions in the summer season, thereby guaranteeing that we get quality footwear that should last the entire run.

"Because we consolidate our efforts, we are able to have fewer orders (less shipping!) and standing relationships with vendors. We even have wholesale accounts set up with some of the vendors we use on a regular basis (Stacy Adams, Scully, and others).

"For the past couple of years, we have someone in the shop with the official title of Costume Design Assistant, but in reality, that person serves more as the next step down from me—more of an Assistant Shop Manager. The Festival pays that person hourly, just as everyone else in the shop."

Design Assistance at Parsons-Meares

Tony Johnson,[11] Head Shopper at Parsons-Meares and freelance costume designer, gives an alternate perspective as he discusses Design Assistants and Associates, and how they work in a large costume shop like Parsons-Meares.

"Large Theatre Show, Main Associate, Associates, and Assistants: When working on large shows for Broadway there is a main associate with other associates or assistants working with them. We use the main associate to get in touch with the designer and to schedule meetings and fittings. We rarely contact the designer directly. If we need clarification about some notes from a meeting, we ask the main associate. The main associate is also the keeper of the designer's schedule for the show. Design meetings are scheduled through them. Sometimes when the designer is unavailable, they will answer our design questions. They coordinate with stage management, wardrobe, and the designer to decide when and where each fitting happens. We also work with the main associate as the primary point person during the bidding process, by sending them the prices and negotiations.

"Other Large Shows, Main Assistant: On other shows, like an ice show, there is a different chain of command. Feld Entertainment is a large entertainment company and they have a main costume supervisor for all of their shows, including, and not limited to, ice shows, circus, and 'live' shows. She is who we do the bidding process with. She also has the final say, over the designer, about which

fabrics and materials are used because she knows what each show requires in terms of being laundered, and how much wear they will get. The assistants make the show bible and request for swatches.

"Other Shows, Main Assistant (when applicable): Finally, there are shows where the assistant is present, but we usually speak directly to the designer. For these types of shows, the assistant is used more like a runner. They drop off costume pieces or fabrics. The assistant is usually contacted when we can't get a hold of the designer. The assistant sends us measurements, makes the show bible, and requests for swatches."

Design Assistance at Santa Fe Opera

Eriko Terao,[12] a freelance costume designer and technician, offers a third perspective on how the Assistant Costume Designers are used in a shop environment. She recently worked at Santa Fe Opera and made the following observations from that shop:

"The Assistant Costume Designer is a person who keeps the shop running during the designer's absence. He/she is also a 'translator' in between artisans and designer. Tasks include:

1. Pull rehearsal costumes and store them in assigned rehearsal costume storage.

2. Pull costumes for designers to go through.

   — Ideally, check measurements and seam allowance in advance. (When I helped to pull costumes for a designer, I wrote garment measurements, seam allowance, and the singer's name on a tag so it would be easier for the designer to make decisions prior to fittings. I am not sure if everyone else did this.) You can make rough design choices based on the designer's research and renderings when pulling.

3. Prepare for fittings.

   — Have garments ready to go in the fitting room . . . not every assistant did this at SFO but I would have research pictures and/or renderings available. Get the fitting started before the designer arrives. Basically, do whatever you need to do to save as much as time possible during the fitting.

Fitting time is very limited, especially with equity actors/performers.

4. Attend rehearsals as needed.

5. Be a messenger in between the designer and the cutter/drapers.

  — Assist cutter/drapers with their needs while the designer is absent.

  — Pass on the designer's notes to drapers and vice versa.

  — Pass on items which the designer has pulled to the assigned team in an organized manner (i.e., buttons in labeled plastic bags; and swatches with labels).

6. Make lists of distressing so the dye shop can start planning the dye schedule.

7. Take notes during dress rehearsals.

  — Share notes with the cutter/drapers, wardrobe supervisor, and shop supervisor."

FIGURE 6.13 *Costume storage/stock at Indiana University.*

The Shop Process

After the costume shop manager has had preliminary conversations with the designer over the first sketches in order to assess the viability of the show (in terms of timescale, personnel, budget, and resources), the process in the shop then moves quickly through to opening night. In the beginning stages, the designer works closest with the shop manager, who will help to assess what can be pulled and/or altered from stock, what the options are for purchasing costume pieces, what rental options might be explored, and when the time and money is best spent building a costume. A shop manager will know how fast their staff can work, and be able to estimate how long the proposed builds should take. Complete costume builds require a lot of time from experienced drapers and stitchers, so this option is often prioritized for hard-to-fit bodies, costumes that can't be found anywhere else, and/or leading characters.

The shop manager is also a good resource for finding fabric, **notions**, trims, and extra costume items. They should have a good handle on the availability of these things locally, so that someone can run out and purchase that day; and what needs to be ordered, from where, for how much, and how long it should take to ship. A designer would do well to listen carefully to the shop manager's advice. This might be the designer's only show in a particular city, or the first show with a theatre, so it is the shop manager who has experience with what has worked, and not worked, with purchases for other shows that have come through their shop. The shop manager has also established relationships with rental companies and vendors, and can assist a designer through the process. They continue to be a valuable resource for the designer throughout the entire process. They will often be the liaison with company management, to schedule fittings and provide rehearsal pieces at stage management's request.

The Draper's Role

After the shop manager and the designer have agreed upon how to source each costume piece, shop managers meet with the shop drapers to divvy up the show's work. All the teams will get a sense of the scale, scope, and style of the design. Assuming multiple drapers, each show is divided between the different teams of workers. A team usually consists of a cutter–draper, a first hand, and stitchers—both machine and hand. The shop manager tries to keep the workload balanced while charging each team with costumes that play to their strengths, so that the best work is produced most efficiently for each show in the shop. Some environments permit each show to be the only one worked on at a time. But many shops juggle multiple shows by different designers at all times.

The next step for the designer is therefore to meet with the drapers or other artisans. They are expected to speak about the show, the concept, and the costumes generally, as well as specifically. This helps to get everyone who is responsible for making costumes onto the same page. The designer may also need to have similar but separate conversations with the dye shop (or anyone who might be doing crafts, tailoring, dyeing, or distressing). In some shops this happens all together; there is one big meeting to explain the design needs for the whole show to everyone. In other shops, the designer may meet individually with each of the more specialized teams, so that the makers can ask specific questions, similar to the process between the draper and the designer now described.

The draper looks at the rendering and analyzes what the designer is trying to achieve. They may do some of their own research. This process involves looking at patterns from the time period, patterns from similar costumes they have previously made, or examining relevant clothing and construction methods that might influence how they would begin their draping job. They will analyze the actor's measurements, and the measurement sheet used is usually quite extensive. The most basic information would include the bust, waist, hip, height, inseam, outseam, and sleeve length. However, given proper time to measure, there are approximately 60 measurements that most costume shops take so that multiple circumferences and lengths of all limbs, trunk, and head are included. This information is shared with the designer so they can use the actor's measurements to pull items or order items for the costume.

The draper wants to know exactly how an actor is shaped so that they can reproduce a reasonable facsimile of their body on a dress form. Several photos of the actor may be taken; a close up of the face, and several full body shots. This helps the draper to see postural idiosyncrasies so they can accommodate for the natural body shape of the actor. The draper pads out a dress form to the size and shape of the actor. This will allow the draper and designer to see the costume on an actor's form in the shop as they work. It is good practice to also try to match skin tone at the first meeting: in case anything needs to be dyed to disappear

FIGURE 6.14 *Example of a detailed measurement form created by Rebecca Kaufman, co-founder of www. periodcorsets.com, and current owner of www.beelignes.com (for custom covered buttons).*

Name:				Date:		Measured by Initials:		
Height		Suit		Glove		Right/Left handed		
Weight		Trouser		Hat		Allergies		
Shoe		Shirt		Jeans		Ears Pierced: Y/N	Tattoos: Y/N	
Widths						**Head and Neck**		
SH to SH Front			SH to SH Back			Head Circumference		
Across Front Scye to Scye			Across Back Scye to Scye			Nape to Hairline		
						Ear to Ear Across Forehead		
Circumferences and Lengths						Ear to Ear Over Top		
Torso						Mid Neck		
Chest or Bust/Expanded			CF Neck to Waist			Neck Base		
Ribcage/Expanded			CF Neck to Floor			**Boot measures**		
Women Bust Pt to Pt			Nape to Waist			Upper Thigh		Ankle
Waist			Nape to below Seat			Middle Thigh		Heel
High Hip			Nape to Knee			Above Knee		Instep
Hip			Nape to Floor			Knee		Ball
			Crotch Depth/Rise			Below Knee		
Legs and Girth						Calf		
Thigh			Waist to Below Knee			Above Ankle		
Knee			Waist to Ankle			**Tailoring Measures**		
Below Knee			Waist to Floor			*Stance*		Front Shoulder
Calf			Inseam			Normal		Over Shoulder
Ankle			Half Girth			Forward		Scye Depth
Instep			Full Girth			Erect		Nat. Waist
Arm						*Shoulder Slope*		Length
Armscye			Neck to Shoulder			Normal		Sleeve
Bicep			SH to Elbow			Steep		Across Back
Elbow			SH to Wrist, Bent			Square		Across Chest
Forearm			Arm Inseam			**Cape Measures**		
Wrist						Around Arms and Shoulder @ SH:		
Hand						Nape to Waist:	Nape to Floor:	

against the actor's skin, the dye person would know what color to match. An experienced dyer–painter might have a ring of skin tone color swatches to compare to the actor in order to help the team to share this information. The shop may also have a ring of hair color swatches for the same purpose, or to choose alternate wig colors.

As the draper begins creating the costumes, there are additional one-on-one conversations between the draper and the designer. Drapers strive to ask questions as they come up, such as:

- What fabric/lining/interfacing would you like to use?

- What undergarments will the actor be wearing?

- Where would you like there to be openings?

- What does the back view look like?

- Are there any quick-change needs?

- Will the insides of the garment be seen while onstage?

- What finishing details would you like to see?

- How historically accurate are you aiming to be?

All of these questions will influence how the maker interprets the designer's rendering. The goal is to recreate the designer's designs as closely as possible. When the draper feels confident that they understand what the designer wants to see, they will move forward with their work.

There should be a clear understanding, early in the process, of what each person is doing for the production and when. To those that see costume construction as an art, there is a beauty in a perfect invisible zipper, in a well-set sleeve, in a balanced skirt, or in creative **style lines**. The artisans that make costumes take pride in what they can accomplish with stitches and fabric manipulation. The makers appreciate the art in a designer's ideas. Both parties should develop a mutual respect for the process, and every person involved should feel like part of a team.

> "Just say what you're thinking—we *want* to give the designer what they want and if they can be open and speak their mind from the start that is very helpful!"
> Katherine Marshall,[1] owner and draper at Tricorne

Oftentimes the next step in the construction process involves the draper quickly producing a half drape of the costume to more specifically discuss the costume with the designer. This is where the draper has put muslin or other draping fabric up on half of the actor's dress form, pinning fabric together to get the desired shape of the garment. They often draw on this half drape to indicate where the neckline is, what the hem is doing, or where embellishments might go. This step is nowhere near a finished product. It is unquestionably a working document. It gives the two artists a three-dimensional medium to look at and discuss. A half drape is helpful because it clarifies that both people understand each other; they are talking about the same shape, proportion, style, fullness, length, and detail. It gives the designer a moment to see how the draper is interpreting their rendering. Since it is not in any finished form, there is inherent freedom to discuss, change, or clarify what the designer really wants. The lack of time and money invested in this step belies the volumes it speaks about the direction in which the draper is taking the costume. Even the most experienced drapers will not always see things the way a designer intended. The designer must speak up and be able to clarify where the differences are. The draper will adjust the direction of their process at this step, and will make their actual patterns after this conversation.

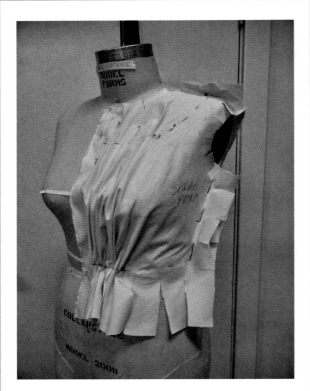

FIGURE 6.15 *A half-draped bodice from a production of* Italian Straw Hat *at the University of Alabama. (Costume design by Donna Meester. Draper: Anne Sorenson.)*

FIGURE 6.16 *Mockup pattern pieces for Jaquenetta's bodice in a production of* Love's Labour's Lost *at Illinois Shakespeare Festival.*

The draper takes on board the designer's comments, and makes corrections to the muslin from the half drape. The shapes will then be put onto paper. Now the draper begins to work with their team, handing the patterns to their first hand. In this mockup phase, the team will work out what the challenges or needs of the costume might be. The designer will be in communication with the team as questions come up. The first fitting is not usually done in the actual chosen fabric; however, it should be made out of fabric that has a similar drape. This will allow the actor and the designer to most accurately see and feel how the costume will hang, move, and look. This mockup for the first fitting is still a conversation piece. It is another way to make sure that the draper has the correct shapes needed to make the final costume. This step in the process allows the costume to go onto the actor so that the best fit and proportion can be definitively decided upon. The first fitting usually happens in the first third of the build time because it is important to leave enough time for finishing the garment in the chosen fabric.

The Fitting Stages

There are usually at least three people in the first fitting of a costume (the mockup fitting); the actor, the draper, and the designer (and occasionally an assistant). It is extremely helpful to have the correct undergarments and accessories at this fitting in case they change any element of the design or shape of the costume. For example, the shape of a skirt is drastically altered by the addition of a bustle, and all bustles are not the same. Without having the real undergarments at the mockup fitting, a dress cut

in the show fabric might not be able to properly cover the top of a bra if the neckline was cut too deep.

In the fitting, the draper and the assistant help the actor to get dressed in the costume pieces. When the draper sees the costume on the actor, they will adjust the costume to get the best fit and style for the design. They might pin out some fullness, or open a seam, or draw in a new neckline. This is still part of the working process. The designer will have their rendering, and possibly research, for reference to compare against the mockup on the actor. The actor will be asked how they feel about fit, and if they are able to move as their character dictates. The designer and the draper will use this information to decide on changes. Together, the designer and the draper will look at the costume on the actor and make sure it is what the designer envisions for the final costume. The designer should be able to see an accurate representation of their rendering in this fitting. The main difference is that it is not in the correct fabric, and may simply be made from a cheaper fabric such as muslin. The costume should fit the actor like it was made for them, because, in fact, it was. First fittings often happen after the actor is well into rehearsal

FIGURE 6.17 *A mockup on an actor, Sara J. Griffin, as Jaquenetta in a production of* Love's Labour's Lost *at Illinois Shakespeare Festival.*

FIGURE 6.18 *The designer (Emilio Sosa), the draper (Artur Allakhverdyan), and the actor (Ephraim Sykes) in a fitting at Artur & Tailors Inc., for a Broadway production of* Motown. *(Photo by Tova Moreno.)*

FIGURE 6.19 *Actor Berklea Going in a fitting for Rosa Bud in a production of* The Mystery of Edwin Drood *at Indiana University. (Costume design by Eriko Terao.)*

and they should have a good idea of what they are doing in this costume, as well as what they are doing before and after. Quick changes can be discussed in case special rigging needs to be accommodated for.

It is very helpful to take photos in this first fitting. Although the draper and the designer or assistant will take notes about what alterations are needed, a fitting can move so quickly that notes may make no sense after you have seen multiple costumes on several actors in one day. "A picture speaks a thousand words," they say, so you should try to take close-up photos of places that are not fitting properly in order to better think about the solution after the fitting. Also take full body shots to make sure the proportions and fit are appropriate. Use of photography helps to move the fitting along, which is important when time is short, but the designer and the draper can also use these photos outside of the fitting room to discuss the costume and what needs to be changed. Photographing each stage of the build and fitting process is therefore good practice.

Proper etiquette in a fitting is vital: it is important to speak carefully and professionally. It is very common for a designer or a draper (especially when they have a pre-established relationship with an actor) to be overly casual, but the conversation should stay focused on the costume. There should be no commentary or joking about the actor's body, shape, or size. The designer and the draper should always be conscious of the people in the room. The actor is a person, who wants to look their best in the role that they are playing onstage. The draper should also be consciously considerate of the designer with whom they are working: it is not a draper's job to comment on any aspect of the design. The team will have time to speak frankly in the shop after the actor has left. Also, the designer and the draper should be careful not to discuss any problems they are having with any other member of the company, be it the artistic team or other actors.

Keeping an actor focused on their role in the show and engaged in small talk can be helpful to keep the actor from unnecessarily fidgeting or picking at their costume. Sometimes, the more an actor stares at themselves in the large, well-lit fitting room mirror, the more problematic they can find the costume. However, Susan Davis,[2] at the Seattle Opera, says that she "pays attention to the places the actor/singer picks at or keeps touching, as it can be a good indicator that something feels odd or suspiciously uncomfortable."

After the first fitting, the draper will take their notes, photos, and the mockup back to their workspace and figure out what needs to be altered before they create the final garment. They will talk to the designer and make sure everyone understands what needs to happen and what has to change. They will alter the patterns while considering closures, hems, interfacings, linings, and all of the elements that will make the finished costume perfect. This is when the first hand will cut the real fabric pieces. They will have discussed specifically with their draper how the garment pieces go together and how they are finished. They should have thoroughly considered the construction of the garment so that if a stitcher has a question, the first hand can answer.

There is usually at least one more fitting in the final fabric. This way the actor, the designer, and the draper can all see the mostly finished garment. Undergarments and shoes are absolutely necessary at this fitting because hems will be marked and the final finishing will be decided upon. The rendering should be in the fitting room for comparison purposes, to make sure this final garment is exactly what was imagined. The costume in real fabric should be a three-dimensional version of the design. Taking photos at this fitting is highly recommended. It allows everyone

FIGURE 6.20 *The final garment fitting for Matthew Weidenbener as* The Giantess *in a production of* Into the Woods *at Indiana University. (Costume design by Kelsey Nichols.)*

FIGURES 6.21 & 6.22 *Costume design for Rosa Bud in a production of* The Mystery of Edwin Drood. *(left) Final rendering by Eriko Terao. (right) Berklea Going in performance at Indiana University. (Costume design by Eriko Terao.)*

FIGURE 6.23 Costumes in the dressing room at Indiana University.

"They only get one fitting, in the real fabric, for the leads. Although this seems difficult to make sure everyone is satisfied with the end result, they accomplish this by making a full mockup and putting it on the dress form. They eliminate the performer from this initial conversation. The reason for this is that the leads only come to town three weeks before dress rehearsal.

"The thing about opera is that the singers are the most valuable asset. It's not a rehearsal process like the theatre. There isn't a lot of development. There is just not time. They are not paid to rehearse. They are paid to perform. Those three weeks they are here to get the performance up."

Susan Davis,[2] costume shop manager at Seattle Opera

to see what has to be done to finish the garment and to get it on stage. If there are multiple chorus people, seeing photos together can help unify hem lengths and finishing touches. Photos next to the rendering, side by side and in the same scale, can be

compared to make sure the draper has done all they can to give the designer what they put on paper.

Finally, the team carries out all the finishing work on the garments: all seams are made clean and secure so that they will not unravel or fray; all linings and closures will be finished; and all hems will be completed. The costume may then need further attention from the painting and distressing department of the shop. Once everyone is satisfied that the costume is finished, it is put on the done rack and is ready for transport to the stage.

WHERE DESIGN MEETS TECHNOLOGY

In academic settings or smaller theatre venues, a costumer may possess equal abilities in both design and technology, and they will use both skills to bring a show to life. Many students starting a career in costuming feel they need to choose one path over the other, but there are undergraduate and graduate training programs that give costumers equal training in both, and there are programs that train each area specifically. This variance in training helps meet the needs and desires of the students and prepares them differently depending on what kind of theatre they pursue. Whether a student wants to do just one, or do both equally, it is always good for students to know a fair amount about how the other area works. There are many pieces to this costume puzzle; the goal is getting them to work together.

Technology Skills

The costume designer and the costume shop work hand-in-hand alongside one another. Although they each have their specialties, there needs to be a common language and basic understanding of the processes and techniques that each utilize. Good costume shop personnel should learn the basics of rendering, research, play analysis, and collaboration with other creative artists. They should also have solid fashion history knowledge.

"It's a dance, sometimes it's like the tango and sometimes it's a waltz. There is a beauty that comes from both. If you don't know anything about your collaborator's part, then you can't appreciate what they are contributing to the process."

Hilary Rosenfeld,[13] freelance costume designer

When shop personnel were interviewed, one of the basic things they found lacking in young designers was good, in-depth knowledge about fabric, what it can do, and how it works. Fabric is the medium through which our art is created. Although a designer might be a wonderful artist—the end product, the art, isn't the sketch: it is a garment made of fabric that appears on the stage. Knowing the limitations and the possibilities of your medium is vital. It is important for a designer to have an understanding of different fibers, different weaves, and different weights of fabric. Knowing what fabric is correct for the garment that is being created for each character is crucial. A draper can do a lot with a poor choice of fabric but it helps the whole project if decisions about fabric are being made from an informed position.

> "I think purposeful, educated choices are more welcome than the fabric choice made off the cuff without regard for construction value. I will say that designers don't need to know how to sew and pattern with *skill and precision*. But, if they have at least a basic understanding of how things go together and how fabric choices impact their design, the working relationship between the technician and the designer will result in a better realized design."
> Rebecca Kaufman,[14] co-founder of www.periodcorsets.com, and current owner of www.beelignes.com

In some shops, there are staff who will help designers to make fabric choices. Susan Davis, costume director of the Seattle Opera, often goes fabric shopping with the designers. As already mentioned, some larger shops have a shopping department or shoppers that specifically do the purchasing. Some specialty artisans, like crafts people, need to do the shopping themselves because figuring out the materials is an integral part of their development process. But in other places, the designer is responsible for purchasing fabric on their own.

> "I don't expect designers to be able to double as dressmakers, but the problem with not educating them in construction is that, as a result, young designers are woefully inexperienced with *fabric*. The way to learn about fabric, which is their true medium, is to make garments. The single most important decision a designer makes is what fabric to use. If you don't have construction experience, you never get your hands on the medium of your art form."
> Nancy Julian,[15] costume shop manager at Alley Theatre

A draper can participate in trouble shooting and planning up front if a designer comes in with a less than ideal fabric choice (for example, a drapey charmeuse to create a highly structured jacket). The shop has tricks in their toolbox (such as interfacing or treating the fabric in a specific way), so the draper can get creative in changing the natural properties of the fabric. The general consensus from costume shop personnel is that it is less appreciated when the designer makes poor material choices without even appearing to know that they are making the construction difficult.

> "It really helps if the designer says something like, 'I know this isn't normal,' or 'This might be asking a lot, but I'd like to . . . ' If they can enlist me/us in the challenge of unusual materials, rather than just assume we can make any design out of any fabric, they'll get a better result."
> Sheila P. Morris,[16] tailor at Denver Center Theatre Company

Learn about fabric. Touch a lot of fabric. It is good practice for young designers to make and keep a fabric swatch ring, to use as an effective communication tool. Collect swatches of everyday and specialty fabric and label them with full information on the back. This helps a designer to learn about fabric and helps them distinguish one fabric from another. It also can help with purchasing fabric in the future; you can keep track of what it is, where you can get it, and how much it costs. Designers need to choose fabric in the show's color scheme to show to the director,

FIGURE 6.24 A fabric swatch ring.

but the shop is much more interested in the correct fabric weight, texture, and weave.

Finally, a designer should have solid knowledge of basic costume construction terms. A costume designer should learn to sew. They do not have to have great skill, or even gain enjoyment from it. There is no need to be able to produce their own designs, unless they choose to do so. But they need to know the basics, and trying their hand at some costume or clothing construction means that that they will know the steps involved in the process. The designer does not need to be skilled in making a beautiful French seam in chiffon, but knowing why that might be done or what it looks like is essential for meaningful communication with the shop.

Digital Skills

Communication has been stressed as one of the most important aspects of creating a positive working environment between the costume designer and the costume shop. Face-to-face communication has been the primary discussion thus far. However nowadays, with the prevalence of digital media, this standard has begun to change. Most people spend inordinate amounts of time in front of their smart phone, tablet, or computer, and most adults are comfortable communicating with many people in their lives through digital means.

Technology is being developed to assist and simplify all sorts of tasks, including many aspects of costume design and technology. Digital mediums have infiltrated the shop–designer dynamic. The first introduction to a designer or to a shop is often what can be found out about them online. Renderings are first seen when sent in digital format. The in-person discussion is sometimes replaced by a digital meeting, phone conversation, or email correspondence. Even having a designer present in a fitting room is occasionally replaced by photos being taken and sent electronically. Although this may have happened due to budget cuts, or perhaps a lack of time to travel great distances, it is now more socially acceptable. People are more comfortable with a digital reality, and the technology is improving so rapidly that digital photography is extraordinarily accurate. It may not feel as personable to look over renderings on your computer screen or to be sitting in separate cities while using Skype, but it is crucial that communication involves everybody in whatever way necessary.

There is a heated debate about the use of social media in the costuming industry. Some people are keen to use social media at every opportunity. For instance, the marketing department want to entice potential audience with "behind the scenes" vantage points, and actors want to share their experience backstage by using the theatre's or show's hashtag. Yet this can become contentious because some designers and technicians believe that their work is being poorly represented if the costumes are not in a finished state. It is therefore important for each company to clarify what is appropriate and acceptable for posting photos on social media.

Digital media can also be used as artistic tools: designers can now render on a computer, create digital collages for color and pattern, and carry out their research online. Pattern-makers can also use computer programs to arrive at the shapes needed to create a costume. Digital fabric printing is being utilized more often. These new developments may change some aspects of costume design and technology, but they do not change the end goal. The artists still need to be able to communicate with one another and express themselves visually, verbally, and in three dimensions. The needs and questions of both designers and shop personnel still need to be answered.

The designer should embrace this new reality, by using photos and other digital communication tools to the show's greatest advantage. The costume shop manager can send photos of relevant stock costumes. The actors can all be photographed, including a facial close up, so body types and shapes can be considered. The long-distance designer can work with the draper so that they both can be present and invested in day-to-day decision-making by asking drapers to take photos as they are starting work on the costumes. If the photographs are not providing the best information for the designer or the shop, there are several avenues to explore. Often, poor camera technique is to blame. Ask the shop to make sure they have proper light; this is often the biggest problem, yet is easy to correct. If you cannot see detail, ask for closer shots to be taken. If distance is needed to look at proportion or hem lengths, the designer should also ask for that perspective. The shop should try to provide photos with good lighting and multiple viewpoints to ensure the best communication.

CONCLUSIONS

The costume designer and the costume maker have an interlaced, interdependent relationship—at the core of which lies respectful communication that encourages trust in each other's art. Creating a costume involves a journey from initial idea, to rendering, to fabric decisions, to mock up, and finally to finished costume. Many people are involved in this process, and recognizing others' skills as complementary to your own is crucial. Learning what each person brings to the project and how best to communicate with them makes for a successful transition through the costume shop. Strong collaboration allows the whole team—and the finished costume—to shine.

On a Personal Note

Use the biggest scissors your hands can manage—small scissors chew up fabric.

QUESTIONS

- In this chapter, communication was discussed at length. What are some of the best communication practices that will help designers to bring their costumes through the shop?

- What questions can designers ask themselves as they begin working with a costume shop?

- With which costume shop personnel does the designer work closely, and what skills does that artist bring to the process?

- How does technology factor into the costume design/costume shop relationship? How might it play a greater role in the future?

NOTES

1. Katherine Marshall, email interview with author, September 9, 2014.
2. Susan Davis, telephone interview with author, July 30, 2014.
3. Mary Nemecek Peterson, telephone interview with author, August 7, 2014.
4. Campbell Baird, email interview with author, August 20, 2014.
5. Kathleen Trott, email interview with author, July 28, 2014.
6. Natalie Kurczewski, email interview with author, September 27, 2015.
7. Killer, email interview with author, September 25, 2014.
8. Martha Ruskai, email interview with author, September 19, 2015.
9. Martha Ruskai and Allison Lowery, *Wig Making and Styling: A Complete Guide for Theatre & Film* (Waltham, MA: Focal Press, 2010).
10. Jennifer L. Bach, email interview with author, September 29, 2015.
11. Tony Johnson, email interview with author, September 29, 2015.
12. Eriko Terao, email interview with author, September 30, 2015.
13. Hilary Rosenfeld, email interview with author, August 5, 2014.
14. Rebecca Kaufman, email interview with author, August 6, 2014.
15. Nancy Julian, email interview with author, August 18, 2014.
16. Sheila P. Morris, email interview with author, August 5, 2014.

scapino

Scapino

FIGURE 7.1 *Watercolor rendering of Scapino by Esther Van Eek for the University of Windsor, ON.*

CHAPTER 7

COSTUME DESIGN TRAINING: CREATING IN OTHER CONTEXTS

Esther Van Eek

It has often been said that clothes make the man. American humorist Mark Twain expanded the idea to, "Clothes make the man. Naked people have little or no influence in society."[1]

Clothing defines us. It is the outward expression of ourselves that we choose to display to the rest of the world. From the first time we play dress up, or when our schoolmates assert what is

the "right" way to dress, and what isn't, we begin our education in the power of clothing. What we opt to wear—whether it is a conservative navy business suit, our favorite well-worn jeans and t-shirt, or the latest designer label form-fitting frock—provides essential clues to our culture, belief system, status, and personality. Without speaking a word aloud, we have spoken volumes to those

FIGURES 7.2–7.4 *The three main reasons we wear what we do—power, comfort, seduction—as advanced by James Laver: (left) the classic and conservative business suit (courtesy of Shutterstock; ©EDHAR); (middle) the comfortable and casual jeans and t-shirt (courtesy of Shutterstock; ©Kudla); and (right) the sheer and seductive couture gown (photo by Luciano Consolini; courtesy of Flickr).*

around us who are looking to know something about us. When we study clothing as historical, sociological, and artistic artefact, it becomes a fundamental manifestation of our very selves.

Understood through these lenses, what people wear takes on much greater significance than current styles of clothing selected for warmth or comfort. Similarly, when imbued with this same richness, costume becomes so much more than an historically accurate outfit selected to flatter the actor's body, and the costume designer can understand their role in a production as much more complex and much more vital to the telling of this specific story and the narrative of these particular characters.

For the early-career designer, the most critical skill, and perhaps the most difficult to teach, is learning to see how a creative artist sees; looking not only at things as they are, but also seeing them for the endless possibilities they present. This requires an open mind and an ease with ambiguity. There are

no single right or wrong answers, but there are certainly choices that are more appropriate and fitting than others. Paradoxically, experienced designers may see limitations or problems too early in their design process to truly explore and take the risks that lead to inspired design. Designers must journey through the world with their eyes, ears, and very pores open to sensory input of all kinds, observing the big picture as well as filing away small details for future reference: impressions, feelings, textures, patterns, gestures, and attitudes. The study of human history may take the designer back 5,000 years, but this study should also be understood to include the history that occurred yesterday, or even five minutes ago. Openness to the world around us will create a deep well from which to draw when designing, and will afford more opportunity for truly creative expression. Cultivating a curious spirit that can see beyond simple problems and solutions, successful designers recognize the emotional impact of good design; they can "see" through the eyes of the audience or consumer to feel what response their work will likely evoke. From this response comes the meaning of the design. The end user or audience member may not be able to articulate the choices and decisions that made a design successful, but they will surely know good design when they see it.

I WANT TO BE A COSTUME DESIGNER

There are some careers that seem to have a clear path of study and training to arrive at the desired state of readiness. On the surface, costume design and costume technology seem to fit that mold. If you discover or develop a passion for theatre, and believe your creative drive will find full expression in costuming for the theatre, there are many training programs to choose from, often within the context of a broader liberal arts education. In addition to literature, philosophy, mathematics, and sciences, these programs will offer the eager student courses as varied as theatre history, costume history, traditional and computer rendering, script analysis, two- and three-dimensional design theory, color theory, costume construction, pattern drafting and draping, stage makeup, costume crafts, and more. Add this classroom knowledge to some practical learning gained by working on department productions as a dresser, wardrobe run crew, a stitcher, a draper, and eventually, an assistant to the designer, and you are all set to conquer the theatre world as a brilliant designer. Or are you?

Training for the Designer

Designers in every field benefit from a very broad range of knowledge and experience in order to add depth, focus, and

FIGURE 7.5 *Costume design for Henri in Tom Stoppard's translation of Gérald Sibleyras' Heroes. Character is conveyed through color choice, texture, pose, and even the inclusion of hand props such as the pipe and cane. (Costume design by Esther Van Eek for Shakespeare & Company, Lenox, MA.)*

direction to their innate creativity. Strictly speaking, designers in many disciplines can begin a career with little or no formal training, yet formal training does certainly offer great advantages in these highly competitive arenas.

While preparation for the costume designer often begins with a four-year liberal arts degree, there are many design training programs offered through colleges, arts academies, or dedicated fashion schools, and these can be more focused and shorter in duration than the Bachelor of Arts or Bachelor of Fine Arts degrees. The resultant degree or certificate may open doors to entry-level positions within the industry. Costume designers who go on to complete an additional two- or three-year Master of Fine Arts degree may pursue careers in teaching, costume shop management, and more.

Hundreds of liberal arts colleges across the United States, along with a growing number of schools in Canada and abroad, offer excellent broad-based educations, often with relatively small class sizes and an emphasis on student engagement and an active, participatory learning environment. Many large universities also offer liberal arts programs in addition to their graduate degree programs, but with a greater priority placed on research. Along with the prestige of name-recognition and the benefits of well-stocked research libraries come very large classes with more limited access to professors, and so larger programs are best suited to an independent learning style. At the other end of the spectrum are the highly specialized, often private schools where intensive professional training is offered in fields such as Makeup, Special Effects (FX) and Hair Design, and Wig Making. Students graduate with functional expertise and a well-developed, specific skillset allowing them quicker entry into the job market, but perhaps without the career mobility of those with liberal arts degrees.

The curriculum for designers, costume and fashion designers among them, may include art history, design theory, and rendering in addition to very targeted skill-building courses such as sewing and tailoring, pattern making, draping, and computer-aided design. Courses in many disparate fields also have a lot to contribute to the designer's training, from literature to psychology, and period styles to marketing. Although the designer may not be an expert in all of these fields, they should be conversant with them and should be able to conduct research comfortably in any of these areas. No degree or certificate program can teach you all you need to know, so seizing opportunities to continue your education through workshops, symposia, involvement in professional organizations, and the like ensures your continued growth and feeds your creative spirit as a designer and an artist.

There is no universal standardized path to acquire all the necessary knowledge and experience needed to succeed in a creative field. Rather, the training and education required in various design fields is dictated by the employer or company for which the designer wishes to work. Sometimes, emphasis is placed solely on the capacity for innovation and versatility displayed in the designer's portfolio. At other times, letters of reference hold immense sway, especially when the designer has apprenticed under or worked with recognized names in the fashion or theatre world. Most often, employers want to see evidence of creative output in the form of a portfolio or website, see proof of productive collaborations with others in the field, and have the assurance of future potential that successful completion of a university or college-level degree brings.

With the ascendance of work teams, a collaborative model that theatre practitioners are very familiar with, so-called "soft skills," are arguably more important than any single course or even major. These include skills such as relationship building, teamwork, problem solving, critical thinking, and communication. Teamed with personal attributes such as a positive attitude, a strong work ethic, developed social skills, and a healthy curiosity, these are the most desirable traits for anyone aiming for a career in design. They are also the best predictors of long-term success in the job market.

Training Complete . . . Now What?

All the education and training in the world does not guarantee a thriving costume design career. Success, and indeed steady employment, can be elusive even to the most talented designer. In the current marketplace, an *adaptable and portable skillset* is more valuable than ever before.

Smaller theatres that were once the training ground for many a young designer have had an increasingly difficult time surviving in a climate of fiscal restraint and funding cutbacks to the arts. Many established theatres have reduced production costs and boosted revenues by mounting fewer shows in-house, re-mounting past successes, and filling out their seasons with touring shows. Already proven successes, these touring shows are brought in as complete packages; sets, costumes, props, and even marketing materials arrive by truck requiring merely to be unloaded and offered to the theatre's patrons. And while opera, dance, film, and TV all provide design opportunities, these art forms have suffered many of the same challenges as theatre. Faced with increasing costs (from raw materials to labor and shipping), and shrinking revenues from declining ticket sales, companies are relying more than ever on grants from the government, charitable foundations, and the generous support of wealthy benefactors. Stiff competition for existing funding, the search for new, more diverse sources of revenue, and the challenge of attracting new subscribers make this a particularly challenging time for arts organizations, in turn making it harder for them to act as incubators for new talent.

Do these trends spell the imminent demise of the costume designer? Why go through all the training required if there is little or no work to be had at the end of it all? Is costume design still a viable career goal? Can you follow your bliss *and* support yourself? These are valid, even necessary, questions prospective designers need to ask themselves. In the face of all the challenges, functional skills need to be complemented by strengths like *critical thinking, communication, and creative problem solving.*

WHAT ELSE CAN I DO?

The title of this book is *The Art and Practice of Costume Design* and it is meant as a guide for aspiring costume designers as seen through the eyes of practicing professionals. However, there are many occupations other than costume design that require a similar skillset, design vocabulary, and critical eye. Indeed, every consumer product, from the chair you are sitting in, to the pen you are taking notes with, to the advertisement that just popped up on your screen, is the result of a series of design decisions. Somebody was responsible for identifying a problem or need and coming up with the solution or product through a process similar in many respects to the process of costume designers. Some people may object to calling theatre a consumer product—

it is an art form, after all—but there is no theatre without an audience.

Fashion design is one such related occupation. Fashion designers create original clothing, footwear, and accessories. They sketch designs, source fabrics, draft patterns, and communicate the construction of their designs. Costume designers have been known to migrate into the world of fashion and vice versa, despite the widely divergent goals driving each area. Some designers are able to work successfully in both areas simultaneously, although this is quite rare. Often, a designer makes a name for themselves in one discipline and then they are hired with much fanfare to design in another. Twentieth century American designer Adrian Adolph Greenberg, commonly known as Adrian, began his training as a fashion designer in New York, but before establishing his career in fashion, was hired to design costumes for film. He enjoyed a very prolific and critically acclaimed career in Hollywood before retiring from film and establishing his own fashion house.

More recently, visionary fashion designers such as Karl Lagerfeld, Christian Lacroix, and Giorgio Armani have created costumes for operas presented at opera houses such as La Scala and the Metropolitan Opera, while also maintaining the demands of their fashion empires.

Award-winning costume designer Janie Bryant trained as an artist and fashion designer. Early in her career, she was hired to design for TV, and one successful collaboration led to another so

FIGURES 7.6 & 7.7 *Two designs by Adrian: (right) a costume designed for the 1939 film* The Woman *(photo by Laura Loveday; courtesy of Flickr); and (far right) a 1945 silk evening ensemble from the* Shades of Picasso *collection (gift of Eleanor Lambert, 1958; courtesy of the Metropolitan Museum of Art, New York).*

 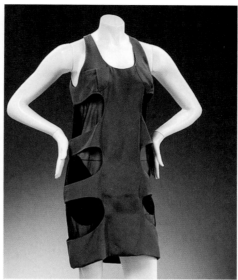

FIGURES 7.8 & 7.9 *Images of the Sixties: (far left) a dress contemporary to the period— a 1960s space-age dress by French designer André Courrèges; and (left) a modern interpretation—the Bette dress from Mary Ping's Spring/ Summer 2007 collection (photo by Isabel Asha Penzlien). (Photos courtesy of the Victoria and Albert Museum, London.)*

that her costume design career took off. The phenomenal success of the TV show *Mad Men*,[2] and Bryant's critical contribution to that success, has led full circle to several design collaborations within the realm of fashion. Comprehensive period research carefully interpreted and applied to compelling characters in *Mad Men* created a renewed interest in the silhouettes and look of the period. Thus, a demand for a modern take on the Sixties was born, right down to the requisite foundation garments without which the shapes could not be recreated. Regardless of the starting point and direction of their journey, the accomplished designer carries with them many tools and a way of thinking that enables them to transition from one focus to another.

Fashion and Costume Design: Related Careers

What follows is a comparison of the practical considerations of costume design with one of its most closely aligned disciplines, fashion design. The many similarities are probably more easily identified than the more subtle but crucial differences. For all that, the skillsets needed to succeed at either career have much in common. Other related careers in creative fields will be touched on, though in less depth.

Pre-dating the advent of talking pictures, there is evidence of cross-pollination between fashion and costume. In some cases, one clearly references the other; and in most cases, each influences the other. A more recent example is the magnetic

performer Dita Von Teese, who has brought about a resurgence in the popularity of burlesque as a legitimate performance genre, and this, in turn, has created a demand for luxe, burlesque-inspired lingerie.

Costume design and fashion design share a great many areas of overlap. Both the costume designer and the fashion designer possess an inquisitive spirit, a passion for wide-ranging research, an interest in the history of clothing, an understanding of psychology, a love of fabrics, and an excellent grasp of the principles and elements of good design. They must be very detail-oriented and enjoy working in fast-paced, ever-changing, and demanding environments. Both must be skilled communicators, verbally and especially visually. Highly organized and able to work within strict time and budget constraints, both must be able to contribute as a member of a team. For the creative soul, the great variety of tasks within these respective job descriptions can be challenging and endlessly engaging.

The key component to success as a designer, and a very elusive one to define, is *creativity*. There is no single, universally accepted definition of creativity. However, there are elements that are essential to any discussion regarding its meaning:

- Originality, imagination, innovation—a move away from what is already known or already exists.

- Effectiveness, value, producing the intended result—a journey beyond the merely practical, to the desirable.

FIGURES 7.10 & 7.11
(right) *Dita Von Teese performing a burlesque routine (photo by Artibop); and (far right) Dita Von Teese modeling burlesque-inspired lingerie from the line bearing her name. (Photos courtesy of Flickr.)*

- Refinement, ingenuity—an idea that is simplified to leave only the essential elements, so what remains is elegance by design.
- Expressiveness, passion—thinking that is emotionally connected, intuitive, and speaks to the intended audience.

> **"Creativity is a wild mind and a disciplined eye."**
> Dorothy Parker,[3] American writer and critic

The costume designer's work varies a great deal because every new play makes different demands and requires finding new solutions. The costume designer may be called upon to recreate a period with great accuracy and attention to detail; a scenario that might not seem to allow for much creative freedom. However, the practiced designer will research the period, seeking first to understand the social, political, and economic forces that were at play in order to set the context for the opening moment of the show, and what follows after the show's conclusion. The designer will devise not an isolated moment in time, but a world abounding in specific detail that gives the audience a rich view of the characters' lives. Deep and thorough research is the foundation of any project. But research does not create a box from which no imagination can escape, nor does it restrict creativity. Rather, it frees the innovative artist to make decisions from a rich variety of

choices secure in the knowledge that for each design choice there is an answer to the question "Why?": Why that cut? Why that color? Why that fit? Why at this time? Costume design, whether for a period play, a modern drama, or a futuristic odyssey, is not about shopping for a flattering outfit for an actor; it is about making truthful choices for a specific inhabitant of the story at that moment in the character's life. Furthermore, the choices should be just as deliberate for the characters in a modern dress drama.

Fashion designers also need to have a deep understanding of history, but they rely on their knowledge and quote from it in a very different way to costume designers. Sometimes, they might pull one detail from a period, and that period-specific detail might form the inspiration for an entire line. Sometimes, an historical period or event will reverberate through a collection in a totally fresh and unexpected way. Over time, the fashion designer will develop their own style which is built on the best of what has come before, not to merely duplicate what has already been done, but to understand it in its historical, social, and political context, and to be inspired by it. Looking at Jean Paul Gaultier's unique and exceptionally innovative designs, his comprehensive grasp of fashion history is readily apparent, but his brilliance as a designer can be fully appreciated in his history-meets-culture-meets-counterculture outlook.

Understanding that fashion history follows a cyclical pattern and reflects a unique set of social, political, and economic factors

FIGURES 7.12 & 7.13 (left) *Costume design for Viola in Shakespeare's* Twelfth Night *set in Prohibition-era Detroit. (Design by Esther Van Eek for the University of Windsor, ON.)* (right) *Modern costume design for Ronnie Brown in* Parasite Drag, *a tragicomedy by Mark Roberts. (Design by Esther Van Eek for Shakespeare & Company, Lenox, MA.)*

FIGURES 7.14 & 7.15 (far left) *Historical inspiration—a mosaic detail from Monreale Cathedral in Palermo, Sicily (photo by Terry Feuerborn, 2011; courtesy of Flickr); and* (left) *modern design—Dolce & Gabbana draw from history and their shared Italian heritage for this "mosaic" dress from the Fall/Winter 2013 collection (in printed silk with sequins and Swarovski crystals); (image given by Dolce & Gabbana, courtesy of the Victoria and Albert Museum, London).*

enables the thoughtful designer to reference styles that have gone before, and put their own unique stamp on them. **Haute couture** designers understand "there is nothing new under the sun,"[4] but they can make an old idea new again when they allow their creativity free reign.

The Beginnings of Haute Couture

In 1858, English couturier Charles Frederick Worth established the first haute couture house in Paris, championing exclusive luxury fashion for the upper-class woman and coining the term "fashion designer"—an artist in lieu of the basic dressmaker. In the face of a sharply declining customer base, few modern designers maintain haute couture houses: those who do recognize their value in adding prestige to their ready-to-wear lines.

There is no doubt that costume in the theatre has evolved from the relatively simple Greek mask made to amplify the voice and magnify the presence of the character onstage, and from the elaborate patron-donated garb of the English Elizabethan stage. But the purpose and process of costume design has evolved very little in the last centuries. The purpose costumes serve within the context of the show and the processes by which the costumes come to be are remarkably unchanged over time. So too are the essential tools of effective design, making them well defined and readily available to be learned and practiced.

Other Career Options

As well as designing costumes for the film and TV industries, other potential sources of work are dance companies and opera companies. These art forms are well suited to those who enjoy working on a grand scale and can "read" music as one reads a script. Designers who develop expertise in areas such as wigs, corsetry, **millinery**, stage makeup, or aging and distressing may find they can augment their design income with work as a specialist in these related areas and, as reputation and positive word-of-mouth spreads, this supplementary area may evolve into their primary focus.

A Costume Director's Journey

Govane Lohbauer,[5] Costume Director at Shakespeare & Company, details her career path:

"I was a stitcher and dresser in the beginning. Once I found out that designing gave me the opportunity to use all of my mind and all the skills that I enjoyed, I continued to look for opportunities to do it.

"I am not formally trained in costume design. I come from the old school of learning as you work, so picking out one aspect of that process would be difficult. Learning as you work is invaluable. Having to design with no budget is the best training of all. You *must* be creative and use all your skills to make a great looking show! It was very instrumental in my career to

FIGURE 7.16 *Costumes designed by Govane Lohbauer for the cast of Molière's* The Learned Ladies *at Shakespeare & Company, Lenox, MA. (Photo by Kevin Sprague, © 2012.)*

have a great mentor or two, and to work with directors who believed in me and gave me opportunities.

"It's difficult to design confidently without very strong stitching skills and an understanding of construction. A love of historical clothing and lifestyles has also stood me in good stead. Strong organizational skills are as useful as being able to draw well. You have to really want to work with people, and enjoy the journey. Costume design is not a selfish, internal art—it is, or should be, outwardly directed. If designers are only focused on the pretty pictures, they do not serve the theatre or the play very well.

"My advice would be to practice your construction skills until they are second nature, and then enjoy the ride. Take jobs for almost no money with little budgets, and make them look fabulous while you build a resume. Don't be afraid of hard work and don't assume that you will be a terrific designer right away, even if your professors say you will. Love what you do and the people you work with, and the rest will follow."

Virtually everywhere that there are live performers, there are makeup artists. Stage makeup functions in much the same way as costume: it is about the creation and development of character. Together with costume and hair, makeup alters or enhances the performer's appearance and completes the perception of character even before the actor delivers their first line.

> "I had no idea of the character. But the moment I was dressed, the clothes and the make-up made me feel the person he was. I began to know him, and by the time I walked onto the stage, he was fully born."
>
> Charlie Chaplin[6] from *My Autobiography*

FIGURE 7.17 *Publicity photo from Charlie Chaplin's 1921 movie The Kid. Pictured here are The Little Tramp and Jackie Coogan. (Courtesy of Wikimedia.)*

If an actor's appearance needs to be significantly changed—by the addition of Cyrano de Bergerac's famously oversized nose, for example—the makeup artist may use **prosthetics**. At other times, only basic corrective makeup is applied (for example, in TV talk shows or newscasts), in order to conceal imperfections and to enhance a performer's appearance on camera. While excellence in stage makeup and special effects relies heavily on the same core competencies as costume design, most costume design programs include only limited instruction in stage makeup and special effects. Pursuing a career in this field usually requires additional training through a cosmetology school or intensive workshops offered by theatrical makeup manufacturers such as Ben Nye, Mehron, and Graftobian. Volunteering to work for local theatres, student films, and independent films will build competence with the particular tools and techniques of this trade, and will grow a portfolio of work and a contact list that will make future professional jobs more likely.

Finally, a designer who is especially adept at rendering may find work as a sketch artist, or a fashion or commercial illustrator.

Other Careers in Design

Accessories Design	Jewelry Design
Blogging about Costumes or Fashion	Pattern Maker
Children's Wear	Production Management: Fashion and Related Industries
Cosmetics and Fragrance Marketing	Project Planning
Custom Dressmaker	Retail Management
Direct and Interactive Marketing	Sales Representative
Entrepreneurship	Sample Making
Event Planning	Technical Design
Fabric Stylist	Textile Development and Marketing
Fashion Buyer	Textile/Surface Design
Fashion Journalism	Trend Research/Analysis
Fashion Photography	Visual Display and Merchandising
Fashion Styling	
International Trade and Marketing for Fashion Industries	

There are less obvious sources of employment that also require the skills of a costume designer. The explosion of the gaming industry has created a market for game character designers and animators who understand fit and fabric drape and movement. There are year-round commercial and custom design opportunities generated by annual Halloween and Mardi Gras

An Illustrator's Journey

Steven Stines,[7] Illustrator, Costume Designer, and Professor, details his career path:

"I grew up watching TV variety shows, especially *Sonny and Cher* and *The Carol Burnett Show*, which were designed by Bob Mackie. Seeing his screen credit was the first time I realized there was such a thing as a costume designer. I was attracted to all that glamour and glitter, and the comedy of many of the variety show costumes. I think I bring that aesthetic to the projects I work on.

"The other point of entry into costume design was seeing the work of Léon Bakst for the Ballets Russes in a book I was given in ninth grade. Bakst got me interested in designing for dance. I never had the aspiration to perform, but my college had a wonderful dance program, and I had a lot of opportunity to design for both dance and musical theatre, which have remained the focus of my career.

"I began college as a journalism major, then made stops along the way in advertising and commercial art before landing in theatre. As it turns out, I continually use all my areas of training, and use them often. I think having explored a number of areas has given me not only a set of skills to earn income outside of theatre, but also a body of knowledge on which to draw when working in theatre design. My drawing and painting skills have allowed me to work extensively as an illustrator, primarily for publishing as opposed to advertising. Like theatre design, illustration is a highly competitive field. That said, what my illustration work has in common with theatre design is that I am telling a story through each image.

"The costume designer must not just be a visual artist, but also have a really thorough understanding of fabric, which is our primary medium. Even though I hate to sew, I can do it. This allows me to have an informed conversation with the people who will build my designs, and to step in when there is a vacuum.

"A skill I wish I possessed in greater measure is diplomacy! The designer needs to be adept at self-promotion and socializing. Something I do think I am good at is keeping records and tracking money. The business managers and accountants at theatres like me, because I make their work less complicated.

"The skills I think are most important include artistry, a high degree of ingenuity in terms of sourcing and shopping, understanding construction, and being responsible about formulating and tracking a budget. Time management is critical. If you miss deadlines you risk not being paid, and certainly you will not be hired a second time."

FIGURE 7.18 *A commercial poster by versatile designer/illustrator Steven Stines for* The Kuglemass Affair. *(Ink on board and Photoshop. Producer: The Musical Writer's Playground, New York. Composer: Seth Weinstein. Book/Lyrics: Jon Karp.)*

events. Marketing for companies from small stand-alone businesses to national franchises, for products as diverse as pizza and sports teams, has spawned the need to create larger-than-life mascots and walk-arounds.

Many other organizations use costumes for presentation and display, perhaps not with enough regularity to warrant staffing their own costume shops, but they provide another excellent source of income for the freelance artist. Investigating and replicating period costumes for museums, historical sites, and living museums—for example, creating the costume for Edwin Hubble, inventor of the Hubble telescope, in an exhibit on the history of observational cosmology—presents exciting and unique research and construction challenges.

Costumes for display in museum dioramas will be subjected to close scrutiny, so they must be accurate in every possible detail: from whether they are stitched by machine or by hand, to whether buttons are made of bone, leather, metal, or plastic. Costumes for living museums where tour guides work costumed in the period the museum represents also come into close contact with the public, and present the additional challenge that

they will be subjected to long periods of wear. They must be built to withstand the rigors of daily wear and tear and repeated washings. Re-enactors, people who participate in re-enactments of historic events—from Medieval to Renaissance to the American Civil War—form another sizable potential market for costumes and accessories. Generally speaking, re-enactors desire a high level of detail and authenticity in design, materials, and construction, to most closely replicate the experience they are re-enacting. Creating replicas of military uniforms, hand-woven and natural dyed garments, footwear, and other gear for participants and spectators at such events put the designer's skills to good use. Success in each of these areas requires rigorous research, and the ability to apply the principles and elements of design, while each area also has unique challenges dictated by the purpose and end use of the costume.

The **cosplay** (costume play) genre has some passionate fans, who dress up and role play as their favorite fictional characters taken from non-theatrical sources such as comic books, graphic novels, manga and animé, video games, and science fiction movies. Cosplayers may attend conventions

FIGURES 7.19 & 7.20 *Detailed period costumes in dioramas for the Smithsonian National Air and Space Museum: (left) Edwin Hubble, and (right) Tycho Brahe. (Costume designs by William Pucilowsky. Photos by Eric Long, Smithsonian National Air and Space Museum, Washington DC.)*

around the world where they are scrutinized for the faithful duplication of the characters they are portraying, and every minute detail is evidence of their commitment to the genre. The immense popularity of this relatively new performance subculture has created a new market for costumes, props, wigs, accessories, and weapons. While some cosplayers enjoy developing their own costumes, there are many more who would rather purchase part or all of the costume due to the use of intricate detail and/or unusual materials involved. Serious cosplayers are willing to pay for higher quality pieces than the mass-produced offerings from party stores. With relative ease and little start-up investment required, an entrepreneurial designer can access large markets for their custom-made cosplay costumes

and handmade accessories via the many craft marketing sites on the internet.

Likewise, designers who are passionate about textiles and comfortable with computer programs such as Photoshop and Illustrator can submit original fabric designs digitally to a number of custom printing companies that will market the designs online and print-to-order any size run on a variety of fabrics.

Of course, many costume designers will have been trained in at least one other area of design for the theatre. In North American universities, Master's level study typically requires a primary and a secondary area of specialization. Historically, training abroad focuses on creating theatre designers or

A Textile Designer's Journey

Elinor Parker,[8] Costume and Textile Designer and Business Owner, details her career path:

"I earned my BFA at The Cooper Union School of Art, where a student could choose to focus in a certain area of art, or could dabble in every area. I studied graphic design, drawing, sculpture, book making, calligraphy, photography, video, art history—just about anything I could get my hands on. Cooper didn't have a theatre program, but they did have a theatre club, The Cooper Dramatic Society. I still remember watching their performance of *The Importance of Being Earnest*. It was amazing, and it wasn't long after that I joined the group. I quickly discovered that my diverse interests in the fine arts translated well to theatrical design.

"When I was an art student I regularly had to present, discuss, and even defend my work in class. Being able to talk about my work, as well as others' work, was an integral part of my education, and those skills translated very well into the theatre world. My drawing skills also proved invaluable. The ability to communicate, both orally and visually, are

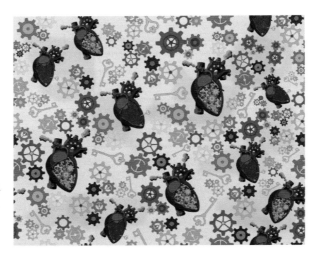

FIGURE 7.21 *An original fabric design by Elinor Parker,* The Heart of the Matter *is available for print on various fabrics, wallpaper, and giftwrap. Self-described chic geek, Elinor Parker markets her designs on websites such as Etsy and Spoonflower, and through her own website, the Costume Wrangler. (Courtesy of Elinor Parker, http://thecostumewrangler.com.)*

traits vital to being a successful designer. It's not enough to have a great idea. A designer has to be able to show and talk about her idea, and discuss it with the director and the rest of the design and production teams. Being able to collaborate is also really important to being a successful designer. You've got to be able to work in a team, voice your opinion, but be open to others' opinions too, and be willing to compromise. What makes a design "good" or "bad"? It's not enough to know you like something. Ask yourself why, and be able to back up that answer with some concrete examples.

"I've moved from teaching and designing in the academic community to owning and running my own businesses, The Costume Wrangler's Closet and Geek Chic Boutique. I design and create custom costumes, clothing, and accessories. I also design many of my own fabrics and get them custom printed through a company called Spoonflower. Even though I'm not part of a collaborative design team, I still have to communicate with customers and collaborate with clients on custom orders. Whether I'm selling online or in person, presenting my work is vital to the success of my business."

scenographers who design all of the visual elements of a production. These additional areas of expertise exponentially increase the probability of steady work. Any and all training that develops a designer's eye and feeds their creativity is worthy in the pursuit of employment and, indeed, excellence. With persistence and an open mind, the varied skillset and process steps of the theatre designer can translate into many other design disciplines in and outside of the theatre.

A New York Designer's Journey

Teresa Snider-Stein,[9] Costume Designer and Professor, details her career path:

"Although I've done many of the jobs in the costume design field, I think of myself primarily as a costume designer. I started in summer stock as a costume intern, where I stitched in the costume shop and even ran the light board for a show. By the third year I was designing the entire season. My summer stock experience was essential to my development as a costume designer. I worked with great professionals, and started to find my voice as I designed numerous productions in quick succession. I also had to work fast!

"After moving to New York I worked in several costume shops, mostly at Parsons-Meares. I started as a shopper there, filled in as a stitcher and first hand, and then worked as a project manager. I earned an MFA at the Yale School of Drama and then moved back to NYC. I worked Off Broadway and Off Off Broadway as a costume designer and as a first or second assistant costume designer on films and a broad range of theatre productions.

"My internship with the legendary Broadway costume designer Patricia Zipprodt was life changing. The opportunity to work with Ms Zipprodt opened my eyes in ways I could never have imagined. I really didn't know how much I didn't know. I did a lot of the prep work—researching, swatching, and the like. I learned how to keep records in a costume 'bible' and function in pressure-cooker dress rehearsals. It was a serious introduction to the 'business.' She encouraged me to go to the Art Students League and draw, draw, draw!

"After nine years as the resident costume designer at Signature Theatre in NYC, I took a position as the assistant costume designer on the *Late Show with David Letterman*. I had two small children at the time, and this opportunity allowed me to have some financial stability and a somewhat predictable schedule.

"I have always been interested in bringing stories and characters to life. I really like finding the key to why someone wears a particular type of clothing and translating what it communicates, visually, to an audience. Costume design is different from fashion design in that there is a human being who needs to be defined, understood, and visually represented to tell a particular story. At the heart of everything is the ability to identify the problem or issue at hand and discover the correct or relevant solution to the specific situation. A strong liberal arts education with some background in history, psychology, art, literature, and global issues is a good place to start. Designers must understand psychology as it applies to character analysis, as well as to working with colleagues. Whether it is in theatre, film, opera, or a music video, it's important to know and understand the power structure so one can successfully accomplish goals in a timely fashion without alienating key players. It's important to know who to ask for information and when. When I'm working I never 'know' everything at the start of any project, but I must identify what I don't know and solve specific problems for this specific project.

"The costume design profession is for those who are compelled to do it because they must, not because it sounds like a cool thing to do. It's for those who have the passion to design. It's hard work, much harder than most would think."

SELLING MY SKILLS: THE DESIGN PORTFOLIO

"A portfolio is a showcase of artistry, special skills, and process."

Rafael Jaen[10] from *Showcase*, p. 2

Whether in traditional physical book or online form, a well-rounded portfolio that showcases your artistry, craftsmanship, unique abilities, and creative process is a tangible result of the years of training in any design field. It is a necessity for gaining an audience with the human resources department, talent recruiter, or creative director of the company for whom you wish to work. Your portfolio is both an historical archive of work you have completed, and also evidence of future potential to attract the kind of client and work you most want.

The following tips will help you to build a strong portfolio:

- Introduce yourself: your portfolio should reflect your personality and invite contact.
- Emphasize quality over quantity: you do not need to include every project—remember you will be judged by your weakest work.
- Keep it simple: your content is the featured attraction, so minimize distractions.
- Showcase your process: initial concept and early sketches illustrate how you think.
- Highlight your role: clearly identify your part in the project and give credit to your collaborators.
- Make it flow: opt for a professional, cohesive, and easy to navigate layout.
- Review and update often: your portfolio is a fluid, evolving project—the best of your **brand**.

The costume designer's portfolio should reflect who they are and show an ability to design in a broad range of genres and styles, both realistic and non-realistic, in order to be most marketable. In face-to-face interviews, the traditional portfolio provides tangible evidence of the creative process. It provides opportunities to elaborate on a project's constraints and how they were resolved. Online portfolios are relatively simple and inexpensive to create

FIGURE 7.22 *Men's knitwear—a fashion design area of specialization—from Australian designer Chris Ran Lin's* Conflict and Fusion *2012 collection. (Photo by Vikk Shayen Wong; courtesy of Chris Ran Lin: http://chrisranlin.com.)*

and allow potential employers and collaborators easy access to your work even before meeting you. Whether building a physical portfolio or an online portfolio, the fundamental rules are the same: show only your best work; be aware that how you present your work is almost as important as the work itself; highlight the part of the project for which you are responsible (for example, "distressed all costumes" or "costumes designed by"); give credit to any other artists whose work is represented and to the photographer who shot the image; keep the content fresh and current; and, most important of all, make it simple to find and contact you.

Fashion designers for the **mass market** will often focus their careers on either menswear, women's wear, or children's wear, and within their chosen area, may specialize even further on a particular type of clothing (for example, maternity wear or men's knitwear). Their portfolios should show a great deal of depth and versatility within that limited area and may need to be revised to reflect current trends in the job market.

Designers in any field need to recognize that they are marketing themselves as an inextricable element of their "brand." Control over the image they project through their presence online, in social media, on websites, as well as in their design portfolios, is essential. Savvy potential employers are very likely to make use of the easy access to information by conducting a quick online search prior to deciding whether you will be granted an interview. Guard your image as carefully as you guard your work.

INTENDED AUDIENCE OR CONSUMER: TELLING VERSUS SELLING

Although there are many areas of overlap in the sensibilities, skills, and training from one design discipline to another, there are also significant differences. These differences are worthy of consideration when pursuing training and employment. Individual preferences and personality traits may make someone better suited to one field than another. Designers who are drawn to narrative and love research and collaboration may find designing for theatre and opera especially fulfilling. Creating for museums and re-enactments will fascinate those who love historical research and exacting detail. Designers with an eye for popular culture and evolving trends will thrive in the world of fashion. The variety of opportunities within the design sphere allows for a great diversity of interests and personalities among designers.

Perhaps the most significant divergence between creative fields of endeavour is revealed in response to the question of function. Who is the **end user**, the consumer, or the **intended audience** for costume and fashion design?

Telling

The costume design process almost always begins with the designers immersing themselves in the script. It is to the story that they owe their greatest allegiance. In the first, second, and even third readings of the play, it is important for designers to stay open to their visceral response to the story and the characters who inhabit it. Before forming firm opinions or beginning to make design decisions, a designer needs to note their impressions of the large picture the story paints. These impressions are formed in response to the language of the play, its rhythms and textures, **themes** and motifs, and the arc of the story. Only after absorbing this information can the designer begin to put these elements together with the director's dramatic interpretation, and then to populate this world with its inhabitants and relationships.

Character information and costume requirements can be gleaned from the playwright's notes and also from the dialogue; in how the characters talk about themselves and each other, and in how the characters talk to each other. Finding each character's place in the story—their role in driving the story forward—and understanding their relationships to the other characters must take place before deciding what costumes will best assist in revealing their importance to the story and assisting the audience to understand it. Indeed, these discoveries happen before getting down to the analysis and research that will eventually support the overall approach to the costumes and, only then, the individual costume choices. The director will add narrative and visual goals and a point of view that may focus on the historical significance of the story, or they may be more interested in the universal truths contained in the play. Perhaps it is a specific theme in the play that makes the story especially timely and compelling.

A well-written story will support many distinctive approaches and visual responses to it. Each encounter with such a play will allow for a unique collaboration and outcome, and a new experience for the audience. Beautiful renderings and desirable clothing are never the ultimate goals of the costume designer. They may be a by-product of the process, but success is measured in how well the costumes support the story. The magic of the design happens only once the costume is inhabited by the actor and brought to life onstage.

Devised and physical theatre, dance and other non-text based work, present unique challenges to the costume designer, but even without a script, the work begins with a central idea, a theme, or a cast of characters that gives the designer a starting point for their research and exploration.

Symbols and symbolic meaning are very important to creating clothing designed for the purpose of establishing character and storytelling. But this is not to say young lovers should always be dressed in pastels, or jealous rivals in green: there is no universal formula. Where the script gives much information about character, the designer can make subtle choices that provide hints, rather than revealing all. Any use of symbols must serve the story and not detract from the actor's work to reveal character. The costume designer with a passion for research and a firm grasp on the elements and principles of design including proportion, line, texture, color, focus, and unity has many tools for creating successful designs.

Selling

The fashion designer has a very different goal from that of the costume designer. In some ways, the principal design goal of

FIGURE 7.23 *A physical theatre ensemble at work:* Revelations *performed by Alvin Ailey Dance Theatre, New York, in 2011. (Courtesy of Flickr.)*

FIGURE 7.24 *This costume with symbolic meaning was designed for Lady Sneerwell, a gossip with deadly aim, in* The School for Scandal. *(Costume design by Esther Van Eek.)*

fashion is antithetical to that of design for the theatre. While success in both fields depends on a comprehensive understanding of the end user or target market, the fashion designer's main objective is to anticipate the "next" —what will appeal to their customer and entice them to buy and wear the newest designs from the latest collection.

The fashion line may have an underlying story or theme that the designer wants to embody, and that theme may serve to unify the collection they are designing, but the story is not the priority. Even the most devoted clients are unlikely to purchase the entire line, so each piece must be irresistible quite apart from its relationship to the wearer. Customers will pick and choose from the offerings based on their own tastes and lifestyles, add the new pieces to their existing wardrobes, and make them their own by how they mix and match and accessorize the pieces.

Whereas theatre costumes are designed for specific productions, guided by unique production concepts, conceived of as a unified whole, and finally driven by the characters and relationships that populate that story, fashion designs originate outside of such strictures and relationships. Each new season's collection and every garment in it must provide the customer with a compelling reason to buy. Fashion is aspirational: it plays on seduction and sells an image of self, turning garments once required for practical purposes into objects of desire. At its best, fashion captures the spirit of its time and when that time moves on, what is "in fashion" becomes "out of fashion."

FIGURES 7.25 & 7.26
Contrasting images of (right) the simplicity of World War II fashion, when austerity measures dictated A-line skirts and shorter hemlines; and (far right) post-war optimism in Christian Dior's sumptuous "New Look" Bar Suit, with its ultra-feminine wasp waist and extravagant skirt. (right: Photo of Maureen Sullivan and Shirley Conn in the uniform of the American Women's Voluntary Services, by Fred Palumbo; courtesy of the Library of Congress. far right: Courtesy of the Metropolitan Museum of Art Online Collection.)

In this context, research takes on a very different role for the fashion designer. A deep appreciation and understanding of history is still foundational to inspired design, but at least as important is an understanding of the driving social and political forces behind the styles, the "why," if you will. Christian Dior's ultra-feminine "New Look" designs with their voluminous skirts and extravagant lengths would not have been so radical or so wildly popular without the preceding period of rationing and austerity. Shapes, styles, and trends come and go, but none without an underlying historical basis.

The fashion designer cannot rely on a crystal ball to foresee what the market will want many months in the future. Over the last several decades, an entire support industry has emerged to assist designers in arriving at necessary decisions about everything from silhouette to fabrication, and from color to graphics and finishes. Without leaving their desks, today's fashion designers can instantly access trends from the haute couture runways of the world's fashion capitals to street style and counterculture movements across the globe as they develop. Instant access to such an overwhelming array of trends and forces on the marketplace creates a high pressure environment where choosing one direction over another involves both great risk and the potential for great gain.

It is only fashion's elite, those designers whose names are already well known, who have the luxury of creating for creativity's sake. For them, each season's new runway collection may boast incredible flights of fancy that are meant to showcase the designer's creative brilliance. Favorable reviews in the fashion press ensure high demand for the designer's more wearable couture lines rooted in the same themes, color palettes, and fabrics. Mass-market versions of the look will be available at high-end retailers, but perhaps in less luxe fabrics and with fewer details. Name recognition brings with it the opportunity for these top designers to enter into licensing agreements with manufacturers of everything from sunglasses to perfume, and from bedding to baby strollers. The designer collects a substantial fee for the use of their name and may or may not have much to do with the actual **aesthetics** of the products that bear their name. This produces something of a fashion democracy; everyone can own something with that designer's logo on it, even if it is only a keychain.

Unlike the few designers occupying fashion's top tier, most fashion designers will labor in virtual anonymity for someone else's label or for a manufacturing company producing ready-to-wear garments under various private labels. For this designer, decisions are always made with the brand and the consumer—the end user—in mind. Whereas the costume designer probes

FIGURE 7.27 *Valentino's incredible versatility on display: 45 Years of Style exhibit, Ara Pacis Augustae, Italy, 2007. (Courtesy of Wikimedia.)*

the script to identify what is required and to design what is appropriate, the fashion designer relies on market analysis to design what is desirable. Important questions for this designer include: Who is my target customer? What will motivate them to choose this garment over the multitude of other garments on the rack? What trends and colors will be most in demand many months from now? A fabulously creative idea that does not sell is a failure. The fashion designer must be far enough ahead to appear to lead, but not so far ahead that the marketplace fails to understand; and they must achieve just the right mix of luxury, desirability, and practical wearability.

Although an understanding of psychology is necessary for both the costume and the fashion designer, it is psychology of the masses that is required in fashion, not of the individual. The public's voracious appetite for the latest, greatest trends is driven by the desire to be "in," to be admired. When the average consumer sees fabulous creations worn by exceedingly chic and impossibly thin models on the runway, and then sees the modified and more wearable designer gowns on the red carpet, this time worn by extremely elegant movie stars, they want a piece of that glamour. And they can have it. What is on the red carpet one day is on the best- or worst-dressed list the next, and **knockoffs** are available soon after that. Once a look is available to the masses, it is no longer appealing to society's elite, and the cycle starts all over again. This evolution of an idea used to take years, then seasons, and then months, but now, due to proliferation of digital media sources, it is only days from the revelation of a new design to retail racks everywhere, even if it is in a somewhat diluted form. This democratization of high fashion at an ever-increasing

FIGURE 7.28 *Haute couture on the red carpet: Lupita Nyong'o wearing Prada to the 2014 Oscars where she won Best Supporting Actress. (Courtesy of Flickr.)*

ANIMAL INSTINCTS AN

UNIVERSAL COLOR
FALL/WINTER 2016

FIGURE 7.29 *A color and trend forecast for Fall/Winter 2016 by Los Angeles based Design Options. (Courtesy of Fran Sude at Design Options: http://design-options.com.)*

pace intensifies the pressure on the designer to remain at the cutting edge of style, and makes their job especially high in stress.

Fashion designers rarely know their customers personally, but they know much about the "typical" buyer within their target demographic. Each garment is meant to have broad appeal to that target group. Color is most likely chosen based on professional trend forecasting services, and is not used to indicate anything about the wearer or their character in the way color may be used in costuming. These forecasting services collect and interpret data from a wide range of sources, then market their research in the form of predictions about color and fabric trends grouped thematically. It is the fortunate designer who will travel to research and collect data to discover these trends for themselves. As with the costume designer, excellent command of the elements and principles of design is crucial for the fashion designer to create clothes that complement the figure and draw attention to the desired feature of the garment or its owner. Proportion, line, color, contrast, texture, emphasis, and balance are all carefully controlled to achieve the desired outcome.

In contrast, proportion, line, color, contrast, texture, emphasis, rhythm, and balance are powerful tools for indicating aspects of character on a stage. They also give the audience strong visual clues about who holds what place in the created world of the play and what is their relationships to the other characters. Think about how color and style conventions differentiate young from old, servant from master, and virtuous from amoral: for example, when a complementary color scheme (colors directly opposite one another on the color wheel as explained in Chapter 3) is used to convey the animosity between the Capulets and the Montagues in *Romeo and Juliet*; or between rival gangs the Sharks and the Jets in *West Side Story*; or between Kate and Petruchio in *Taming of the Shrew*. Shifts in the designer's color palette can add richness and depth to the story, subtly communicating evolving relationships.

WORK ENVIRONMENTS

Successful costume and fashion design both involve many more people than the individual designer: they are both collaborative efforts. From very early in the process, the costume designer works to create a vision for the costumes that keep them in line with what the director and the rest of the design team imagine the world of the play to be. Knowing the inhabitants of the play will reveal information about their world and vice versa. This process of conception and development involves a great deal of communication with words, and especially with visual images. Therefore using sketches and other visual images to support presentations to the director and the other members of the production team reduces the likelihood of misunderstandings, and serves to ensure that all involved are on the same page.

As each designer develops their approach to the play, shared images can serve to strengthen meaningful connections within the play and within the team. Without this open exchange of ideas, there is the possibility of one design area moving ahead of the rest, and starting to dictate the direction of the rest of the team. But frequent design and production meetings under the guiding hand of the director and the production manager ensure that each voice is heard in balance. Often, creative ideas from one design area will not only affect the choices in another design area, but will trigger more inspired and unified solutions to the problems presented by the play, the venue, or the budget. When this collaboration is working at its best, the result is a production whose individual parts are so interwoven as to be inseparable—a production that speaks the truth of the story in a more compelling way than any one member of the team imagined it could.

Costume designers often work in close proximity to the costume shop where the fittings will occur and the costumes will be built. This allows for a continuous flow of information with the shop supervisor, the drapers, and others whose job it is to turn the renderings into three-dimensional versions ready for the stage. Prompt answers to questions that may arise during the construction and fitting phases of the process will ensure that the production continues on schedule. This is very important in a process where each design is made to fit one character and one actor's body, and so a multitude of decisions must be made for each design and with each fitting.

In the fashion industry, while collaborative relationships are the ideal, it is more the norm to have a hierarchical structure with the designer near to the top. The fashion designer's work environment can vary a great deal from a one-person studio to a studio team with a creative director overseeing the work of many "in-house" designers, each of whom may have a specialized area of responsibility. With many mass-market companies producing their goods overseas, the designers of these garments may no longer be in the same place or even the same country as the stitchers or the **samples sewers**. It is therefore important that the specification sheet (or **spec sheet**) conveys all the information with no room open for misinterpretation.

Instead of an expressive costume rendering with a pose that indicates something of the character and style of the production, as produced in costume design, the fashion rendering or "plate" idealizes the human form by stretching a seven- or eight-head tall proportionate figure to ten or eleven heads tall (and with the difference accounted for in the impossibly long legs of the model).

FIGURE 7.30 *Vanessa Williams being fitted by designer Carmen Marc Valvo for her appearance in* The Heart Truth's Red Dress Collections *at New York's Fashion Week, 2004. (Courtesy of Wikimedia Commons.)*

The fashion plate thus serves as a marketing tool more than as a production guide. Instead, spec sheets contain a "**flat**" or technical drawing which is meant to clearly show the features of the garment such as closures, pockets, and collar style, right down to details like the location of all topstitching. In addition to all of that information, the fabric, thread, findings, and embellishments are itemized, costed, and tallied along with the production steps required for manufacture of the garment. The designer is often responsible for overseeing the production of prototypes or samples that will accompany the spec sheet to the manufacturing plant. They must then liaise with the manufacturer throughout the production process to ensure that each garment in the production run is consistent with the sample in fit, appearance, and quality.

The structure and work relationships in fashion design, while endlessly varied in size and form, are typically more stratified

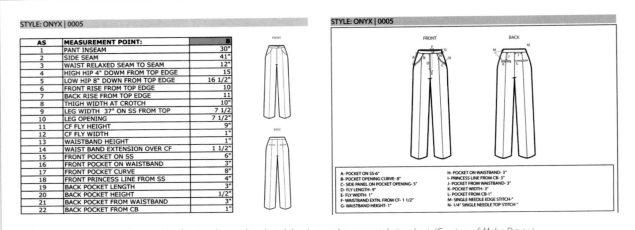

STYLE: ONYX | 0005

AS	MEASUREMENT POINT:	8
1	PANT INSEAM	30"
2	SIDE SEAM	41"
3	WAIST RELAXED SEAM TO SEAM	12"
4	HIGH HIP 4" DOWM FROM TOP EDGE	15
5	LOW HIP 8" DOWN FROM TOP EDGE	16 1/2"
6	FRONT RISE FROM TOP EDGE	10
7	BACK RISE FROM TOP EDGE	11
8	THIGH WIDTH AT CROTCH	10"
9	LEG WIDTH 37" ON SS FROM TOP	7 1/2
10	LEG OPENING	7 1/2"
11	CF FLY HEIGHT	9"
12	CF FLY WIDTH	1"
13	WAISTBAND HEIGHT	1"
14	WAIST BAND EXTENSION OVER CF	1 1/2"
15	FRONT POCKET ON SS	6"
16	FRONT POCKET ON WAISTBAND	3"
17	FRONT POCKET CURVE	8"
18	FRONT PRINCESS LINE FROM SS	4"
19	BACK POCKET LENGTH	3"
20	BACK POCKET HEIGHT	1/2"
21	BACK POCKET FROM WAISTBAND	3"
22	BACK POCKET FROM CB	1"

STYLE: ONYX | 0005

A- POCKET ON SS-6"
B- POCKET OPENING CURVE- 8"
C- SIDE PANEL ON POCKET OPENING- 5"
D- FLY LENGTH- 9"
E- FLY WIDTH- 1"
F- WAISTBAND EXTN. FROM CF- 1 1/2"
G- WAISTBAND HEIGHT- 1"

H- POCKET ON WAISTBAND- 3"
I- PRINCESS LINE FROM CB- 3"
J- POCKET FROM WAISTBAND- 3"
K- POCKET WIDTH- 3"
L- POCKET FROM CB-1"
M- SINGLE NEEDLE EDGE STITCH-"
N- 1/4" SINGLE NEEDLE TOP STITCH "

FIGURES 7.31 & 7.32 *An example of a spec sheet with technical drawings, and a garment design sheet. (Courtesy of Meha Davey.)*

than occurs in theatre. While the designer is responsible for arguably the most important aspect of the company's success (i.e., the design of garments people either want to buy or choose not to), they still need to answer to the creative director, the head of marketing, and the sales team. Interpersonal skills are an undeniable asset for any designer, but the creative designer who prefers to labor alone, rather than work as one member of a

collaborative team, may find the structure of a fashion house to be a more comfortable fit.

STEPS IN THE PROCESS

Every designer has a process by which they generate ideas and create solutions to the problems that they have been hired

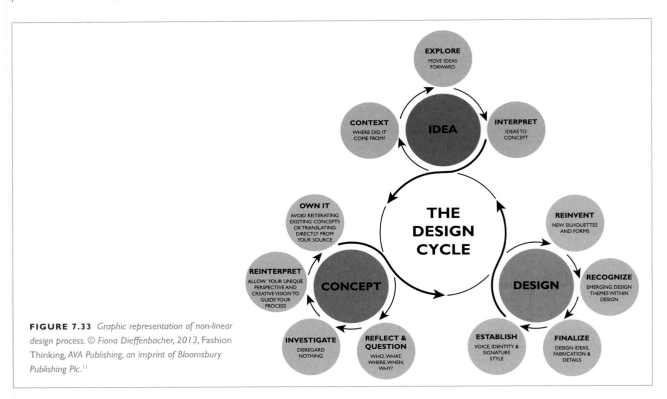

FIGURE 7.33 *Graphic representation of non-linear design process.* © Fiona Dieffenbacher, 2013, Fashion Thinking, AVA Publishing, an imprint of Bloomsbury Publishing Plc.[11]

to handle. In part, the process is a very personal and internal response to the challenges the play or garment line presents. This process is very rarely linear and is dictated to some degree by the needs of the rest of the creative team and the timeframe within which the solutions must be brought to the stage or to the market. That said, the steps creative people take to arrive at a design solution are remarkably similar across the different design disciplines.

Development of Ideas

Once the central problem is identified, there is a period of research and brainstorming. This stage is about **ideation**—taking in information from a wide range of sources, and thinking of as many potential solutions and approaches as possible. The object is to generate a large number of ideas without pre-judging them, and staying open to possibility, imagination, and creativity. This phase is likely to involve many more quick sketches than finished renderings, and more gathering of inspirational images and textures than editing.

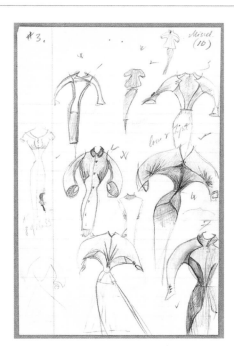

FIGURE 7.34 *A sketchbook page brainstorming ideas for day dresses by designer Charles James (1906–1978). (Courtesy of Brooklyn Museum Costume Collection at The Metropolitan Museum of Art, New York. Gift of Mrs Clive Runnels and Mrs Edward L. Ryerson, 1957. © Charles B.H. James and Louise D.B. James.)*

The costume designer thinks in terms of relationships between one character and another, of characterization, and the **story arc** of each character. This may involve the evolution of how a character is portrayed from the onset of the story to the end, possibly requiring changes to the character's age, shape, or size. Whatever the costume solution, it will be unique to this story, this character, and this actor, and must appear as though the character chose the clothes themselves.

In contrast, fashion designers think in terms of mass appeal and of groups of related garments that form a **line**. They typically produce clothes to standardized measurements—think small, medium, and large—and yet their designs must flatter the infinite shapes, sizes, and variations of the human body. Design concepts will be applied to a targeted group, not to specific individuals, although the line's success depends on mass appeal to those same individuals. Inspiration for the designer may come from trends identified through personal experience, travel and research, trend reporting companies, or any number of other influences—world events, popular culture revealed through music, street style, current blockbuster movies, or popular TV shows—almost anything can spark an idea worth exploring.

In the next stage, constraints need to be identified. There are the constraints imposed on the characters by the playwright, commonly referred to as the given circumstances, but here it is the limitations imposed by time available, deadlines, budget, and other resources including the availability of skilled labor, that need to be considered. To some degree, these constraints are also present at the beginning of the process, but they can inhibit creativity if they are made the focus at too early a stage. Designers need to be aware of the impact all design decisions make on the cost of a garment, because even seemingly small changes can make a large difference to the fiscal bottom line, especially when the number of garments is factored in. A fashion designer is often working from between one season to over a year ahead of when the lines will actually be available on store shelves. But costumes are more likely to be designed only a few months, or even just a few weeks, ahead of opening night. The costume designer also needs to add how a costume will be worn to this list of constraints, flagging any exceptional physical action or quick changes that require extra consideration in the design and planning of the costume.

FIGURES 7.35 & 7.36 *Costume designs for Hippolyta* (left) *and Titania* (right) *in* A Midsummer Night's Dream *were designed with special consideration for quick changes. The actor wore a wig built on a snug thermoplastic cap over her own asymmetrical braid, and a fairy dress with only magnetic closures. (Costume designs by Esther Van Eek for the University of Windsor, ON.)*

Evaluation of Ideas

Ideas generated in the brainstorming phase of design must now be evaluated and edited down to the practical, viable, and fitting. For many, this is the most angst-ridden part of the process since it requires discarding some wonderful design ideas that simply do not serve the story or the brand, or are not feasible within the limits that have been identified. The remaining fashion designs are further honed and edited in cooperation with representatives of sales and marketing, and, in the case of designs for a private label or license, with representatives of those concerned parties too. Changes may be requested or designs rejected outright. However, the costume designer has fewer interests to answer to at this stage of development. The director may request changes to bring the costumes more in line with the interpretive approach to the script or with the other design elements, and will have final say over which costumes get produced. Developing designs as a conversation, a back and forth exchange, is certainly preferable to a dictated solution. There may be several presentations, discussions, and re-renders before final designs are approved for production.

Realization of Designs

Once the final costume designs are selected and finishing touches are added to the renderings, the costume designer or the design assistant will shop for fabrics that best capture the desired hand, drape, color palette, and construction qualities for each design. Swatches of these fabrics are attached to the renderings so the shop can sort through the large variety of small yardages that make up a typical show. Costume production can start as soon as the renderings and fabrics are available. **Mockups**, also called muslins or toiles, are made up in inexpensive fabrics to check for proper fit and drape before the show fabrics get cut.

Once the fashion designer has received final approval for the line—and there may be several in development at the same

FIGURE 7.37 *Costume design for Sylvestro in* Scapino. *Swatches attached to the rendering provide production information for the costume shop. (Costume design by Esther Van Eek for the University of Windsor, ON.)*

time—every fabric, thread, and **finding** must be accounted for, and every step of the production planned for in great detail and recorded on the specification sheet. The designer may be the person responsible for drafting the initial pattern, or there may be a person whose sole job it is to create patterns, usually with a computer-aided design program. In mass-market production plants, the designer would then work with a sample sewer to make up a prototype of each design. This is done in a sample size—a size in the middle of the range of sizes to be produced. Samples provide one more opportunity to make adjustments to the look and fit of a garment before the pattern gets graded up and down into the full size range and all of the pieces move to the production floor. Changes at the sample stage are much less expensive to make than after 3000 garments have been cut.

Presenting the Designs

The costume designer will have several opportunities to present their designs after the director has signed off on them: at the first read-through with the cast, at the design meeting with shop personnel, and in one-on-one fittings with the actors. In this last setting, the renderings can be invaluable as the basis for a discussion of character, and how the design supports the actor in their role. The lengthy period of reading, research, sketching, sharing, and eventually rendering the costumes finally results in a cohesive group of three-dimensional garments—the design ideas brought to fruition. The actual costumes are often not on view

FIGURE 7.38 *Models and Creative Director Jason Scarlatti walk the runway at 2(X)IST Spring/Summer 2016 collection in New York. (Courtesy of Shutterstock. ©Lev Radin.)*

until the show has moved into dress rehearsals, just days before the show opens. This may also be the first time the designer sees the costumes on the actors, onstage, and in relation to one another—on set and under lights is a very exciting moment! To learn whether the show is deemed a success, the costume designer may have to wait for audience reactions and critics' reviews of the work. Excellent costumes should not stand out from the other elements of the show, so an intrinsic sense of good design is a more reliable gauge of success than any external critiques. Possibly the greatest compliment a costume designer will ever receive comes from the actor who says that donning the costume feels like putting on the character.

The fashion designer is more likely to present finished sample garments, rather than renderings, to the company's sales force and retail buyers. Some companies will produce the line in numbers, already anticipating sales. Increasingly common is the effort to "cut to order" so there is no waste and no over-runs that will eventually need to be sold at a discount. This approach requires a very responsive manufacturing plant and the ability to ship quickly from source to retail. The sample, then, must be an appealing and accurate representation of the final garment's look, feel, and fit. While seeing your designed garments on store racks is an undeniable rush, spotting someone wearing your work is an even bigger thrill! Yet success for the fashion designer will be judged by the numbers; the bottom line of sales. It is often said that designers are only as good as their last collection, and the public is a very fickle bunch indeed.

FINAL THOUGHTS

In today's job market, there is wisdom in investing in education and building skills that can be applied in more than one context or design discipline. When you consider that every consumer product is the result of somebody's design process, creativity is a valuable commodity. Developing and honing the tools of visual literacy; identifying and embracing the creative challenge presented by each new project; learning to imagine what is possible; practicing collaboration; and fine-tuning your interpersonal abilities—these are the essential skills of the successful designer. Mastering these skills will serve as a strong foundation, no matter what the medium. While pursuing a career in design will demand a great deal of energy, courage, flexibility, and commitment, few other professions offer such a variety of experiences and potential for discovery and growth. The only constant is change!

On a Personal Note

The designer's challenge—to create high quality solutions that can be produced quickly and on budget. It can be necessary to remind colleagues that when two of the three constraints take precedence, the third will suffer.

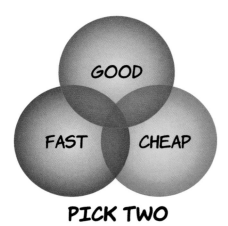

FIGURE 7.39 *Good–Fast–Cheap Venn diagram. (Courtesy of Esther Van Eek.)*

In other words:

- If a project must be done to exacting standards and must be completed quickly, the solution is likely to be expensive.

- If a project must be fast and cheap, the quality will suffer.

- If a tight budget is non-negotiable yet the work must be high caliber, the solution will take longer to realize.

QUESTIONS

- The author begins this chapter with the statement, "Clothing defines us … What we opt to wear … provides essential clues to our culture, belief system, status, and personality." What does the clothing you are wearing say about you?

- Identify skills in addition to those discussed in this chapter that would contribute significantly to making a successful designer. Are these skills unique to one design discipline, or do they cross the disciplines?

- In what ways do your personal interests and temperament suggest an affinity to one design discipline over another?

NOTES

1. See: www.twainquotes.com/Clothes.html.
2. *Mad Men*, AMC Network, 2007–2015, Lionsgate Television, created by Matthew Weiner.
3. See: www.azquotes.com/quote/797965.
4. Ecclesiastes 1:9.
5. Govane Lohbauer, email interview with author, August 22, 2015.
6. Charlie Chaplin, *My Autobiography* (Neversink, NY: Melville House, 1964).
7. Steven Stines, email interview with author, August 18, 2015.
8. Elinor Parker, email interview with author, August 2, 2015.
9. Teresa Snider-Stein, email interview with author, August 10, 2015.
10. Rafael Jaen, *Showcase: Developing, Maintaining, and Presenting a Design-Tech Portfolio for Theatre and Allied Fields* (Waltham, MA: Focal Press, 2012).
11. Fiona Dieffenbacher, *Fashion Thinking* (Worthing, UK: AVA Publishing, 2013).

FIGURE 8.1 *The Witch and Rapunzel from leading UK contemporary dance company balletLORENT's Rapunzel, which toured the UK to much acclaim in 2012–2015. (Costume design by Michele Clapton. Photo by Ravi Deepres.)*

CHAPTER 8

SHOW BUSINESS: NO ONE CALLS IT "SHOW ART"

Holly Poe Durbin

THE INFLUENCE OF COSTUME DESIGN

Many people encounter the power of wearing costumes for the first time without knowing it: playing some form of make-believe. It is natural for children to imitate what they see, creating their own costumes with items at hand. In the contemporary world the first characters and images they see are some form of media entertainment. Children first imitate their media heroes with logo clothing, character kits, and Halloween costumes. Most traditional Halloween "guising" costumes came to North America with European immigrants in the early 1900s and at that time emphasized the holiday's folk origins in devils, ghosts, and monster costumes. These early Halloween costumes were made at home using simple found elements. In the 1930s American companies began mass producing costumes for sale in stores as trick-or-treating swept the country. Children drifted away from folk characters in which they no longer really believed, switching to favorite characters from comic strips, radio, and movies.

The first film costumes to be licensed were Walt Disney's *Snow White and the Seven Dwarves* characters,[1] and this trend has grown stronger in the current media-saturated culture. It is testament to the imaginative power of effective characters and costumes—people want to identify with unforgettable characters. The phenomenon is also proof of the great powers in American retailing. Trend studies of Halloween costumes show that by the 1990s, increasing numbers of costumes were sold to adults, and Halloween ranked second only to Christmas as an economic marketplace. The National Retail Federation noted that, in 2014, over two-thirds of Halloween celebrants wore some sort of costume and total spending on all Halloween goods sailed past the $7 billion mark.[2] Today, the vast majority of regular clothing

for children includes some branded elements or references to entertainment persona, some even including wings, princess dresses, or full superhero garb available for everyday wear. Beginning in the 1980s, a large percentage of the American adult clothing market also included some marking identifying the wearer with an image—a sports team, a small jockey on a

FIGURE 8.2 *Two early cartoon characters illustrate fantasy characters used to market a persona. Richard Outcault's 1902 cartoon character Buster Brown became the official mascot of the Buster Brown Shoe Company. Clothing retailers subsequently called this style of suit a Buster Brown. His sister Mary Jane gave her name to the flat shoe with an instep strap. (Courtesy of Digital Comic Museum.)*

horse, or a fashion name. In the 2000s, this adult identification with media characters went one step further, allowing people to personally interact with their favorite media characters through imitation using cosplay and **live action role playing (LARP)**. Clothing merchandising licensing creates billions of dollars in the United States alone, with Disney leading the way. In 2013 the Disney Consumer Products division launched fashion apparel for adults with Spanish retailers Mango and Zara featuring Disney and Marvel characters. These companies are banking, in no uncertain terms, on the communicative power of clothing to craft and present a character.[3]

Widespread familiarity with one form of costume is a double-edged sword for professional costume designers. Many of these everyday costume items are made very cheaply to compete in the mass market, or are the result of imaginative but amateur do-it-yourself projects. The average person has been conditioned to believe, therefore, that the costumes are hastily or poorly made with affordable retail fabrics and relatively little formal training. No other aspect of entertainment consistently competes with such a juggernaut of cheap materials and ideas. Yet the average person has done enough carpentry to know it requires skill and dangerous equipment; they would not touch electricity or design their own lighting; many cannot successfully operate their own computers, much less create complex automation or special effects. As a result, professional costume designers must extensively educate their producers and colleagues on what they do, and how much training and practice goes into creating an effective character and costume design.

The Costume Design Profession

One of the dichotomies of any creative work is the inevitable push and pull between producing creative work and staying in business long enough to present that work to an audience. Those two elements can sometimes seem like polar opposites, and they form the most basic challenge many creative organizations face. This need to mind the financial bottom line provides one of the oldest sentences in Hollywood, uttered to almost every beginner "They don't call it show *art*, kid. It's show *business*." There are famous stories of wildly original and creative people burning and crashing in the business, and producers can be extremely leery of creative geniuses who may be too expensive or disorganized to support. On the other hand, there are just as many—or more— examples of mediocre, formulaic shows guilty of "bottom line" thinking; proving that leadership by a committee of accountants can sap the creative life from any project.

> "Costume designers create and shape the characters alongside the actors. They also directly influence and shape the aesthetic of the movies with palette, print, and silhouette choices. I feel that the costume designer should start at the same time as the production designer. Usually these two department heads work closely together on the palette and visual tone of the movie."
>
> Sophie de Rakoff[4] from *Film Independent*

Costume designers must also find a balance between creativity and the extraordinary amount of organizational work and project management needed to complete a project. How do costume designers approach this? "Everyone finds their own way. You could ask that question of five of us, and each person will deal with it differently," explains costume designer Isis Mussenden,[5] whose work includes costume designs for *The Wolverine*, *Shrek* and *The Chronicles of Narnia*. "You are, no matter what, the head of your department. You are responsible creatively and logistically to pull it off. That is your job."

Beginning a career seems mysterious to many beginning costume designers. How to break into the business? What aspect of the business is right? Like many professions, the entry-level jobs are key, and job applicants may have to be willing to go to the city or location where much of their desired industry is concentrated during summers, internships, and first jobs. Many jobs in the field are not advertised, so knowing *where* to look for those first positions is daunting. This chapter will discuss many aspects of the costume design profession so that early-career costume designers can expand their thinking about where to look for those first jobs.

Costume design itself does not have a central clearing house that operates across all levels, as does the American Medical Association. Instead, there are disparate unions, associations, and businesses that identify with their media type, such as film or theatre. Costume design is one job *within* that larger practice. One example is the Themed Entertainment Association, a central entity for companies that create immersive or environmentally based entertainment. Companies that specialize in that style of work look for costume professionals with experience in themed entertainment, and the special requirements that those projects require. Those interested in special practices such as creating ballet costumes or theme park **walk-around** characters will have to work with established providers to learn the techniques from the ground up. There are certainly exceptions to this rule, such as star costume designers with a recognizable point of view. Producers *will* seek that particular designer to bring their voice to a new project, regardless of medium or location. But the vast majority of costume designers work within the parameters of a specific practice, develop specialties, or cross between related areas such as many types of live theatre, or film and TV, or live theatre and themed entertainment. There are increasing exceptions to this rule, and the boundaries are getting thinner every year as technology redefines entertainment.

As with all professions, networking within each application is key. Broadway producers rarely call a designer based outside of New York out of the blue, unless they have a track record proving knowledge of the process, finished work that a producer can see, and a name that keeps popping up. A Los Angeles based producer, for instance, will rarely call a costume designer based in Memphis to give them a big break unless there is a pre-existing connection through colleagues that vouch for the designer. Thanks to the proliferation of regional and university theatres, nationwide film locations, local and online video programming, and themed entertainment venues, more entry-level opportunities are available across the country that will lead to connections, or provide engaging creative careers outside of the major markets. All jobs, however, require some sort of track record, contacts, and/or experience so that the beginner can prove their capability and demonstrate potential.

Karen Weller,[6] a costume designer and partner in the themed entertainment design company The Costume Connection, advises the aspiring designer to keep an open mind about entry-level positions. Working in vintage stores, fabric stores, stitching for local theatres, and taking advantage of the wide array of summer theatre opportunities are all excellent ways to build a foundation. "Of course, in order to advance within the field, one needs to sharpen leadership abilities and financial expertise. At the risk of taking the glamor out of the creative aspects, it is a business and as such must operate efficiently and economically—with regard to both materials and labor—whether you are producing a one-time parade experience, or an entire theme park with many attractions and entertainment venues. Those experienced in theatre are no strangers to the concept of balancing time, cost, and quality in the pursuit of a successful product."

Working up the ladder in a costume shop or wardrobe department is the best way to learn the basic skills any designer will need. Learning the construction process and fitting methods sharpens a designer's skills to assess work quality and budgets. Juggling fitting schedules with sometimes conflicting labor requirements teaches the young professional how to interact with rehearsals, union rules, and goal setting. Purchasing fabrics and garments introduces the young designer to sourcing methods and departmental accounting. Working in a rental house or costume

stock teaches how to categorize historical garments accurately and to properly assess the time involved in pulling garments. Rental houses also offer the opportunity to study many finished garments and other designers' methods. Salvador Perez, the President of the **Costume Designers Guild (Local 892)** notes: "I started as a stitcher and worked my way up from stitcher to workroom supervisor to assistant costume designer then started to costume design. I even worked as a set costumer once on a non-union film. . . . A great costume designer should have worked their way up. It will give them the experience and knowledge to be a better costume designer."[7] Most beginning designers will combine several of these approaches to support themselves and to learn from others, overlapping all manner of jobs. "I would assist, then stitch in the shop, then go do a low budget show on my own in a small, controlled environment" recalls film costume designer Mussenden,[5] who began her career working in New York theatre under Jane Greenwood and Ann Roth.

During a recent gathering of costume designers to discuss the future of their profession, one successful designer noted: "The best way to look at a career is to consider the entire arc—you will spend three to five years, say, in a shop learning the ropes of construction and fitting, and as a shopper or costumer in stock learning about ready-made garments and how each brand really fits. Learn to tell the hallmarks of quality in garments, and make contacts. Then branch out to assisting a designer on the next logical step on the trajectory. No one will be a successful designer right out of school." Another noted: "I probably wasn't a really good assistant designer until I was in my 30s. It takes a lot of judgement."

There has never been a wider array of arts and entertainment forms using the talents of professional costume designers. Costume designers now choose to work in every kind of career, such as educating or empowering community members using theatre as an outreach tool, as does the Cornerstone Theater in Los Angeles. Designers create haunted house experiences in Halloween attractions all over the United States; or touring spectacles such as ice shows and circus performances; or they use costumes as an immersive education tool in historical re-enactments and museums. Other designers pursue traditional forms of entertainment such as ballet, opera and plays, films and TV, theme parks and attractions, online series, animation, video games, or cruise-ship shows. And increasingly, costume designers must understand the financial and technical requirements of more than one venue or platform, as many areas of entertainment blur the lines that used to separate different kinds of stories.

FIGURE 8.3 *Costume design by Alan Armstrong for Sir John Falstaff, Henry IV Part I, Repertory Theater of St. Louis, MO. The rendering includes the swatches of fabric, suede and leather, for the construction of a very detailed costume. (Courtesy of Alan Armstrong.)*

The Artist's Point of View

Regardless of the art form costume designers work within, their artistry remains the same: the costume designers' canvas is the performer and the subject of their art work is the script. Costume designers create characters with complex personal histories using the language of clothing the audience will consciously or subconsciously understand. The characters must believably inhabit a visually unified story world created in collaboration with the director and other designers on the team, following visual rules set up for that story. No single element can stand out, unless intended to do so. But designers are not just literal interpreters of the storyline. A designer's work is always an interpretation of the intent, or an illusion. Realism on stage or screen is not truly real. The costumes often fit better than in real life, accommodating movement and fast changes. Duplicates are used to counteract damage. The color palette and textures are tightly controlled, and each garment contributes to the dramatic intent of a scene.

Creative teams express an *artistic point of view* when they create each story world, often beginning with where the story falls on the spectrum of realism to exaggeration; and this decision will communicate strong visual clues to the larger themes of the work. Audience members often fail to realize the costume designer is expressing an artistic point of view when making these decisions, particularly when the costume design suits the story so well. "You would have to be standing in the middle of Macy's not to have a point of view," declared the Oscar and Tony winning costume designer Ann Roth,[8] whose specialty is building believable characters with actors such as Meryl Streep, Nicole Kidman, and Gwyneth Paltrow. For *Places in the Heart*, a 1984 film set on a farm during the Depression, Roth fit actress Sally Fields into a correct period 1930s girdle as her character, Edna Spaulding, goes into town to request a bank loan. Roth knew that women in that era would have wiggled into the proper girdle to be seen in town, and this would affect the way they walked and sat down. How does this decision express an artistic point of view? This film was widely admired for its authenticity and film critic Vincent Canby praised this work for its "junk detector" or the ability to recreate American life at that time.[9] Another director–costume designer team might take a different approach toward the same material. They may choose to suggest people in other eras were just like the contemporary audience; for that point of view true period garments and more formal movement would be incorrect. This interpretation might call for a mixture of period and contemporary styles, or characters that wear contemporary costume with period-inspired elements. This type of decision is a subtle, yet very powerful version of artistic point of view.

Costume designer Colleen Atwood is an example of an identifiable point of view. She often works with stories featuring off-kilter characters who do not belong in a world that values conformity; her characters embody traits of gothic misfits or even lovable monsters. Yet it is the so-called normal people who might turn out to be the monsters. The 1990 Tim Burton film *Edward Scissorhands* contrasts these two types of worlds most clearly: Edward, the childlike misfit, tries unsuccessfully to fit into a candy colored suburban neighborhood of tract homes and trapped minds. The characters are a conglomeration of exaggerated mid-century archetypes who wear bright colors, creating a world just exaggerated enough for the audience to believe that a Frankenstein-like character could exist. Atwood's work on *Lemony Snicket's A Series of Unfortunate Events* (2004) with director Brad Silberling, carries this gothic exaggeration even further, commenting on a fear-mongering mainstream society. Atwood is a master of the color black, a notoriously difficult color to use in film as it often obliterates details. Her costume design for *Lemony Snicket* is a masterful interpretation of the gothic genre.

FIGURE 8.4 *Johnny Depp in* Edward Scissorhands, *1991. (Director: Tim Burton. Costume design by Colleen Atwood. Courtesy of 20th Century Fox. Photo: The Kobal Collection at Art Resource, NY.)*

"When I read a script and start to think about a character, a hazy picture forms in my mind which I then try to clarify on paper, working around it until I get the effect that I want. I see the character first of all in shapes and colors, and the details come later."

June Hudson, Costume Designer for *Doctor Who*,
from *Reading Between Designs*, p. 7[10]

An example of a visual point of view carried to an extreme is the color scheme used by director Yimou Zhang in the film *Hero* (2002) with costumes designed by Emi Wada. The film tells the story of an assassin overcoming powerful rivals in three different versions. Each iteration tells the story from a different point of view until the audience pieces together the truth. As the story repeats, the color scheme changes utilizing a grey monochromatic scale, one significant black and white sequence, saturated red and

yellow scenes, and azure blue and green. The conclusion appears in white, as all embellishments and deceptions strip away to reveal the truth. Director Zhang planned the colors for purely aesthetic reasons, but the effect was so powerful cinema fans speculated widely about symbolic meanings for each choice, finding their own deeper interpretations in the work.

Costume Designs Amplify the Truth

Costume designers bring another essential skill to each project: a sophisticated understanding of story mechanics. Why is each character in the story?—to act as the voice of reason; or to provide an element of chaos in an otherwise orderly world? Should the audience trust this character? Does an innocent-seeming character turn out to be a surprise villain at the end? Triggering the correct emotional response from the audience at the right moment is a key part of creating an effective story. Roth recalled the huge effect entertainment costumes had on her, as a

FIGURE 8.5 *Maggie Cheung as Flying Snow and Zhang Ziyi as Moon in Hero/Ying Xiong, 2002. (Director: Zhang Yimou. Costume design by Emi Wada. Courtesy of Beijing New Picture/Elite Group. Photo: The Kobal Collection at Art Resource, NY.)*

child, when she first saw the costumes in a 1941 musical movie titled *Sun Valley Serenade* starring Sonia Henie, a Norwegian Olympic champion figure skater turned Hollywood star. "They were utterly glorious and contributed immeasurably to the spirit of the picture. I had no idea who designed them, but I think of them still. Truly great costumes amplify the truth of the tales they tell with compassion and specificity. They should distill and heighten reality; after all, we have only two hours to illuminate entire lives."[11]

It is easy to understand showy costumes, and to be impressed with fantasy projects. But many projects feature contemporary costumes, and some audiences wonder if using contemporary clothing is costume design. "Contemporary costume design is often overlooked" designer Anna Wyckoff acknowledges in the *Costume Designers Guild* magazine (p. 26); and many costume designers have also noted the lack of understanding for what they contribute to a contemporary story.[12] Aggie Guerard Rodgers (*American Graffiti*, *Cocoon*, and *The Color Purple*) notes (p. 24): "I am the costume designer on every show I'm on. Whether I'm going to [clothing store] Maxfield Bleu or having it made in a shop, it's still my design. I feel very strongly that even if I shop the entire show, what I'm doing is using—let's say ten other designers' work—I'm using their art for my art."[13] Designer Mark Bridges reinforces this point, describing his approach to *Fifty Shades of Grey*. The much anticipated film version of the hit book would face a very opinionated audience with preconceived ideas about the characters: "It was a big responsibility to either be true, or to allow the costumes to be nonspecific enough that the audience finds them possible . . . The way I approached this film was to try to illustrate who the people are while trying to give it a timeless quality." (p. 26).[12] Bridges, and many other costume designers, say they try to avoid overly trendy or identifiable fashions because they will quickly date a film. Studios invest millions of dollars in a story they hope will play for years across several platforms. A classic, more timeless look will stretch the life of a film, as well as ring true with millions of audience members around the world.

Costume Designer Renée Kalfus describes her approach to contemporary costume for the most recent film version of *Annie* (p. 28): "Every single piece of clothing was built, **overdyed**, manipulated, torn, then re-sewn, patched, and embroidered to have the look of hand-me-downs. I worked the same way I would work on a period film." She also created a color to overdye the clothes that she dubbed "ten years of bad laundry" to unify the costume color palette. This is "part of what we try to do . . . We try to heighten elements, even when they are real."[12]

The Goals of Costume Design

- Create characters with complex personal histories using the language of clothing.

- Create a visually unified story world in collaboration with the director and other designers.

- Express an artistic point of view appropriate to the project.

- Enhance the story by eliciting emotional responses from the audience.

- Balance both the creative and logistical demands for the specific project.

THEATRE FOR EDUCATION, OUTREACH, AND COMMUNITY ACTIVISM

Luis Valdez, director, actor, and playwright of many plays including *Zoot Suit* and the film *La Bamba*, tells the story of how a mask made by a teacher for a school play transformed his life. As a child, his parents were migrant farm workers, and young Luis started working in the fields at the age of six. During one very short stay in first grade, a teacher transformed one of his rare personal possessions—a brown paper lunch sack—into a **paper-mâché** painted mask that riveted his imagination. The teacher built a costume and enlisted him to act a role in the school play. But the day he was to perform, the family was evicted from their labor camp after the cotton harvest and they climbed into their truck to drive away. "I felt this hole open up in my chest, it could have destroyed me . . . and that hole became the hungry mouth of my creativity . . . I took with me the secret of paper-mâché. That six-year-old is still alive in me, and with that, the anger, the residual anger of being kicked out of the labor camp . . . and for the last 65 years I've been pouring out plays and scripts and poems and stories." (p. 13)[14] He went on to found *El Teatro Campesino*, one of the earliest contemporary outreach theatres working within its community for social justice.

"Any theater that has a result in mind is not having a conversation."

Michael John Garcés,[15] Artistic Director of the Cornerstone Theater Company

---

As seen in its effect on Valdez, the power of a live performance on young minds is immeasurable. Theatres and the costume designers who choose to work in this rewarding field wish to focus on social issues, cultural conversations, personal empowerment, or other imperatives. Costume designs range widely; from elaborate portrayals of period or cultural garments to the use of non-traditional materials or upcycled found objects; or work with everyday garments to suggest illusions of fantasy. The Cornerstone Theater Company is one of the oldest community-based ensemble theatre companies producing new plays using a unique collaborative process between theatre professionals and members of the community. Their work equates aesthetic practice with social justice, artistic expression with civic engagement, and access to creative expression with individual and community health. They produce both single plays, and projects in extended series, such as the Justice Cycle or the Hunger Cycle. Plays such as *Flor* explore migrant labor issues through an imagined meeting between generations of contemporary workers from Mexico and the depression-era workers fleeing the Oklahoma dust bowl; and *Touch the Water* blends contemporary characters with Native American myths to explore urban environmental issues.

Cornerstone is currently working on a six-year cycle of nine new plays addressing food equity, food availability, urban food deserts, food addictions, and the redemptive power of feeding the community.

Another company actively engaged in community health is Kaiser Permanente, a managed healthcare and insurance provider, whose doctors and nurses see the direct result of poor food supply or dietary disasters in their communities. They have created a Community Benefits Division to address a wide range of public health issues, including an Educational Theatre featuring professional writers, directors, actors, and designers. These short plays and workshops are carefully adjusted to the developmental stages of primary, middle school, and high school students. Troupes of professional, full-time actors travel to schools and community centers performing completely free of charge.

> "If an audience member tries to steal the shoes backstage after the show, then we're doing something right."
> Michael Millar,[16] Production Manager, Kaiser Permanente Educational Theatre

This careful calibration to childhood development includes not only the format and subject matter of the play, but also the type of design that will appeal to children at each stage of growth. "Kids are very sophisticated and visually acute," explains Michael Millar,[16] the Production Manager overseeing five professional touring programs in Southern California. "They will disengage if we give them any reason, or if they don't see themselves in the characters," he notes. The educational shows cannot scrimp on production values, because "our competition is TV, video games, movies, and game shows." Costume design plays a crucial role in this form of theatre to create empathetic characters, and this challenge is most acute among middle school and high school audiences. Costumes must accurately reflect up-to-the-moment school trends. "If **Ed Hardy** t-shirts were popular last year, we can't use them this year because the kids *know*. We make arrangements with local high schools for our costume designers to shadow students, to learn what the kids are doing and saying now." The result is student audiences that are excited, engaged, ask questions, and even ask for help because they see themselves in the characters. "The kids will listen to what our actors/health educators say—not their teachers or parents."

Millar hires approximately nine designers each year to create or update educational theatre tours. Although located in Los Angeles and surrounded by designers with film, TV, and music video experience, he prefers to hire applicants with a theatre background. Those with theatre experience understand the unique challenges of building a live story well—the value of smooth scenic transitions and costume changes, durability for touring, and perfect timing. Shows must fit into a school's class schedule; even with sophisticated equipment and support systems, shows are always constrained by curtain times. "There's no stopping the camera in live theater," Millar emphasizes.

FIGURE 8.6 California: The Tempest (Bridge Tour), *Cornerstone Theater Company. (Director: Michael John Garcés. Costume design by Garry Lennon. Photo courtesy of Cornerstone Theater Company.)*

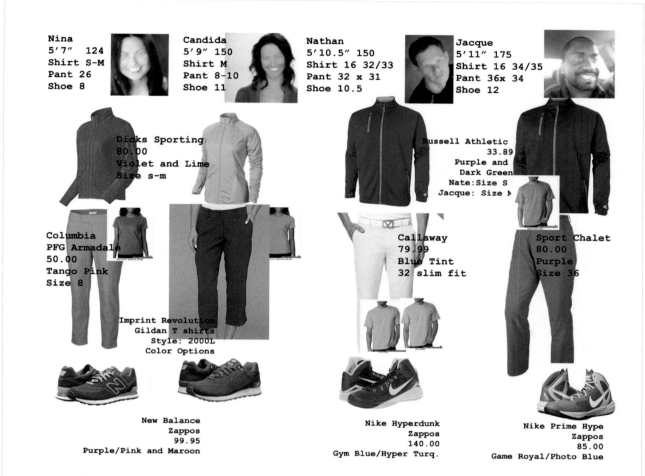

FIGURE 8.7 *Costume design tear sheets specifying the use of sourced garments for* The Amazing Food Detective, *Kaiser Permanente Educational Theatre, Southern California. (Costume design by Jessica Champagne-Hansen.)*

Other forms of educational or community theatre include teaching or creating shows in after-school programs, performing arts schools, colleges, and universities, or small **Theatre for Young Audiences** touring shows in **regional theatres**. One creative challenge that education costume designers must embrace is the non-realistic intent of casting decisions. Commercial theatre, film, and TV casting agents must consider outward attributes such as age, gender, body type, or visible attributes when casting. Educational or community casting decisions may favor intangible attributes, such as restricting the casting pool to just students in one theatre program who are about the same age range, or opening the casting call to include members of a target community, or casting performers who are much younger or older than the characters they will portray.

Performers may have advanced training or no experience at all. The educational or activist costume designer must develop skills to work with their specific cast of performers, usually employing some form of stylization in the design. Other skills include the ability to change an actor's physical attributes with padding, visual tricks, or make-up to transform the performer into character.

Educational and activist theatre offers other challenges for the costume designer. Educational theatre often tries to give as many students as possible the opportunity to participate in the performance, dividing roles between actors, or creating larger ensembles to fill out the acting roster. Many commercial or regional theatre producers will seek to do just the opposite: combine or eliminate roles without jeopardizing the story in order to avoid additional salaries. Educational costume designers

FIGURE 8.8 Touch the Water, *Cornerstone Theater Company.* *(Director: Juliette Carillo. Costume design by Soojin Lee. Photo courtesy of Cornerstone Theater Company.)*

will find themselves creatively stretching their budget and instituting organization systems to accommodate unusually large casts or additional performers added late in the rehearsal, or crews that are learning skills on the job.

This performance field is experiencing rapid growth, and is sometimes called **Applied Theatre** or Participatory Drama. Recently expanding into other media formats, digital technology allows ordinary people to create video telling their own stories or documenting their own experience and heritage. Facilitators provide the funding and a framework, often teaching members of the community to create stories themselves, or creating alongside members of the community. Some applications include using theatre, film, and puppetry with therapeutic goals in prisons, hospitals, rehabilitation centers, and marginalized communities. Designers working in these circumstances can be responsible for more than just costumes, taking on a wide array of creative,

therapeutic, or producing responsibilities. These stories also provide more opportunities to create items that cross the boundaries of costumes, to include crafts and props such as puppets and masks.

Many cities have experimental or radical theatre companies offering similar opportunities to interested designers. Increasing numbers of cultural anchor institutions also explore performance as an agent of change: universities, performing arts venues, and museums sponsor this style of outreach, or are increasingly interested in doing so. There are a few training programs available to those interested in developing such approaches, ranging from short workshops to masters degrees.

The internet offers opportunities to designers that go well beyond designing avatars and characters, and may have widespread implications for applied theatre. One example is the widespread adaptation of *Second Life*, a rich avatar environment, to serve as host for educational communities. Experimental online works include groups creating scenes caught on a network of security cameras to question the pervasive use of cameras in public places; and a massive online text-based chat room drama by the Hamnet Players. One experimental educational work was titled *To the Spice Islands*, at Charles Sturt University with campuses throughout Australia. The story was inspired by the wreck of the Dutch ship *Batavia* off the Australian coast in 1629. Students took on roles as marine archeologists to piece together the historic events, creating an experience that was deeply meaningful to the participants. These kinds of stories are told without an audience, and indeed it may be that no one ever sees the story in its entirety.[17] These online experiences are in their infancy, but are causing interest as a future component of education, activist or applied theatre, and costume designers interested in this area will be part of creating a new form of entertainment.

CREATING COSTUMES FOR COMMERCIAL THEATRE

When the average audience member thinks of **commercial theatre**, they might think first of London or **Broadway** shows and the large touring companies of musicals winding their way across the country. The American Theatre Wing's annual **Tony Awards** is the official "face" of live theatre, luring over 15 million viewers to the TV broadcast, so the general public might use the term "Broadway" incorrectly to mean any professional production in New York. But that term actually applies only to the 40 professional theatres located in the theatre district and Lincoln Center in Manhattan. Although located within a small footprint on the map, Broadway shows wield a powerful impact on the American cultural landscape.

In the last decades, the practice of commercial theatre has broadened to include new entities such as a global entertainment corporation headed by the Walt Disney Company, Cirque du Soleil, and even cruise-ship lines producing reduced versions of Broadway shows. Hence a more relevant division for understanding American theatre is the distinction between professional commercial theatre and professional not-for-profit theatre.[18] Commercial theatre, whether based in New York or elsewhere, is typically created by a partnership or corporation founded to produce one work at a time or one genre of work.

Many audiences experience commercial theatre by seeing one of the numerous shows produced by Cirque du Soleil. Cirque is a privately held entertainment company whose shows reach millions of people each year. Their shows tour in stadiums or custom-built tents, and offer permanent companies in Las Vegas. Cirque du Soleil has a reputation for promoting people from within their ranks and they pride themselves on the same family feel created by traditional circus performers throughout time. Many Cirque employees begin in crew positions that offer a wide range of experiences, particularly in wardrobe. Dressers participate in the repair of unusual costume items and accessories

FIGURE 8.9 *Arthur Kennedy, Mildred Dunnock, and Lee J. Cobb in the original Broadway production of* Death of a Salesman, *1949. (Director: Elia Kazan. Costume design by Julia Sze. Photo by Eileen Darby. Courtesy of Broadway Photographs, The Shields Collection, Dr David S. Shields, McClintock Professor, University of South Carolina.)*

that can teach a number of special skills unique only to the Cirque experience. Learning their approaches and systems is a crucial step to advancement.

More and more plays transfer to New York for **Off Broadway** or Broadway runs from regional theatres, and some take the original design team with them. A regional theatre may also hire a New York designer to work on their initial production, and then take it to Broadway. The Broadway community can be somewhat cozy, and producers and directors keep an eye out for the designers who have good reputations for delivering work that

FIGURES 8.10 & 8.11 (top) *Costume rendering for the front and back of Joseph's coat, designed by Jennifer Caprio, for the Andrew Lloyd Webber/Tim Rice* Joseph and the Amazing Technicolor Dreamcoat *national tour. (Courtesy of Jennifer Caprio.)* (bottom) *The finished robe, in collaboration with Projection Designer Daniel Brodie. (Photo by Daniel Brodie.)*

they admire. The costume designer who wants to work with Off Broadway theatres or on Broadway itself will find most success by moving to New York. Many early-career designers begin as shoppers or in other positions for one of the costume houses, or as rentals workers for a rental house. Once they learn how to put together a show in New York, they can become effective assistants to more established designers. Aspiring designers combine these jobs with designing shows of their own in small budget **Off-Off Broadway** theatres. Every business is unique, but New York theatre can feel like an especially small community.

Martin Platt,[19] a producer of the most recent revival of *Dames at Sea* and the Tony Award winning *Vanya and Sonia and Masha and Spike* worked extensively in regional theatre before moving to Broadway. He notes some differences between working commercially and working in a regional theatre; a main difference being in how creative teams are assembled for a project. For Broadway shows: "The author has to approve everybody, although they don't usually weigh in much on the designers. They are more concerned with the director and choreographer—but they do have to approve the designers eventually." The director, choreographer, and producer approve the designers more specifically by suggesting people with whom they have worked before, or the team will try "brainstorming." For *Vanya and Sonia and Masha and Spike,* Platt notes, "We talked about several designers we thought would be right for the production, and the best mix on the team." To make it into this brainstorming conversation, a designer has to have a body of work that the producers or directors know, or be known by other designers already on the team. Producers must also consider who will "work well with the director's personality, and really enjoy doing the show." Once the author approves of the director and likely design teams, then the director has final approval over casting and the actual designers that will be hired. Producers are involved in every step of the process, sometimes more overtly, but often in the background. "Producers can veto a choice, but they can't impose people unless there is a special concern." Platt notes, "Producers can fire anyone, too, without the author's approval. But they can't hire a new person without the author's approval."

Platt also offers insights into attributes costume designers working at this level should possess. "Working on Broadway, the stakes are higher" he explains. And, for any project, "the designer has to be right for the show. No one can direct or design every show that comes along." Part of maturing in this business is "turning down work that is *never* going to bring out the best in you." Platt explains that high visibility and high stakes also require excellent communication skills. With so much money invested in

a show, producers and directors want to know exactly what a show is going to look like. "So we look for somebody who will get what you are saying." He notes that a costume designer must be able to parse what a producer, director, and creative team really *mean*, not what they are saying: "Which is frequently not the same thing," he admits.

> "Besides having all the general skills—like the encyclopedic knowledge of costume and history—communication skills are the most important thing a costume designer can have."
> Martin Platt[19] from a personal interview

Mastering communication and knowing your own voice comes with experience. After decades in the business, Platt has a word of caution for costume designers: "I don't think designers always know how little some of their partners know about costumes: the process, how to read sketches. There are directors and certainly a lot of producers who don't know how to do that." Of course, there are some with a firm grasp on all the aspects of a show, but a surprising number do not have any experience with costume. Platt sees that problems begin when "everyone approves sketches and then the costume appears, and no one understood it would really look like *that*."

Platt acknowledges that costume designers invest a lot of their training in learning to create renderings, and they often go to great lengths to draw effective illustrations. But a drawing may not always be the best communication tool. "Their collaborators don't know what questions to ask, such as "Is this costume heavy?" Then the actor puts it on, and now the actor can't move in it and everyone is surprised, even though there had been a swatch attached to the sketch, and everyone dutifully felt the swatch." He suggests spending time to find a way to make the sketch come alive for the rest of the team, or spending less time trying to create impact with just an illustration style. He prefers to see good character work in a sketch, but he often sees sketches that feature movement, especially with women's costumes. "That's not what the costume is going to look like when the actor is standing on the stage talking or singing for 45 minutes. That's what it will look like in a twirl they will do just once." The rest of the time, he notes, the costume will hang like a limp rag. "You want to see what the costume will really look like—not exaggerated with sparkles flying off."

Platt notes another element of working in commercial theatre: "the only goal is to make the show as good as it possibly can be. Nothing else is important." Whereas in many non-profit

FIGURE 8.12 *Fay Templeton as Gabriel in a production of* Evangeline, *1885. Even in its earliest days, glamorous costumes were an important visual element of Broadway musicals. The producers of* Evangeline *first toured a limited production in order to raise money for the elaborate costumes required in the New York production. (Photo by Napoleon Sarony, Harvard Theater Collection. Courtesy of Broadway Photographs, Dr David S. Shields, McClintock Professor, University of South Carolina.)*

In commercial theatre, "... it is so hard to put things together financially," Platt explains. The budget is also fixed, but on a different level. Platt reveals that the costume budget for the current production of *Dames at Sea* could be, for example, around $150,000. "That is really the number, and you really expect your production manager and the designer to work toward that number for you." But, once well into the process, "... if something is not working, you change it. And you change it again. And if every time you make a change, it's another $5000 or $10,000 for costumes for somebody, you can't *not* do it." The producers and investors have saved an extra $1 million or so to cover all changes, because changes are inevitable. "If you get it wrong, the investors lose their money, and you don't get to do your next show."

Commercial production companies approach costume logistics in many ways. At one end of this spectrum is Cirque du Soleil, who maintain a large resident costume shop with 300 artisans in their international headquarters in Montreal. But most other commercial theatre producers subcontract the work to individual costume shops. While many of these shops are located primarily in New York, Chicago, and Los Angeles, there are regional shops starting to build a business because costs are more affordable outside large cities. Costume designers must be very savvy in leading projects through several shops at one time. It is not uncommon for the menswear to be built in a tailoring shop, the women's wear contracted to another shop, and specialty, crafts, or dance costumes built by yet a third business.

Many costume designers start their careers in one or several costume shops, apprenticing as shoppers, assistants, stitchers, or dyers. Along with learning materials and purchasing, these positions allow an early-career professional to learn how to negotiate different personalities and timetables. Some large shows are now sending garments overseas for specialty work such as beading, and this may continue to grow for projects with enough lead time to allow for the extended shipping time.

CREATING COSTUMES FOR NON-PROFIT THEATRE

The New York theatrical establishment effectively dominated the creative content and allied arts, such as costume design and manufacture, until the mid-20th century. Although there were a few early theatres around the country now known as the **Little Theatre movement,** by the early 1950s many theatre artists began to question this monopoly in earnest. Artists such as Margo Jones in Dallas and Zelda Fichandler in Washington DC thought (p. 25) "... something was amiss. What was essentially a collective and cumulative art form was represented in the United

theatres there is an over-riding sense of "that's good enough" because there are finite resources, or the theatre is bound to certain rules from their Board of Directors, or the next show has to move into the shop by a certain time. The typical non-profit theatre works with a fixed budget, regardless of whether that budget is adequate to produce the show. A large regional theatre may be able to commit $5,000 to a small cast, modern dress show, while a smaller theatre may have $5,000 for 150 costumes. The budget is based on the theatre's own history or financial situation; perhaps they have a lot of costumes in stock to reuse, or previous designers have consistently delivered budgets cheaply by begging and borrowing costumes. The costume designer is expected to conform to the needs of the budget rather than the best way to design the show.

FIGURE 8.13 *The Old Vat, Arena Stage, 1956–1961. Regional theatre pioneer Zelda Fichandler and founders of the Arena Stage convert part of the Old Heurich Brewery into a 500 seat theatre-in-the-round, 1956. (Courtesy of Arena Stage.)*

States by the hit-or-miss, make-a-pudding, smash-a-pudding system of Broadway production."[20] These pioneers created theatres around the country to present professional productions, taking advantage of relatively recent legal changes for establishing not-for-profit organizations. Their mission was to fully produce shows in-house, as part of mixed seasons offering some new work and some classics.

By the 1980s large regional theatres had matured. They began to complete the circle by sending original works back to New York for their Broadway debut. One particularly prolific theatre was the LaJolla Playhouse, developing 13 plays that moved to New York, such as *Thoroughly Modern Millie*, *Dracula*, and *Jersey Boys*. The regional movement gained so much notice that in 2003

Time Magazine extensively covered these theatres in an article sensationally titled "Bigger Than Broadway!": "Many have gleaming new theatres, with two or even three stages, and state-of-the-art production facilities that put to shame the cramped old boxes on Broadway." The article notes "these companies are pursuing whole chunks of the repertory that New York, with its commercial pressures and unforgiving critics, largely ignores. And local audiences are getting a better taste of the possibilities of theatre than most New Yorkers get in an entire season."[21]

By 2014 Theatre Communications Group (TCG) counted over 1,700 non-profit theatres representing a large artistic and employment opportunity for theatre artists of every type.[22]

Some of the larger theatres established their own costume shops, and many current professionals began their careers in regional theatres that perform during the summer or across the year. Early in the regional theatre movement many directors, actors, and designers were part of a permanent resident company. Many theatres have moved away from this model and now pull their creative teams from a national pool, holding auditions in cities such as Los Angeles, Chicago, and New York, as well as their own local communities. Many theatres are large institutions responsible for producing a season of plays, administering the business and physical assets such as multiple buildings, raising money to subsidize expenses, offering community or educational outreach, and even offering training programs for students. Each area offers employment opportunities, with costume personnel involved in many of these functions.

A THEATRICAL MACHINE

The **artistic director** has responsibility for planning each season and hiring directors for specific shows in the season. The theatre artistic director or **production manager** will sometimes match a costume designer to a director, or approve a director's request to use a specific team of designers. Most theatres try to maintain a careful balance between local and out-of-town designers, and can be generous in giving designers their first significant jobs, particularly in the outreach programs or smaller studio theatres. Many costume designers have worked their way through the regional or summer theatres, beginning in the costume shop to learn every aspect of the field, gaining experience and contacts along the way.

Regional theatres are sophisticated producing organizations that move complex puzzle pieces to create large seasons on time, under budget, and aspiring to a high level of artistry. The Repertory Theatre of St. Louis and the Cincinnati Playhouse are excellent examples of the complicated theatrical machinery required to produce full seasons. Both maintain a complex operation with multiple venues: a bigger main stage theatre for larger or more mainstream plays, a smaller studio theatre for experimental plays or new works, and a touring Theatre for Young Audiences season. These organizations also oversee satellite spaces for storage or scenic construction. A small resident staff works on several projects at once, employing overhire workers for large shows, and scaling back the operation for smaller shows.

Alphabet Soup: Interpreting LORT, TCG, and USA

Each theatre develops a distinct personality influenced by its leaders and home community. While most present a mixture of genres during the performing season, some prefer to commission new or edgy work, others offer more musicals, or a mixture of classics. Some operate as mini-Broadway houses, producing some of the latest New York hits for their home audience. In its 2003 article on regional theatre, *Time Magazine*[21] reported: "One of the things you find is that there's a low level of audience pretension," says Richard Greenberg, who has developed plays like *Three Days of Rain* and *The Violet Hour* at South Coast Repertory in California's Orange County. "There's a receptiveness about the audience. Their responses are pure. And that's especially good early on, when you're not so sure." While it may be impossible to categorize all regional theatres as a whole, it can be even harder to research such scattered venues for possible employment opportunities. Finding jobs requires some detective work; it is most useful to begin with the theatre associations. The League of Resident Theatres (**LORT**) and **Theatre Communications Group (TCG)** are two of the largest. LORT is the largest professional theatre association in the United States and operates as the legal entity for negotiating bargaining agreements with its counterpart organizations, **Actors Equity Association (AEA)**, **Stage Directors and Choreographers Society (SDC)**, and **United Scenic Artists (USA)**—the union representing theatrical designers. Before LORT, individual theatres used to create their own contracts for all talent resulting in wide variances and practices.

LORT currently consists of 74 member theatres with an established category system to affiliate similar theatres into groups; most categories use the average box office receipts and seating capacity as a way to determine group membership. The categories include A, B+, B, C (C1 and C2 options available) and D. These categories help theatres identify other institutions with similar concerns, and create a universal system for setting a range of directing fees, acting and stage management salaries, and designer fees for each category. Both LORT and USA list current bargaining agreements on their websites; USA also posts the rate sheets sorted by region and the type of project.

TCG is a wider membership and advocacy organization including theatres, individual artists from every aspect of live theatre, educators, and students. They offer publications such as books, scripts, and the magazine *American Theatre* which features a play script in each issue along with a list of member theatres and their current work. TCG also publishes **ARTSEARCH**, a premier job listing service featuring over 3,000 job postings per year in regional, educational, and summer arts organizations.

FIGURE 8.14 *Costume design for the Porter in Macbeth. (Watercolor, Prismacolor, graphite and relevant research. Costume design by Alan Armstrong, Alabama Shakespeare Festival. Courtesy of Alan Armstrong.)*

Resident Costume Shops

Regional theatres serve as a major training ground for costume professionals; seasoned professionals guide the beginners on their team, and early-career costumers learn professional practices. Many theatres maintain a resident costume shop; those located in large labor markets often keep a small cohort as permanent staff, hiring additional positions as needed for specific shows. These positions are called "overhire" jobs, or sometimes "jobbing out" if the costume maker works in their own studio. Staff and overhire positions include drapers, tailors, dyers and fabric painters, milliners, specialty crafts artisans, first hands and stitchers, shoppers, and general organizational duties. Many designers who ultimately work in other fields such as film or themed entertainment got their start in a non-profit theatre.

If a theatre is located in an area with a smaller available labor pool, the costume shop might choose to hire a larger full-time staff with needed specialties in order to ensure that they are always available. While this was, at one time, a common practice, many shops now pursue the opposite strategy. They hire fewer specialized personnel, instead preferring those with organizational and general skills who can do a number of jobs, and keeping only a skeleton crew of skilled labor. The rise of the internet store is changing how costume designers source garments. Within the last five years, a number of costume makers have debuted sophisticated and reliable services online, making it possible to order both custom-made and ready-made garments for historical

or contemporary shows. And, conversely, it is also possible for a theatrical costume maker to augment their income or leave the employ of a costume shop altogether to establish their own business.

Oregon Shakespeare Festival is a well-regarded large theatre organization: in 2003 *Time Magazine* named it one of the top five regional theatres in America.[21] Many costume designers, shop managers, and shop staff began their careers as apprentices or in entry-level jobs here or other places like it. Oregon Shakespeare mounts 11 to 12 shows in a rotating **repertory** model with an approximate total of 900 performances per season. Their location, large shows, and commitment to high production values mean their costume department employs over 70 people as costume designers, assistant designers, organizational and management positions, and costume construction positions such as draper, tailor, first hand, stitcher, crafts and dyer, along with wardrobe crews to run the performances. A comprehensive program of fellowships, assistantships, internships, and residencies offers outstanding opportunities for many levels of beginning career theatre artists.

A medium-sized regional theatre is the Cincinnati Playhouse, producing 11 shows on two stages; the Marx Theatre with a seating capacity of 626 and the Shelterhouse with a smaller stage and more intimate seating of 225 patrons. A typical season might include a small two-person show, a very large holiday show such as *A Christmas Carol*, and a variety of new works, family programming, and recent Broadway hits.

Costume Shop Manager Gordon DeVinney is ultimately responsible for planning the entire season of shows, as well as scheduling the labor and resources for each show, and working with the individual designers. The Cincinnati Playhouse and the Repertory Theatre of St. Louis share co-productions, and in that case he and the costume shop manager in St. Louis are responsible for all the logistics of those projects. He is responsible for delivering each project to the stage on time regardless of production or rehearsal challenges. The costume shop employs a small resident staff and DeVinney augments that with extra people from the local area. Like many theatres, the costume department operates in two shifts: a day crew in the shop builds shows, and the night crew runs shows in wardrobe, hair, and makeup. He will also utilize makers in other cities, such as a tailor in Chicago, sending suits back and forth for fitting and finishing. Entry-level jobs for the Playhouse include stitchers, first hands, and general costume stock and shopping assistants. DeVinney is a costume designer too, and may design one or more of the shows in the Playhouse season, or special events throughout the year.

FIGURE 8.15 *Online store "Lucky Zelda," created by theatrical costume draper Catherine Esera, features her line of custom-made and vintage items. (Screen capture by Holly Poe Durbin.)*

FIGURE 8.16 *Period ladies jacket for* ShipWrecked!: *understanding proper fit is an essential element of successful costumes. (Draped by Cindy Witherspoon, Cincinnati Playhouse in the Park. Costume design and photo by Holly Poe Durbin.)*

One example of a smaller regional theatre is the Geffen Playhouse in Los Angeles. Its main stage venue, the Gil Cates Theater, seats 512 and its smaller flexible space theatre seats a maximum of 149 people. Located on the west side of Los Angeles, it has access to many support resources, such as rental houses, made-to-order costume shops, vintage suppliers, and many freelancers working on a show-by-show basis. There is only one resident costume staff member, the wardrobe supervisor. Each costume designer works with the wardrobe supervisor to define the needs of that specific project—where will made-to-order items be built? Who will do alterations? Does the theatre have a regular relationship with a wig maker or dyers, or should the costume designer call on their own network?

Many regional theatre costume shops will work with interns, although not all have the resources to offer well paid internships and those with a small staff may not have a formal structure to extensively teach interns. However, there is a lot to be learned by being in the room with working professionals. Volunteering with a regional costume shop while still in college is an excellent way to get an introduction to the kinds of jobs and skills that costume shops use.

Summer Theatres

Some professional costumers swing between two regular performance seasons: a regional theatre that operates from fall through spring, and a summer theatre or opera season. Summer theatres offer classic training methods, and many designers begin their careers in this way. Some summer theatres are also members of LORT or TCG and will be listed on their websites, but others may not be members. A comprehensive list of summer theatre opportunities can be found on the websites of the Educational Theatre Association or Cengage Learning.[23] Summer festivals and theatres run the gamut from large, fully professional organizations, to semi-professional or educational endeavors employing large numbers of students and theatre educators. An understanding of the LORT category system can help the early-career professional to climb the ladder from a smaller theatre to a larger one in order to advance their skills and network.

Working for a summer theatre is the traditional entry-level route for most people interested in live theatre. The creative team and department heads do the vast majority of planning and hiring before the season begins. Directors, actors, designers, and shop and show running staff then converge from all around the country to work on a condensed season, presenting multiple shows rapidly. College students have the opportunity to work with more experienced mentors, and try several types of jobs during the course of the season. They observe the kinds of jobs they might like to have in future, and what kind of skills those jobs require. These summers often feel like a trial by fire, but they teach advanced planning methods, and how to streamline process. People may leave early for other jobs, and those left behind often step into a new promotion to fill the gap—a time-honored way to work up the ranks, and learn every part of the costume design process.

Independent Theatre Companies

There are many more theatres than those presenting a full regional theatre season, or those that belong to LORT or TCG. There are also a large number of independent theatre companies doing excellent work who do not own buildings, and must rent their performance spaces. New York has a lively Off Broadway, Off-Off Broadway, and **Showcase Theatre** scene,

FIGURE 8.17 *Costume design for Mrs Ann Lovely in* A Bold Stroke for a Wife. *(Collage with watercolor, pencil, fabric, lace, and photocopied elements. Costume design by Alan Armstrong, Alabama Shakespeare Festival. Courtesy of Alan Armstrong.)*

FIGURE 8.18 *Paul Kalina, Adrian Danzig, and Molly Brennan in 500 Clown Frankenstein. (Costume design by Tatjana Radisic. Photo by Michael Brosilow.)*

festivals, musical theatres, and historical dramas), and The Shakespeare Theatre Association (listing over 100 members worldwide), can help an early-career costumer to create a list of theatres to investigate. Some theatre companies book their performances through touring organizations to play on college campuses and other community venues. The following additional sources maintain job boards accessible for free or through a subscription:

- The Southeastern Theatre Conference (SETC)
- United States Institute for Theatre Technology (USITT)
- StageJobsPro.com
- Indeed.com: Backstage Jobs
- OffstageJobs.com
- Theatre Communications Group
- Opera America

COSTUME DESIGN FOR OPERA, MUSICAL THEATRE, AND DANCE

There is an old saying that when emotions grow larger than words can express, characters burst into song. And when singing is not enough, they break into dance. John Adams, a renowned composer and conductor said "Opera is the art form that goes to the max: it is the most emotional, it goes the furthest . . . music is, ultimately, about *feeling*. And that may be why people go the opera house."[24]

Opera and dance are international art forms; different companies around the world may share the same singers or dancers for their roles. Directors and designers may also be international, following a production from one opera house or theatre to another, and dance companies often undertake extended national or international tours. Opera companies often share resources and ideas so all may benefit. Many opera companies are members of Opera America, the member service and advocacy organization. They publish an extensive website of resources, including job listings, grants, and a design contest for early-career design teams, as well as publishing the magazine *Opera America*.

Opera combines all the performed arts in one performance: song, music, acting, and historically, also dance. Dance is a more varied art form, with companies specializing in specific styles. Dance/USA is the largest membership service and advocacy organization with 500 member groups. Musical theatre and operetta have a long history and many styles of presentation, including film musicals. Musicals form a large part of the Broadway experience and for many theatre goers, the musical *is* Broadway.

and Los Angeles supports a large 99-Seat Waiver movement. Many of these companies have permanent company members or work with a coterie of like-minded artists to develop shows. Independent theatres may not pay enough to fully support the designers or actors for each project, but this system offers a classic way to get a "foot in the door"; making connections, getting your work seen, and meeting others working in the area who may help with future work.

Independent theatres are excellent resources for an early-career designer, but it often requires tenacity and face-to-face meetings to find a position. Many of the jobs are secured through word-of-mouth or local connections, and some producers advertise through networks geared toward their own region, such as the online services OffStageJobs.com, where jobs are sorted by location. An internet search of organizations such as **The Institute of Outdoor Theatre** (a member organization serving Shakespeare

Like opera and dance, revivals of classic works are common with creative reimaginings an enjoyable part of the experience for its fans. Just as with opera, there is a great deal of written literature for aficionados to study about the art form. The National Alliance of Musical Theatre (NAMT) is the member service and advocacy group that provides resources and information.

The best-known opera companies began as temples of 19th century grand opera tradition, such as the Paris Opera, La Scala, the Royal Opera in London, and the Metropolitan Opera in New York. These companies play to very large audiences with seating capacities as large as 2,000. Such large scale performances require great vocal and orchestral power, and compelling production values. The spectacle of opera has been an important part of the grand opera tradition. Musical theatres and ballet may also fill large stages, but the seating capacity of the theatre is seldom as large as grand opera.

Unlike many plays, there is a very well-known repertoire for opera, ballet, and musical theatre and fewer new works debuting each year. Audiences can be quite sophisticated, learning about a production before they see it in performance. They may well have seen other productions. Opera is the one art form where audiences are accustomed to listening and watching works performed in languages different from their own. The extensive training and smaller pool of singers and dancers performing this repertoire means that many opera companies must draw from an international pool of singers. Casting for vocal range and dance skill means that many traditional casting factors may be overlooked, such as age, physical type, and nationality. These elements directly affect the costume designers approach to any project. For instance, it is much more common to work with middle-aged opera singers cast as young ill-fated lovers than it would be in theatre or film.

Casting variations are more acceptable in all the musical arts because the suspension of disbelief is already enormous: characters are singing or dancing—feats we seldom see in daily life. The dramatic situations are heightened to match the presentational format of performance. Costume designers must be proficient in designing for music: the mood or intent may be more evident in music than the libretto. Much is determined by the length and placement of the music, and all action must occur with split second timing. While musical traditions may dictate specific approaches, design for music is in many ways more freeing. There is usually more emphasis on emotional impact, glamor and figure correction, and fabrics and trims that reflect light or float with movement. Costume designers creating these art forms will have two visionary voices to collaborate with: the stage director and the choreographer.

Opera, Musicals, and Dance by the Numbers

All forms of musical performance may feature a large chorus or ensemble. If the music calls for a powerful effect, the chorus or **corps** can be an extremely large presence, from 20 to 100 people, and this creates a unique challenge for the costume department. Before approaching the design, the intent behind these numbers should be clear. Does the chorus or corps represent one voice or character, such as a group that that will perform in unison? If that is the case, do the costumes closely resemble each other? Or is the chorus or corps a group of individual characters, such as all the town folk in a village or guests at a party? If so, are the costumes visually different from each other? Will the costumes be rented from another production, and what is the best way to create components for so many costumes? Smaller or experimental companies have begun approaching shows differently, deliberately trying to change the need for a large chorus. They may ask a chorus to sing offstage, or create a reduced ensemble. Some opera companies will only present works that feature small cast sizes, or experimental works. A costume designer may be asked to create new solutions as part of reconceiving an opera.

FIGURE 8.19 *Michael Dean singing the role of Araspe in Handel's opera Tolomeo. Costume design by Bonnie J. Kruger for the International Handel-Festspiele in Göttingen, Germany. (Photo by Bonnie J. Kruger.)*

Designing for musical performance requires complex logistics over the life of a production. Ensembles of matching costumes are usually required, and there are specific approaches in the costume design that may be determined by the script or by traditions set by the original production. There are many technical considerations working with singers and dancers. Some productions are conceived as co-productions (often shortened to "co-pros") between partner companies in order to help offset the very great investment in costumes. Companies may also create a new production knowing they will revive it several times over the next ten years, again recouping more from their investment.

The costume designer may have to design costumes which will look appropriate for several different singers or dancers contracted for a role over time. And some co-pros can take years to make the appointed rounds of venues, with the costumes starting to show wear and tear. Dance companies may tour repeatedly, with little money to replace ageing or ill-fitting costumes. Anticipating these circumstances can be an important budget- and labor-saving device, as well as ensuring a less stressful transition from company to company.

The costumes may be kept to be rented out as a full package to other opera companies, or eventually sold to rental houses such as Malabar Ltd in Toronto, Canada. A look at the Malabar website reveals over 100 opera productions for rental, with several operas listed more than once in order to accommodate completely different designs or eras. Opera America and Dance/USA provide a resource library of costumes and scenic packages available for rental from all its member companies.

Costumes may be periodically refreshed and replaced, but planning for longevity and frequent alterations is a crucial aspect of any opera costume design. Opera and ballet productions take on a long life for many reasons. First, the effort to design and make large numbers of costumes is labor intensive. "Most opera productions require one to two years' lead time," says costume designer Dunya Ramicova,[25] who has designed dozens of operas. The time to procure principal singers, cast the company, obtain a slot in a performance season, search for resources, and rehearse an orchestra and chorus all add up to a much longer preparation period than many live theatre events.

Opera fans all over the world will follow the designs of a particularly exciting new production in *Opera News* or the *Opera Magazine,* and subsequent productions may be influenced by the initial interpretation. "Working with a new opera or play is my favorite kind of design," notes Ramicova. "[This kind of new work] . . . is breaking new ground and frequently one's work sets the standard for all future productions."

FIGURE 8.20 *Costume design for Zoroastro in Handel's Orlando. Designed by Bonnie J. Kruger for the International Handel-Festspiele in Göttingen, Germany. Kruger has created a number of opera costumes in the same Baroque style. Remaking items from this inventory results in a unified approach for her productions and allows the producers to recoup their investment. (Courtesy of Bonnie J. Kruger.)*

An opera, dance, or musical theatre company's resident costume director or costume coordinators can play a strong role in planning large scale projects: researching rentals for partial or full packages; fitting large numbers of singers at once; overseeing specialty costume builds and footwear; and managing a large costume stock and rentals to other companies. A costume director may be deeply involved in future season production planning; traveling to other companies to assess the suitability of a rental package; and assessing future workloads. Costume directors also need to possess advanced design skills in order to build new costumes for principal singers or dancers that must match an existing package, or to revive a prior production after the original designer is no longer available.

Musical performance companies all have their own personalities, as do regional theatres, but most strive to offer

FIGURES 8.21 & 8.22 *Costume designs for a production of the opera* Tosca: *(left)* Baron Scarpia *and (right)* Tosca. *(Costume design by Jennifer Caprio, Mill City Summer Opera, 2014. Courtesy of Jennifer Caprio.)*

a balance of experimental and traditional work, appealing to both the more sophisticated audience members who have seen multiple productions, and also to the new audience members who would like to see a traditional classic for the first time. Many opera and dance companies have large community outreach or education components, offering performances in schools or in underserved communities. These smaller projects are an excellent way for an early-career designer to begin work in this art form.

Repeated Performances

Opera has a repertoire well known to many of its audience members. There is a natural tension between upholding performance traditions and wanting to explore new areas of the work; yet opera audiences have come to expect new productions of favorite traditional works. Director Jonathan Miller dedicated an entire book to exploring why some types of performances are revived over and over, with ballet, Shakespeare's plays, and

opera notable examples of this practice. "It seems to me precisely because [they] are interpretations, rather than copies, that they have survived . . . The work has enjoyed an extraordinary afterlife unforeseeable by the author at the time of writing." (p. 55).[26] Many opera companies may feature the same titles at the same time, but upon comparison each production will be very different.

Opera designers in particular must be adept at envisioning how the same story can be told in new ways. One recent example of this principle at work is the Los Angeles Opera's two recent versions of Mozart's *The Magic Flute*, a fairytale featuring exotic creatures and locations that presents the opportunity for wildly imaginative interpretations. Seeing how each new production will present this favorite story is part of the fun for audiences, and can bring prestige to individual opera companies. During the 20th century, some opera companies invited famous artists or designers not normally associated with stage design to create a new production of this opera. Each is so distinctive that they are referred to by the artist's name, rather than by the stage director. Notable designs include: a 1967 Metropolitan Opera production designed by painter Marc Chagall; a 1978 Glyndebourne Festival Opera production with sets and costumes designed by painter David Hockney; a 1981 Houston Grand Opera production designed by beloved children's book author and illustrator Maurice Sendak; and, more recently, a 2012 Washington National Opera production designed by Japanese ceramicist Jun Kaneko.[27] The Los Angeles Opera, in turn, invited Gerald Scarfe, a British political cartoonist known for his puppets and art direction, to create *The Magic Flute* for the 1993 season. It featured costumes that created larger-than-life silhouettes, enlarging the singers' bodies. The bright colors and addition of black lines on many edges called to mind his work as an illustrator. The LA Opera scheduled a fifth revival in the 2013–2014 season, but at the last minute substituted a new production created by Barrie Kosky, Susanne Andrade, and Paul Barritt for the Berlin Komische Oper in 2012. First spotted on a scouting trip in Germany by the President of the LA Opera, this new production was inspired by the silent movies of the 1920s and 1930s and seemed the perfect fit for the home of Hollywood. It combined animation with live action, and featured stunning scenes of singers interacting with hand-drawn animated characters.[28]

Opera and dance creators are well in the vanguard of experimenting with new forms or technology. One interesting new production is *Hercules vs Vampires*. Opera Theater Oregon partnered with Portland based Filmusik to combine a 1961 Italian film originally titled *Hercules in the Haunted World* with live singers and orchestra. The creative team theorized that the stories used in low budget cult cinema were just as outsized and dramatic as many classic opera plots. The production included the full movie, starring the 1958 Mr Universe bodybuilder Reg Park, screened behind live singers in what Opera Oregon terms "Operascope." The new commissioned score by Patrick Morganelli was substituted for the film's original soundtrack, with dialogue sung by live singers at the same time as the characters on the screen spoke. The performance offerings included related events such as a costume party, and popcorn vendors did a brisk business in the lobby. The performance was a sensation with critics that drew enthusiastic youthful audiences and also appealed to a film-industry crowd. Film director Mario Bava's work was "Low-budget but no joke . . . [he] put his mad stamp on Quentin Tarantino, Tim Burton, the Beastie Boys, and Joe Dante."[29]

Opera and dance have long been presented in a festival atmosphere, many performing during the summer. Festivals are a good way to see or work on several projects in a short period of time. Some companies use the festival to present fully produced work in repertory, others create chamber pieces or debut new works. Opera festivals must hire a costume staff sufficient to present several works in repertory, and this can offer excellent training. The Santa Fe Opera maintains a particularly well-regarded Apprentice Program in their large costume, crafts, and wig shops.

COSTUME FOR FILM, TV, AND THE WEB

Film costume design has experienced a renaissance in publicity not seen since the Hollywood Studio era, thanks to the extra materials on DVD releases of films; the tireless efforts of the Costume Designers Guild; and the recent proliferation of blogs by film costume aficionados or designers themselves. Mussenden,[5] a film costume designer (including movies such as *The Chronicles of Narnia, Shrek, Shrek 2,* and *Wolverine*) explains: "In the 90s we were starting to realize if we don't publicize ourselves, no one is ever going to know what we do. We were constantly asked 'Do the actors bring their own clothes?' The publicity *has* gotten the layman to understand what we do, and to understand the complexity of it and how much we're involved." Worldwide exhibitions of film costumes have also contributed to public understanding of the costume design process.

Until recently, anyone interested in working in film had to move to Los Angeles or New York to break into the business. But that is no longer the case, with production companies and studios established in Canada, Georgia, Louisiana, North Carolina, New Mexico, and Texas. In 2013 Louisiana lured the most major studio films and larger independent productions. California and Canada ranked second, but more than 40 states in the United States and 12 other countries offer tax credits and other incentives to entice film makers.[30] More locations mean that more people can work in film without having to move to one central location, and more than 1,000 Film Commission offices have opened across the United States to assist film makers with local crew, locations, and other production support services. Film crews can now create an entire career away from New York or Los Angeles, or gain experience before deciding to relocate to a major market.

Film costume design has evolved away from the studio system of the golden age, where resident and guest designers worked with a large workroom staff and huge costume stock to create films. When the studio system dissolved in the 1970s, many independent production companies sprang up in their place, and the studios themselves now concentrate less on production and more on development, deal making, and distribution. Some production companies organize to create a single film, intending to dissolve later. These companies do not want to invest in assets or equipment, and each film is financed separately. While it can take years to negotiate the development process, as soon as the

FIGURE 8.23 *Tilda Swinton as The White Witch and Skandar Keynes as Edmund. Chronicles of Narnia: The Lion, The Witch and the Wardrobe, 2005. Director: Andrew Adamson. (Costume design by Isis Mussenden. Courtesy of Walt Disney Pictures/Walden Media. Photo: The Kobal Collection at Art Resource, NY.)*

money is put together, a huge company of people must swing into action to start up, prepare, shoot, and wrap in a matter of months. That may mean building the infrastructure from scratch each and every time the designer begins a new project. Lead times are decreasing and locations are more far flung, so costume designers have to deploy a team and marshal resources rapidly. Hence, a designer's ability to manage logistics, as well as the artistic concerns, is a key element of each job. Producers may be absolutely unaware of the costume process and its needs, yet they perform a more overt presence in daily operations by micro-managing or sometimes refusing to use resources or methods proposed by the designer. With all these pressures, costume designers try to work with valued team members again and again; they have to trust their crew to handle a lot of tasks efficiently. TV shows produce on an even faster cycle, with each episode put together within a 7 to 10 day production period. Recently, TV shows have started shooting several episodes simultaneously, contributing to an even more hectic pace.

Two people generally head the costume department: the costume designer and the wardrobe supervisor, and both are equally responsible for delivering the costumes to the camera on time. As Mussenden[5] explains "You are, no matter what, the head of your department. You are responsible creatively and logistically to pull it off. That is your job." Television designer Chrisi Karvonides-Dushenko (who worked on *American Horror Story*) notes that demonstrating an understanding of the logistics can be part of the interview for some projects: "If I can't propose *how* a show can be done in the interview, then I have no business being in the room."[31] Indeed, the job is so complex that "the personal characteristics of a successful costumer in terms of intelligence, problem solving ability, creativity, management abilities, and leadership abilities are such that, if they were so motivated, they are capable of running a large country," designer Stephanie Schoelzel notes wryly.[32]

Daunting as it may sound, costume design for film is a rewarding career that many would like to try. New technologies

FIGURE 8.24 *Triphammer, a recurring character in the streaming series* Powers *for Sony PlayStation Network. (Costume design by Wendy Greiner. Illustrator: Mariano A. Diaz.)*

in digital design and recording are encouraging more crossover projects between film and live performance, and hence many costume designers may work in some aspect of film regardless of the medium of the final performance. Every designer approaches this amalgam of logistics and art differently: "Some go right to the color palette first . . . some people are drawn to the lead character first." Mussenden[5] continues, "I can't begin until I have an end. What is the truth in this script? What story are we trying to tell? I approach it very much like an actor or a director. I can't even think about a piece of clothing until I break down the script. How many days, where we are, the economic level, and how many changes they have. It's different if they have three changes or 42 changes—the stakes are higher, then . . . Some people leave it to their script supervisor to break down the script, but I can't

do that. It's part of my process. Until I know whether the big change is a three-minute scene or a forty-minute one, that's when I know where I'm telling my story. And . . . how to spend the energies and money." Costume designer Sophie de Rakoff (who has worked on *Legally Blonde* and *Legally Blonde 2*) notes that: "Ground Zero for all costume designers is character and how to realize this. When you know your character, you know their wardrobe. [For this reason] Costume designers often have a very intimate relationship with the actors, sometimes as intimate as the director's."[4]

> "I truly believe everyone needs to know Illustrator or Photoshop. That is a prerequisite. I find that a young person coming into the business that doesn't understand that—there is no excuse."
>
> Isis Mussenden[5] from a personal interview

Mussenden[5] has advice for those looking for entry-level positions in film costume design. "They need to organize information well. How to organize, how to shrink files and send them in the best resolution for an iPad—that's how all information is shared these days." Technology is also used to tinker with fitting photos: "Directors and producers can't read a fitting photo, and do not understand that the part sticking out with the safety pins will be gone. They worry the actor will look fat, when they are really looking at extra fabric." She uses an assistant with Photoshop skills to smooth out the alterations on the photos to show what the costume *will* look like when it is finished. "I choose the best photos, and they organize [the presentation] and send it on to the director. And it's a good check for me, to see the decisions I made will work." Although the Technical PA position is relatively new, and is not yet regulated by any union, it is an ideal way to join a design team and learn the ropes. For example, the TV series *Brooklyn Nine-Nine* hired a Technical PA to screen-capture purchased clothing from online sources and wrap those garments around the actors' bodies in Photoshop in order to communicate what the characters would look like to the director, producer, and actors.

Although Mussenden is comfortable with many aspects of digital work after working on *Shrek* and *The Chronicles of Narnia*, she points out that the costume design profession is in transition, with many established designers unable to use the required software. "They don't have time to sit down to learn it. . . . Young people entering the profession can get jobs if they demonstrate those skills. Everyone needs a person to do all that." Those interested in costume supervisor work have to be proficient in at least one costume management software program, such as CostumePro and CPlotPro. The latest innovation, SyncOnSet, is available as a free download to individuals, who can learn to use it on their own or take a number of workshops. Costume designers working in independent film with a smaller team may have to use this software themselves in order to manage their department.

Another skill costume designers must master is an understanding of fitting and construction. While they may never do these tasks themselves, a clear understanding of construction will help a designer to achieve a final look through their fabric choices, and their understanding of the human body. Like many designers, Mussenden started her career in a theatrical costume shop. Her first job was stitching for the New York Shakespeare Festival. "You learn the human body by draping it, and drawing it," she notes. "You can flat pattern to your heart's desire, but until you see what the fabric is going to do, you can't tell. Will it bounce? Is the skirt going to look twice as wide because of the fabric, or will it fall like a wet noodle?" After working with the head draper, she was spotted by Jane Greenwood, who hired her to work in her office, the Costume Depot, for seven months. "She taught me how to research, [and] how to pinpoint [exactly what the costume should look like]."

At the beginning of their career, costume designers may work for free on small student films or short independent projects, while augmenting their income with crew work on other films, or working in costume rental houses, or indeed any number of day jobs. These first jobs teach the beginning professional how to anticipate the pacing of productions, how each item will appear through a camera lens, how the typical film arranges into departments and responsibilities, and how to communicate with the other personnel. With experience and connections, early-career designers then transition into low budget independent film, commercials, and music videos, also joining another designer's team on higher budget projects as they progress in the field. Designers post their reels online to document their working style. Mussenden notes that she spent ten years working her way up through the system, and there are many new opportunities now available through web series. For many designers, these early assignments are usually working with contemporary clothing, and they will soon learn several 20th century decades or genre styles, such as mastering the immediate character identification necessary for episodic stories like TV sitcom *The Big Bang Theory;* or learning to create the more complex character arcs evident in longer feature films.

For those wishing to start a career in film and TV, designers Holly Cole and Kristin Burke have written a definitive book explaining the entire process, entitled *Costuming for Film: The Art and the Craft,*[33] with over 570 pages of detail. For a shorter introduction to the theory of film costume design, consult Richard La Motte's book *Costume Design 101: The Art and Business of Costume Design for Film and Television.*[34]

Costume Designer, Costume Stylist, Wardrobe Supervisor, Costumer, Concept Artist

Throughout film history, there has been a grey area between the roles of costume designer, costume supervisor and, with the advent of films derived from comics or fantasy franchises, the concept artist. From its earliest days, film costume designers were used to create elaborate period looks for high budget films based on literature or stage plays. These were called "prestige" films, and they often featured famous stage stars appearing on screen, such as Sarah Bernhardt. One designer who created both sets and costumes was Natasha Rambova, who is credited with introducing the Art Deco visual style to the American mass public in the 1921 film *Camille.*

Each studio established costume manufacturing workrooms to create these films and costume their stars. At the same time, they also maintained large wardrobe inventories of garments to use in contemporary dress films or low budget projects.

FIGURE 8.25 *Film still from Camille, 1921. Art Direction and Costume Design by Natasha Rambova. (Metro Pictures Corporation. Courtesy of Wikimedia Commons.)*

Background characters, if not fully designed for the production, were costumed by the Wardrobe Supervisor and their staff, titled Costumers. Costumers worked in the studio warehouse and were authorized to pull together character looks using items in stock. Other costumers worked on set to handle and maintain the costumes during shooting and wrap. Studios did not always assign a designer to their lower budget films, instead substituting a wardrobe supervisor and costumers. This historical split of duties creates a tension still alive today, when a producer tries to cut expenses by eliminating the costume designer or releasing them early from a project, opting instead to use a wardrobe supervisor to assemble costumes from available sources.

In recent decades some projects have adapted a position created in the fashion and print professions: the Stylist. The stylist crafts marketable images using existing fashion or costume elements and is an essential part of promoting fashion in print or on the runway. Commercials, music videos, and red-carpet gowns were the initial crossover media for stylists who became costume designers. Arianna Phillips' career as a costume designer owes much to the impact she created as Madonna's stylist.

The latest development to muddy these waters is the immense popularity of film series adapted from branded characters, such as comic book superheroes. Many of these characters are initially drawn by concept artists during the story development phase, perhaps even before a script is finished. When the project has a green-light, a costume designer may be handed a series of sketches to bring to life, or may be asked to design costumes for all the human characters, but not be involved in the superhero costumes. One costume designer who has negotiated this ground well is Alexandra Byrne, who designed the costumes for *The Avengers* and *Guardians of the Galaxy*. She explains that adding a human actor into the mix will change everything. "You always, always start with the comics . . . Marvel has a visual development team and they are the experts on the comic book characters. But, also, the crucial part of creating one of these characters is the casting. So, you can draw and draw

FIGURES 8.26 & 8.27 *Two characters in the Powers comic series, and a streaming series on Sony's PlayStation Network. (left) Zora (Costume design by Wendy Greiner; Illustration by Liuba Randolph). (right) Retro Girl (Costume design by Wendy Greiner; Illustration by Oksana Nedavniaya).*

away, and design and do all you want—until you've got your casting, you don't know what the physicalization of this character is going to be … and making it into a practical action garment becomes another whole thing."[35]

COSTUMES AND ANIMATED PERFORMANCE

Animated characters as we now know them have come a long way since the first one in 1911, Winsor McCay's **Little Nemo**. The character and costume were developed as one concept expressed largely through exaggerated silhouette and hand-drawn lines. Costumes served as iconic identification, much like a clown suit, and most early characters did not change their clothing from story to story. One exception to this approach was *Betty Boop,*

created in 1930 as a spoof of Jazz Age flapper girls.[36] Although she wore an iconic look—a strapless, short dress with a garter—she would also wear entirely different costumes for certain plots, such as a grass skirt with only a lei to cover her torso.

Traditional, or hand-drawn, two-dimensional animation emphasized fluid movement to create the illusion that characters had come to life. The technique relied on simplification to work properly. Characters were not dressed with much regard to historical or cultural accuracy, and a look back at some of the original animated stories strike contemporary audiences as culturally insensitive. The role of costumes on characters began to change dramatically with the advent of CGI (computer generated imagery). "There is a growing awareness in animation (overlapping into live-action CG animation) that clothing on animated

---

Unraveling Costume Job Terminology

- Costume Designers: create both the individual characters in a story and the overall picture of texture, color, and tone for the larger costume conceptual approach. In film, they function as one of the two Department Heads, with the Wardrobe Supervisor. In live theatre, the Costume Designer often also creates the makeup and hair styles, working with makeup and hair artists to complete those looks.

- Assistant or Associate Costume Designers: work with the Lead Designer to complete a specified aspect of the design, as defined by each association. Some examples include assisting with sourcing, or taking charge of specific types of costumes such as a chorus, military uniforms, or menswear.

- Stylists: use existing fashion garments and costume elements to create marketable images in the fashion print or on the runway, or to create a wardrobe for a specific person or special event.

- Wardrobe Supervisors: work as the financial and operations part of a film team, responsible for daily operations, logistics, and personnel. In live theatre, a Wardrobe Supervisor may be another term used for a Costume Director, particularly for theatres who do not employ a full-time staff. Touring productions use a Wardrobe Supervisor to accompany the tour to oversee local or traveling crews and to maintain the costumes.

- Costume Directors: usually employed by an institution as the Department Head. They have more extensive duties than a Costume Shop Manager, including strategic planning for multiple or large scale projects, some design duties, and budget forecasting and tracking.

- Costumers: perform different functions depending on location or medium. In live theatre, a Costumer can be a general term for crew members working in the costume department. Themed Entertainment Costumers oversee the costumes in a particular attraction or live show. Film Costumers operate in several ways: handling garments in a rental warehouse; pulling character costumes under the direction of a Designer or Wardrobe Supervisor; preparing film costumes in a staging area; or operating on the set of a film or photo shoot to dress actors, and handle and maintain costumes in front of the camera.

- Costume Illustrators: create renderings under the direction of a Costume Designer to communicate the finished look of a character. Union Illustrators are represented by the **Costume Designers Guild**.

- Concept Artists: work as part of the pre-visualization process for a film, video game, or animation. Originally derived from the process of creating film storyboards or comic books, the position transitioned into use for complex fantasy projects requiring lengthy visual development, such as animation or themed entertainment. Concept Artists may define the general approach for branded assets (characters), such as superheroes, before a Costume Designer joins the team.

characters can no longer merely be part of the graphically-silhouetted character itself. [Technology had now] necessitated treating clothing as almost a separate entity with its own properties and behaviors," observes Jean Gillmore, the costume designer for Disney's *Frozen*.[37]

Ogres are Like Onions

One landmark breakthrough for animated characters was the Dreamworks hit *Shrek*. The project required three years to make and incorporated more sophisticated facial animation, combined with a more complex background and a larger number of effects, than any animated film before it. The visual style consciously combined stylization and the illusion of realism to strike the right visual balance in a story that combined human characters with fantasy and animal characters. Visual effects supervisor Ken Bielenberg explained the overall approach: "There are so many things that go into creating believable humans. The audience is not terribly forgiving of human characters because everyone consciously or not is studying human behavior every day. And if we don't get the major aspects correct, something is going to feel wrong. One of the things we have to do is . . . find the level of stylization that would be appropriate for the design of the film. It seems like it would be obvious looking at the end product, but it wasn't obvious at the time . . . We weren't trying to make a photo-real movie, it was a stylized realism."[38] The skin and clothing textures were legendary accomplishments, as soft surfaces are the most difficult to create with CGI. Bielenberg continues, "The clothing was a big challenge . . . We decided to do tight fitting clothing using our proprietary tool—layering clothing is fairly difficult. We had to figure out getting the right things to wrinkle as the characters move."

> "That was how it started—Fiona's skirt was the first piece in CG animation to work independently of the anatomy. And from there we took off."
>
> Isis Mussenden[5] from a personal interview

FIGURE 8.28 *Cameron Diaz as Princess Fiona and Mike Myers as Shrek. Shrek, 2001. Director: Andrew Adamson/Vicky Jenson. Costume Design by Isis Mussenden. Courtesy of Deamworks LLC. Photo: The Kobal Collection at Art Resource, NY.*

Veteran film costume designer Mussenden[5] designed the costumes for both *Shrek* and *Shrek 2*. The technology was in its infancy, and she helped to develop some of the new techniques. She notes that in animation the creative teams "drew everything and fed it to the animators . . . that were creating the software for rendering fabrics; and educating them on trims." Mussenden had to learn to work with animators who began with a maquette of the body. Before *Shrek*, every costume had been moved by the three-dimensional framework of anatomy below it. The costume, in other words, was a type of layer over the figure, explaining the tightly fitted clothing with a few wrinkles added that most animated characters wear. But the *Shrek* creators wanted a more realistic approach. "They knew Fiona was going to wear a dress which moves independently from her anatomy [but] they did not know where to begin," Mussenden recalls. One of the *Shrek* producers had worked with Mussenden years ago on another project and asked her to help them bridge this gap. "So I started with Fiona's dress. I made a one-quarter scale pattern for the skirt. They needed to know what the volume was, because it was 3D not 2D. Where does it hit on the hip, and where does it move out? Where is the fullness? We worked with a dancer, and I worked with a pattern maker. So I would design and we would pattern and we'd give them patterns with all the seams at the one-quarter scale. The seams were labeled A to A and B to B, C to C, D to D. And they would match it up on the computer."

Background characters in animation function somewhat like those in film; they have a less specific look. In animation, they are called *generic* looks. "I would build a file of three silhouettes of skirts, two silhouettes of blouses, four sleeves—almost like **Colorforms**—to put together." As the animation progressed with a need for 200 people outside the castle, Mussenden would assess the scene requirements. She determined if the audience will see the first 20, or first 50, background characters: beyond that, "We're going to see a lot of heads, so we need more headdresses." She was a stickler as regards making the generic crowd appear to have individual characteristics, and used the usual design tools: "One was silhouette, just like Costuming 101, then texture and color. Those were the three things I needed to concentrate on—just like I would in a live action film. I took a lot of my live action sensibility and used it in CG animation to make it interesting; and I took my CG animation knowledge, which is how to multiply things, and took that back to live action for *Narnia*."

Animation is a complete design experience that few real life costume designers get to practice; creating the shoes, the jewelry, and every textile pattern from scratch. But even in this process there are limitations: "You have different parameters of things you can and can't do. As my producer would always remind me 'It's not that we *can't* do it, but *that* [idea] would take 100 hours of time whereas *this* [idea] would take four.' So it was a budgetary thing. But at the same time, I didn't have to make 17 skirts because it was live action and there are so many stunt doubles and photo doubles,' Mussenden notes.

Each new animated film wants to incorporate a higher standard in detail and believability. Claudia Chung, the Simulation Director for Disney's 2012 feature *Brave*, discusses their method for creating virtual clothing. Using the same method Mussenden described for *Shrek*, the *Brave* animators modeled the garments in three dimensions first, and then virtually sewed the garments together around the characters body. "All our tailors take actual sewing classes . . . Our tailors have their own identity. They think of themselves as tailors. If you look at the way we credit them, we credit them as tailors or simulation artists. What I have noticed over the last ten years is that more and more people are choosing tailoring or simulation as a discipline . . . I'm hoping even more people become interested after *Brave*," Chung says.[39]

One hundred years after *Little Nemo*, Disney's animated feature *Frozen* became "the most elaborate costume-animated CG film to date," says Art Director Mike Giaimo. Two sisters grow from childhood to adulthood, navigating difficult social dilemmas and adventure. The costume changes follow live theatrical tradition, rather than the animation tradition of establishing iconic looks. This costume design process is thoroughly documented in *Tyranny of Style*, a blog dedicated to the study of costume design in entertainment. Art Director Giamo brought in Jean Gillmore to create the characters' extensive wardrobes. Gillmore began her career as a Character Designer, a position that is a cross between Animator and Concept Artist. "This was not a titled position for me on this picture—you'll find me lumped in with the other Visual Development artist credits," she explains. "I never set out to be a Costume Designer for animation . . . but I always had a love and interest in historical/ethnic costume . . . so was often handed the task of researching the period/place for details. On top of my animation career, I used to design and sew costumes to wear on the side, so that too taught me a lot about construction and materials. Guess it was fate."[37]

The design process for *Frozen* followed the usual steps of gathering research that helped Gillmore to understand and translate a high level of detail using "innumerable photos and odd pieces of actual garments and trim . . . My general approach was to meld the historic silhouettes of 1840 Western Europe (give or take) with the shapes and garment relationships and details of folk costume in early Norway, c. 19th century . . . At one point I gathered some images of the crisp, graphic shapes typical of

Dior fashions, thinking maybe that would help Mike [Giamo] articulate . . . his shape language for the entire picture. It did."

Video Games Reinvent Reality

"If you're not screaming at the screen, whoever made that game might not get to make another one" says the game designer and producer Tom Meigs. While this may be a slight exaggeration, he lists the goals for the typical game as "developing innovative, re-playable, highly addictive, and lasting play."[40] Now considered in its seventh generation, gaming is maturing; with story and aesthetic points trumping sustained action.

Game development and design, just like performance genres, is a complex web of interdependent functions created by very large teams. Character design is an important part of consumer appeal, and costume design is a specialty as technology evolves to feature more realistic detail. Rockstar Games, a leader in the game industry, hired a costume designer for *Grand Theft Auto Five*. They turned to Lyn Paolo, an Emmy Award winning TV designer (for example, *Scandal*, *Homefront*, and *The West Wing*), and her experience is documented on the costume blog *Tyranny of Style*. Rockstar Games kept most of the details a secret to protect their game until its release date, so Paolo worked from detailed

concept boards. "We scanned the real people in real time and in 3D into the computers and those images were then altered, adjusted for the game so one person could become several people."[41]

"Once we have the concept boards, we then discuss each character with the design team [then] I went to work finding an array of clothing that defined each character," Paolo described her process. After she sketched what the characters would wear, the animators made 3D scans of each person in the game. "We created a database of many accessories so that Rockstar would have a lot of images to pull and add to each character as the game progressed." Paolo compared the process to designing a film or TV show, noting: "It is not as complicated in terms of alterations because often before a character is scanned, we can just pin clothes and not have to alter them in such a detailed way as I would on a show . . . Fit is not as important and we can tweak things." The animation process allowed her the opportunity to change color and tone after each character is scanned.

The newest digital innovation widely available to costume and character designers is Marvelous Designer, a three-dimensional pattern-based design tool, using the idea of digital tailoring that has been described by Mussenden and Claudia Chung. It was used to create the character designs for the game

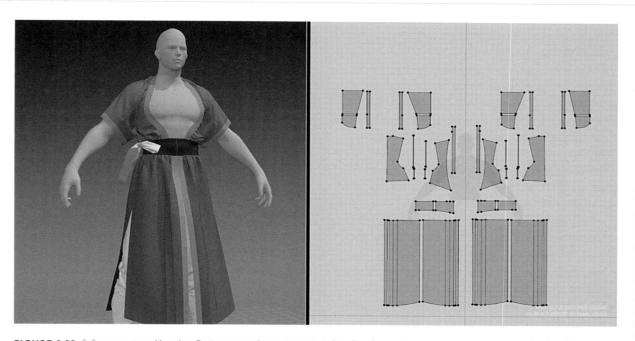

FIGURE 8.29 *Software company Marvelous Designer created many innovations that allow designers to wrap garment patterns around a virtual character to create a costume. (Senior Character Artist at Pearl Abyss: YoontekOh. Screen capture courtesy of Marvelous Designer, CLO Virtual Fashion Inc.)*

Assassin's Creed Revelations and *Unity* and by Weta Digital Studios to create background characters in *The Hobbit*. This software is unusual in that those with an understanding of garment patterns and how clothing is worn will have a distinct advantage when learning how to use it. This approach may be the future of costume design for many styles of projects.

COSTUMES FOR THEMED ENTERTAINMENT

Those who work in theme parks can easily explain their job satisfaction. "The best live theater show I ever did was seen by maybe 20,000 people. But the smallest thing I did for a theme park touches millions of lives around the world—my work is in their family photos!" explained one costume designer who works in both areas. Karen Rivera,[42] the Head of Costume Production at Universal Studios Hollywood, noticed that when the Transformers characters walk into the park every day "Everyone wants their pictures taken with them! They are so unique and they have been done so well, even adults become children again. And that's the idea—to present world class entertainment." In a time saturated with small media devices and blurring distinctions between professional and amateur content, themed entertainment offers well-executed playful human interaction.

Themed entertainment is a broad term encompassing a global industry more accurately referred to as *experiential entertainment*. The Themed Entertainment Association (TEA) describes their nearly 1,000 members as the creators, developers, designers, and producers of compelling places and experiences. Once limited to a few parks and attractions, this form of entertainment expanded rapidly during the 1980s to include all manner of destinations: resorts, restaurants, casinos, cruise-ship lines, museums, discovery centers, zoos, haunted houses, and retail stores. For decades, the industry leader in immersive themed entertainment was the Walt Disney Company, when the 1955 opening of Disneyland transformed the successful animation, TV, and music studio into pioneers of a new form of entertainment. Industry insiders currently argue that Universal Studios may have set a new high standard with the 2014 Diagon Alley expansion of The Wizarding World of Harry Potter in Orlando, Florida. "Historically, Disney set the standard for immersiveness and Universal led the way in the visceral," notes Kile Ozier, a Creative Director and Concept Developer, "but with the opening of the Harry Potter attractions, the bar has been raised".[43] Many major theme parks created unique identities to appeal to different markets. The Walt Disney Company expanded to six resort destinations featuring their unique interpretation of traditional fairytales. Universal Studios expanded to four resorts capitalizing

FIGURE 8.30 *Costumed characters Optimus Prime and Bumble Bee from* The Transformers® *appear at regular intervals to amaze their fans in the Universal Studios theme parks. (Photo by Prayitno Hadinata.)*

on their historic role in movies, but Legoland also appeals to children and the eternally young, while parks such as Magic Mountain and Six Flags specialize in thrill rides and roller coasters set in themed environments.

The Experiential Story

"Experience design is largely non-scripted," explains Phil Hettema,[44] who has directed the design and production of theme parks, rides, and shows for over 35 years. Writers or producers provide a guiding narrative, but designers must be excellent interpreters in order to create the final experience. The immersive experience must be "immediately accessible to the audience through non-verbal, emotional impact," Hettema notes, "we must rip you from your world and put you in ours." Experiential design, he explains, is one of the most collaborative design fields. "It's not a linear process, it is interdisciplinary, somewhat like a jazz band with all members improvising, or like creating a video game where there are multiple purposes." Experiential design, therefore, is creating an entire world for the visitor to step into, and telling a story with visual clues. "It is a constant battle between complexity and clarity. And good design is born from that reasonable conflict." Costume designers also negotiate the unscripted nature of a project; they must work with all the information their audience already knows about each character.

Experiential storytelling differs dramatically from much traditional live theatre that relies on a fixed playing space. The theatre audience sits around a poetic space, and performers enter to act parts of the story. Jumps in time or place are designated by pauses in the action, dimming lights, new scenic elements brought into the space, or other transitions to reset the space. Experiential entertainment is structured the opposite way—every sequence of the story is set into its own fully developed environment. The audience travels through the story on a designated path or track, and seeing ahead on the ride or path is like peeking ahead in a book. These architectural roots for stories can now be seen in themed restaurants, museums, and shopping malls.

Just as with commercial theatre or film, themed or experiential design is irrevocably intertwined with financial considerations that must be duly considered from the start. The successful designer will determine early in the process what factors drive the decisions. Is it *time*: a schedule that cannot fall behind? This might be the case for seasonal attractions such as Halloween haunted houses, when an attraction that opens 30 days late is of no use, no matter how innovative the design details. Another version of this scenario is a themed environment project nearing its construction completion that must add live shows or other costumes late in the overall process. Is the driving factor *quality*?: a client may be looking for a flagship experience. Such was the case for The Wizarding World of Harry Potter, whose high quality versions of the worlds created for the most successful book and movie franchise in history drew millions of visitors from around the world, setting new attendance records. Author J.K. Rowling and Universal Studios understood that disappointing a global constituency of All-Things-Harry could have ruined the entire brand for millions of people. Or is the driving decision *cost*?: there may be an admission price point the producer cannot cross, thereby limiting the amount of short-term investment. In this case, the designer must consider ways to get as much of the budget in front of the audience as possible, instead of making decisions that could be too expensive over the life of the project.

"At the risk of taking the glamor out of the creative aspects, it *is* a business and must operate efficiently and economically—with regard to both materials and labor—whether you are producing a one-time parade experience, or an entire theme park with many attractions and entertainment venues," explains Karen Weller,[45] a costuming veteran who has worked with Universal Studios in

Japan and Singapore, and is currently a partner in The Costume Connection. "Those experienced in theater are no strangers to the concept of balancing time, cost, and quality in the pursuit of a successful product."

The Design Development

Themed entertainment projects are enormous undertakings that can require years to fully develop and build. Financial analysts speculate Universal spent $265 million dollars on The Wizarding World of Harry Potter, with an additional $400 million dollars for the Diagon Alley extension.[46] With such large undertakings and so much money at stake, a theme park will contract many of the physical and creative steps to other firms, each with different specializations: for example, landscape engineering, architectural theming, ride or mechanical engineering, special effects, entertainment production, and costume design and production. The theme park owner or the developer begins with some idea of the general content: rides and attractions based on a movie franchise, or the rights to use characters originally created for other media such as films or comics. The preliminary design begins with a site visit and feasibility study: real estate planning, land and road developers, legal and permit research, repurposing of older assets, and initial budgets. An important outcome of this phase is the overall physical layout of the attraction called a "bubble diagram," and perhaps some early concept art. This art may be drawn by development company illustrators, or by other artists, in order to communicate the major components. These drawings suggest the basic direction well before individual designers are involved in the project.

Each element indicated on the bubble diagram may be, in turn, subcontracted to other design firms, where the creative staff might inherit that preliminary concept art from early meetings or several proposals. The disjointed approach and long lead times create large communication challenges from the very start. Phil Hettema, a renowned theme park designer, described these challenges when speaking to a group of designers at a recent conference. "We can be working on a site three years before they've written the show to go into it" he notes, so the design firm must fill in a lot of information gaps to proceed.[44] The first step is to break the large project into smaller parts to prevent feeling overwhelmed. Such parts might include: the waiting area for the line outside a ride or attraction; an interior waiting area that sets the story using walk-through techniques; an elevator up or down to the start of the ride; the individual segments of the ride; and the off-loading area. Most importantly, each area must contribute something to the overall story.

Every firm employs creative personnel and designers who assemble all the background information to create a "**project brief**," which provides overarching guidance. After extensive research and preparation, the next step is to hold a brainstorming session called a design "**charrette**" to flesh out the initial general concepts into producible ideas. Each layer of the planning process hones the big plan into distinct areas within the park, the buildings, or the attractions, and then the décor that contributes to the story, called "**theming**," is considered. It is at this relatively late date that costume designers often join the process. Bonnie Sinclair,[47] a veteran costume designer for themed entertainment, notes that even though they may join the process last, the park characters are often a strong element of any experiential entertainment.

> "People never leave a theme park wanting to be a castle … They want to be one of the characters they've just seen."
>
> Bonnie Sinclair[47] from a personal interview

Costume designers are particularly interested in what kind of character will tell each part of the story most effectively: an animatronic character, live performers, pre-filmed video of live action performance, and the ride operators themselves. Every element must enhance the experience, with visitors piecing a story together as they move through the park or attraction. The designers conduct extensive artistic, cultural, and literary research on the given theme, even going so far as to visit far flung locales for inspiration, if possible. Cultural advisers consult with the theme park producer and design firms to prevent accidental offenses to the visitors, or to outline climate concerns in each location.

The costume designer for themed entertainment begins their process in the same way as every costume designer: with their own research, creating mood boards for initial artistic communication, followed by several steps to create the final designs. But costume designers Weller and Sinclair note that they also have to be very proactive when they join the multi-year process already under way. Recognizing that the buildings themselves were designed years before the parade or show to fill it, they need to assess the overall costume protocol, and not just the design. Sinclair once discovered that a building created to store and stage a parade presented severe obstacles. The dressing rooms had been located on the top floor to use space efficiently, but once the performers dressed in their large dragon costumes, they could not fit down the staircase. Furthermore, the fully decorated and assembled floats could not fit through the exterior doors with all the elements in place.

Every themed entertainment costumer must be comfortable with several formats, and be particularly skilled at communication so that they can collaborate with the unusually high number of parties involved in each decision. Themed entertainment costume designers categorize the characters they create in two ways: general characters, and specific branded characters such as Mickey Mouse, Shrek, or Harry Potter, whose appearance must meet strict guidelines. Consequently, many more levels of authority will have approvals over each design, such as company executives, agents and rights holders, and legal consultants. Ideas may be refused or amended for arcane reasons, but the costume designer must acquiesce. Each step adds many considerations and can create time delays when the clock is ticking towards opening day.

Practical Considerations for Costumes

Many characters in themed entertainment are anthropomorphic mixtures of human, fantasy, or animal forms, creating interesting challenges for the costumer and the performer. Designing and building these **character costumes**, sometimes referred to as "walk-arounds," requires special artistry, knowledge of ergonomics, and health and safety considerations. These costumes should meld with human physiognomy, but will disguise—to one extent or another—how a person inhabits the interior. Even well-crafted character costumes can still be incredibly difficult to wear. In spite of hidden eye screens for the performer to see where they are going, visibility is often limited. Fans and cooling vests can be built into large costumes, but the outdoor work in most theme parks still creates a hot, sweaty environment. Performers in hot costumes will enter the park to interact in character for controlled times such as 15 to 30 minutes, and then leave through hidden paths for an extended break. The costumes themselves also endure rugged climate conditions such as sun-fading and rain, as well as special effects, such as bromine used in water shows as a purifier, that will fade materials or render them brittle.

There are a number of hidden functional considerations that must be introduced into character costume design, such as whether a performer must dress or undress without help. The costume must break down in special sections for dressing, maintenance, and storage. Some large character costumes, for example, have removable hoops or padded under structures called "pods" so the storage area can accommodate many duplicates. "When we introduce new characters to the park we have to plan enough room to store *that* many large items," notes Rivera,[42] the Manager of Production-Entertainment Costuming for Universal Studios, Hollywood. Some of the very large character

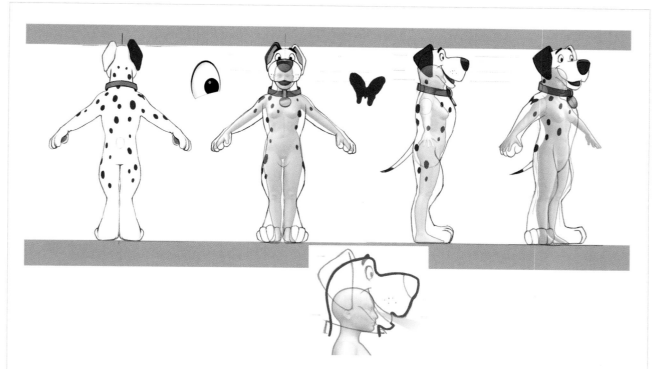

FIGURE 8.31 *Costume design for the costumed character Lucky the Rescue Dog. This schematic drawing indicates sightline, and size and proportions in relation to the performer. Costume Designer Bonnie Sinclair uses this style of sketch as a blueprint for construction and fit. (Courtesy of the Herschend Family Corporation.)*

costumes she must consider include: Marge Simpson, whose body and hair towers well over 7 feet; the Despicable Me Minions who have short and very wide padded frames; and the staggering Transformers figures such as Optimus Prime, whose costume is over 10 feet tall. Built by Michael Curry Design, the Transformer costume parts are so cleverly assembled it is difficult to determine where the human performer sits inside the complex construction, allowing viewers to believe they are actually seeing a large robot. Performers inside these types of costumes must also meet specific requirements regarding height, weight, shoe size range, and ability to operate the mechanisms.

One important feature of any theme park experience is Operations Costumes: the ensembles designed for employees in the park. Most visitors neglect to give this large part of their experience much thought, but employee appearance must also contribute to the story, work within a specific area or attraction, operate as the public face of the park, and serve as functional clothing. Managing operations costumes requires more than knowing what the costume should look like; the costume designer must be familiar with both garment manufacture techniques

used in fashion and those used in theatrical costume design. Some examples of these skills include: understanding the role of prototypes; creating garments for affordable mass manufacture; predicting how size range grading may affect the design; negotiating manufacture with specific vendors who may require spec sheets, a prototype, or patterns; surface embellishment such as embroidery or printing and sublimation; and resourcing materials in large quantities. "In order to advance within the field, one needs to sharpen leadership abilities and financial expertise," Weller[45] recommends.

Haunts and Horrors

In 1973 Knott's Berry Farm, a Western-themed amusement park in Southern California, introduced its nighttime alter ego Knott's Scary Farm to produce an annual Halloween Haunt.[48] This seasonal attraction intended to tempt prior guests into repeat visits, and widen the park's appeal to teen and adult audiences. It set a new standard for an otherwise seasonal Halloween industry largely run by low budget independent presenters of local haunted houses or mazes. The concept was so successful, it spread to other theme parks and attractions, creating a new wave of employment for experiential entertainment creators of every kind.

Theme parks and stand-alone Halloween attractions are now packed with visitors lining up to see favorite attractions or new additions. The parks are subdivided into scare zones or mazes (a portable haunted house style experience), and some

FIGURES 8.32–8.37 *Costume designs for operations wardrobe to be worn by employees within a themed environment. Unrealized project, inspired by costumes for the HBO hit series, Game of Thrones. (Costume design by R. Gwyneth Conaway Bennison.)*

feature live shows. By 2014 Knott's Scary Farm produced ten fully themed mazes featuring new content or reworking existing ideas aptly named Voodoo, The Gunslinger's Grave, Black Magic, and Pinocchio Unstrung. Universal Studios began their own Halloween Horror Nights in 1991—a logical extension of their place in film history with monster and horror films such as the classic *Frankenstein*. Their 2014 season featured a maze based on the hit TV show *The Walking Dead*, and the 1981 film *An American Werewolf in London*. Combining puppetry, "scare-actors," and three-dimensional video, it proved to be a crowd pleaser. The Walt Disney Company creates a family friendly Halloween, featuring their classic Haunted Mansion, as well as characters from *Nightmare Before Christmas*. These haunted themed attractions provide a large seasonal opportunity for actors, costumers, makeup artists, and puppeteers. The wardrobe departments begin work for Halloween during the summer, providing about three months to revamp returning attractions and to prepare new ones. The independent haunted attraction business itself expanded in the past 20 years with haunted houses or mazes growing in cities or regions without major theme parks. These haunted venues run the gamut from creating temporary pop-ups in parks and parking lots to sophisticated haunt companies such as Midnight Productions, featuring the 40,000 square foot attraction The 13th Gate, in Baton Rouge, Louisiana.

Experiential entertainment now influences traditional theatrical performances through the innovative and wildly successful efforts of immersive theatre company Punchdrunk. The London-based company created *Sleep No More*, a site-specific version of Shakespeare's *Macbeth*, first in London, and then in New York. Actors create scenes within the environment, and true to theme park format, the audience moves from space to space. Taking a cue from both themed entertainment and video games, the environment itself holds clues for the audience to examine. Punchdrunk's latest show, *The Drowned Man: A Hollywood Fable*, took place in a building near Paddington Station in London. The company transformed the dreary offices into an eerie Hollywood studio of the 1960s, loosely adapting another classic script for the narrative, Buchner's play *Woyzeck*. Both productions ask the audience to experience only some portions of the story, possibly returning several times to piece together the entire experience.

Starting a career in themed entertainment requires, like any other profession, a network of contacts. Many theme parks will hire entry-level costumers as wardrobe issue and maintenance, checking costumes in and out to the various performers who work in the park. But Rivera[42] stresses: "The chances are small you will be working in the theme park itself. That is not where

---

Mickey's Ten Commandments

1. Know your audience: Don't bore people, talk down to them, or lose them by assuming that they know what you know.

2. Wear your guest's shoes: Insist that designers, staff, and your board members experience your facility as visitors as often as possible.

3. Organize the flow of people and ideas: Use good storytelling techniques, tell good stories not lectures, lay out your exhibit with a clear logic.

4. Create a weenie: Lead visitors from one area to another by creating visual magnets and giving visitors rewards for making the journey.

5. Communicate with visual literacy: Make good use of all the non-verbal ways of communication—color, shape, form, and texture.

6. Avoid overload: Resist the temptation to tell too much, to have too many objects; don't force people to swallow more than they can digest; try to stimulate and provide guidance to those who want more.

7. Tell one story at a time: If you have a lot of information, divide it into distinct, logical, organized stories; people can absorb and retain information more clearly if the path to the next concept is clear and logical.

8. Avoid contradiction: Clear institutional identity helps give you the competitive edge; the public needs to know who you are and what differentiates you from other institutions they may have seen.

9. For every ounce of treatment, provide a ton of fun: How do you woo people from all other temptations? Give people plenty of opportunity to enjoy themselves by emphasizing ways that let people participate in the experience, and by making your environment rich and appealing to all senses.

10. Keep it up: Never underestimate the importance of cleanliness and routine maintenance; people expect to get a good show every time; people will comment more on broken and dirty stuff.

Martin Sklar, *One Little Spark! Mickey's Ten Commandments and The Road to Imagineering* (White Plains, NY: Disney Publishing, 2015).[49]

most of the items are made anymore." She notes that with a few exceptions, most costumes are created by sub-contractors, specialty shops, or the same made-to-order costume shops used in theatre or film. "That is where the jobs really are," she reveals, because there are not enough craftspeople to work on the huge numbers of shows and characters that a theme park will use. Weller[45] notes "Whether you strive to develop expertise with defined technical skills, or pursue skills for involvement in a broader role, it is an enthusiasm for what you do, a respectable work ethic, and an ability to collaborate well with others that will help make you a valuable contributor wherever your career adventures take you."

Costume design originates as part of a narrative, but in some cases it will take on wider meanings than the story that gave birth to it, and stories that resonate with the wider culture owe some of their appeal to the engaging costume designs. Costume designs may transcend the life of the story, influencing cultural tastes independently of the original story. The designs for the TV and film versions of the *Star Trek* franchise are a strong case of transcendence, influencing how science fiction would look for many other narratives. Other examples include *The Lord of the Rings* and *The Game of Thrones*, each redefining the traditional appearance of stories set during a version of medieval lore.

A COSTUME DESIGNER PREPARES

There is no one single experience the costume designer may expect across the huge spectrum of working in live or recorded performances. The resources each project commands varies widely from a large modern costume shop and a full staff to a small, barely equipped wardrobe room or trailer. The designer may be expected to act as department head as well as creative head, may have to hire their own crew, or may work within a large, corporate infrastructure. One of the most important skills costume designers must hone is the ability to assess and organize each project to work with the available resources and timetable. Working in any capacity with different size projects will give the early-career costume designer the means to compare various methods. It is important to intern with a larger organization to learn the height of current practice, and it is equally important to experience independent projects with the challenge of maintaining an artistic vision with little money or labor. It can be equally challenging to work with larger, complex organizations juggling many shows at once or communicating across the globe.

How the designer begins a project can be just as crucial as the final result, and this is especially important when beginning a

working relationship with a new organization. Contact someone who has worked there before to assess the working situation or learn about challenges ahead of time. Create a list of questions for the producer, production manager, and costume shop manager. Never assume any performing organization will do things the way others do; every organization creates—or lacks—systems reflecting their own business practices. Many costume designers have taken jobs only to discover they were expected to do different tasks than they had assumed.

Many costume designers openly acknowledge that they must educate their producers about the complex job of providing performance costumes, particularly if presented with an unreasonably low budget, a short preparation period, or a lack of proper equipment and supplies. Most producers are *not* experts in costume design and preparation, and that is why they hire people who *are* experts. Producers are, however, aware that each project will present unique circumstances, and understanding the art of budgeting will help the designer to propose reasonable alternatives. All costume designers should develop an "inner weasel" that they can use to overcome obstacles. Educating the producer about the specific project also avoids the thing everyone hates the most: surprises. One head of a costume rental house confessed she spends a distressing amount of time on the telephone with producers who are reluctant to pay the final bill. "They did not understand what the *whole* cost of a project would be, so they end up blaming the costume designer," she notices.

"We depend on the designer and costume supervisor to provide realistic numbers," explains Millar,[16] Production Manager of Kaiser Permanente Educational Theatre. "The more information we have up front, the better we can plan accordingly. The budget number is usually negotiable in both directions because that number was chosen before we even knew the scope of the design. Of course we expect them to hit our number within reason, but if we know about *all* the variables ahead of time, we can make choices, or maybe find a little bit more money," he advises.

The New Job Checklist is just one tool to remind designers of the entire scope of a project and what kind of questions to ask producers at the very beginning. "If a problem shows up at the 11th hour that will cost a lot of money, chances are it will get cut because there is nothing we can do," Millar explains. Presenting the large view of a project gives a designer credibility in the eyes of the producer and establishes trust. As early-career designers create more shows, they will learn the issues they will face repeatedly and can learn to plan ahead. One whose work calls for complex fabric treatments will develop a different list from a designer who prefers to use vintage garments.

		COSTUME DESIGN NEW JOB OVERVIEW/CHECKLIST

PHASE ONE: *Define Scope of the Project with Producer/Production Manager*

		Define dates carefully—techs, shoot dates, dress rehearsals, previews, open, strike/wrap
		Full schedule for ALL the departments and how this show fits into that large picture
		Negotiate responsibilities from start to strike (see sections below)
		Contact info—Dept Heads, shops, office, etc
		Producer's expectations for show—spectacle, intimate, etc
		Casting dates and contacts for preliminary measurements, use of understudies, swings, doubles, extras
		Actor availability—fitting & rehearsal schedule—Equity/Non-Equity
		Labor schedule or considerations for crew—union, staff, volunteers, interns
		Budget and reporting method of purchases, petty cash, reimbursement, POs, credit card
		Use of personal vehicle and reimbursement
		Negotiate crew & staffing—team, construction, wigs & makeup, running crew, strike
		Costume facilities and equipment in shops, providing a kit, kit rental
		Expected early publicity or photo calls scheduled, use of renderings in PR, social media protocols
		Open accounts with vendors, existing relationships for goods and services
		Travel and housing, travel to rental or shopping sources
		Type and size of costume stock available, reciprocal usage agreements
		Being paid—contract triggers, invoice submission, union contract, riders, etc
		Hidden costs in costume budget—supplies allocations, dry cleaning, actor contract stipulations?
		Preferred online sharing methods—DropBox, Google Drive, Box, etc
		Required protocols for all purchasing and/or tax-exempt requirements

PHASE TWO: *Artistic Planning with Director*

		Script and design approaches
		Special FX with other departments? CG/animation/video/stunts/camera crews/duplicates
		Budget priorities, concessions or request more resources
		Determine casting breakdown with roles assigned to each actor, doubling, swings, combined roles
		Finalize costume designs
		Negotiate communication process—fitting photos, others involved in decisions?

PHASE THREE: *Logistics Planning with Costume Shop Manager/ Wardrobe Supervisor/ Vendors*

		Review and confirm all items discussed with Producer/Production Manager
		Determine in-shop due dates: rentals, fabrics, likely rush charges, use of upcharges or inhouse materials
		Number of costumes, groups or types, determine likely number of builds
		Determine pre-production labor, running crews, or other labor needs and availability for this show
		Desired period silhouette, type of foundations required, special accessories or modifications for stunts, movement
		Location or onsite services, labor, and supplies—who will work in what locale, what are the necessary jobs?

FIGURE 8.38 *The New Job Checklist helps designers to thoroughly assess the parameters of a new job.*

		Microphone/sound requirements—placement, matching mic pacs, etc
		Movement or fight requirements—choreographer, fight director, padding, stunts, other doubles
		Wig, hair and makeup, collaboration researched & determined
		Final Piece list generated for each actor, who is responsible for show paperwork, etc
PHASE FOUR: Green-light and Strategies		
		Finished design communication available to all parties—color sketches and fabrics, or appropriate visual communication such as character collages, shopping sheets, or technical drawings
		Costume sources identified: built, rented or purchased, vendors identified, costumes ordered or located
		Last minute budget items—rentals, restocking fees, dry cleaning, etc
		Determine made-to-order process and deadlines
		Build list, crafts list finalized
		Final in-shop dates with vendors, fabrics, rentals, purchases, begin fitting date
PHASE FIVE: Made-to-Order Start Dates/Rehearsal Expectations/Pre-Production or Early Production		
		Table meetings with cutters and vendors to define each item
		Fabric modification methods, materials, labor
		Production meetings
		Expectations for rehearsal costumes, reacting to rehearsal notes
PHASE SIX: Technical or Dress Rehearsals, Shoot Dates, Previews, Opening, Strike Wrap		
		Quick change rehearsal process (live performance) or double performers needed?
		Load in to dressing rooms, locations, crew, calls, equipment
		Providing wardrobe track or running sheets, actor dressing lists, set continuity sheets, etc
		Union considerations, call times, dinner breaks
		Designer responsibilities and notes sessions—who, when, where
		Preview day rehearsal schedule/shoot days/wardrobe turn around for costumes
		Maintenance during run or shoot—designers expectations for each character
		Return of unused or cycle out short-term rentals to avoid overcharges
		Photography and documentation of actors in costumes
		Budget wrap and close out purchasing
		Strike process and responsibilities

FIGURE 8.38 *continued.*

Some designers have learned that they can increase their own worth to the producer by supplying needed items themselves; they keep an inventory of vintage items, jewelry, specialty garments and accessories, and even materials and supplies. Taking a cue from working in independent film, some costume designers provide a large "**set kit**" to augment the project even when working in live theatre. These extra items serve several purposes: the designer can stretch the budget when using their own items so they may purchase something else; the show will have a more polished or upscale look than the budget might allow; or the designer may augment a lower design fee by renting or selling goods to the show. Some designers will arrange to keep some items built or purchased for the show in exchange for waiving a labor fee or for the use of their own stock. Costume designers should be aware these practices have positive economic value to an organization, but should be careful to negotiate this arrangement in advance. Designers who do not plan to provide additional services should also make this clear at the outset of any independent project to avoid assumptions by the producer. This conversation is particularly important to determine who is responsible for building costumes or overseeing vendors. Many experienced costume designers keep a very strong eye toward parity in a production team; if the scenic designer or art director is not responsible for extra duties, the costume designer should not automatically assume extra duties as part of the design job.

In the contemporary world, more designers may have to view themselves as small businesses providing creative services, and sometimes actual goods, to their projects. Designers who specialize in many freelance or independent projects may wish to research the requirements for a business license or permit from their local city or franchise tax office. A business license allows a designer to purchase goods at wholesale and resell them to the project. Some designers choose to pass the savings along to the project, again stretching their budget, or they may choose to add a small markup to the purchase price to cover overheads such as book-keeping fees. Non-union designers may find themselves employing assistants or other help without union guidance on the practice and should understand the liability and tax issues. Freelance models of employment are increasing, and the **Freelancers Union** is an excellent place to research these considerations.

Understanding simple business practice is a wise investment of time for any costume designer. As department head for many projects, the designer may oversee a large or complex budget. Small business experience is especially useful for situations where costume designers are expected to pre-purchase fabrics or clothing for later reimbursement. Fronting money without a petty cash allotment is technically loaning money to the producer. It is a very risky proposition and many designers tell horror stories about producers who did not repay on time—or ever. Should this occur, a designer who can prove ownership of the items may have the small consolation of reclaiming and reselling them to recoup some of their loss, or adding them to their own inventory. Invoicing for purchased garments also separates the designer's fee from tangible goods. "Invoice for those goods separately, and indicate we should *not* include it on the 1099 tax document, or you will be taxed accordingly by the government," Millar[16] advises. Any designer who wishes to work as a freelance artist should gain business experience through courses or workshops; there are a number of free options available online.

Learning Costume Resources

Another valuable asset costume designers must develop is excellent resourcing. Before working in any city it is essential to know the suppliers, or hire an intern or assistant who does. Sometimes the first film experience that theatrical costume people have is joining a film crew in town to shoot for a short time. Locals are often hired to shop and advise on local resources. The ability to move around town quickly using public transportation or driving in an organized manner, no matter where a costume designer or assistant works, is also an essential skill. A current source list and the ability to read maps to override sometimes silly directions provided by a GPS will save the designer untold agony, moving the work along quickly. A strong overview of an area allows the designer to choreograph daily rounds with travel routes and closing times in mind, avoiding time consuming crossing back and forth. Always find reasons to visit new sources as part of doing research for a show. Producers, production managers, and directors need a designer who can operate in a fast paced environment; and they will feel more confident with a job applicant who knows both local and national sourcing.

There are several large listings available to guide costume designers toward industry standard vendors, but a costume designer must always have outside or personal sources beyond these lists. For more information, consult these sources:

- *The Entertainment Sourcebook: An Insider's Guide on Where to Find Everything*
- *Shopping LA: The Insider's Sourcebook for Film & Fashion*
- *Costuming for Film: The Art and The Craft*
- *Hollywood Creative Directory*
- variety411.com/us/new-york (The Production Services Resource for New York)
- variety411.com/us/los-angeles (The Production Services Resource for Los Angeles)
- Manhattan Wardrobe Supply (www.wardrobesupplies.com)
- www.creativehandbook.com
- www.reelcreations.com
- www.shoots.com
- www.showbizjobs.com

Look for the Union Label

Eventually any freelance costume designer will consider joining a union to qualify for more jobs, to be taken seriously in the industry, and to benefit from collective bargaining. Many freelance costume designers have found that to make a living wage in any form of entertainment, they must belong to one or more unions who guarantee minimum earnings, monitor working conditions, gain alerts to employers who have broken prior agreements, and offer benefits. There is a confusing array of unions in entertainment, and both local and national entities have jurisdictions in different states. The ability to put oneself on the work list for day work or other employment opportunities eases those gaps between projects and broadens one's network. Some unions still allow a designer to work in non-union situations.

There are overarching types of unions, although some variations occur by location. In general, unions for costume people are divided into two general categories: Costume Designers & Illustrators, and Costume Makers & Crew. The unions are also further divided by region with national offices and local chapters. The main unions are:

- **Costume Designers Guild (Local 892)**: Film and TV Designers in Los Angeles, Costume Design Assistants, Costume Illustrators, and Commercial Designers. There are four ways to qualify for the union, depending on category. Generally, designers and assistants must have one credit for a commercially released film or TV production, show a portfolio, and produce three letters of recommendation.
- **Motion Picture Costumers Union (Local 705)**: Film and TV Finished Costumes Men's or Women's, Custom-Made Costumes Men's or Women's, Live TV Costumer, Costume House Costumer. With six different categories, qualifying can be confusing, but generally working 30 days in a union costume house is the classic entry point.
- **United Scenic Artists, 829 (USA)**: National Theatrical Designers, plus Film & TV Designers in New York. There are several ways to qualify for the union. A designer or assistant working in a theatre with a Collective Bargaining Agreement may apply directly, or show a portfolio, or produce letters of recommendation from members in good standing.
- **Wardrobe Local 764 (IATSE) New York**: Film, TV, and Broadway Theatre Finished Wardrobe, and Custom-Made Costumes for Radio City Music Hall and The Metropolitan Opera workrooms.

- **International Ladies Garment Workers Union (ILGWU)**: Film, TV, and Broadway Theatre Custom-Made Costumes.

ADVICE FOR EARLY-CAREER COSTUME DESIGNERS

An important part of preparing for any career is communicating your skills and abilities to those who are hiring. In spite of an ever-expanding array of job boards for design and backstage advertisements, a very large portion of the jobs in show business are never advertised. Each project is unique and it is difficult to maintain quality, as anyone who has ever seen a bad piece of theatre, film, or TV can attest. Some projects fail and, unfortunately, in show business the failure is a public one. Theatre, film, and TV are also extremely expensive to produce—with so much at stake, teams form on the basis of trust. As this chapter has shown, hiring begins with creators asking themselves and each other who they already know or know something about. New opportunities open up all the time, however, when collaborators or team members are already busy and they recommend someone else. A good recommendation is one of the most prized elements for show business, and very little else matters. It is for this reason that many people will start their careers working for no or low pay in student films or internships: a good recommendation will bring opportunities for years to come. Interspersing these first opportunities with schooling is a smart decision because the aspiring designer can graduate into better entry-level jobs. However, lingering in no or low pay jobs for too long will have a negative effect: establishing your reputation for low level work, and also falsely training producers to believe costume personnel should work for very little money.

Recommendations and Resumes

There are two parts to earning a good recommendation: earning that reference through hard work, and keeping it through consistent, positive interactions in the performance community. Professional behaviors are key, and include such essential rules as never thoughtlessly speaking poorly of a colleague from a past project. Producers and directors expect a productive team, and will balk if they hear about past bad attitudes. This professional world is a small one and almost everyone is just a few degrees of separation from each other.

A good resume addresses both the past and the future: it documents prior work, and holds clues to *how* you might be expected to work in the future. Past jobs tell future employers

NAME, COSTUME DESIGN
WEBSITE, EMAIL, OTHER CONTACT INFORMATION

THEATRE

The Power of Light	Star Theater, Off Broadway, NY, 2016 *in process*	Director: Martin Chow
The Codex	Midwest Repertory Theater, 2015	Director: Brandon Jimenez
As You Like It	Shakespeare Center, Memphis, 2013	Director: Mary Saberson
The Kids Show	Maine Summer Theater, 2009	Director: Martin Chow

FILM/TELEVISION/WEB

The Candy Jar	Eat My Hat Productions, see Imdb page, 2014 Short Film, international festival screenings	Director: Mark Supter
Building the Dream	Vertical Line Productions, 2011 PBS Documentary with Historical Re-enactment sequences *Regional Emmy Nomination—Best Documentary*	Director: May Powell
Last Chance	Northstar Entertainment Group, 2010 Netflix Pilot Episode of "Turn of the Screw"	Director: Bill Regal

RELATED POSITIONS & SKILLS

Crafts Head	Midwest Repertory Theater, 2005–10 Millinery, fabric dye & color matching, masks, general crafts
Crafts Artisan	Maine Summer Theater, 1999–2003
Other Skills	Photoshop CS6, Basic editing iDVD, Fluent in Spanish *Please see my website www.AboutMe. com for further examples*

EDUCATIONAL THEATRE—UNIVERSITY OF THE MIDWEST 1998–2001

Christmas Carol	Assistant Costume Designer, Jane Jefferson Faculty Designer
Hamlet	Wardrobe Crew Head, Dresser
Oklahoma	Costume Crafts, Dyer

EDUCATION

University of the Midwest, BA	Theatre and History (double major) 2001

REFERENCES

Brandon Jimenez, Director boxingday@gmail.com	Mary Jefferson, Artistic Director Jeffersonairplane@gmail.org	Martin Chow, Director eyesonyou@comcast.net

FIGURE 8.39 *Sample resume featuring work divided into media format categories.*

NAME, COSTUME DESIGN
WEBSITE, EMAIL, OTHER CONTACT INFORMATION

COMMERCIALS/MUSIC VIDEOS

Jepson Ravitz Agency

DirecTV/ The Wallenda Story	Director: James Jewell, 2015
Bad Heart Band/Can't Stop	Director: Pons Soon, 2015
Wonder Pinkett/One Hit Wonder	Director: Gillian O'Brien, 2014

Star Theater, Off Broadway NY

The Power of Light	Director: Martin Chow, 2016 in process

Midwest Repertory Theater, St Louis

The Codex	Director: Brandon Jimenez, 2010
As You Like It	Director: Mary Jefferson, 2009
The Kids Show	Director: Martin Chow, 2007

OPERA

Summer Opera Theater, Atlanta

Grand Duchess	Asst. Costume Designer, Jun-ha Soon, Director: Adali Rolf, 2014
Carmen, Apprentice Scene	Director: Imelda Juarez, 2013
Rigoletto, Apprentice Scene	Director: Abebi Lorne, 2012

RELATED POSITIONS & SKILLS

First Hand	Shakespeare Center Theater, Atlanta 2005–07
	Millinery, fabric dye & color matching, masks, general crafts
Stitcher	Maine Summer Theater, 1999–2003
Other Skills	Photoshop CS6, Basic editing iDVD, Fluent in Spanish
	Please see my website www.AboutMe. com for further examples

EDUCATIONAL THEATRE—UNIVERSITY OF THE MIDWEST 1998–2001

Christmas Carol	Assistant Costume Designer, Jane Jefferson Faculty Designer
Hamlet	Wardrobe Crew Head, Dresser

EDUCATION

University of the Midwest, BA	Theatre and History (double major) 2001

REFERENCES

Brandon Jimenez, Director	Mary Jefferson, Artistic Director	Martin Chow, Director
boxingday@gmail.com	Jeffersonairplane@gmail.org	eyesonyou@comcast.net

FIGURE 8.40 *Sample resume featuring work divided into performance venue categories.*

about the type of venue or organization with which you have worked before, and therefore they may deduce the level of professionalism they could expect from your work. For instance, if the applicant lists working in regional theatre or feature films, it is reasonable to conclude that the applicant understands higher quality expectations; whereas a specialty in experimental or devised theatre communicates a willingness to think in new ways or collaborate closely with performers and ensembles. The names of collaborators will also hold clues—high profile directors or actors can denote a certain level of accomplishment or style of working.

Not every designer will use the same style of resume, and some will keep separate resumes featuring different types of work. A designer who also teaches at the university level, for instance, may keep a professional resume for their design work, and a university mandated curriculum vitae form for their teaching accomplishments. The designer who augments their income as a graphic artist may keep two separate resumes with an acknowledgement of the other skillset on each one. The key to arranging any resume, just like any creative endeavor, is to understand the intended audience. Producers and directors want to glean the *type* of creative project on any resume— has this designer worked on a similar type of project before, or do they demonstrate the potential to understand this project?

Conventional wisdom for business resumes does not hold true for the entertainment resume. Business or corporate job seekers list work experience in chronological order, and may include items like goal statements. Potential corporate employers like to see consistency; they may not understand gaps in the record. However, fitful employment is not unusual in entertainment where a large number of people are self-employed or work several jobs at once. In fact, a chronological listing by itself could result in a confused and scattered picture. The designer's resume must be arranged differently—as a record of creative work, not mere employment. An excellent example of this idea is any costume designer's listing on the Internet Movie Database (www.IMDb.com) or Internet Broadway Database (www.IBDB.com). New projects accumulate at the top of the list within designated categories. This arrangement places maximum impact on the job title. Job title categories also work well for the freelancer with multiple skills or jobs, such as a designer who works regularly as an assistant, or a costume shop manager who works as a wardrobe supervisor in film.

Choosing the correct format for the resume is an exercise in efficient communication. What is the best way to reflect an individual designer's work? The designer who crosses media may choose to list projects by the genre or format. This approach emphasizes an understanding of media requirements (see Figure 8.39).

Some designers work repeatedly for a specific set of venues, such as local theatres, regional theatres, or independent producers. In this instance it can be advantageous to craft a resume sorted by venue or company categories with multiple projects listed for each one (see Figure 8.40).

It is vital for early-career designers to separate their professional projects from educational projects. Potential employers can and do empathize with the entry-level job applicant; some want to help students to start careers. However, employers must be reassured that the applicant understands the distinctions between school work and professional work; burying an important professional summer job in a long list of school assignments is confusing and may indicate a poor understanding of the professional field. Another essential element of a successful early-career resume is listing work experience using the correct terminology: research the actual job titles accepted in the industry for theatre, film or TV, or theme parks. A good internship with a larger organization will also teach the early-career designer proper job titles. The resume should stay reasonably updated, regardless of format: online text, downloadable print copy, or hard paper copy. Day jobs, such as working in a fabric store or doing graphic design work, not only pay the rent but may also add to the designer's accumulated experience. Jobs such as these are best listed in a separate category labeled Related Experience.

Design Portfolios

> "A website is essential. We don't have time to schedule interviews with every designer just to find out who they are, especially if they are new in the business."
>
> Jonathan Banks,[50] Artistic Director
> of The Mint Theater, New York

Social media, and photography and art sharing sites are increasingly important to make early connections, but there is *no substitute* for a dedicated archive of your work. Relying on sharing sites may associate your work with pop-up windows featuring styles radically different to your own; not every potential employer can look past this visual confusion.

The major goals of any portfolio are to feature visual examples of work, to supply talking points for conversation during

FIGURE 8.41 *Taking the time to document a body of work with good quality photographs will create an authoritative, interesting portfolio that stands out from others. Reproduction 1907 corset created by MFA student Erin Abbenante at the University of North Carolina, Chapel Hill. Corset made with 12" busk and 22 spiral steel bones, metal grommets, coutil, pink and yellow silk, and dyed-to-match elastic garters. (Courtesy of Erin Abbenante.)*

convert a physical book into a new format. However, those entering the job market and competing for jobs are expected to establish and maintain an online presence, and failure to do so may create a suspicion that the designer is out of step with the creative world. The concept of personal branding comes naturally to many early-career designers raised as digital natives, but careful attention must be paid to the quality of that brand.

CONCLUSION

There has never been a wider choice of careers to explore as a costume designer, or more opportunities to apply the same set of skills to different media. Even with such wide choices, every job will draw from the solid foundation of skills described in this book. The beginning costume designer should take a long view of the possibilities, taking as many different jobs as possible to explore what media or process suits their individual skills and temperament. Even day jobs taken to tide a designer through the challenges of starting a career will add value.

an interview, to supply a resume, and to offer current contact information. There are numerous website template and web-hosting services that appeal to busy designers who do not have time to learn coding or site design. Some sites offer free hosting that may appeal to the early-career designer who is still exploring exact needs and formats, such as www.carbonmade.com, www.weebly.com, and www.wix.com. It is wise to avoid a lot of complex site design elements at first, instead focusing on a straightforward style that features your work and is easy to update frequently.

Fewer designers emphasize a physical "book" of their work, and this practice can be a hallmark of generational views on the subject. Established designers may seldom or never show their portfolio if they consistently find work with the same collaborators or through word-of-mouth. Designers with a large body of work that has not been digitized may see no need to

---

The Importance of Varied Experiences

Karen Weller[45] notes what these experiences can teach the young designer:

"Working as a sales clerk can afford you insights to the consuming public; being a labor scheduler can give you insights to managing time and personnel; working in fabric stores can expand one's knowledge of the tools of our trade; experience in costume rental houses can refine knowledge of costume history; working in a theme park wardrobe issue service can build your awareness of garment use lifespans; working on alterations can establish a better understanding of garment fit; experience as a cutter can help you envision the structure of future designs; being a shopper can help build vendor resources; and being a shop manager gains experience in managing budget, time, and personnel. There are many combinations of experiences that can lead you to a multitude of opportunities. My own adventures have taken me from being a volunteer stitcher for a children's show in undergraduate school to designing and developing wardrobe and costume programs for theme parks globally. You may not know exactly where your path will take you, so work to build experiences that will help you be prepared when interesting opportunities do come along."

FIGURE 8.42 *Costume designs for the evolution of Mephistopheles in Gunoud's opera Faust. Design by Holly Poe Durbin, as a portfolio project for a contest. Continuing participation in contests or challenges such as those offered by Opera America or DeviantArt, the online art community, give a designer the opportunity to produce new work and sharpen skills beyond those needed for a specific production.*

On a Personal Note

Working in costume design can be an incredibly rich life lived with passion, filled with creative partners, and drenched with compelling purpose. I was reminded of this recently when a director and I held a design meeting in a landmark Los Angeles lunch spot. We chose it partially because the location was half way between us in distance, but also because this restaurant featured huge, old-fashioned wooden tables and benches. We spread our images and books and papers and computers all over this large table. Our meeting lasted a couple of hours, with excited gestures and bouts of inspiration between bites of original French dip sandwiches. Toward the end, a fellow diner approached us. He apologized for interrupting, and said: "I don't know what you do for a living—but I wish my job had *half* that much passion. It was such a pleasure to listen to the two of you."

QUESTIONS

- What are some of the key considerations for finding an entry-level job in costume?

- What are some of the goals of costume design within its storytelling function?

- What types of entertainment fields typically employ costume professionals?

- What are some typical job titles for those who work in the costume industry?

- What are some of the ways in which costume professionals can prepare for a career?

NOTES

1. Richard Mueller, Jr., "Snow White Costumes By Fishbach," *Playthings Magazine*, June 1938: p. 47.

2. "Halloween Headquarters," *National Retail Federation*, 2014. https://nrf.com (accessed December 29, 2014).

3. Ratna Bhusan, "Disney Consumer Products Launches High-Fashion Apparel for Grown Ups," *The Economic Times*, July 1, 2013. articles.economictimes.indiatimes.com (accessed December 10, 2014).

4. Lee Jameson, "Find Answers: Costume Designer Sophie de

Rakoff," *Film Independent*, May 7, 2013. www.filmindependent.org (accessed January 10, 2015).

5. Isis Mussenden, personal interview with author, August 15, 2014.

6. Karen Weller, personal interview with author, January 10, 2015.

7. Joe Kucharski, "A Look at the Costume Designers Guild with President Salvador Perez," *Tyranny of Style*, May 7, 2015. www.tyrannyofstyle.com (accessed May 10, 2015).

8. Ann Roth, personal interview with author and Bonnie J. Kruger, January 25, 2011.

9. Vincent Canby, "Places in the Heart," *New York Times*, September 21, 1984. www.nytimes.com (accessed January 10, 2011).

10. Piers D. Britton and Simon J. Barker, *Reading Between Designs: Visual Imagery and the Generation of Meaning in The Avengers, The Prisoner, and Doctor Who* (Austin, TX: University of Texas Press, 2003).

11. Ann Roth, "The Best Movie Costumes of All Time," *Rome (Georgia) News-Tribune*, February 27, 2004.

12. Anna Wyckoff, "The Case for Contemporary Costume Design," *The Costume Designer*, Winter 2015.

13. Valli Herman, "Aggie Guerard Rodgers," *The Costume Designer*, Winter 2015.

14. Luis Valdez, "USITT Keynote Address 2012," *TD&T*, 48.3, 2012.

15. Michael John Garcés, "About Cornerstone Theater Company," *Cornerstone Theater*, n.d. www.cornerstonetheater.org (accessed January 10, 2015).

16. Michael Millar, personal interview with author, January 20, 2015.

17. Toni Sant and Kim Flintoff, "The Internet as a Dramatic Medium," *Interactive and Improvisational Drama: Varieties of Applied Theatre and Performance*, July 24, 2007. www.interactiveimprov.com (accessed January 22, 2015).

18. Tim Donahue and Jim Patterson, *Stage Money: The Business of the Professional Theater* (Columbia, SC: University of South Carolina Press, 2010).

19. Martin Platt, personal interview with author, August 8, 2014.

20. Joseph Wesley Zeigler, *Regional Theatre: The Revolutionary Stage* (Minneapolis, MN: University of Minnesota Press, 1973).

21. Richard Zoglin, "Bigger than Broadway!" *Time Magazine*, May 27, 2003. www.time.com (accessed January 10, 2015).

22. Theatre Communications Group, "Theatre Facts 2013," n.d. www.tcg.org (accessed June 22, 2015).

23. Educational Theatre Association: www.schooltheatre.org/home (accessed February 8, 2016); and Cengage Learning: "Professional Theatre Companies (Summer)" www.cengage.com/resource_uploads/static_resources/0495898074/24674/summer_theatre_companies.html (accessed February 8, 2016).

24. Tom Morris and John Adams, "2014–15 New Production Videos: Interview with Director Tom Morris and Composer John Adams," *Metropolitan Opera*, n.d. www.youtube.com (accessed August 12, 2014).

25. Dunya Ramicova, "Interview with Lynn Pecktal," *American Theatre*, n.d. www.DunyaRamicova.com (accessed August 15, 2014).

26. Jonathan Miller, *Subsequent Performances* (New York: Viking Press, 1986).

27. George Heymont, "A Most Magical New Flute," *Huffington Post*, August 15, 2012. www.huffingtonpost.com (accessed August 10, 2014).

28. Mike Boehm, "LA Opera to Import a 'Magic Flute' Influenced by Silent Films," *Los Angeles Times*, June 4, 2013. www.latimes.com (accessed August 12, 2014).

29. Tim Appelo, "LA Opera Goes Technicolor in Morganelli's Musical Reboot of a Cult Horror Epic," *The Hollywood Reporter*, April 23, 2015. www.hollywoodreporter.com (accessed August 10, 2015).

30. Todd Cunningham, "What State is the Movie Making Capital of the World? Hint: It's not California or New York," *The Wrap*, March 6, 2014. www.thewrap.com (accessed March 6, 2014).

31. Chrisi Karvonides-Duschenko, et al., "Inside the Process: Award Winning Costume Designers Speak," Panel Discussion. Bowers Museum: Santa Ana, California. March 10, 2013.

32. Stephanie Schoelzel, "Costumers, Costume Designers & the Unions: An Historical Event: A Brief Look at the History of the Costume Unions in the United States." www.StephStuff.com, 1999 (accessed July 19, 2014).

33. Holly Cole and Kristin M. Burke, *Costuming for Film: The Art and the Craft* (Los Angeles: Silman-James Press, 2005).

34. Richard La Motte, *Costume Design 101: The Art and Business of Costume Design for Film and Television* (Studio City, CA: Michael Siese Productions, 2001).

35. Mike Ryan, "'It's Sort of Liberace Meets Billy Idol' The Costumes of *Guardians of the Galaxy*." www.ScreenCrush.com, August 1, 2014 (accessed August 14, 2014).

36. King Features Syndicate, "Betty Boop Biography." www.bettyboop.com, n.d. (accessed July 19, 2014).

37. Joe Kucharski, "Costume Design in Animation—Disney's *Frozen*," *Tyranny of Style*, January 7, 2014. www.tyrannyofstyle.com (accessed May 10, 2015).

38. Iain Blair, "The Making of *Shrek*," *Digitalanimators*, May 5, 2001. www.digitalanimators.com (accessed August 16, 2012).

39. Christopher Laverty, "Brave: Costume in Animation—Interview with Claudia Chung," *Clothes On Film*, August 16, 2012. www.clothesonfilm.com (accessed August 16, 2012).

40. Tom Meigs, *Ultimate Game Design, Building Game Worlds* (Emeryville, CA: McGraw-Hill/Osborne, 2003).

41. Joe Kucharski, "On the Upswing: Costume Design for Video Games," *Tyranny of Style*, n.d. www.tyrannyofstyle.com (accessed May 10, 2015).

42. Karen Rivera, personal interview with author, January 11, 2014.

43. Kile Ozier, "Game Change: A Call for Quality in the UAE," *Entertainment Designer*, December 29, 2014. www.entertainmentdesigner.com (accessed May 12, 2015).

44. Phil Hettema, "Theme Park Design: the Big Idea," Panel Presentation. Annual USITT Conference: Long Beach, California. March 30, 2012.

45. Karen Weller, personal interview with author, January 11, 2014.

46. Brooks Barnes, "Universal Lifts the Veil on a Harry Potter Park," *New York Times*, September 15, 2009. www.nytimes.com (accessed May 12, 2015).

47. Bonnie Sinclair, personal interview with author, November 2, 2012.

48. Knott's Berry Farm, "Knott's Berry Farm History," n.d. www.knotts.com (accessed January 12, 2014).

49. Martin Sklar, *One Little Spark! Mickey's Ten Commandments and The Road to Imagineering* (White Plains, NY: Disney Publishing, 2015).

50. Jonathan Banks, "Portfolios for Designers," Panel Presentation. Annual University Resident Theatre Association National Unified Auditions and Interviews: New York. January 26, 2013.

GLOSSARY

Acrylic Paint   Paint that has a polymer base, is water-soluble when wet, and water-resistant when it dries.

Action Chart   A document used to track each character and/ or performer throughout the sequence of events in a production. This could be simple: breaking an opera into three acts where the characters have only one or no changes between each act; or more complicated: a highly physical musical theatre production with quick changes, or a farce where quick changes contribute to comic timing. The action chart is typically created by the costume designer well before sketches to ensure that they are designing according to the dramatic action of the storytelling.

Actors Equity Association (AEA)   Known largely by the short name Equity, AEA is the labor union representing actors and stage managers in the United States. It negotiates the wages and working conditions for live theatrical shows and provides benefits such as health insurance and pension plans to member performers. For more information, visit the website: www. actorsequity.org.

Additive Color Theory   The color theory that theatrical lighting design utilizes in which the mixing of colored light produces white light. The primary colors of additive color theory for light are red, green, and blue. The secondary colors of additive color theory for light are cyan, magenta, and yellow. This theory is often referred to as RGB.

Aesthetic   The appreciation of beauty and ideas governing taste at a given time and place.

Analogous Color Scheme   Colors that live side-by-side on the traditional (RYB) color wheel and share a primary color. Also commonly referred to as adjacent color.

Applied Theatre   Creating drama outside of traditional performance venues to raise awareness of social, political, educational, health, or cultural issues; includes a wide range of practices and styles of performance. Examples include working within marginalized communities to give voice to common issues such as prisons, underserved neighborhoods, or other voiceless communities.

Art Deco   Style prevalent in art, design, and architecture in the 1920s and 1930s; it is marked by geometric line, bold colors, and the influence of ancient and eastern art and of streamlined machinery.

Artistic Director   An executive position responsible for the artistic vision for a theatre company; includes choosing an overarching theme or mission for the body of work, curating a season, and hiring directors and other artists.

Art Nouveau   Late 19th century style seen in art, design, and architecture; it is marked by sensuous, organic line, and the portrayal of movement and light.

ARTSEARCH   A premier job listing service featuring over 3,000 job postings per year in regional, educational, and summer theatre, and related arts organizations. For more information, visit the website: www.tcg.org/artsearch. See also Theatre Communications Groups.

Balance   The principle of design that describes the placement of shapes, forms, colors, textures, and space in a way that makes the work of art feel steady and even. Balance can be symmetrical, asymmetrical, or radial.

Ballets Russes   A dance company that presented the work of Russian dancers, designers, and composers in Western Europe and America from 1909–1930. The vivid colors and exotic style of the designs influenced art and design in the Art Deco period.

Bias   Cut on the diagonal; true bias being exactly at 45 degrees between grain and cross grain.

Bid   Price for constructing a costume, provided by the shop, and based on the designer's rendering and other information.

Brainstorming   A technique used for collaboration by incorporating methods of interaction between two or more people. The method generally involves a group of people who have an idea or issue to address, or a problem to solve, and utilizes divergent and convergent perspectives to formulate a variety of potential solutions.

Brand   The name and features of a product or group of products that distinguish them from others, ideally making them more desirable.

Break (in pants)   Horizontal crease(s) above the hem of pants where they hit the foot, determined by the length of the inseam.

Bristol Board   Drawing paper available in a variety of weights and both smooth (plate) and textured (vellum) finish, made for use with most drawing and color media.

Broadway   An umbrella term used to describe any show within the New York theatre district between Avenue of the Americas and 9th Avenue, and from West 41st Street to West 53rd Street, and The Lincoln Center. The Broadway League, a theatrical producers' organization, holds the power of negotiation with the 14 labor unions representing workers involved in Broadway and Touring Broadway productions. For more information, visit the website: www.broadwayleague.com.

Burberry   A company founded by Thomas Burberry in the United Kingdom, known for its distinct tartan plaid.

Character Costumes/Walk-arounds   A term used in themed entertainment or experiential entertainment for oversize costumes worn by actors that portray non-human or larger-than-life characters such as Mickey Mouse, Snoopy, or the Minions. The term Walk-Around originated to separate immovable animatronic characters from those created to move and interact with the audience or guests.

Characteristics of Line   Line traits including width, length, direction, focus, and feeling; they are used to convey specifics about character, place, time, and construction needs.

Charrete (proper pronunciation *shuh-ret*, common American pronunciation *chah-ret*)   An intense brainstorming meeting for a project with all interested parties in one place; the intent being to create new ideas and present solutions.

Chiffon   Lightweight fabric, usually silk or polyester, that has a gossamer feel.

Choreographer   An individual who creates the original movement for a dramatic event. This could include a wide range of performance genres from ballet and contemporary dance, to period movement in a play, or highly specialized dance styles for musical theatre and other genres, such as tap or hip-hop.

Closure   Refers to how a garment is kept closed at any opening. Types include:

- Buttons: primarily two or four hole flat buttons or shank buttons, they are used in conjunction with a button hole.

- Snaps: a male and female part working together to close a garment, they come in many sizes, from very tiny to the very large "whopper popper." They are also used in the form of snap tape, which is snaps evenly spaced set into twill tape for the convenience of machine sewing (rather than sewing them individually by hand).

- Hook and eye or Hook and bar: another two part closure, a hook holds onto either the eye/loop or bar. These also come in varied sizes and in a "tape" version. Velcro is the trade name for hook and loop tape, which is essentially a narrow bit of fabric, one side being tiny hooks and the other side being tiny loops. The two sides stick together to hold an opening closed.

- Zippers: a common closure that can be set into an opening in a variety of ways. It is a device that is made of two rows of metal or plastic teeth and another piece that slides over the teeth to make them fit together or come apart. Zippers can be applied in different ways, including: lapped, invisible, centered/exposed, or separating.

Collaboration   The act of sharing ideas and methodology with other artists and practitioners, resulting in cooperative endeavor and/or artistic production.

Collage   Artwork created by adhering elements, including paper, fabric, and photos, to a background. A collage may also be created digitally by piecing and layering scanned elements.

Color   The quality of light that an object reflects; it can be measured by hue, saturation, and intensity.

Color Forecast In fashion, home décor, and other industries whose products are designed to appeal to the mass market, a well-researched analysis of the trends and influences that shape the evolution of color in design.

Colorforms® A children's toy invented by Harry and Patricia Kislevitz in 1951. Flat die-cut plastic shapes that adhere to a plastic board. A player combines or repositions the shapes to create larger images of his or her own design.

Commercial Theatre Producing theatre with a goal to make a profit for the investors. Since the growth of Non-Profit Theatre, this category is now sometimes referred to as For-Profit Theatre.

Communication An interaction between two or more people that creates interpersonal contact by discovering similarities and differences in thought and process.

Complementary Colors Colors located directly opposite each other on the traditional (RYB) color wheel.

Composer An individual who creates original music, often for the purpose of dramatic storytelling. This might include composing opera or musical theatre (while the librettist writes the dialogue); yet it can also include a person who creates an original soundtrack or score for theatre, dance, film, or devised work.

Contour Line Marks that both describe the interior portion of an object and help to define the exterior shape. Contour lines can be used in the rendering stage to describe shadow and pattern within a draped garment, creating depth and life within the established shape, while reinforcing the outer edges of a garment.

Contrapposto A pose used in classical art where the weight is concentrated on one foot, pushing the body out of vertical and horizontal alignment.

Cool Colors Colors located from green to violet on the traditional (RYB) color wheel.

Corduroy Ribbed cotton fabric, its velvety tufted texture originates from the Egyptians in AD 200 as a weave known as "fustian."

Corps (corps de ballet) The ensemble of dancers performing as a synchronized group, often portraying background characters.

Cosplay A fusion of the words "Costume" and "Play"; dressing up in direct imitation of an existing fictional character from a sci-fi, comic book, or anime character. Recent Cosplay innovations include crossing concepts such as taking a current character back in time, for instance Victorian Sailor Moon.

Costume Designers Guild (Local 892) A labor union for Costume Designers, Assistant Costume Designers, and Costume Illustrators in film, TV, commercials, and music videos, with jurisdiction in the United States and Canada. The vast majority of its members live in Los Angeles, and it is one of the historic Hollywood Locals that form the backbone of the Californian film industry.

Costume Director The head of a large Costume Department, overseeing all aspects and personnel needed for costume construction, show crews, maintenance, and storage. The Costume Director participates in future season planning, budgeting, and interdepartmental collaboration, and may step into the design role to complete rental packages or to accommodate new performers.

Costume Plot An inventory of every item that each actor wears, and when they wear it, during the production. The most successful costume plots include information about quick changes, how the costume might be worn (for example, in a disheveled manner), as well as information regarding exits, entrances, pre-sets, and special effects (such as the use of blood or battery packs). The more detailed and well-outlined a costume plot, the more helpful it will be for the backstage wardrobe crew to maintain the integrity of the costume design and the timing of costume changes.

Craft Work In a costume shop, a role that encompasses the use of unusual materials that the designer has specified. Traditional sewing and garment construction may not be needed when working with these unconventional materials, such as foam, glue, felt, thermoplastics, wire frames, plastics, metals, wood or bamboo, and rods and reeds.

Croquis French term for "sketch," referring to a quickly drawn picture of the body. Also, an outline drawing of a body on which clothing can be drawn.

Cross Grain Term describing something that is perpendicular to the selvage edge of a fabric.

Cutter–Draper In a costume shop, the individual responsible for overseeing the creation of the desired costumes. They may build entirely new garments, or alter existing garments to improve fit for costumes that are pulled or rented.

Dhoti A type of long loincloth worn by men in India.

Dior (pronunciation *dee-or*)   The couture fashion house created by Christian Dior, active in Paris from 1946 to his death in 1957. The House of Dior continues today with other Head Designers. When used as a single word "Dior" generally refers to the height of Christian Dior's considerable global influence on mid-century fashion.

Direction   Where on the page the line starts and is traveling; the intentional placement of a particular line with regard to the outer edges of a page. A line can be horizontal, vertical, or diagonal. A line can radiate from a center. Lines may also curve or zigzag across the page.

Director   The individual who has been given the authority to oversee and guide the artistic vision and aesthetic of a particular production or event. Their vision provides an overarching idea, which informs all other aspects of a production.

Dramaturge   A member of the production team whose main responsibilities include research on the play, the playwright, translation, and past productions. May also act as a mediator between the playwright and the Director on new productions.

Draper   The costume technologist who creates the patterns for a costume, based on a designer's drawing and instructions.

Drybrush   Painting technique using a minimal amount of paint and little or no water, allowing the color and texture of the paper's surface to show.

Dynamic Shape   A shape that appears to be in motion; can be found in fabric pattern, and the use of particular trims.

Ed Hardy   The American subculture graphic artist, Don Ed Hardy, who worked primarily in tattoo design and tattoo-influenced graphic design, publishing over 25 books of artwork. Hardy licensed his brand in the early 2000s, spreading his work from prints to all manner of consumer brands. Ed Hardy clothing rose in popularity after Saks Fifth Avenue partnered with him to create clothing and accessories.

Embellishment   Details applied to a costume, including embroidery, appliqué, trim, and beading.

Emphasis   The principle of design created when a section or part of the art piece pulls in the viewer's eye. Focal point and subordination are symbiotic components of emphasis.

End User   The person who uses a product after it has been fully developed and marketed.

Feeling   This denotes the sharpness, smoothness, jaggedness, and/or graceful nature of a line.

Fibers and Filaments   Individual threadlike pieces that are twisted together into yarns to become the basis for woven cloth. Usually divided into two different groups: natural (cotton, linen, wool, silk, and hemp) and manufactured (polyester, acetate, and rayon).

Fight Director   An individual who creates the original movement for a variety of performance genres that require conflict. This may include physical altercations between two or more actors; the use of weapons; or even a highly violent attack, such as dragging a character across the stage to communicate an assault. The Fight Director must be trained and certified to ensure that techniques and protocols are in place for safety, as injury or even death can occur.

Final Rendering   A drawing that uses more finished quality media such as watercolor, pastels, marker, or digital software, in order to flesh out the nuances and details of a costume idea. Ultimately this drawing includes clothing and accessories, and the pose of the figure evokes a sense of action or storytelling that is consistent with the genre and the mood/spirit of the production.

Finding   Garment components other than the fashion fabric, including closures, trims, and labels.

First (or Second) Hand   In a costume shop, the individual who works alongside the cutter–draper. Taking patterns from the cutter–draper, they fit them onto the chosen fabric, therefore being the "first hands" on the chosen fabric.

Fixative   Clear spray used to coat and protect artwork.

Flat   In the fashion industry, technical drawings that accurately illustrate a garment's front, back, and side views, including its proportions and construction details. May be drawn by hand or computer generated.

Focal Point   The component of the principle of emphasis that describes the exact area of a composition that the artist deliberately chooses to accentuate.

Focus   A characteristic of the line created by the type of drawing instrument and the pressure or energy applied to the implement at the time the line is put to the page by the designer's hand. Can be described as sharp, blurry, fuzzy, choppy, or irregular, and numerous other adjectives.

Form   A three-dimensional object with true height, width, and length, for example: cubes, cylinders, spheres, pyramids, and prisms. Form for the costume designer is the actor's actual body in the costume.

Freelancers Union   A voluntary constituency founded in 1994 with the erosion of social support systems and traditional employment benefits. Members form a large consumer group that can negotiate socio-economic structures on behalf of the individual such as providing insurance, reducing risk, professional growth events, and business education. For more information, visit the website: www.freelancersunion.org.

Garment Features   All of the structural details that create line and shape: pockets, collars, darts, tucks, cuffs, peplums, and various seams and décor.

Geometric Shape   A category of shapes created by various lines that meet to form an angle or a line that is continuously bent in one direction until it touches itself. Some basic examples of geometric shapes are: circles, squares, rectangles, triangles, trapezoids, and ovals.

Gesture Line   A type of line that is filled with motion and energy, to capture movement in the fabric and in the body of the character being drawn. These lines denote the action of running, laughing, crying, waving, and dancing, for example.

Gobo   A sheet or screen (usually metal) placed over a light source in order to create shapes or textures when the light passes through the openings in the gobo onto the stage.

Gouache   Water-soluble paint designed to be opaque when used; it can be diluted to be translucent and used much like watercolor. It is also available in an acrylic formula.

Gradients   A smooth blend of value from dark to light, or, of color, from hue to hue.

Graphite   A mineral that is a form of carbon; commonly misidentified as "lead," graphite is the pigment part of a pencil.

Gusset   Fabric added to a garment (usually in the underarm), giving some extra fabric to allow for increased movement. The shape is often either diamond or football-shaped.

Half-Tone   A color with an intermediate value between light and dark; in describing paper, it usually refers to a neutral color like tan or gray.

Hanfu   The traditional dress of the Han Chinese people.

Haute Couture   Literally French for "high sewing," but meaning high fashion.

Hennin   A conical or heart-shaped hat, often with a flowing veil.

Hue   The twelve basic colors of the traditional color wheel (RYB) in their purest form, void of white, black, or grey pigment. A pure or saturated hue is bright and has high intensity.

IATSE   A labor union, the International Alliance of Theatrical Stage Employees, that represents people working in theatre, film and TV in many capacities, including wardrobe and costume construction.

Ideation   The process of generating, developing, and communicating (and some say realization of) new ideas, often used as a synonym for brainstorming. This process may occur within a group or as part of an individual's design process.

Implied Line   A line type created when two different or distinct objects/clothing items neighbor each other, and their outer edges meet to form a line.

Implied Texture   The use of various drawing techniques to make a blank (two-dimensional) page look as though its surface is smooth, rough, soft, or any number of consistencies, as it correlates to the hand of the costume fabric.

Institute of Outdoor Theatre   An international organization founded in 1963 to serve the unique needs of outdoor drama presenters, such as Shakespeare festivals, historical dramas, religious pageants, and other forms of theatre presented outdoors. The Institute provides member support services as well as a comprehensive list of presenters. For more information, visit the website: www.outdoor-theatre.org.

Intended Audience   The group of people for whom a product is designed or a production is developed.

Kilt   A traditional Scottish skirt.

Knockoff   A cheap, inferior, or unlicensed copy of something, especially high-end designer items.

Lapel, Notch   The lapel has a downward angle where it is sewn to the top collar, creating an open angle or notch. This is the most common lapel on a man's suit.

Lapel, Peak   The lapel has an upward angle where it is sewn to the top collar, echoing the shape of the collar's edge. This lapel is common on double-breasted jackets and formalwear.

Lapel, Shawl (shawl collar)   There is no angle and sometimes no seam in the lapel as it extends to form the collar. The edge is curved. This lapel is found on smoking and dinner jackets.

Length   The characteristic of line that describes the distance a line travels on a page, picture plane, or space.

Libretto   Musical theatre and opera use two forms of the script to create a performance. The libretto contains the spoken works, or text; the score contains the music for the performance.

Lighting Designer   A specialist who provides the illumination of the mise-en-scene, enhancing both the aesthetic and the storytelling through use of lighting technology and/or modifying natural light in a theatrical space depending on the needs of the production. Sequence and timing of cues along with the intensity of lighting are critical artistic attributes of a lighting design.

Line (drawing)   A mark or series of marks that takes the viewer's eye from one point to another.

Line (fashion)   Often understood to mean a group of related garments within a collection, for example a line of dresses presented by a high-end designer in their Fall collection. The collection may contain dresses, suits, separates, and accessories.

Line Types   See Sketch; Gesture; Outline; Contour; and Implied Line.

Little Nemo   The main character of the 1905–1911 comic strip *Little Nemo in Slumberland* created by Winsor McCay. McCay was a seminal comic strip artist who influenced the work of generations of artists.

Little Theatre Movement   A precursor to the contemporary Community Theatre, Applied Theatre, and the Regional Theatre movements, this movement began in the early 1900s to create theatre on the local level. Individual groups were founded by groups of amateurs with or without formal training in theatre, and the content often revolved around classics or socially relevant narratives. These theatres were also a reaction against the commercialism of national tours and melodramas, which were the main sources of theatrical entertainment at the time. The movement flourished between the 1920s and 1950s.

Live Action Role Play (LARP)   A live, interactive game organized around groups of people assuming a specific character in a mutually agreed fantasy social construct. The characters may be historically based, as with the Society of Creative Anachronism (SCA) and historical military units, or may be fantasy based.

LORT (League of Resident Theatres)   The largest professional theatre association in the United States, operating as the legal entity for negotiating bargaining agreements with its counterpart organizations, Actors Equity Association (AEA), Stage Directors and Choreographers Society (SDC), and United Scenic Artists (USA)—the union representing theatrical designers. This membership organization also pursues mutually beneficial actions on behalf of all its constituents, such as lobbying and commissioning studies, or furthering member education. For further information, visit the website: www.lort.org.

Marie Antoinette (1755–1793)   Queen of France in the late 18th century.

Mass Market   A large undifferentiated group of consumers or end users of a given product.

Measure of a Line   The length and width of a particular line.

Milliner   One who designs or makes hats and headpieces.

Millinery   The craft of designing and manufacturing hats, specifically women's hats.

Mixed Media   A term applied to a piece of art made with more than one form of paint, or a combination of paint and other elements (for instance, pencil, chalk, ink, or applied details).

Mockup (toile or muslin)   The first version of a designed garment made in less expensive fabric in order to test the design and pattern.

Monochromatic Color Scheme   The shades and tints of one color.

Motif   A recurring idea, image, or element that supports a specific theme.

Movement   The principle of design that describes where on the visual plane the viewer's eye is being directed by the artist or designer. The use of various types of line or implied line created by specifically arranged shapes, shape edges, color, and value in a work of art create this path.

Negative Space   The area that surrounds a primary object in a piece of art. In costume design it is the space around the character drawn on a blank page or the darkness around a character in the spotlight on a stage.

New Work   Any live performance that utilizes original text, music, or choreography and has a living author, composer, librettist, or choreographer who is ideally available for consultation or collaboration.

Notch Lapel   See Lapel, Notch

Notions   Sewing accessories that are needed to complete work on a costume; examples include buttons, elastic, thread, hooks and bars, and seam binding tape.

Off Broadway   This term bears both a general meaning for a type of theatre movement and a legal meaning governing contract negotiations between creative team members and producers. As a general term, it refers to theatre in New York with seating capacities of 99 to 499 seats operating with lower producing budgets. Off Broadway shows are often experimental, ensemble pieces, new scripts, or a reinvention of large cast classics not seeking a large commercial audience appeal. Members are officially represented in contract negotiations by the Off Broadway League. For more information, visit the website: www. offbroadway.org.

Off-Off Broadway   This term bears both a general meaning for a type of theatre movement and a legal meaning governing contract negotiations between creative team members and producers. In the general sense, this term describes small, non-union experimental theatres in New York with a maximum of 99 seats in found spaces or converted spaces.

Ombré   From the French word for "shadow"; in paint or dye, a smooth transition from one color to another, or from light to dark values.

Organic Shape   A category of enclosed space that is free form, irregular, and conveys an energy of movement. These shapes are associated with things seen in the natural world. Shapes that are varied in nature such as apples, pears, leaves, shells, or butternut squash. These shapes are curvilinear, and possess a flowing quality and a calming feeling.

Outline   A type of line creating the outer edge of an object, capturing the silhouette of a particular garment or period clothing.

Overdye   A process where a dyed garment or fabric is dyed a second time to alter the original color or add a patina, an ombré effect, or other overtones.

Paint Elevations   Color scale samples of scenery or scenic elements provided to the client as an indication of the painting style to be used.

Paper Mâché (papier mâché)   A hardened substance made of torn paper pieces mixed with water and glue. The material is hard when dry, but will revert to a mushy substance if soaked in water.

Pastels   Sticks of compressed powdered pigment used for drawing; also available in an oil-based stick and as pencils.

Pattern   The principle of design that describes the regular replication or reiteration of shape, line, or form throughout the plane of the entire work of art. This principle is closely related to repetition and rhythm.

Peak Lapel   See Lapel, Peak.

Plate, Costume   See Rendering.

Playwright   The original creator of the storyline and dialogue that culminates in a play. The language of the world of the play is crafted in a style and/or method to create dramatic tension and to engage the audience in the action onstage.

Pointillism   A painting technique that uses paint applied in small dabs or dots of many colors. The viewer's eye then blends the colors and perceives solid images in the composition.

Positive Space   The area inhabited by the primary object that is the focal point of a two-dimensional setting; the costumed character/figure on the rendering, or under directional or selective lighting.

Preliminary Sketch   A drawing representing an early draft or a progression of an idea in physical form, usually in pen or pencil. This drawing is usually quick, varied in size or detail, and may be shared with a director, another designer, or a cutter–draper at some point during the process.

Primary Colors   Red, yellow, and blue pigments of the subtractive theory, often referred to as RYB primaries or traditional color wheel primaries.

Princess Seams   Shaped seams that are used in place of darts: they extend from either the shoulder or the armscye to midway between the center front or center back and side seams in order to provide a more contoured fit.

Principles of Design   The nine principles that organize the elements in a work of art are balance, emphasis, movement, pattern, repetition, proportion, rhythm, variety, and unity.

Production Manager   A theatrical Production Manager coordinates the planning for a project or a full season of plays. Each theatre defines the term broadly, with some sharing artistic oversight in hiring the designers, stage managers, and crew, and overseeing all the department heads. Others oversee the operational side of a producing organization.

Project Brief   A formal or informal document defining the scope of any project and responsibilities, including a description of the job, due dates, team members, protocols for approvals, and finances. Freelancers must often create this brief for themselves if definitions are not provided by a union, or if a producer uses a template contract that is purposely vague.

Projection Designer   A specialist who builds an environment through images projected in some way upon the physical space of a production. The quality of the images in content, composition, and resolution are only a part of their critical role in storytelling. Like other designers, the timing and execution of cues set, or at the very least complement, the tone and rhythm of a production.

Proportion   The principle of design that considers the size and relationship of all the individual parts that make up a whole object or a single form. It has a symbiotic relationship with the principle of scale.

Prosthetics   Artificial body parts or applied dimensional pieces that are used as makeup and special effects.

Readable   A term applied to an image that can be understood by the average viewer. Or onstage, to a detail (for example, a pattern or a trim) that can be perceived from a distance by the audience.

Realization   The process of taking a costume design through the shop and building it so that it can be worn onstage.

Regional Theatre   Professional theatres that produce their own seasons for a local audience. The terms Resident Theatre and Regional Theatre are sometimes used interchangeably, although a resident theatre uses an ensemble of affiliated artists, and a regional theatre denotes a theatre outside of New York's Broadway district. The largest theatres are members of the League of Resident Theatres (see LORT).

Rendering   A piece of visual art that portrays the idea and details of a costume design; it may be created in a variety of traditional or digital techniques. It is also called a "sketch" or a "costume plate."

Repertory Theatre   A producing organization that creates work to be presented on alternating days or in a specific rotation. Many regional theatres or opera companies contain the word "repertory" in their names, but no longer present two or more works on the same stage, alternating nights. The contemporary use of the term most often refers to the simultaneous use of a main or large stage, and a small or experimental stage, or even the addition of an educational touring company or academy stage. Theatres may present several in-house works at once.

Repetition   The principle of design that revolves around the creation of feeling and activity through the use of patterns created by objects, forms, and values.

Research Board   Paper or digital presentation of historical, inspirational, and character-based reference material related to a costume design; it may also include images of garments available to be purchased or pulled from stock.

Resolution   The number of pixels per inch displayed on a computer screen or used in printing. The higher the number, the better the quality of the image.

Rhythm   The principle of design that examines the mood created by the carefully orchestrated repetition of one or more elements into a varied and energetic visual plane. Two basic rhythm types are linear and gradation.

Ruff   Found in Elizabethan and Jacobean eras; a starched, frill collar.

Samples Sewer   Experienced and highly skilled stitcher responsible for executing the designer's sketches, specifications, and patterns into prototypes and sales and manufacturing samples.

Sari   Long decorative fabric worn wrapped around the female body; traditional dress in India.

Scale   The principle of design in which the size relationship of one object to another object in a single work of art or a given visual plane is examined.

Scenic Designer   A specialist who provides the fundamental organization of the space and landscape of a given production. The Scenic Designer creates a space that provides for movement, and enhances the integrity of the storytelling by expressing the nuances that determine time, place, and overall mise-en-scene.

Scumbling   Applying and blending paint in a seemingly random or irregular manner.

Secondary Colors   Orange, green, and violet pigments of the subtractive color theory, often referred to as RYB secondary colors.

Set Kit   A term originating in the film industry that is now applied across the board to independent theatre or other forms of entertainment. A collection of tools and supplies gathered as a portable workshop for a behind-the-camera or off-stage worker. Set kit or box rental augments a worker's weekly pay to include the use of wardrobe supplies, expendables, and permanent supplies. Costume set kits can be extensive, filling a storage unit, and may include enough supplies and equipment to outfit a wardrobe trailer or to augment the meager in-house supplies of a 99 seat theatre. Although the majority of a set kit is functional (such as weather protection, garment steamers, irons, sewing machines, tools, wardrobe supplies, paint, dye, etc.), some costume designers keep garments, jewelry, and other accessories that will extend smaller budgets. It may take many years to build up a set kit, and it greatly enhances the ease of daily work.

Shades   Pure pigment hues that have degrees of black pigment added to them. Shades of a hue work their way toward black. Can be utilized to depict shadows and depth on a rendering.

Shalwar Kameez   A long tunic worn over baggy pants; generic term for traditional dress in India and Pakistan.

Shape   Space that is two dimensional, self-contained, and created by a single line or several lines. The basic categories of shape are organic, geometric, positive, negative, and dynamic.

Shawl Lapel   See Lapel, Shawl.

Showcase Theatre/99-Seat Waiver Theatre   A term for a small budget, small seating capacity theatre where most of the artists work for free or for minimal transportation costs. Creative unions may have agreements exempting the producer from union minimum rates, or the theatre may hire only non-union or beginning artists. A classic first stepping stone for artists in their early career. The term "Showcase" is more common on the East Coast of the United States, and the term "99-Seat Waiver" is more common on the West Coast.

Silhouette   The outer edges of the character's body and the clothing drawn on the body. In fashion, the new silhouette at the beginning of the season describes the shoulder width, waistline, skirt length, etc.—especially as they differ from previous seasons. In a production, the silhouette will often establish time and place even before any dialogue has been spoken.

Sketch   See Rendering.

Sketch Artist   One who creates the rendering for a designer, either working from the designer's ideas and instructions, or creating the design from scratch.

Sketch Line   A shorter line with an airy quality; it may imply the shape of an object, texture of a fabric, or facial features, to name a few.

Sound Designer   A specialist who provides the soundscape for a production, whether live, recorded, or a combination of both. The soundscape enhances the mood and spirit of the storytelling. As in lighting, the sequence and timing of cues in combination with the intensity and mixing of the sound are key artistic attributes of a sound design.

Space   The area a shape or form encompasses, together with its surroundings.

Spattering   Flicking or splashing drops of paint onto a surface.

Spec Sheet (Specification Sheet)   In the fashion industry, a spreadsheet containing all the relevant measurement and construction data needed to produce a garment, thus allowing for accuracy and consistency in design, fit, and costing. Likely to include flats, fabric swatches, and sample production information.

Split Complementary Color Schemes   Two complementary hues on the traditional (RYB) color wheel, and only one of their analogous or adjacent pairs.

Stage Directors and Choreographers Society (SDC)   The theatrical union for American professional stage directors and choreographers; it has legal jurisdiction to negotiate contracts on behalf of its members with signatory professional theatres such as Broadway, Off Broadway, Association of Non-Profit Theatre Companies, League of Resident Theatres, etc. For more information, visit the website: http://sdcweb.org.

Starch   A white, odorless substance derived from plants used to stiffen fabric.

Static Shape   This type of shape is grounded and at rest, showing no real or implied motion.

Stitcher   In a costume shop, the individual responsible for sewing a costume together, or stitching the alterations. They must be proficient in a variety of hand stitches, and skillful in the use of a sewing machine.

Story Arc   Overarching storyline; chronological order of events by which the story unfolds.

Style (to style a costume; stylist)   To use pre-existing garments, combining them into a designed look or a costume.

Style Lines   An implied line created by the seaming of two distinct and different fabrics on a particular garment. Also referred to as a "construction seam."

Subordination   The component of the principle of emphasis that describes the areas or other elements in the composition that are intentionally muted, in order to lead the viewer's eye to the focal point.

Subtractive Color Theory   The mixing of paint or pigment that transforms the three primary colors/hues of red, yellow, and blue into secondary (orange, green, violet) and tertiary (yellow-orange, red-orange, red-violet, blue-violet, blue-green, and yellow-green) colors that make up the twelve colors of the traditional (RYB) color wheel. When two colors are mixed together, one of these pigments will no longer reflect a particular color of white light; it is "subtracted" and this allows the new color to be created. Subtractive color theory allows the designer to manipulate and transform these twelve pigments into the various colors of our everyday lives.

Swatch   A sample of fabric, trim, or other materials used to create a costume; it is attached to the sketch or included with other records for the costume shop.

Symbols/Symbolic Meaning   A visual image, object, or element that signifies something else.

Ten-Out-Of-Twelves   In the final technical rehearsal period of a production, a company will often schedule a rehearsal for 12 hours, with a 2 hour break. (The break may be two 1 hour breaks, or one 2 hour break.) It is an opportunity for the artistic team, technologists, run crews, and actors to work together in an intensive rehearsal process in order to plan and practice scenic and costume changes, lighting and sound cues, and unusual demands such as quick changes or special effects.

Tertiary Colors   The six colors created by mixing primary and secondary hues/colors to create six other hues/colors. The tertiary colors are: yellow-orange, orange-red, red-violet, violet-blue, blue-green, and green-yellow.

Texture   What the surface of an object feels like to the human hand. With regard to fabric in costume and fashion design, it is often referred to as the hand of the fabric.

Theatre Communications Group (TCG)   A wide membership and advocacy organization in the United States including theatres, individual artists from every aspect of live theatre, educators, and students. TCG creates an annual conference, maintains an ambitious publications arm, produces the magazine *American Theatre*, and offers an employment service called ARTSEARCH. For more information, visit the website: www.tcg.org.

Theatre for Young Audiences (TYA)   A term applied both to a style of performance and a national service organization of theatres and producers promoting and advocating live theatrical productions specifically created for younger audiences. Some organizations, such as the Minneapolis Children's Theatre or Kaiser Permanente Educational Theatre produce only young audience shows. Other theatres include an educational or entertainment component in their season. For more information, visit the website: http://assitej-usa.org.

Theme   In theatre the central idea or thought that is explored in a play.

Theming   A short-hand term for the application of a single visual concept to a venue and costumes in order to create an illusion. The terms Themed Entertainment and Experiential Entertainment derive from this idea, creating a top-to-bottom unique experience.

Thumbnail   Small drawings of costumes focusing on silhouette and color palette, as well as the overall stage picture and visual relationships of the characters.

Tints   Pure pigment hues that have degrees of white pigment added to them, causing the original hue to get progressively lighter. Tints can be used as low-, medium-, and highlights of that particular hue in a rendering.

Tone   The muting of a pure pigment hue at full saturation by adding its complementary color or gray, thereby reducing its vibrancy.

Tony Awards   Awards bestowed by the American Theatre Wing for excellence in Broadway Theatre. The award is named after Antoinette Perry, an early 20th century actress and director who co-founded the American Theatre Wing.

Train   An expanse of fabric extending past floor length behind, or on the back of, a garment.

Trapunto   A quilting technique in which padding is inserted between the quilted layers in order to create dimension.

Triadic Color Schemes   The use of three colors that are equally spaced on the traditional (RYB) color wheel.

Tropical Weight Wool   Wool, or wool blend fabric that is lighter in weight, often 4 or 5 ounce.

Twill Weave   A plain weave that produces a diagonal wale on one side; examples include denim, drill, and serge.

Union Stamp   The mark added to a costume sketch by a member of the design union

United Scenic Artists, 829 (USA)   The union representing designers, scenic artists, and craftspeople working in New York film, television and commercials, American theatre, opera, dance, and industrials. For more information, visit the website: www.usa829.org.

Unity   The principle of design that describes the achievement of a sense of oneness within the work of art, creating a sense of harmony and completeness.

Value   The lightness or darkness of a color, and ultimately the entire composition. Value can be found in both two- and three-dimensional art.

Vantage Point   A perspective or view of an object, event, or idea taken by any given member of a collaborative team which is based on their opinion, socio-historical experiences, or other reasoning. This is sometimes referred to as a "point-of-view" or POV.

Variety   The principle of design in which the combination and calculated use of several design elements is organized by various principles to create difference. Variety creates visual interest and holds the viewer's attention.

Vellum   Translucent paper made in imitation of fine parchment (also called vellum) and used for drawing and hand-drafting.

Walk-arounds   See Character Costumes/Walk-arounds

Wardrobe Person   An individual responsible for maintaining costumes once a production has progressed to dress rehearsal. This position works primarily backstage, helping the actors to get in and out of their costumes.

Warm Colors   Colors located from red to yellow on the traditional (RYB) color wheel.

Warp   The threads of a strong and high quality fabric that are pulled taut lengthwise or longitudinally on a loom in the fabric creation process. In costume construction, this is often the straight of grain on a piece of fabric.

Watercolor   Paint that is made useable by mixing with water and is usually translucent when applied to paper; also refers to a painting made by using this paint. It is available in dry cakes, paste, or concentrated liquid.

Weft   The filling yarns that are woven over and under the warp, running cross grain on a piece of fabric. Weft yarns are usually fuzzier and more uneven due to the twisting of filaments, contributing considerably to the texture of a fabric.

Wellingtons   Rubber rain boots, common in the United Kingdom.

Width   The characteristic of line that defines the thickness or thinness that can be achieved when drawing a line from point A to point B; provides a feeling of weight.

INDEX

Note: Figures in *italic* type indicate relevant illustrations.

synergy 157
synthetic fabrics 52–3
Sze, Julia *233*

T

tailors *see* stitchers
Tale of Lady Thi Kinh, The 171
Tango 141
Tartuffe xiii
Tashman, Lilyan *71*
Taylor, Elizabeth *139*
tear sheets/mood boards *231*
Technical PAs 249
technology 192–4, 247; *see also* digital
    environment
television 247–52, *249*, *251*
Tempest, The 86, 106
Templeton, Fay *236*
ten-out-of-twelves 164, 284
Terao, Eriko 185–6, *190–1*
terminology of costume jobs 252
terracotta pencils 82
tertiary colors 49, 284
textile designers 208, *208*
texture 39, 50–3, 284; implied 51, *279*
theatre associations/unions 238, 241, 265,
    266
Theatre Communications Group (TCG) 238,
    284
Theatre for Young Audiences (TYA) 231, 284
theatre history, rendering in 68–73, *68–73*
themed entertainment (character costumes/
    walk-arounds) 224, 256–62, *256*, *259–60*,
    276, 284
themes 31, 211, 284
They're Playing Our Song 111
threads, warp and weft 51, 285
Three Sisters, The 132
thumbnails 98, *98*, 159, *159*, 284
time of day and season 7–9, *8*
tints 49, 284
Titterington, Zachary *64*
Titus Andronicus 114
Tolomeo 244
tone 49, 284
Tony Awards 232, 284
Tortoriello, Lani *161*
Tosca 246
To the Spice Islands 232
Touch the Water 232
Toulouse-Lautrec, Henri de *41*
tradition and religion 34–5
training *see* careers and training
trains 15, 284
transfer paper 99

Transformers, The 256, *256*, *259*
transgendered characters 13, *14*
trapunto *63*, 284
Traviata, La 62, 153, *159–60*
triadic color schemes 50, 284
Tripp, Tony *102*
tropical weight wool 9, 284
Trott, Kathleen 179
True West 114
trust, designer–shop relationship 176
t-shirts 9
Tsu, Susan 79, *106*, *113*, *128*
Turganska, Malgosia *141*
Twelfth Night 203
twill weaves 52, 284
2(X)IST *219*

U

undergarments/understructures 47–8, *48*, 94,
    140, 189
uniforms 13–14
union stamps 122, 159, *160*, 284
unions/theatre associations 238, 241, 265, 266
United Scenic Artists (USA) 162, 238, 266,
    284
unity 39, 57, 285
Universal Studios 256, 258–9, 261
Utah Shakespeare Festival 184–5
utility principle 33

V

Valdez, Luis 229
Valentino *213*
value, color 39, 53–4, *54*, *55*, 285
Van Eek, Esther xiii, *xiii*, *8*, *196*, *198*, *203*, *212*,
    218–19
vantage points 149, 151, 285
Vanya and Sonia and Masha and Spike 3, 235
variety 39, 57, 285
Vaudeville performers *59*
vellum 75, 100–1, 285
video game characters 255–6, *255*
Vincent 155
virtual characters *see* digital environment
Voelpel, Fred 80
Von Teese, Dita 201, *202*
Voyage, The 60, 74
Vu, Bich *42*

W

Wada, Emi 228, *228*
walk-arounds *see* themed entertainment
Wardrobe Local 764 (IATSE) New York 266

wardrobe persons 164, 183–4, *184*, 251, 252,
    285
warm colors 49, 285
warp threads 51, 285
watercolor 73–4, *73–5*, 82–3, *82–3*, 87, 114–15,
    115–17, 160, 285; gouache 83–5, *83–5*,
    279; *see also* rendering
watercolor papers 75–9, *75–9*
Watson, Court *90–1*, *122*, *134*
weapons 156–7
weaving process 51
website services, careers 269–70
weft threads 51, 285
Weiße Rose 122
Weller, Karen 225, 257, 262, 270
Wellingtons 10, 285
Whatever Happened to Baby Jane? 59, 140
Whidden, Amanda 65
White Christmas 126
Wickedly Ever After 137
width, line 40, 285
Wiebers, Leon *23*
wigs *see* hair, wigs and makeup
Wild Party, The 22
"Wilhelm" 70, *71*
Williams, Vanessa *215*
Wilson, Tyler *83*, *114*
Wizarding World of Harry Potter, Orlando
    256, 257
Woman, The 200
Woman's Robe à la Française and Petticoat 47
Woman Strolling (Seurat) 44
wool fabrics 52
work environments 214–16, *215–16*; *see also*
    costume shops
workers' clothing 15
Working 90
World Wars I and II 10, 12, *212*
worsted wools 52
Worth, Charles Frederick 204

Y

yarns 51
YoontekOh *255*
You Can't Take It With You xvi, 81

Z

Zegra, Jungle Empress 93
Zhang Yimou 228, *228*
Ziegfeld Follies 71
Zipprodt, Patricia 209
Zodiac 117
Z-twist fabrics 51